THE
CONDEMNATION
OF LITTLE B

Also by Elaine Brown
A Taste of Power

THE CONDEMNATION OF LITTLE B

Elaine Brown

BEACON PRESS Boston

Beacon Press
25 Beacon Street
Boston, Massachusetts 02108-2892
www.beacon.org

Beacon Press books are published under the auspices of
the Unitarian Universalist Association of Congregations.

Printed in the United States of America
06 05 04 03 02   8 7 6 5 4 3 2 1

This book is printed on acid-free paper that meets
the uncoated paper ANSI/NISO specifications for
permanence as revised in 1992.

Text design by Melodie Wertelet/mwdesign
Composition by Wilsted & Taylor Publishing Services

Library of Congress Cataloging-in-Publication Data

Brown, Elaine.
     The condemnation of Little B / Elaine Brown.
        p. cm.
     Includes bibliographical references.
     ISBN 0-8070-0974-1 (alk. paper)
     1. Lewis, Michael, 1983 or 4– 2. Murder—
Georgia—Atlanta. 3. Murder in mass media.
4. Discrimination in criminal justice adminis-
tration—Georgia—Atlanta. 5. African
American juvenile delinquents—Georgia—
Atlanta—Public opinion. 6. Atlanta (Ga.)—
Race relations. I. Title.
HV6534.A7 B76 2002
364.15'23'09758231—dc21   2001037943

For Michael
Until you're free

Contents

I
SCAPEGOAT

[1] Black Man-Child

The shooting was a familiar tragedy in "Black Mecca," the name some
black people had bestowed on the city of Atlanta, home of the defunct
Civil Rights movement. Such an incident hardly merited more than an
obligatory mention in the local newspaper's crime reports or obituary
notices—which was, in fact, how it had been first reported in the *Atlanta Journal-Constitution*. It was, after all, just another killing in the
black ghetto, euphemistically known now as the inner city.

Suddenly, however, the death of Darrell Woods became significant,
far more significant than his short life ever had been. The newspaper
began to serialize the story in front-page installments. It was now "the
senseless killing of a family man." Maria Elena Fernandez, the young
journalist who would make her name with this story, knew instinctively
that in 1997 a black "family man" was singularly newsworthy. In contrast to the statistically stereotypical young black male, Woods was
nearly a hero in his seeming ordinariness—the kind of man who was a
rare source of black pride.

The heinousness of the crime became heavier than homicide. It
seemed to snuff out hope in a dark field of black despair. It was not
merely that it occurred just as the city—the whole country—was cele-
brating the life of Dr. Martin Luther King Jr. It was not even its untimely
juxtaposition with the heady aftermath of Atlanta's success as host of
the Centennial Olympic Games. It was that this crime had resulted in an
irreplaceable loss, the loss of a responsible black man, a black father and
husband who worked for a living. His widow reminded us, "The only
thing Darrell wanted was to raise his family and have a home. He didn't
ask for handouts. We were raising our sons to be men. We didn't want

to raise no thugs." [1] Adding insult to injury, this hardworking black father had been killed, shot three times, in front of his young sons. Still,
the death of Woods did not rise to the point of public outrage, not until
the arrest, seven days later.

The horror of it seemed clear then. A thirteen-year-old boy was arrested. He was surely black, blacks whispered to each other on the te-
lepathic grapevine. Woods had been shot in a rough neighborhood, the
inner-city community of Vine City. There was really no question, then,
that the suspect was a black boy. Thereafter, the crime exploded into a
sensational spectacle.

Fernandez and her colleagues now exposed this reprobate in daily
headlines. The early press coverage revealed that the boy known as Little B was, as suspected, a troublemaker. "He's a thug," Atlanta police
major Mickey Lloyd would be quoted over and over as saying in the first
articles about Little B, which began to appear two days after his arrest.
When police arrived to take the boy into custody, Lloyd explained, "he
was acting like the thug that he is." Then there was the fact that, as the
victim's mother said, this thug had "slaughtered a man down like a dog
in front of his kids." [2]

Black Atlanta shook its head in shame, a shudder I was sure I felt in
my own apartment. Racists rested their case. This was exactly the kind
of scenario that had spawned the new tough-on-crime laws. Here was a
workingman, the reports continued, a machine operator, who had simply stopped at a corner store with his wife and two small boys to buy a
soft drink to accompany the family's takeout dinner. Waiting in the family car with his kids while his wife purchased the soda, Woods had been
shot and killed, in front of his children. The city's mayor, Bill Campbell,
who had offered a two-thousand-dollar reward "to persuade a witness
to formally identify the teenager," seemed overcome as he announced,
"There is no joy in Atlanta today. . . . The tragedy of the two young boys'
witnessing their father's murder is compounded by the fact that another
boy apparently killed him. My son is thirteen. It's hard for us to imagine
that a thirteen-year-old would have the will to kill another human being
in cold blood, as the facts of this case suggest." [3]

Before police provided an explanation for the shooting, other details
were published that punctuated the monstrousness of this crime. The
victim's widow had been several weeks pregnant and had suffered a

miscarriage the day after Little B's arrest. At the funeral, the victim's mother had been obliged to set aside her own grief to console her two-year-old grandson as he reached into the coffin to touch his father's lifeless body.

The next major headline quoted Little B's brother, Jason Morgan, as saying of him, "He's bad." [4] Morgan was himself being held in jail as a suspected accessory to the murder. Others agreed with Morgan's characterization. Eric Mills, a twenty-one-year-old friend of Morgan's who had been arrested as the original suspect in the murder and was now being held as an accessory, reportedly told police that he had witnessed the shooting. He had tried, he said, but been unable to stop Little B, even though he pleaded with him, "Little B, don't do that." Morgan validated his friend's account: "I don't know if he did this, but Eric says he told my brother not to do it, so he must have done it." [5] Furthermore, juvenile court records—which Ms. Fernandez had been able to obtain in spite of laws prohibiting their publication—suggested that Little B was a "repeat offender." He had been brought before a judge twelve times since he was ten, she told readers. Finally, police leaked their theory about the shooting: Little B had done it to gain respect, they speculated, and to prove his "manhood."

The *Atlanta Journal-Constitution* daily bombarded the city with headlines referring to these unconfirmed reports that this boy, this "thug," had ritualistically killed to prove his "manhood." The Little B accusation was beginning to take on a familiar tone, echoing an age-old refrain about the savagery of black boys, recalling the dark histories of Emmett Till and the Scottsboro Boys.

What was most startling about this steady demonization of Little B, though, was the silence of blacks themselves, especially the local black leadership. Not a single voice was lifted from the pulpit or the podium to challenge the premise or the implications of the wild assertions being made about this black boy, not to mention the pretrial presumption of his *guilt* contained therein. This silence suggested that blacks who had slipped into the mainstream of society were drinking from the tributary of racism that still flowed there.

These same blacks had vociferously demanded fair treatment in the O. J. Simpson case, had stood by Simpson and understood and rejected the racist stereotyping of him—the image of the black man as beast. But in the case of Little B, there was no demand that judgment be reserved pending the outcome of the trial, no cry to halt the vilification campaign at least until there had been a full investigation of the facts. There was only this hush of seeming shame, an obsequious acquiescence to all the public speculation about the savage nature of Little B, who had surely committed this "senseless killing."

This image of him thus came to be imprinted on the mass mind. In the first days of February, the *Journal-Constitution* ran a front-page feature that opened with the lines "Barely a teenager, the thirteen-year-old known around the Vine City neighborhood as 'Little B' wanted to be thought of as a man. A tough man." [6] The feature's author, Fernandez, noted that in comparison, "Darrell Woods, twenty-three, father of two and a loving husband, had a different vision of maturity: He worked hard, dreamed of owning a home, and wanted to provide for his family." While quoting both police sources and members of the victim's family, Fernandez's article did not include a statement by anyone who might have had a different vision of the boy who was still only a suspect in the crime.

Now came the first of the opinion pieces about the collateral atrocities of Little B's crime, following up on the collective article wherein the *Atlanta Constitution*'s editorial board had noted that "society must protect itself from such children, even if it means locking them up for most of their lives." [7] A black editor named Jeff Dickerson accused Little B of contributing to the destruction of the black family, in an essay entitled "Another Black Father Dies." [8] Dickerson forcefully assailed "the thirteen-year-old 'thug'" known as Little B, who was charged with killing a "black father," and argued that this murder was a cautionary tale about the catastrophic consequences attendant on the sweeping breakdown of the black family over the previous decade or so. The trend affected not only all of Atlanta but indeed the entire nation: "Thirteen-year-olds [without fathers] out there gunning down real fathers—which the black community boasts so few of."

Next came the features-cum-editorials dramatizing the demonic nature of the boy. Reporter Dave Kindred remarked on the maliciousness of the crime: "Police said the boy shot an unarmed man three times." And not only had "the shooter" killed an unarmed man, but he had also "shot the man with his two small children in the car." Moreover, "the shooter, whoever it was, did more than kill a man. The man's [pregnant] wife . . . had a miscarriage [as a result]. So the shooter killed a man and a baby." Kindred went on to examine the degenerate history of the suspected "shooter," Little B: "Friends say the boy's mother lost him to the streets and didn't much care. He didn't go to school. . . . Police called him a thug. His brother said . . . 'He's bad.' " He quoted the Suhs, the Korean immigrants who owned the store in front of which Woods's murder had occurred, who recounted their efforts to help Little B: "I told him," Mr. Suh said, " 'If you're hungry and have no credit, I'll give you credit. Don't steal.' " But his wife, Myong Suh, said Little B was "too wild." [9]

Finally Atlanta saw him: Little B. In connection with his first court appearance, the newspaper printed a photograph of the back of his head on its front page. The hearing was on the issue of whether or not Little B could or would be tried as an adult. A new law gave prosecutors absolute discretion, in a certain category of crimes, to try children as adults from the age of thirteen. The photographic glimpse of Little B showed that his head was small, and his shoulders narrow. He appeared to be just a whisper of a boy, barely pubescent. His faceless photograph seemed to illustrate the irrelevancy of his life, except as he had come to be held forth as an exemplum of social decay, of black shame. Only days had passed since his arrest, but clearly he had already been judged guilty. His lawyer was a young black woman named Patrice Grant, who appeared alongside Little B in the photograph; her expression was compassionate, and her touch on his shoulder looked ever so gentle. The caption identified the boy as "the thirteen-year-old who reportedly killed a man for 'disrespecting him.' " The headline announced the outcome of the hearing: " 'Little B' faces judge. Sobbing 'tough' teen to be tried as adult in killing." [10]

In the coming days, more came to be disclosed about the background of this boy who had become the focus of public disdain and outrage—the boy whom Kindred had summarily indicted as an "evil in our town." According to Atlanta school officials, Little B had "not been enrolled for two years." [11] At the same time, as Fernandez reiterated, he had "appeared twelve times in Fulton County Juvenile Court," commencing with an assault charge when he was ten years old. Then the issue of manhood as motivation was scrutinized, based on Atlanta police detective S. E. Lawter's testimony at the last hearing: "Little B became angry when he twice asked Woods to turn off his headlights and Woods refused. . . . By not dimming his lights, the man in the car disrespected Little B." Furthermore, Lawter testified, "Little B told his mother 'that he shot the man.' " [12] The case seemed closed. It was February 6, less than two weeks after the arrest. The trial would begin in November.

Despite the fact that there seemed to be nothing left to report on the matter, stories about Little B continued to fill the pages of the *Atlanta Journal-Constitution,* thence to be carried over into the unabated public outrage. There was the piece that held up the boy's two-year absence from school as a means to examine the widespread problem of inner-city truancy and its ramifications. There was the commentary concerning Little B's seeming sociopathic nature—his "thuggery"—as validated not only by the police, the Korean grocer, and even his own brother, but also by a host of neighbors who desired anonymity on account of obscure fears.

The most striking article in this sequence was the one that bore the headline "A Teen's Choice: Accused Killer Wanted Life on the Street." [13] This was effectively a profile of a woman who identified herself as "Little B's legal guardian." Marilyn Reed explained that because she had known Little B's mother, Valerie Johnson, for years, and knew how hard Johnson was trying to overcome her "drug problem," she had taken in Little B herself, at least until October of 1995. After acting as the boy's guardian for a year, however, and doing the best she could by him during that period, she had concluded that Little B could not be helped: he *wanted* to be a "thug." It was Mrs. Reed's contention that Little B had had choices, opportunities he had rejected; he had, for example, refused to stay in school. And in the end he had run away from his guardian's home and from the stable home life she had provided for him. There was no mention of Little B's guardianship after October 1995.

Later it would be disclosed that during those last two years before his arrest, when he was absent from school and not living with Mrs. Reed, Michael Lewis—"Little B"—had been under the guardianship of the state, in the form of the Department of Family and Children Services (DFACS). When Michael was eleven years old, DFACS had sought and obtained a court order declaring Valerie Johnson an unfit mother. There was no father on the scene. No information was forthcoming as to what

DFACS had done as his guardian after that court order was issued. As it turned out, Michael had lived pretty much on the street from the time he was eleven until he was arrested at thirteen, in January 1997.

As the month of February passed, and as these newspaper articles about Little B began to form a mountain, I came to realize that the rage in them, as it echoed in the street, was about something bigger than this murder case. This became evident, for example, in an editorial advocating the "toughening" of juvenile crime laws by lowering to ten the age at which a child could be sentenced to "boot camp"—a change proposed by black state senator David Scott and endorsed by Atlanta police chief Beverly Harvard. Scott's proposal had become even more compelling, the editorial argued, in light of this latest case, since "murder suspect 'Little B' . . . had been before juvenile authorities twelve times in two years but had never been sentenced." Targeting Little B and others like him, the new bill would at least, and at last, "get them off the street." *Something* had to be done, the editorial insisted: "It's a sad testament that today in the city of Atlanta, people are under siege [from kids]." [14] Then there was the subsequent *Journal-Constitution* editorial in which black journalist Fredrick D. Robinson grieved over his own fear of young black street toughs and excoriated rampant "black-on-black" crime: "Even if every white racist turned from their [*sic*] racist ways, the Little B's of the world wouldn't disappear," Robinson wrote. [15]

And this was the point, finally. The outrage was not about the death of Darrell Woods; it was about the very existence of the "Little B's of the world," these nonfictional Bigger Thomases and guilty Emmett Tills. Now some blacks were even calling for the rope.

Little B came to be held symbolically responsible for the complete deterioration of the Vine City area in which he had grown up, whose streets he had wandered alone for those last couple of years. This became clear in another *Journal-Constitution* article, which held up the case of Little B as an example of just how far Vine City had fallen, a decline attested to by the reminiscences of a seventy-five-year-old resident: "This used to be a beautiful community . . . [with] dress shops, shoe shops . . . and a beauty parlor." [16]

My own rage, by then, was pounding. This child, this black boy, had become a scapegoat for the poverty and despair still suffered by Atlanta's black masses; he was being castigated in much the same way that the biblical goat of Aaron had been cast out into the wilderness with all the sins of the children of Israel heaped upon his head. I was aware of course, that across the nation black children like Michael Lewis were being singled out by angry whites and a certain segment of the black population as proof that something was wrong with black America. Now, it seemed, through Little B's irredeemable transgressions, we knew what that "something" was. As black *Journal-Constitution* editorial writer Fredrick Robinson had opined, the problem was no longer a matter of "lack of opportunity." Rather, he suggested, some other element, an apparently sinister one, had "seep[ed] into the soul of inner-city culture," bringing with it a loss of "self-respect, self-love and personal responsibility." [17]

As I witnessed the wrath rising in the city over this boy, ceaselessly spilling from the headlines and television reports into the streets, my reaction turned from rage to sorrow. I was not so much angry now over how swiftly this boy had been damned; I was more anguished by thoughts of what thirteen-year-old Michael Lewis must be feeling, suspended as he was over an abyss of absolute abandonment in the universe he occupied. I could remember feeling something like that myself as a child. I could remember trembling in fearful aloneness, feeling unwanted in the world into which I had been born, black and female and poor, circumscribed to a Philadelphia ghetto and predestined to isolation from the mainstream of society, a whites-only preserve.

Now there was silence from the black quarter over the injustice of the public trial and condemnation of Little B. Nobody who had a voice, neither the blacks nor the liberal whites, seemed willing even to honor the legal notion that Michael Lewis should be presumed innocent. With the exception of a single early appearance by his mother, at the hearing where it was determined that Michael would be "tried as a man," no family members came to see about him. And even she, as caught by the photographer's lens, seemed insensate, her gaze empty of everything, a diet of crack cocaine having left her gaunt, with sunken cheeks and perhaps a frozen heart. But she was all he had. Nobody else claimed him.

Nobody had a dream for a boy like him anymore. This knowledge filled me with sorrow.

Then I remembered the touch of the young black attorney in that first photograph, the gentle protection of her hand on his shoulder. I set out to find Patrice Grant. She had a broad and genuine smile, and a commitment to her client, Little B. Her commitment seemed bigger than her smile, more vital than her youth, more beautiful than her brown face, framed by a cascade of braids. She was a graduate of prestigious Emory University Law School. Unlike most of those few blacks who were her professional peers, Patrice had not chosen to grab for the golden ring of the corporate world. She had determined to bide, as I saw it. That is, Patrice Grant was holding on to a forgotten dream, a flame of justice, no matter how feeble it had become, no matter how alone she might be in so doing. When I finally saw her standing there in the meager offices of the Fulton County conflict defender, she seemed pathetically idealistic. Indeed, lawyer and client made a sorry pair: she was his only hope, and he her charge, to whose defense she was dedicated. I wanted to join their ragtag army. Patrice hugged me and welcomed me. Then she told me that Little B was innocent.

[2] The Murder Case

"I didn't kill that man. I didn't kill nobody, ma'am," Michael Lewis told me when I saw him briefly some months later. "I didn't even know what they wanted. I just opened the door, and they came on in and told me to put up my hands. I kept asking them what I'd done. My heart was beating fast."

None of this was the answer to any question I had posed or even had in mind, I thought, scrutinizing the tenderness of his age and his manner, an inculcated Georgia gentility attended by an indigenous drawl. There was no hair on his face, which was a Hershey's Kiss, small and dark and sweet. The hair on his head was close-cropped, neat, framing small ears and nose, complementing smooth lips. His expression, like his gaze, was reserved, but for the hint of a smile that revealed stark white teeth.

I was not really interested in the truth about the murder, for I had begun to understand more in that regard than I wanted to. There had been a river of unsolicited revelations from Gary Guichard, and I did not want to know more. Guichard was the other attorney from the Fulton County conflict defender's office assigned to handle Michael's defense; he was, in fact, the lead attorney on the team, assisted by Patrice Grant.

The office of the conflict defender had been created a few years before to guarantee the right of legal defense to indigent criminal suspects in cases where a conflict of interest existed between or among defendants represented by the public defender's office. The conflict defender's office also handled the rising number of cases in which juveniles were tried as adults. In 1994, a new piece of legislation, proposed by then-governor Zell Miller and sponsored by representatives Mark Taylor (soon to become the state's lieutenant governor) and Robert Brown, a black legislator from Macon, authorized the state to try children as young as thirteen as adults for a certain category of crimes, collectively referred to as the seven deadly sins. This legislation, still commonly known as SB (Senate Bill) 440, became effective in early 1995.

Guichard had suggested to me, almost immediately after we met, that he knew who had really killed Darrell Woods; he said that Michael knew and had told him, and that he wanted Michael to tell the truth about what he knew. But Michael was afraid, Guichard added.

Gary Guichard was a thirtyish, caramel-colored black who wore suits that fitted him like sausage skins. He did not seem to possess the street savvy necessary for a criminal defense attorney. Although he had never met me before, he willingly talked to me about his theory of the murder and his plan for Michael's defense, which was to point a finger at someone else as the killer. He would help Michael set aside his fears, he said, and accept that this strategy would mean victory. Guichard also told me during that first meeting that he intended to surprise the prosecutor and the whole courtroom with Michael's testimony at trial. He would do it, he elaborated, in the same sensational way that Perry Mason had always shocked television audiences by exposing the real killers in *his* cases, often forcing confessions in "open court." Parenthetically, Guichard told me that it was in fact the *Perry Mason* television series that had first inspired him to pursue a career as a criminal defense attorney.

The next time I met Guichard, he was trying to find Valerie. Valerie Johnson, also known as Valerie Morgan, was a crack addict and prostitute whose innumerable brushes with the law had resulted in as many arrests. Almost incidentally, she was Michael's mother. She had, two years before, lost legal custody of Michael in the court hearing in which she had been deemed an unfit mother. Long before that, she had lost touch with her own humanity, having made the proverbially Faustian deal with a drug dealer. A deal with the police was an afterthought, even if that afterthought condemned her thirteen-year-old son. She had reportedly just signed a statement saying that Michael had "confessed" to her; Guichard wanted to talk with her about it.

Guichard, Patrice Grant, and I all met for lunch at Sylvia's, the upscale soul-food franchise that sat at a busy intersection amid Atlanta's downtown government office buildings. Marvin Dixon, the investigator for the case, joined us. In stark contrast to Guichard, Dixon was street-wise. He had grown up in Atlanta and knew the streets and people of the Bluff, as that part of the Vine City district in which the murder had oc-curred was known. Dixon even had police contacts in the area. He was, moreover, familiar with the particular corner of the Bluff where Woods had been killed a few months before—a corner known as New Jack City.

Life in the Bluff was simple and raw, Dixon testified over a plate of barbecued chicken swimming in sauce, piled high with collard greens. Every activity there related, in the end, to only one activity: the selling and buying of drugs, including not only crack cocaine but also pow-der cocaine, heroin, and marijuana. Indeed, Dixon suggested that ad-dicts, users, and dealers throughout Atlanta regarded New Jack City as a sort of one-stop, drive-through drug supermarket. This fact alone had aroused numerous suspicions about Woods's killing in Dixon's investi-gative mind.

"Let me show you what I mean," he said after lunch, speaking in the soft, closed-lipped way of a man who could draw information from the darkest crevices of the city, a street-corner confidant. Dixon slid his wiry body smoothly into the driver's seat of his Mercedes, laughing with a crooked smile at my comment that he looked as if he could be Little B's father. (Michael's real father was, tragically typically, an unknown phantom.) Dixon's suit was gray, like his car, and sharp, in the vernacu-lar of my day, as were his polished shoes and white shirt. Guichard sat up front with him, while Patrice Grant and I rode together in the rear—Muslim-style, we joked with each other.

Swishing away from Sylvia's, we drove west in the expanse of traffic lanes of Techwood Boulevard, soon passing the massive CNN Center. Within seconds we were assaulted by the giant red roof of the Georgia Dome Sports Arena, which dominates the horizon, reigning over the network of boulevards and freeway arteries that converge there, at once segregating and integrating the city. Passing this sprawl, we seemed in danger of being swallowed up by the dome's gargantuan parking en-trance, a gaping mouth waiting to be fed the cars of the mostly white sports enthusiasts who would arrive there from suburban Atlanta for a Falcons game, borne on the safety of concrete shoulders. From there we followed a serpentine route to our intended destination. Dixon navi-gated with ease, carrying us through the maze of streets into the core of the Bluff. None of the rest of us, all Atlanta transplants, would have been able to find it on our own. As a native of the asphalt ghetto streets of Philadelphia, I had to resist making a spontaneous association, as we entered the area, between the savage growth of grass and trees all around and a middle-class community.

Soon enough, the illusion created by the greenery disappeared, leaving the stark reality of raw sewage. The Bluff housed the bottom of life in Atlanta. Dixon transported us through its bowels, a stygian journey along streams of charred dwellings and vacant lots, past shuffling bodies expressing despair in the April sunlight. Life was conspicuously irrelevant and cheap in the Bluff, a dark parallel universe to the Atlanta that beamed only blocks beyond in a shimmering skyline of corporate growth. The Bluff's only link to *that* Atlanta was the dope dealers operating there, whose profits proffered them passage out. There were two or three walking each block, recognizable by anyone with eyes, all glaring back at us, outfitted rather uniformly in Nike sports ensembles accessorized with diamond earrings and solid-gold necklaces, watches, rings, and dental crowns—bastard African chieftains of another day, linking time and space by means of pastel-colored personal pagers and the latest in cellular telephones.

Eric Mills, known as Big E and named in news reports as a key witness in the Woods murder case, had been one of that population of dope dealers, Dixon explained to me over his shoulder as we slowly wound through the Bluff's blocks of cutoff streets to the corner of Griffin Street and Meldrum that was called New Jack City. Were we the police, or social workers, or customers? so many empty, staring eyes seemed to wonder. I myself began to wonder, aloud, why anyone would stop at the grandiosely named Henry's Supermarket there to buy a soda. There was a chorus of laughter inside the Mercedes. Why, I went on, had Darrell Woods chosen *this* store, on *this* corner, particularly after dark? Could his death have been a murder rather than an arbitrary street killing, if such a distinction could be made in light of the finality of the result? This last question was chillingly punctuated when Dixon broke in with the rather surprising (to me) information that it had been Kenya Woods, Darrell's twenty-three-year-old wife, who had driven the car to Henry's that fateful night.

The newspaper accounts had left the impression that the young

Mrs. Woods, being pregnant, had craved a soda, as pregnant women are wont to do, and that Woods had accommodated his wife's craving by stopping at the first place he could find. But no mere craving, I thought, remembering my own pregnancy, seemed capable of compelling a stop at New Jack City—unless it was for marijuana or cocaine or heroin, which were, of course, all sold there, and certainly in greater abundance than Atlanta's own Coca-Cola. Although there was nothing to suggest that Kenya Woods had any such inclination, I was not alone in my newly inspired suspicions about the notion of buying a soda at Henry's— which had seemed to me to constitute an original idea when I voiced them.

Dixon told us that his investigation had uncovered the fact that the widow Woods had reported her husband to the police on numerous occasions for battery—and specifically, battery of *her*. This was in stark conflict with the image that had been projected citywide by the press— the portrait Mrs. Woods herself had painted, of a loving marriage tragically cut short by a senseless, vicious act. In fact, Woods's beatings of his wife were one of the reasons they had, only months before, left their apartment in College Park, an area a good distance away and easily a grade or so better, to move into the Bluff. Even though Kenya had told reporters, as she would testify in court, that she and Darrell had left their College Park apartment to save money toward, variously, buying a new house or enabling her to continue her education, they had actually been evicted. And they had been evicted not only because of nonpayment of rent but also because the landlord had received too many complaints from neighbors about the disturbances caused by the husband's beatings of the wife. Dixon had a copy of the eviction notice, along with the neighbors' written accounts of the incidents.

As Dixon deftly wheeled his car past Henry's, following Guichard's latest thought on where "Val" might be, he offered his observations freely. That was where Kenya and Darrell had lived, he said, pointing out a nondescript gray, wood-paneled duplex on a little street that bore the big name of Western Avenue. I noted that it was impossible to drive onto Griffin Street from Western Avenue, which ran only a few blocks east and west and dead-ended at Vine Street, some blocks east of Griffin. A waist-high chain-link fence secured by a giant lock cut off the small driveway to the right of the duplex where the family had lived. One of the neighbors, an old man, had told Dixon that the Woodses had had a Toyota Land Cruiser parked behind that fence until some men came and removed it, the night before the killing.

The women were out by the time we returned to New Jack City, and children's faces could be seen peering out from behind the porch doors and barred windows of the helter-skelter landscape. Some of the women had situated themselves in folding chairs across from Henry's. We rolled by, still searching for Val. They sat in their chairs, possessed by the potion called crack that had rendered them apparitions of their former selves, waiting for the vampire's fix. Nighttime would be the right time, when food stamps and any other thing of any value could be traded for cash, which could in turn be traded for crack, exchanges that occurred just outside Henry's door.

Some of the women shuffled back and forth across the small streets that intersected there, creating, along with a born-again madman preaching on one corner, an incredible cacophony. The one with the iridescent pink fluffy slippers, sitting in her chair in a prominent place on the corner opposite Henry's—emaciated, like all the other women— would be a witness against Michael, Patrice Grant told me.

Like all the rest, this woman was waiting for the pusher man. The main man who ran this dark spot was unavailable, though others yet worked the surrounding alleyways that passed for streets. She seemed, still, to be this man's eyes and ears. But Big E had not been servicing the corner since January. He and two of his lieutenants were in jail, as was another associate: Michael's half-brother, Jason Morgan, known as J-Boy.

Another gaunt and ghostly figure of a woman suddenly appeared as we were about to circle the area again. She was a friend of Valerie Johnson's. Dixon stopped the car at Guichard's command. Guichard beckoned to her. She shuffled over to the car and leaned down to talk to him through the open passenger window. She was a nervous squirrel, glancing back and forth while speaking with the attorney. Her eyes were shaded by the bill of the baseball cap she wore, which somehow complemented the men's pants and golf shirt that hung from her body; her dark skin was now ashen. Val was around the corner, she swore in a raspy whisper, presenting a toothless grin. Yes, yes, she would tell her that Guichard wanted to see her. She would be right back.

Guichard's apparent expectation that Valerie Johnson would soon appear amazed me. All of us were certainly suspect to the inhabitants there, if not as police or social workers then surely as something "official," something that stood outside of and thus threatened their desperate way of life. Nobody would be volunteering to talk to such outsiders. Valerie Johnson, of course, did not appear, though her friend actually did return after about fifteen minutes to report that Val had just left the place where she had thought she was; she had in fact been there only moments before, the friend swore. Nobody knew where she had gone.

As Dixon drove off, Guichard hollered back to the expressionless friend to tell Val to call him. This would not happen—not that day, not ever. Valerie Johnson had already signed her statement for the district attorney, maintaining that her son Michael had "confessed" to her that he had killed Darrell Woods. Though the prosecutor would be unable to introduce this questionable statement as evidence at trial, she would never disavow it. Despite her shadow existence, Valerie Johnson was clinging to life, as enabled by a man who could imprison her, the district attorney, and a man on whom she had long been dependent, Big E.

Something was wrong, it seemed to me, with the story of Darrell Woods's murder. A few days after our visit to the Bluff, I went to Captain D's fast-food fish takeout in the West End, on Ralph David Abernathy Boulevard, which used to be Gordon Street before the death of the famous civil rights leader. Despite some trepidation, I had decided to drive the same route Kenya Woods had presumably driven on the night her husband was killed. She had reported that with her children in tow she had picked up Woods at his place of employment as a machine operator at around six-thirty that evening, and that from there the family had gone on to Captain D's to buy dinner. En route home from the restaurant, she had gotten thirsty and had stopped at Henry's, at around seven-twenty, to buy a soda. While driving, I made notes.

Going east on Abernathy toward Ashby Street, right after Captain D's and on the same side of the street, I spotted a Wendy's franchise. Had I gone a few blocks west instead, I would have encountered the giant Kroger supermarket, referred to by some in this black community as the "Be-Be" (pronounced "Bay-Bay") Kroger, on account of the seeming predominance of older black ladies who shop there. Traveling east, though, within two blocks I arrived at Ashby Street, where I turned left to go north. Another block further east on Abernathy was Lee Street, where there was a much-frequented Krispy Kreme donut shop and, across from that, the rambling West End Mall. Contiguous to the mall were a Taco Bell drive-through, a BP gas station, and a Church's Chicken outlet. All of these places sold sodas.

Driving north on Ashby toward Western Avenue, where the Woodses had lived, I passed a strip mall on my left in the first block, and then another, a block later, just before the I-20 freeway entrance. Passing under the freeway overpass, I noted an Exxon gas station and mini-market and then, at Westview, the Mrs. Winner's Chicken & Biscuits and Domino Pizza locations patronized by students from neighboring More-house, Clark-Atlanta, and Spelman colleges. Soon I saw a Superette mar-ket, across from another Church's Chicken. At the busy intersection with Martin Luther King Jr. Boulevard, there were a McDonald's, a Ken-tucky Fried Chicken, a BP gas station, a Quick Stop market, an Amoco gas station, and the Ashby Street Rib Shack, all of which would surely have been open at around seven on a January evening, and all of which sold a wide variety of sodas in relatively secure settings.

Rather than continue north to Bankhead Avenue, an extension of Bankhead Highway, which had given its name to the popular Bankhead Bounce, the dance that black kids all over the nation were then doing, I took the next logical step and turned right, going east, on Simpson Street. Western Avenue was two short blocks north of Simpson.

The corner of Ashby and Simpson still maintained a pulse, a final re-minder that it had once been full of life. Now it was barely hanging on, its slow demise being at once its chief activity, like a cancer victim busy with chemotherapy. The dominant chemical here, of course, was crack cocaine. My friend Marva would later tell me that Monique's Variety Store, the deteriorating market that dominated the four corners, used to be a really popular place back in the day, before the crack era. In any case, Monique's still sold sodas, as did the small store across from it on Ashby and the little market a few blocks away on Simpson, at the inter-section with James P. Brawley. More significantly, I concluded as I drove along Simpson, eyeing the children playing dangerously close to the street in front of the raised wooden duplexes that filled in the huge gaps left by any number of condemned and abandoned properties, it was impossible to be blind to the possibilities of purchasing a soft drink on this bustling boulevard and, at the same time, possess the vision to spot the lights of Henry's on Griffin Street, around seven blocks north of Simpson. Yet Kenya Woods had stated, and would maintain, that being new to the neighborhood, she had simply stumbled upon Henry's that evening, attracted by the market's lights. Incredibly, at the corner of Simpson and Griffin Street itself, she would have had to pass, or pass up, the Simpson Plaza's small liquor store to turn left onto Griffin, and then maneuver the car along the seven blocks of this narrow dark passageway to buy her soda at Henry's—a purchase that would cost her husband his life.

It took *me* several more trips to turn that corner—that is, to find the courage to make that left turn onto Griffin Street. It seemed evident to me that there could be no good reason to leave the relative safety of Simpson Street and make that turn, unless one lived or had business there. Otherwise that turn was a dangerous proposition, for the only real business operating there, and operating at the most brutal level, was the drug trade. I knew the danger of Griffin Street instinctively; the same danger had existed in East Oakland when I was living there, had wound through the ghetto—the precrack ghetto—of North Philly during my youth, and persisted in every urban ghetto across the nation at the end of the twentieth century. I knew the danger of interfering with the business of what Huey Newton called the illegitimate black capitalists, the ghetto entrepreneurs who, denied bank loans and other business opportunities on account of their race, carved out what was left of America's economic pie for themselves in the crude fashion of the robber barons and Mafiosi of another day. So it was with Griffin Street's drug entrepreneurs. Legitimacy might come bearing a calm civility, but it was only for those ruthless enough to rule the marketplace. All of this had to be clear to anybody who turned onto those blocks of Griffin Street, whether from Bankhead or from Simpson—and no less clear to the innumerable black and white college students who bought retail drugs there than it was to the small-time dope distributors who bought wholesale, or to the natives and neighboring addicts. Everybody who made that turn had to appreciate what was happening on that stretch of pavement. So the question in my mind was what *really* could have motivated Kenya Woods to drive her red Mitsubishi down Griffin Street the night her husband was gunned down in front of her children. Then, too, I wondered this: If these blocks were known as a heavy drug-trafficking area—as the prosecutor in the case would repeat over and over during Michael Lewis's trial—and if they formed one of the most lawless districts in the city in terms not only of drug trafficking but also of prostitution, why had the officers of the Atlanta Police Department's Zone 1 done next to nothing about the problem?

No one had to speculate long about the ambition of Paul Howard, the recently elected district attorney of Fulton County. Howard was a member of that elite legion of anonymous blacks who were the direct beneficiaries of the Civil Rights movement. He had graduated from the Emory University School of Law in 1976, a time when more blacks than ever were being admitted into colleges and professional schools across America, little victories of the hard battles fought by blacks to institute programs of affirmative action. It was, too, a time when Atlanta had just elected its first black mayor. Howard's career as a lawyer was undistinguished thereafter, the curriculum vitae of a legal bureaucrat, including a stint as a deputy solicitor for the Atlanta Municipal Court and another as an assistant district attorney for Fulton County, the entity that incorporates the bulk of the city of Atlanta. Notwithstanding this history, Howard seemed to possess an extraordinary drive for personal achievement. In this sense, at least, he was reminiscent of Clarence Thomas, another black boy from rural Georgia—Pin Point to Howard's Waynesboro. Howard's ambition had been evidenced in his quest to become the first black district attorney ever elected in the state of Georgia. He had vigorously sought and obtained the strong support of established black politicians, including not only the current mayor, Bill Campbell, but also Atlanta's influential first black mayor, Maynard Jackson. After defeating a black woman, Louise Hornsby, in the Democratic primary, he had gone on to win against his white Republican opponent.

Howard, who proudly referred to himself as a Morehouse man, a graduate of that historically black college for men that was also the alma mater of Dr. Martin Luther King Jr., was sworn into office in January 1997, at Morehouse's Martin Luther King Jr. International Chapel.

There, speaking with the barely detectable lisp produced by his mal-formed and thickly mustached upper lip, he told his supporters, a gath-ering of mostly middle-class blacks, that he would "reestablish a com-munity of justice." Howard had never really articulated a plan for such a reestablishment, his clearest campaign goal having been to become a "first black."

In the scheme of things, the Fulton County district attorney's office was the most important in Georgia, Atlanta being the hub of the county, the state, and, in fact, the region. Howard may not have had a plan, but he had made a promise or two. For the blacks who had supported him, his victory satisfied his promise to represent his race, on the most basic level. But Howard had also campaigned on a promise to get tough on crime, speaking in the jargon of the day—tougher than his Republican rival, former Bartow County assistant district attorney Brett Ladd, and perhaps even than the outgoing Fulton County district attorney, Lewis Slaton, who was retiring. While the blacks of Atlanta who still voted were surely proud of this "first," no matter what his agenda might be, and hopeful with regard to his promise to "reestablish" justice, the white majority of Howard's constituency were relying on his *other* promise.

In the latter part of 1996, when Howard was waging his election campaign, Atlanta still claimed the notorious distinction of having both the fourth-highest overall crime rate and *the* highest violent crime rate in the nation. The fact that the city had survived that summer's Centennial Olympic Games with little incident, aside from the infamous Olympic Park bombing, seemed to some a virtual miracle. At the same time, the larger success of the Games had allowed Atlanta to rise again, like the phoenix that is its symbol, to the brink of greatness. The crime rate, the high crime rate, now stood as the sole hindrance to the city's claim to its Olympian legacy and to what many saw as its divine destiny to be the hub and economic center of the so-called New South—a spark-ling crown jewel that could and would lure more and more big busi-ness and trade and tourism to its bosom. Atlanta had to seize the day, to cleanse itself, or at least its image, of this taint.

At the time, crime in Atlanta, as in the rest of America, had a color. Or in any event, crime *statistics* had a color, and that color was black. Although blacks comprised only about 13 percent of the total population of the United States, more than *half* of those convicted of crimes were black. In Georgia, around 70 percent of the prison population was black.[1] Moreover, of the children arrested and tried as adults in Fulton County and neighboring DeKalb County, 94 percent were black.[2] There had been no question, then, as to the meaning of Paul Howard's promise to get "tough on crime." The phrase was a barely coded message understood all over America to mean "tough on inner-city blacks charged with crimes," or "on black crime in the inner city," or "on black criminals." Indeed, Howard had, as one commentary in the *Atlanta Business Chronicle* stated at the height of his campaign, postured himself more as "running for sheriff."[3] Post-Olympics, Howard's pledge bore extraordinary weight, much of which now rested on his victorious shoulders. The city's powerful *Fortune* 500 businessmen were waiting.

Meanwhile, however, the black bureaucratic pyramid of the city's government, topped by the mayor and police chief Beverly Harvard (the first black woman police chief of a major city), was teetering precariously on the question of whether or not it could provide the right environment for post-Olympics business interests. Failure at this crucial juncture would cause the pyramid to crumble and fall, and plunge the remains of its black bureaucracy into a fall from grace like that of blacks previously so situated in New York, Chicago, Philadelphia, and Los Angeles, all of whom had been replaced by right-leaning whites. Howard's ability to deliver on his promise was the linchpin in their very survival.

In the context of these two great sets of interests—black and white, government and business—which were, in the end, joined, Howard's promise made him the man of the hour.

Within days of his being sworn in as the first new district attorney of *any* color in Fulton County in thirty years (the length of Slayton's tenure), the case of the shooting death of Darrell Woods came across Howard's desk. That it was not a particularly outstanding case on its merits was reflected in the brevity of the initial printed report of the murder in the *Atlanta Journal-Constitution*. Perhaps the only distinction between it and other, apparently similar shootings in the most drug-infested and poorest ghetto districts of Atlanta, Vine City and the Bluff, was the fact that the victim's small children had witnessed the killing. Perhaps, for that matter, it was that the victim, as a young black man, had even *had* a wife and children with whom he lived in a nuclear family unit. The commonness of this type of crime was such that even Woods's own family had experienced it before: only a year or so earlier, Darrell's cousin Michael Cortez Woods had been likewise gunned down and killed. But in the rightist political atmosphere that charged the nation in the post-Reagan years, when family values and tough-on-crime notions were intertwined cultural sound bites, and in a city that was holding its economic breath waiting to claim its divine destiny, and in a political milieu that seemed to be the last bastion of black elected officials in the twentieth century, this case gave Howard an immediate opportunity to make good on his campaign promise and at the same time make a name for himself.

Adding excitement to the pot, the mayor suddenly announced that he was offering a two-thousand-dollar reward for information about the killer of this black husband and father, a reward matched by Bishop Eddie Long, the superstar minister of one of Atlanta's new-age black megachurches, New Birth Missionary Baptist. Soon—one week to the day after Woods's murder—Eric Mills, Big E, was arrested as the prime suspect. Also arrested in connection with the murder was Jason Morgan, or J-Boy. These arrests were made on the strength of a sudden rush of reports provided by a host of informants-cum-addicts desperate to get their hands on four thousand dollars. Whatever the weakness of this information, the case would have made a politically compelling one for Howard. Big E had already been convicted the previous year for drug possession, a conviction for which he was still on probation. J-Boy, too, was on probation for drug possession, and was facing charges for stealing a handgun, in an incident dating from November 1996. Big E was also looking at two new felony charges for possession of drugs with intent to sell. Under the state's penal code, a first-time conviction for this felony carried a sentence of five to thirty years, and a second conviction, ten to forty. Furthermore, Georgia was a "two-strike" state, meaning that a second conviction for certain crimes would automatically result in life in prison without the possibility of parole. While drug dealing was not one of those "two-strike" crimes, there were recidivist statutes that could be combined with the drug felonies, which, when appended to his previous conviction, could still bring down a sentence of life in prison for Big E, who was twenty-one years old. Before the end of the day on which those arrests were made, however, a new suspect was being targeted by police as the killer of Darrell Woods. And by nightfall Big E had become the state's star witness—an eyewitness, even—against that new suspect, Michael Lewis. He would be able to bolster his statement with the testimony of two of his lieutenants, who were then in jail on their own drug charges, and with that of a woman in pink fluffy slippers who often sat in a folding chair out on Griffin Street.

Everybody in New Jack City, including the police, would come to endorse Big E's version of the events of that night, or a variation of it. Everybody would corroborate the motive Big E would provide, or some variation—a motive that would become a mob mantra within days. Even Valerie Johnson, riding in the police car later, would support this accusation; moreover, she would try, on the way to the Fulton County Youth Detention Center, to persuade her son, as she herself had perhaps been persuaded, to confess.

Howard had a stunning case, one that would serve as an opening salvo to announce his new position and his intention to fulfill his campaign promise. If that case rested solely on the testimony of a man facing a life sentence in prison, well, so be it. Little B was a black street tough who had killed Woods, a working black man, a husband and father, to prove his toughness, his manhood. Little B was the perfect perpetrator in the eyes of all concerned. A warrant was issued for his arrest for the murder of Darrell Woods, who had himself been known, on the street, as Little D.

All of Michael Lewis's short life, they had come for him. From the time his home had become a crack house when he was in third grade, they had come. They had come to arrest Val for prostitution or drugs, or to arrest her other son, J-Boy, for drugs or whatever. They had come three times to take Little B to court for deprivation hearings on the fitness of his mother. Once they had come to arrest him for shoplifting, and once, when he was ten, for a schoolyard fight that was recorded as a battery. Three other times they had come to get him as a "runaway," once as "ungovernable" and once for "disorderly conduct," but never for truancy, though he had not been in school for two years by this time. He was a throwaway boy, never worth very much, except maybe now, as a perfect scapegoat for the ambitions and expediencies of Eric Mills, the

Atlanta police, Paul Howard, Bill Campbell, and any number of *Fortune* 500 companies. When they came this time, he had no idea what it was about.

Surely the black and white detectives who came to arrest Michael that late afternoon were as overwhelmed as I would later be by the putrid smell emanating from the open sewer line that ran along the front of the filthy apartment complex. This was where Michael "stayed," they had been told—presumably by Big E and J-Boy. Having been on the streets since he was eleven, without the benefit of housing or any other basic support from DFACS or the juvenile court or the school system or any community church or other institution, Little B "stayed" here or there. Recently it had been there, at J-Boy's place on Holly Street. So that was where he was when the police came and knocked on the front door with its peeling red paint. Val appeared, ready to ride with him in one of the police cars outside.

"Who is it?" they would testify he answered quietly from the other side of the red door. "Police," they politely responded, or so they would say. He thought they were there about his brother or his mother, as usual. He had come back to the apartment not long before, after spending most of the day in the malls with his brother's baby's mama, Shalance Battle. Noticing that Morgan's handgun had been left lying out in the open, he protectively tossed it out of sight of the doorway onto a couch. Then he opened the door. He did not run. He did not resist. That they had in fact come for him, that it was *he* who was under arrest, still seemed a normal part of life in his universe, until the detectives completed the sentence by saying, "for the murder of Darrell Woods." He had never heard of Darrell Woods. He had never killed anyone. His heart was beating fast, he would later say.

Within hours, Valerie Johnson would tell the police that her son had confessed to her; within days, she would tell them that he had admitted knowing where the murder weapon was hidden, in back of the complex where J-Boy lived, where the police had arrested him. Returning to retrieve the gun, a rifle, the police would find it in the exact spot Michael's mother had described, even though by then more than a week had passed since the murder. Howard could rest his case.

<hr>

When Michael's arrest was announced, the city cheered. Everybody knew it had been someone like Little B. When Paul Howard declared his intention to try Little B as an adult, as per the provisions of the new law, the city cheered again. The mayor spoke of rooting out evil and proclaimed in a press conference a few days after the arrest, "We believe the person responsible has been found." [4] The blacks of New Birth Missionary Baptist and the like, like those in the bureaucratic pyramid, sighed with relief at being absolved of shame. *This* was the face of evil in the black community and in the city. The businessmen were satisfied.

Even in the Cas-A-Spell beauty shop that day, there was a fiery rage over the case, a rage that seemed to me, as I sat under the dryer, hotter than the straightening combs pressing the black women's hair. All the patrons were shouting to one another, none appearing to see what was on the street outside, out on Ralph David Abernathy Boulevard, where deferred dreams strolled by in the silence created by the shop's giant front windows. There were the regulars, as it were, including the man with the mangled hair who scratched his crotch through the gaping hole in the pants he wore, and seemingly must have worn all of his life, pacing up and down the street. There were the numberless others strutting by in the parade, the toothless, drug-addicted worn women, the unemployed young blacks bouncing by to their music, the shuffling old people invariably carrying an abundance of used shopping bags, the nondescript community consumers trying to find a bargain at the Dollar Store, or some long and shiny synthetic hair at the beauty-supply place, or a filling meal at the McDonald's next door or the Subway across the street.

"I'm so sick of these little niggers that mess up our communities," one woman said as the razor cleaned up her kitchen, the rough edges of hair at the nape of her neck.

"If the boy did the crime, he got to do the time."

"Yeah, killed a brother, a good brother!"

"He wanted to act like a man; now let him see what it's like to be treated like a man," another said, reading from the latest story in the *Atlanta Journal-Constitution* to verify and validate her position.

The dryer's heat on my head mercifully allowed me to fall unnoticed into a stupor of sorrow.

[3] Evil in the City

"Say," he began that day, inimitably, with the spirit of Nat King Cole's enchanted "Nature Boy," "you think I'm really evil?"

Was it really a question? I wondered in silence.

Hearing me somehow, he answered, "I mean, a lot of people say that 'bout me."

This was, of course, after the conviction. The jury had taken only a few hours to reach its verdict. It was the first week of his life sentence. His life had been spared because he was just fourteen years old, only a boy, and the state could not impose the death penalty. He had already been transferred to the Lee Arrendale State Prison, a maximum-security facility in the little town of Alto, tucked deep in the beautiful North Georgia Mountains, north of Gainesville. A onetime harbor for the Ku Klux Klan, this mountainous region was still home to a rural population of majority white, mostly poor people. The prison was the "company" that had reinvented the town and its environs, lifting their languishing population from the jaws of extinction.

It was hard to reckon with the beauty residing there, juxtaposed as it was with so much real evil, resting in the mountains' memory and in the steel and concrete of Lee Arrendale State Prison. This boy, Michael Lewis, had seriously questioned, there in the stillness of his prison, surrounded by the serenity of those hills, whether he was evil.

Atlanta's mayor, Bill Campbell, had broadcast the same theme, almost as a clarion call. It was nearly a year before, immediately following the arrest of this boy, whose name was now indelibly written in the historical record as "Little B." Little B was an evil in the city, the mayor had proclaimed. His words had echoed from City Hall to the editorial pages of the *Atlanta Journal-Constitution* and been carried through the streets of Atlanta and out to the suburban, lily-white enclaves: Little B was "evil." The very utterance seemed to me an expression of some sort of primal fear of the beast within. It was as though Little B were a mythical wolf-boy. It was as though some dark spirit hovering in an ether world had placed an imprint upon his being, or some sort of satanic genetic code had been embedded in his skin and soul, all unexorcisable.

When I caught my breath, I answered him, saying simply, "No." Then I added, "If there is evil here, Michael, it's not in you."

Since Michael had not killed this man, he seemed to have no other explanation for how his life had gone from bad to worse. It was surely difficult to comprehend being plunged from his already Dickensian existence into the abyss of life in prison, after only fourteen years of living. It must have been easy to believe this was a matter beyond the world of men and their political expediencies, some sort of kafkaesque nightmare. Thus the word *evil* had come to him, issuing from the mayor's mouth through the press to the courtroom and jury, and now eating away at him within his new prison. *Something* was evil; even *he* had begun to think it was inside him.

───

The stereotyping of black kids, especially boys, as menaces to society was enjoying a revival in American life at the time of Michael's trial. Subliminal messages hinting at some deviant quality inherent to black boys were flooding the nation's editorial pages and headlines like racist Rorschach tests.

Among the proliferation of *Journal-Constitution* editorials written about Michael was one published only a week after his arrest, which developed the syllogistic conclusion, supported by nothing more than its two cited cases, that Michael was the latest exemplar of a new breed of "scary" kids. These were "young killers . . . living outside the bounds of *normal* social interaction, *tiny thugs* who would kill at the slightest insult—or sometimes without any provocation" (emphasis added).[1]

In the myriad of similar pieces that followed, the newspaper painted a dark portrait of Michael as an "evil in our town," a "teen thug," a "predator," possessed of an "irresistible urge" to walk on the dark side—"seduced," like other "boys in Black America," by the "allure" of ghetto streets of "unspeakable savagery." The Reagan and Bush years had tempted Americans with the heady proposition that the country's ills were confined to street crime, and that the intoxicating solution to the problem was simply to "get tough on crime." As the country's white majority moved further to the right with Reagan and Bush, the definition of crime became more specifically urban and black: it was a thing rooted in the ghetto, and the exclusive province of its occupants, as evidenced by the alleged inundation of the country by crimes perpetrated by young black street toughs. (Ironically, of course, the early Reagan years had also shepherded a boundless supply of crack cocaine into the empty markets of the country's black communities, setting off the infamous ghetto drug wars that would ravage them over the next decade.) Public careers now turned on the question of toughness on crime, which itself became a kind of drug to which politicians, police, and established social commentators became codependently addicted. With the problem and the solution thus identified, the addiction fed upon itself and invented a new, dark mythology tying black youth to what was deemed to be, by the time Bill Clinton took office in 1993, a juvenile crime wave— or more particularly, in the code of the day, an *"urban"* juvenile crime wave.

The nation's most prestigious and widely respected and read journals were harbingers of these bad tidings, whipping up what had become a public frenzy. In August 1998, the *New York Times* seemed to surge ahead of the pack with its coverage of the arrest of two black boys from Chicago for the rape and murder of an eleven-year-old girl. In a sensational front-page story, the *Times* transformed this Chicago crime report into an issue of national significance. The story was founded solely upon the local police department's theory and reports about the murder and the accused perpetrators, who were seven and eight years old. The police theory, the *Times* reported, held that these young boys had raped and killed the girl in connection with their theft of her bicycle—her "blue bicycle," as the headline poignantly lamented. The story was accompanied by a large, sweet color photograph of the dead child, her innocent brown face subliminally cuing the reader to infer the color of the boys charged with her death, whose faces could not be shown. It was hard to summon a memory of any other time the *Times* might have allocated page-one space to a color photograph of a black child.[2]

The point of the story was captured in a subhead that identified the boys as "Perhaps the youngest Americans ever charged with murder," and in a quote from Chicago's mayor, the son and namesake of the city's infamous political boss Richard Daley: "The ages of these offenders is [sic] very frightening." The writer, Pam Belluck, established a presumption of guilt by providing an elaborately detailed description of the bestial acts the boys were accused of having committed. The victim, Ryan Harris, and the older boy, anonymous but for the fact that he was black and eight years old, had been seen riding their bicycles together on the morning of the day of the murder, according to the police. At some point they had encountered the seven-year-old boy, who likewise remained otherwise unidentified. Suddenly, the article reported, the seven-year-old had begun to throw rocks at Ryan, one of which struck her in the head. According to detectives, the boys then dragged the unconscious girl to a wooded area, pulled down her underpants, stuffed them into her mouth, "molested" her, and strangled her to death.

There apparently was no question of the boys' culpability, Belluck's piece noted, for the police had obtained "confessions" from both of them. With the question of guilt thus resolved, Belluck, through additional police quotes, attempted to trace the roots of the boys' monstrous acts. Ryan, she explained, ordinarily lived in a "working-class" Chicago suburb, but she had been spending the summer with relatives in the "impoverished" section of the city where she was murdered. The boys, in contrast, were native products of that ghetto's streets.

No doubt in an effort to balance the story, Belluck included a few brief statements by neighbors who refused to believe that these boys could have really committed such a heinous crime. The article's dominant theme, though, washed over such comments, and that theme prevailed. The story ended with a summary of the national debate over appropriate arrest procedures for young criminals.

For its part, the *Atlanta Journal-Constitution* followed up reports of this Chicago story with a full editorial page bearing the title "Conversation Starter," in which the editors invited public response.[3] The question posed was, "How Should Courts Handle the Unthinkable?" the "unthinkable" being the fact that very young (presumably black) boys were now roaming the streets and killing people. Joining the *Times* in its complete disregard for the presumption of innocence or journalistic ethics, the editorial board clarified any confusion readers might have had as to the nature and meaning of the question being raised: "In a country growing more accustomed to baby-faced murderers, this horrible Chicago case still shocks."

Similar stories about the two boys consumed other newspaper columns, radio talk shows, and nightly television broadcasts across the nation in mid-August 1998. In early September, however, the charges against them were quietly dropped. A more likely perpetrator, a grown man who was by then in jail on other, similar charges, had been identified. Floyd Durr, thirty years old, would soon admit to raping little Ryan and would later be charged with her murder.[4]

The sound of silence that subsequently fell over the nation on the subject of these boys amounted to a *thud*. It was impossible to find even a whispered recantation in the media of the hysterical, wholesale condemnation of the pair. No newspaper editorial page invited public response to the reckless, racist presumption of guilt that had been trumpeted in such bold headlines and so many column inches only weeks before. Even in the face of the real rapist's admission, there was no editorial examination of the facts of the case or revisitation of how it was that so many could so easily have concluded that these very young boys—these very young *black* boys—were responsible for, let alone physically *capable* of producing, the semen found on the poor girl's body (a point their ghetto neighbors had tried to raise in the few sentences they were afforded in the established press). There were, if anything, mere blurbs in the nation's newspapers about the charges' having been dropped against the boys. In the main, there was only the proverbially deafening silence, particularly on the proposition advanced by this Chicago story, that America was being overrun by boy predators, black boy predators, who stood poised to end the nation's innocence.

It was not until February 1999 that a lone voice broke the silence. It was that of liberal writer Alex Kotlowitz, who published a massive, confessional piece in *The New Yorker* magazine.[5] Therein he attempted to explain why America (including himself), or white America (including himself), had been so willing to summarily damn those two black boys. It would be some months more before, as *Time* magazine would report in a piece on its "Crime" page, Cook County prosecutors charged Durr, a convicted sex offender, with the murder of Ryan Harris. Durr, who had previously confessed to the child's rape, was now positively linked to her murder through DNA testing. The boys were thus completely exonerated. While bemoaning the "trauma" they had suffered by being so wrongfully accused, *Time* writer Ron Stodghill II also included in his coverage a kind of sidebar portrait of the family of one of the boys, which seemed to offer an explanation for the confusion. He wrote, "Rosetta Crawford, the boy's grandmother and family matriarch, took a drag on her cigarette and said softly, 'Somehow we became the most hated people in the world.' "[6]

These Chicago boys were not the first youngsters on the receiving end of the country's visible renewal of the wholesale condemnation of black youth that had marked its pre–Civil Rights history. In 1997, for example, in Oakland County, Michigan, Nathaniel Jamal Abraham was charged with first-degree murder. In an AP wire-service story, Nathaniel was referred to suggestively by county assistant prosecutor Lisa Tomko as "no ordinary eleven-year old boy."[7] For his part, police captain Greg Formanczyk professed to feel "shock and disbelief that someone that young and small could be a suspect in that type of crime." According to police, it was a "random shooting," a claim that veiled the case in the increasingly popular imagery of the black boy as predator, out searching for something to kill, choosing his prey "randomly."[8]

Even a trivial incident could bring down serious consequences on a black boy. In West Palm Beach, Florida, in 1998, fifteen-year-old Anthony Laster was charged with "strong-arm robbery" on the strength of an accusation that he had "snatched two dollars" from the pocket of a classmate. Arrested, charged, and held over for trial "as an adult," he remained in jail for weeks, until the absurdity of the case attracted the attention of the popular *60 Minutes* television program. At that point, and especially after it was made public that the alleged victim had conceded that Anthony had not so much intimidated him as made him "mad," prosecutors were obliged to drop the case.

More seriously, in 1996, Shareef Cousin was sentenced to death in Louisiana when he was only sixteen, making him one of the youngest people in America on death row, condemned, awaiting execution in the infamous Louisiana State Prison at Angola. One of the star deputies under New Orleans prosecutor Harry Connick Sr. (father of the entertainer) was able to get a conviction in the case without producing any physical evidence. He convinced the jury that Shareef was guilty based solely on "tentative" eyewitness testimony, primarily that of the victim's girl-friend, who said she remembered Shareef's "gaze"—an assertion later called into question by her admission that on the night of the murder-robbery she had not been wearing the contact lenses she needed in or-der to see.[9] All too typically, the man Shareef was accused of killing had been white: according to a report published by the NAACP Legal Defense Fund, fully two-thirds of the seventy-two juveniles on death row in America in 1999 were children of color—predominantly black—while two-thirds of the victims in these capital cases had been white.[10] Between 1976, when the death penalty was reinstated in the United States, and 1996, 318 defendants were tried, convicted, and executed for the deaths of 426 victims. Nearly 40 percent of those victims were black and 55 percent were white, yet only a little over 1 percent of the whites executed had been convicted of killing black victims, while—despite the presumed increase in "black-on-black" crime—*twice* as many blacks were executed for killing white victims as were put to death for killing other blacks.[11] What was even more compelling about this particular case, though, according to Shareef's appellate attorney, Clive Stafford-Smith of the Crisis Assistance Center in New Orleans, was that the boy's basketball coach swore he had been playing a game at the time of the murder-robbery.[12] Moreover, a videotape of that game confirmed the time and showed Shareef playing. Still, it was not until 1999 that this in-controvertible evidence finally persuaded an appellate court to overturn Shareef's conviction. He was set free after spending half his teen years at Angola, facing execution for a crime he had not committed.

Although it is primarily black boys who have come to exemplify such evil, black girls have not been exempted. There was, for instance, the 1996 case of Lacresha Murray, who, at eleven, was charged with murder in Austin, Texas. Accused of killing a baby, Lacresha, like the two boys in Chicago, made a "false confession" after being subjected to intense, isolated police grilling—in her case over a period of four days. In fact, she was innocent, and lucky enough to have supporters who fought to get her case reopened and her conviction overturned, though the process took three years.

Others have been much less fortunate—for example, fourteen-year-old Anisha Walker, who was convicted in Arlington County, Texas, for the 1997 shooting death of a forty-one-year-old man. The *Dallas Morning News* quoted Arlington police detective John Stanton as suggesting that Anisha did not have "the appearance nor [*sic*] attitude of a young girl." [13] This seemed to provide the prosecutor with the justification to make her the youngest person in the county ever tried as an adult, the first tried under a new state law, passed in 1995, authorizing prosecutors to try children as young as fourteen as adults. The law, authored by Arlington's Republican state representative, Toby Goodman, and vigorously supported by then-governor George W. Bush, reflected the dominant social attitude in the county and the state. That Anisha was the first in the home district of the bill's author to be prosecuted under the law also reflected its intent, which was to get girls like her—from whom, Goodman asserted, "the public ha[d] a right to be safe"—off the streets.

Bryan Buchanan, Anisha's defense attorney, shed a different light on the matter. In a telephone interview, he stated that his client, who had been forced into prostitution at an even younger age by older men, had been hired off the street by the Nigerian immigrant she was charged with killing. Instead of paying her, he had held her prisoner in his apartment for days, repeatedly raping and beating her. Finally she had found the will and a way to shoot the man and escape. Buchanan concluded that it was because she was so tragically poor and black that seemingly nobody in the county could imagine that Anisha deserved to exercise the right of self-defense and therefore to be adjudged innocent. [14]

The case that set the precedent for all the others in this new trend of indicting and punishing black children as "superpredators" was that of eleven-year-old Robert "Yummy" Sandifer, in 1994. Yummy's face provided *Time* magazine with its cover image for a story on the purported birth of a new breed of young urban killers. Yummy was exploited, too, by the recently elected president, Bill Clinton, to exemplify what he claimed was a growing problem in the United States, which had led him to declare, in his September 10, 1994, radio address, a National Gang Violence Prevention Week. More significantly, Yummy was used by Clinton to garner and bolster Republican support for his 1994 Crime Bill, which toughened the nation's laws relating to juvenile crime offenders and introduced innovative procedures for punishing them, including the creation of boot camps and drug courts. Yummy was the reason, according to Clinton, that America had to become "tough on crime." [15]

Perhaps the most interesting thing about Yummy's case and the infamy being heaped upon him in the press was this: not only had he never been charged with, tried for, or convicted of the murder of which he stood publicly accused, but also, and even more curiously, he was dead. Within days of allegedly having killed a fourteen-year-old girl, Shavon Dean, Yummy had himself been killed. Nevertheless, *Time* magazine devoted its cover story to unsubstantiated reports that Yummy had murdered this other black child. The *Time* theory was that he had been fulfilling a gang initiation requirement to kill, but had missed his intended target and accidentally shot and killed Shavon instead. In the days after the incident, street rumors had reportedly spread that Yummy was planning to turn himself in to the police. Before such a scenario could play itself out, however, he was found under a bridge, shot to death, presumably by other gang members eager to keep him from talking.

Yummy's tragic death, which paralleled the tragedy of his short life (he had been homeless and abandoned by the time he was eight), could not keep him from being held up for public denunciation as a ruthless killer. The *Time* reporters apparently scoured the blighted Roseland community of Chicago's South Side to talk with Yummy's neighbors, unearthing an anonymous source who offered the opinion that the boy had been a "sociopath." *Time* writer Julie Grace provided a description of the sociopathic Yummy: a "4'8", 68-pound runt . . . pedaling through the streets on his seatless black bike, in high-price tennis shoes and big, baggy clothes . . . [with a] 'nappy' hairstyle—intimidat[ing] the neighborhood with his use of knives, fire and guns . . . he would steal, sell drugs, set fires." Finally, the manager of a local corner store voiced sentiments about Yummy that seemed to echo those of the nation: "They should have hung him in the middle of the street." [16]

It was no surprise that *Time* had stepped into the vanguard of a new national discussion about the country's black "problem." In its cover story about Yummy, the powerful weekly cultivated a new idiom for white racism, which had been muted by the "politically correct" language and behavior promoted in the late 1960s, the 1970s, and the 1980s by the last gasps of liberals. Now, with *Time*'s "report" on the rise of a new breed of criminal in America—the young black "superpredator"— racist stereotyping and denigration of blacks could regain their place in the social discourse and landscape. *Time*'s founder, Henry Luce, had established this journalistic tradition. According to his biography, Luce had "not hesitated to use his magazines to reflect the principles in which he believe[d, as a] . . . Republican . . . defender of big business, a foe of big labor." [17] It was Luce, after all, who had been the architect of the notion that the twentieth century was the "American Century," in which America—that is, the white, right-wing America defined by Luce—would claim its "manifest destiny" to lead and dominate the world.

――――――

The promulgation of the stereotype of the black boy as a social evil is at once a product of the press and a reflection of deeper social realities. This does not, however, diminish the powerful role of the media in providing American racism with a vocabulary and a definition in the post–Civil Rights movement era.

The Western press is known as the Fourth Estate, the fourth arm of the ruling social class. Like American common law, the power of the press derives historically from English and French social structure. The process began in the fourteenth century, when Western monarchs, seeking to abate imminent popular threats to their absolute power, ordained the clergy, first, as an "Estate," or arm, of themselves, securing their rule by "divine right." Next came the nomination of the nobility as a Second "Estate," a new partner in power. The end of the eighteenth century, and the opening of new worlds, brought the desperate establishment of a third auxiliary, an entity alleged to represent the common people; it was this Third Estate that dominated the leadership of the French and American revolutions. The Fourth Estate, the press, was the last branch of the ruling power structure.

While the preindustrial monarchies of the West have withered into relative irrelevancy, there remains, unquestionably, an elite class of people that rules America. Its voice is the American press. Its primary mission is to articulate and defend the interests of big corporations and important individuals, whose advertising dollars, after all, support newspaper and magazine distribution and television and radio programming. The press in America, as an extension of the powerful, has come to define the day.

Even as Michael Lewis was being held up by the local press as an evil presence in society, and offered up to the prosecutor and to politicians as a singular sacrifice for their common agenda regarding juvenile crime, a teen time bomb was exploding in America's heartland. Nice white boys, true sons of America, children of the Bible Belt and suburbia, were committing multiple mass murders so bold and so brutal that they could be neither concealed nor whitewashed. The dominant voices in America, the press and politicians, seemed stunned by these murders, though not necessarily outraged. This time the question was, "What's happening to our children?"

On October 1, 1997—a month or so before Michael was to stand trial—sixteen-year old Luke Woodham, of Pearl, Mississippi, stabbed his fifty-year-old mother to death in her bed. He then went to school— Pearl High—where he fatally shot two fellow students and wounded seven others. Woodham admitted to these heinous acts but pled not guilty by reason of being "possessed." He was tried as an adult, convicted, and sentenced to life in prison in June 1998. Notwithstanding this, or the paralyzing effect on national life of the rash of mass murders perpetrated by other white boys in the period between Woodham's murders and his sentencing, the press portrayed him, upon his conviction, not as himself an evil boy but rather as the innocent victim of an evil, demonic "cult."

In particular, it was an Associated Press wire story about Woodham, circulated through most of the nation's newspapers during his trial, that promulgated this theory. Identifying him in fairly conservative language, as "a teenager accused of fatally stabbing his mother and gunning down two classmates," the wire-service report focused on psychological analyses of Woodham provided by defense experts, relating to his "possession." Through this story and its spin-offs, Woodham attained the status of a "psychologically disturbed young man." Indeed, he was deemed "vulnerable" to being "exploited" by certain older boys who, according to police investigators, "led a cultlike group of teenagers." The end result of this vulnerability to demonic influences was, the AP story explained, that Woodham "woke up that morning and . . . [saw] demons." Evidently this was how he came to be "surprised" when, moments later, he "opened his eyes" to find his mother "lying in her bed," not only fatally stabbed by him but also bludgeoned with a baseball bat.[18] The AP photograph of Woodham picked up by the *Atlanta Journal-Constitution* on the day of his first conviction, for the murder of his mother, bore as its caption a quote from him: "Everything happens for a reason, it's God's will." [19]

Woodham's case was only the first in a series of like multiple murders that would grip the nation over the next few years. All of the perpetrators, all of them white teenage boys, would be defined in the press as possessed, misunderstood, alienated, isolated, or lonely—but never "evil."

Just months after Woodham murdered his mother and two classmates, fourteen-year-old Michael Carneal, son of a locally prominent lawyer and elder in the Lutheran church of West Paducah, Kentucky, fired onto a Christian prayer circle of his fellow students at Heath High School, killing three of them. Carneal's murderous rampage, in which five others were also wounded, was described in the press as "a mystery, perhaps even to the boy himself. . . . Some wondered whether they would ever have an answer." The town's sheriff noted, "He said he was sorry." While one minister was quoted as saying, "I believe there is a real demonic force that would drive someone to do this," the Reverend Paul Donner of the St. Paul Lutheran Church insisted, "I'm firmly convinced Michael Carneal is a Christian." [20]

Only months after *that,* on March 24, 1998, thirteen-year-old Mitchell Johnson and eleven-year-old Andrew Golden, armed with four handguns and three high-powered rifles and outfitted in camouflage gear, ambushed fellow students at Westside Middle School in Jonesboro, Arkansas, and opened fire on them. They killed four girls and one teacher and wounded eleven other children. These killings became the cover story of every major journal in the country, and the subject of unending electronic media reports. *Newsweek* magazine sublimated its coverage of the thirtieth anniversary of the assassination of Dr. Martin Luther King Jr. in order to devote nearly an entire issue to the Jonesboro incident. The resulting story was a variation on the new American theme: "What makes kids kill."

The *Newsweek* piece concluded that only confusion reigned in such cases, because, in the words of one of Johnson's teachers, "For the most part, . . . kids [like Johnson] are sheltered and innocent." The writers reported that on being apprehended, Johnson "kept saying he was sorry."

While Golden was said to act "insouciant" in public, he was described as privately "sobbing in his cell." The article closed by hammering home its point one last time: "Everyone says the same thing in Jonesboro now, the relatives of the suspects, of the victims, townspeople and teachers. They're sorry it happened, and it was so very, very senseless." [21]

Although Johnson was the same age as Little B at the time of his arrest, he was tried as a juvenile along with the younger Golden. After pleading guilty, both were sentenced to confinement in juvenile facilities until the age of eighteen, at which point they will, each of them, be released. For Johnson, this will mean five years of incarceration.

A year later, in May 1999, in the wake of the notorious similar tragedy in Littleton, Colorado, *Newsweek* published an opinion piece by Johnson's father, Scott, about his son's incarceration. A friendly color photograph of the author accompanied the essay, in which the senior Johnson, speaking as a kind of self-appointed spokesman for parents of white boy killers, expressed his profound puzzlement about what had "gone wrong" and how "it could have happened" to *his* child. He pleaded with America to understand these "desperate kids in need of attention," though he stressed that in the end, his greatest concern was for Mitchell's future: he worried, he wrote, about what kind of person his son—who had ambushed and murdered five people and wounded eleven others—would be upon his eventual release, having been housed in a facility "full of young gangbangers." [22]

The growing cadre of confused parents came to include, only a month after the Jonesboro killings, those of fourteen-year-old Andrew Wurst. Wurst, carrying his father's .25 caliber handgun, went to the eighth-grade graduation dance at Parker Middle School in Edinboro, Pennsylvania, on Friday night, April 24, 1998, and opened fire on the celebrants. He killed one teacher and wounded two students and another teacher. An AP wire story, while quoting friends of the boy's as saying that he had, in the past, "joked about killing people," noted that Wurst "apparently didn't say he planned to kill at the dance." As to "answers," then, the story quoted friends of Wurst's who described him as having "a troubled home life and combative parents." Finally, the superintendent of the school district, seeming to speak for one and all, said, "The sad part of this whole thing is I don't have any answers." [23]

Four weeks later, on the morning of May 20, 1998, fifteen-year-old Kipland "Kip" Kinkel, after brutally murdering both his mother and his father and stuffing their bodies into a crawl space in the family home along with some undetonated bombs, went off to school. Armed with his father's .22 caliber Ruger semiautomatic handgun and 9-millimeter Glock pistol and his own automatic rifle, Kinkel walked into the cafeteria of Thurston High in Springfield, Oregon, and began firing on the students gathered there. He killed two of them and wounded twenty-five more before being tackled and stopped. Despite this bloodbath, as well as his booby-trapping of the family home and his assaulting the police who arrested him with a hunting knife he had taped to his chest, he was characterized in wire-service stories as a "freckle-face[d] teenager." [24]

A feature article by *Providence Journal* columnist Froma Harrop explained, furthermore, that though Kip "lived in a new bedroom community . . . that embodie[d] the Northwest ideal[, a] . . . woodsy development . . . called Shangri-La," he was a "geographically isolated child." "Youngsters, especially, must socialize," Harrop asserted, "but that becomes hard to do in exurbia." She concluded that "it [was] not a coincidence that the great majority of schoolhouse shootings . . . [had] taken place in lonely exurbia." [25]

Less than six months later, on November 2, 1998, a fifteen-year-old Atlanta suburbanite named Jonathan Miller, a student at Etowah High School, pummeled and kicked a thirteen-year-old middle-school student into a coma. Two days later, the thirteen-year-old died, and the charge against Miller was increased from assault to murder. Miller's case is particularly interesting because he was tried on the same charge as Little B and in a neighboring judicial district just outside Atlanta.

Miller, however, unlike Michael Lewis, was never branded a "thug," even though the factual issue of whether or not he had beaten his victim was not a matter of debate. He was never identified as an "evil in the city." Indeed, in the *Atlanta Journal-Constitution*'s coverage of his trial, Miller was referred to simply as a "youth," who was, moreover, said to be "suffering" from "attention-deficit disorder." Furthermore, the newspaper criticized the "unusual" media attention that had been devoted to Miller's case, which had surely, it suggested, tainted the prospective jury; it even went so far as to assume specific responsibility for this presumedly unfair pretrial publicity. A May 1, 1999, feature on Miller's trial proceedings noted, "The *Atlanta Journal-Constitution* began printing a weekly edition of Cherokee [County—where Miller resided and was being tried] news in 1997. . . . Metropolitan Atlanta reporters began coming to Cherokee more often. . . . That has given the Miller case more media attention than it might have received years ago." [26]

More to the point, though, was the May 13, 1999, *Journal-Constitution* editorial on Miller's conviction, as an adult, for murder. The piece was entitled "Punishment Too Harsh." [29] In it Miller was cast by the editors as a "troubled child who need[ed] help" and who should not, therefore, have been held to the same standard for the same crime as, say, a boy like Little B. The editors, led by black editorial-page editor Cynthia Tucker, established this point of comparison in the very opening paragraph of their postconviction opinion piece on Miller: "The mandatory life sentence [Miller received] does not fit the *criminal*" (emphasis added). In addition, they wrote, the charge of "murder" was inappropriate in this case, where a "charge of involuntary manslaughter would have [better] fit the crime." In any event, the editors argued, Miller's age—though he was two years *older* than Little B at the time of his arrest—"should have been a mitigating factor." In the end, however, the *Journal-Constitution* staffers charged that what had been most damning for Miller—more than the pretrial publicity or anything else—was the ambience in the nation when he went to trial, in May 1999. Only weeks before, on April 20, 1999, two other white teenage boys had perpetrated the massacre at Columbine High School in Littleton, Colorado.

Columbine seniors Eric Harris, eighteen, and Dylan Klebold, seventeen, were the authors of the most violent and lethal "school shootings" in the history of the United States. While the *Atlanta Journal-Constitution* would contend that this infamous incident had created an explosive atmosphere that proved detrimental to Jonathan Miller, national sentiment, including the paper's own editorials, had been quite sympathetic toward the youthful suburban killers.

Although Harris and Klebold had randomly murdered twelve students and one teacher before turning their guns on themselves, the majority of America's citizens seemed to feel, to judge by the volumes of articles and hours of television and radio-talk-show discussions on the topic, more troubled than outraged by the episode—more sorrowful than horrified, and more forgiving, even, than judgmental.

The bold, front-page headline over the *Journal-Constitution*'s first report about the murders quoted a Littleton resident to sum up the national mood: " 'Make sense of it? We can't.' " One of the two page-one stories attending this headline, a republication of a *New York Times* piece, was headed "Teenagers didn't give off *aura* of murderers" (emphasis added).[28] This feature was replete with quotes from the murderers' friends, mostly referring to how really "ordinary" these "boys" had been: "They wanted to portray themselves as *rebels* or *villains*. But mostly they were . . . *losers*." The "jump" headline highlighted the feelings of one of Klebold's friends: "He really felt unloved."

America's hearts and minds, so vengeful and bitter not so long before, so outraged as to have forced swift passage of a body of Draconian juvenile-crime laws directed at black youth, seemed suddenly to have been healed of their wrath and rage and to have found forgiveness. This generosity about the Littleton teenagers stood in stark contrast to past responses to black boys such as Yummy or Little B—and even more so given the absence of an even remotely comparable case (that is, a mass murder) involving black boys.

Within only two days of the Columbine killings, the nation had evidently reached a consensus that when white boys killed it was a matter of "alienation." With the issue thus defined, a full-blown examination of teen angst became the centerpiece of national discussion. Sympathy for the Columbine *victims* came to be forfeited in favor of a meditative concern over the anguish of the "American teenagers" who had killed them. This raised a rhetorical question in my mind: What might the response have been had the murderers been black boys and the victims the same whites who had been killed, or, alternatively, had the murderers and victims all been black?

Five days after the shootings, on April 25, 1999, the *New York Times* filled its Sunday pages with analyses, including one by reporter Timothy Egan on the theme of the alienated American teenager, entitled "The Trouble with Looking For Signs of Trouble."[29] Egan pondered the difficulty of trying to distinguish one such American teen from another when searching for signs of a murderous heart. Showing unusual restraint in his use of language in connection with the murders committed by the Littleton boys, Egan wrote, "As educators develop a profile of a child who may murder his classmates, they are wading into the same territory [where] airport security personnel, police departments and Federal agents have already gone—often with unhappy results." One such recent, unhappy result cited by Egan was the criticism leveled at New Jersey governor Christine Todd Whitman for giving state troopers free rein to develop a profile of the typical drug dealer—whom they had chosen to portray as a black man. This profile had recently been used to "improperly" justify the wildly disproportionate number of stops and searches of blacks by state troopers on New Jersey's highways and by-ways, an outcome for which Whitman had been forced to make a public apology.

The point of Egan's piece was that it was hard to recognize that a white juvenile might kill, given that across the nation, all police profiles of young criminals pointed to black or, occasionally, Hispanic boys. But rather than draw the obvious conclusion—that were such a profile to be developed for teen mass murderers, it would inevitably describe a suburban white boy—Egan offered an alternative interpretation: "Often the *invisible* student is the one most likely to explode—not the gang member, bully or loudmouth."

That same Sunday, conservative commentator George Will demonstrated a remarkable ability to become instantly soft on crime—at least when it was perpetrated by suburban white boys. Offering his thoughts on the Colorado massacre on the ABC network television news show *Meet the Press,* Will made the observation that one common thread among the recent school shootings was that they had all occurred at public schools. There had been no such murders at private schools, where students wore uniforms.

A few days later, on April 28, Katie Couric, host of NBC television's *Today* show, came forward with her own view, expressing concern for the families of the perpetrators: "We often forget that they [the killers' parents] are victims too."

Time magazine, which had featured Yummy Sandifer on its cover only five years before as the face of the "superpredator" stalking the streets of America, summed up the new national perplexity over these teen killers. Juxtaposed with bright photographs of Harris and Klebold, the stark *Time* cover blurb read "The Monsters Next Door . . . What Made Them Do It." The question of "why" had never come up in the cover story about Yummy—an omission made even more interesting by the fact that the lead reporter for both pieces was Julie Grace. Grace had seemed anything *but* troubled by deeper questions about Yummy's persona, having summarily damned him as a "sociopath." Now, however, Grace and the *Time* team put together a piece written by Nancy Gibbs, in which they wondered in print "what turned two boys' souls into poison" and asked "why smart, privileged kids rot inside." [30]

Even as metropolitan Atlanta reflected on Columbine through the filter of the media, breathing a sigh of relief that its own teen killers presumably remained in the "inner city," one month to the day after the Littleton murders, fifteen-year-old Anthony "T. J." Solomon walked into Rockdale County's Heritage High School with a rifle and a handgun and shot into a crowd of three hundred students. In its first, front-page story under a headline screaming "It Happened Here," the *Atlanta Journal-Constitution* reported, "The shooting happened in suburban Atlanta, in a school known for parental involvement and good academics . . . in a middle-class community." [31] Solomon seriously wounded six students—though killing none, as Heritage High officials hurriedly noted with bizarre pride.

The newspaper recounted the story of Solomon's arrest with unusual compassion—particularly in comparison to its coverage of the arrest of Little B, just over two years earlier. Declining to reveal Solomon's name out of respect for the tenderness of his age, these first lead stories referred to him only as a "Boy Scout," whom staff reporter Craig Schneider deemed to be "suicidal." Schneider's piece noted the community's eerie relief that "no one was killed when a suicidal high school student, upset over breaking up with his girlfriend, turned his anger on the world." He was, Schneider suggested, a "disgruntled boy [who] came to Heritage High School . . . with two guns, a broken heart and a terrible agenda."

In the months following the Heritage High shooting, in coverage relating to the charges against the "Boy Scout" and to the legal issue of whether he would be tried as an adult—as Georgia law seemed to require—Solomon was depicted in the press as "suffer[ing] from long-term, untreated and major depression." [32] The *Atlanta Journal-Constitution* published a lengthy editorial by staff writer R. Robin Mc-

Donald entitled "Punishing Choices: How to Try Teens Charged with Major Crimes?" It was a question that had never once been raised in the newspaper's fifty-plus stories on the "evil" boy known as Little B.

With brazen candor McDonald revealed why the subject had never been broached in relation to Michael Lewis: "The contrasting image of a would-be killer and a depressed, distraught and lonely youngster [like Solomon] . . . is at the heart of the debate over how Georgia treats its young, violent juvenile offenders." McDonald then unabashedly explained precisely what she meant by a "contrasting image": "Virtually no one disagrees that juveniles who intentionally commit violent crimes"—though under the law a "crime" can exist *only* where there is "intent"—"[or] who are habitual criminals should be locked away." Lest anyone fail to take her point, McDonald's two-page commentary was accompanied by a large photographic display that positioned pictures of Jonathan Miller and Michael Lewis side by side. Miller, the white boy from suburban Atlanta who had been convicted of killing a younger boy at a school-bus stop, was identified in the caption as being "responsible for a beating death in Cherokee County." By "contrast," Michael was referenced in the caption as "Michael Lewis, known as Little B, who shot a father to death in front of his two children in Vine City."

McDonald concluded her piece with a quote from state senator David Scott. Scott, a black man, had been a strong supporter of Georgia's harsh juvenile-crime law, known as Senate Bill 440, which mandates, among other things, a *ten-year* prison sentence for any child convicted of *armed robbery.* Reflecting on these depressed, distraught, and lonely youngsters, Scott now wondered rhetorically, along with McDonald, "Who is responsible for the child at Heritage High School doing what he did? . . . Who do we hold accountable?" [33]

Such soul searching seems, however, to have been reserved for reflection on a white boy who shot dozens of kids at Heritage High; or a white boy who beat a younger, smaller boy to death at a bus stop; or white boys who killed classmates at Columbine High in Colorado and Pearl High in Mississippi and Heath High in Kentucky and Westside Middle School in Arkansas and Parker Middle School in Pennsylvania and Thurston High School in Oregon. Indeed, according to a report issued by

Building Blocks for Youth, a "qualitative analysis of all cover stories in *Time* and *Newsweek* between 1946 and 1995 determined that the term 'young Black males' [had become] synonymous with the word 'criminal.' "[34]

The reality has followed the image. According to a report published by the Washington, D.C.–based Youth Law Center, while black children age ten to seventeen constitute just 15 percent of the total U.S. population in that age group, they account for 26 percent of all juvenile arrests, 32 percent of delinquency referrals to juvenile court, 41 percent of juveniles detained in delinquency cases, 46 percent of juveniles in correctional institutions, and 52 percent of juveniles transferred to adult criminal court.[35] The same report also indicated that "in 1991 the long-term custody rate for African-American youth was nearly five times the rate for white youth, and in 1995 a black youth was seven times as likely to be held in a public detention facility as a white youth." Further, it documented that "black youth are also much more likely to end up in prisons with adult offenders."

II
SHADOW OF THE DOME

[4] Atlanta: Hub of the New South

Prosecutor Paul Howard seemed to know, instinctively, how valuable it would be to hold forth Little B as the exemplar of what was wrong in Atlanta. It was a wrong he had personally pledged to right. Looking beyond advancing his own career interests as the state's first black district attorney, Howard also understood his role in serving the big economic interests of Atlanta. He had become an obsequious Jonah, comfortable in the belly of the whale. Atlanta's confederation of powerful white businessmen was prepared either to swallow whole or to kill anything that threatened to undermine the Olympic promise. And at the beginning of 1997, when Howard took office and Darrell Woods was killed in the Bluff, Atlanta appeared to be standing on the brink of the destiny it had attended for more than a century.

―――――――

Union army general William Tecumseh Sherman's burning of Atlanta in November 1864 marked the effective end of the Confederacy. With it came not only the official demise of slavery but also the death of "King Cotton," rendering Georgia, in particular, economically moribund. At best this was an inglorious emasculation of the South, so many of whose sons had been the nation's founding fathers. Undaunted and unforgiving, the South pledged to rise again. It would have to suffer the Great Depression and two world wars, however, to become the economic equal of the rest of America.

In 1860, only a year before the Civil War erupted, two of three males in the United States worth $100,000 or more lived in the South, as Claud Anderson notes in his book *Black Labor, White Wealth*. This southern wealth was attributable solely to the ownership of land and slaves, and was grounded in the cultivation and production of cotton and cotton goods, distributed nationally and internationally. The South was not alone in profiting from slave-produced cotton and its byproducts: New England had three times as many textile mills as the entire South, which mills processed one quarter of all slave-produced cotton. This industry provided northern populations with clothes, fabric, income, and other benefits and silenced the northern white majority on the issue of slavery. Indeed, in that predawn of the Civil War, capital investment in black slaves, at $7 billion, exceeded all other American business investments "in the North, South and the federal budget combined." [1]

Georgia was considered the "Empire State of the South" on account of its powerful slave-supported economy, dominated by King Cotton. This was true even though it was the youngest of the original thirteen states.

When Englishman James Edward Oglethorpe and the consortium of businessmen with whom he was in league, the Georgia Trustees, created Georgia in 1733, slavery was officially prohibited in the colony. This was not a moral stance, for Oglethorpe himself owned slaves in the Carolinas and was a partner in the Royal African Company, a slave-trading enterprise. Rather, the stated intent of Oglethorpe and the trustees was to build a lily-white colony of hardworking Protestant Englishmen, free of reliance upon slaves. It would be a kind of white man's oasis in the midst of South Carolina and Florida, where, on the one hand, the slave-dependent economy was producing a potentially formidable slave population, and, on the other, runaway slaves were being harbored by enemies of the English crown. Only two years after England granted the trustees the Georgia charter, however, a protest against the ban on slavery began to gain ground. Soon the ban was lifted and the way opened to the institution of large plantations in Georgia.

Over the next decades, the center of the country's slave population moved from Virginia to Georgia, mostly because cotton plantation had shifted on account of exhausted soil. In his definitive work on the subject, *The Way It Was in the South: The Black Experience in Georgia*, Donald L. Grant reports that by 1812 cotton production dominated Georgia's economy. Georgia had become the *world's* leading cotton producer.[2]

This cotton boom and the discovery of gold in the Appalachian

Mountains triggered the desire to establish more white settlements in Georgia, an ambition that, almost incidentally, required the final removal of the Indians from its territories. State and federal laws were passed mandating the surrender of all Cherokee lands to the United States and, by 1838, the "relocation" of the native people themselves to the far side of the Mississippi River. Some fourteen thousand Cherokees were accordingly rounded up by the army and led out of Georgia in a forced exodus that left one in four dead, claimed by the wintry trek that the Cherokees would come to call the Trail of Tears.

In the first decades of the nineteenth century, over a thousand miles of railroad track were laid in Georgia, making it the transportation hub of the South.[3] Atlanta developed itself into a regional junction for the rail transport of goods, finally connecting the country's Atlantic coast with its interior. Although the nearby Chattahoochee River was unnavigable, and the land was difficult to cultivate, the city enjoyed the geographic advantage of being situated at the intersection of three granite ridges at the foot of the Appalachian Mountains. This pivotal point gave rise to Atlanta, which started out as the small train depot that marked the spot; in fact, as the town grew up around the depot, it was first named Terminus. A white settlement that had few and mostly domestic slaves (though it hosted slave markets and auctions), it became the bustling home to river-ferry operators and tavern owners along the stagecoach routes used by migrating farmers, adventurers, traders, and later gold prospectors, land speculators, and railroad workers. By the 1850s, it was the seat of a new county, Fulton, named for Robert Fulton, inventor of the steamboat. And by 1860 it was a burgeoning railroad town, the fourth-largest city in the state. The following year, when Georgia became the fifth state to join the new entity known as the Confederate States of America, Fulton County sent more volunteers than any other county to fight in the War between the States.

In the four years of the Civil War, Atlanta's population more than doubled, increasing from nine thousand to twenty-two thousand. The city became the third largest in the entire Confederacy, outranked only by the seaport of New Orleans and the Confederate capital of Richmond, Virginia.[4] It grew because its terrain was a protected interior, far from the fighting, and because it was the hub of Confederate transportation, linking two of the three major railroad lines that bound together the eleven

Confederate states. This was why the fall and burning of Atlanta brought the Confederacy to its knees.

The South was economically devastated by the loss of slave labor attendant on its defeat in the Civil War. The termination of slavery wiped out millions upon millions of dollars in southern "assets" and capital. Slave-produced cotton was all Georgia knew. The response of the broken Confederacy was to try to restore its past glory through brutal postwar resistance, manifested in the Black Codes, a codified rejection of black enfranchisement in spite of the new constitutional amendments, and in the attempted reinvention of slavery in the form of sharecropping. This was all supported by the newly organized Ku Klux Klan and other white terrorist groups, and underwritten by the still-silent northern majority and the benign neglect of the federal government, especially the president, Andrew Johnson.

Having not itself been dependent on slave labor, though certainly profiting from it, Atlanta, more than most, had the will and the ability to resurrect itself from the ashes. It came to see itself as the leader of a New South.

A new political order arose, dominated by Democrats, whom the dying Lincoln Republicans referred to as the Bourbons. This was an aggressive, business-minded planter-merchant clique that included several Confederate generals. While their focus was on profits and the coming industrialization of the South, theirs was a white supremacist philosophy. These New South entrepreneurs, who considered themselves "Redeemers" sent to usher in daybreak after "the long and cheerless night of [Reconstruction] misrule," were in the vanguard in terms of using any means necessary to get Atlanta and the South back on their economic feet. By forcing through legislation that allowed prisoners to be "farmed out" on five-year leases, for example, they created a new, legitimized system of slavery to fill cheap-labor shortages and rebuild Georgia. Nearly all of the convicts in the labor pool were blacks, who were "leased out" in those postemancipation years to work on the construction of, among other necessary enterprises, the Georgia and Alabama Railroad and the Macon and Brunswick Railroad lines.[5] Such Machiavellian expediency came to be known as the Atlanta Spirit—a civic-sounding name for the notion that whatever was good for business was good for Atlanta.

In 1895, the city, now the capital of Georgia, hosted the biggest of three post–Civil War events in this ongoing campaign toward resurrection. At the Cotton States and International Exposition that year, Atlanta promoted itself as the center of the "New South," the bastion of a new, *diversified* economy and a "changing" South.

The term "New South" had been earlier popularized by Henry W. Grady, then the editor of the most important newspaper in Georgia, the *Atlanta Constitution,* and the voice of the Bourbons. The term, like the 1895 exposition, represented a plea for the investment of *northern* capital into the devastated southern economy. The South had been born again, the message went, and was now ready to be a full partner in the Union. Northern investors could be assured that this was a *new* South, one that embraced industrialization and rejected slavery, a place where, as Grady said, "mutual confidence and goodwill between blacks and whites had replaced the doubt and distrust of the past." Furthermore, by investing in the New South, northern whites could be relieved of the burden of the millions of ex-slaves who would surely otherwise head north. Such investment would provide the means for blacks to stay where they were—there in the New South, where southern whites understood them. The son of a prosperous slave owner who had died in the Civil War, Grady spoke forcefully on this question, harmonizing the industrialization of a New South with the sentimentalized, Bourbon-class view of the Old South, asserting in just one of his many speeches that in *his* South, "each has his place and fills it, and is satisfied. . . . As a matter of course, this implies the clear and unmistakable domination of the white race in the South."[6]

Despite such promotion, the very name of the 1895 exposition revealed Georgia's (and the South's) continued, problematic dependence on cotton; indeed, in the last two decades of the nineteenth century nearly half of the state's cultivated acreage was devoted to this crop. The exposition did, however, draw more than eight hundred thousand visitors. It was highlighted, as such, by the historic speech of Booker T. Washington, in which the black leader, commander of the so-called Tuskegee Machine, urged the whites of the New South to accept a new economic interdependency between the races, in exchange for which blacks would accede to social segregation and continued disfranchisement. This New South, Washington asserted—in a statement that brought his audience to its feet—demanded compromise on the part of both blacks and whites, but ultimately it would allow the whole South to rise out of the devastation of the Civil War. It was his idea, and his promise, that "in all things that are purely social we can be as separate as the fingers, yet one as the hand in all things essential to mutual progress."[7]

While race mattered in the New South, the more pressing issue was economic development. As Horace Mann Bond pointed out in his study of Alabama after 1868, the southern economy had the immediate and greatest potential to garner an "accumulation of capital . . . [through the] exploitation of . . . natural resources." The South held coal, iron, and other unexploited power reserves needed in the new industries, a bounty long known, as Bond explained, to "the bankers in Philadelphia and New York, and even in London and Paris. . . . The only thing lacking was transportation." Thus, as Howard Zinn notes in this regard in his acclaimed *A People's History of the United States,* "northern bankers began appearing in the directories of southern railroad lines." (By 1875, for example, J. P. Morgan was a director of several lines in Alabama and Georgia.) The moment the Bourbons had been waiting for, when, in the words of an 1886 *New York Daily Tribune* article, "Northern capitalists would be convinced not only of the safety but of the immense profits to be gained from the investment of their money in developing the fabulously rich coal and iron resources of Alabama, Tennessee, and Georgia [had] come at last."[8]

Despite all that, however, there was no industrial transformation of the southern economy. Cotton continued to be king, its mills dominating Georgia manufacturing; only the later march of the boll weevil would wean the state, and the region, from cotton dependency. By the turn of the century, Georgia was populated mostly by poverty—Tobacco Road whites and sharecropping blacks in almost equal number. Even total black disfranchisement and oppression, settled by the 1896 Supreme Court decision in *Plessy v. Ferguson,* whereby Jim Crow laws were upheld and American apartheid was instituted, had not delivered the South.

This only intensified white rage over black emancipation, which grew so explosive at that dawn of the twentieth century that it erupted into one of the bloodiest post–Civil War incidents in America—the 1906

Atlanta riot, a violent white-on-black uprising—and spurred escalation of the rampant lynching of blacks. Still, prior to World War I, there were almost no economic successes for Georgia or, for that matter, for the rest of the old Confederacy—the development of the Coca-Cola formula by Atlanta's John Pemberton in the latter part of the nineteenth century being a rare, and relatively modest, exception. Unwilling to surrender the "lost cause" of the Confederacy, and unable to finance its industrial dreams, Georgia remained dependent on cotton production, while J. P. Morgan and other northern financiers exploited and profited from its other resources and seized ownership of its railroads.[9] As the *Atlanta Journal-Constitution* would editorialize late in 1999, "For much of this century, Georgia has struggled to get out of the mud, to get out of poverty, to get past racism."[10]

It was World War I, finally, that provided hope. The conflict required cotton, so cotton prices soared, and southern farmers rode high. Soon enough, however, peace reduced the price of all commodities, including cotton. And then, just a few years later, the boll weevil, on its eastward trek from Texas, arrived in and laid waste to Georgia's cotton fields.

Atlanta itself held on to its "New South" economic spirit, struggling, with some success, to prove that it was a hub of commerce. This drive culminated, in 1925, in a "Forward Atlanta" advertising campaign, which crafted the city's identity and honed the old ideal of "Atlanta Spirit"—the Bourbon notion that what was good for business was good for Atlanta. By the end of the 1925 campaign, more than seven hundred new businesses had moved to Atlanta, including Macy's, Sears Roebuck, and General Motors.[11]

The South itself would nonetheless remain in ruins, its lot unimproved even by Franklin Roosevelt's Civilian Conservation Corps employment plan and other New Deal programs. Roosevelt's 1938 National Emergency Board report concluded that the region was "the nation's Number 1 economic problem."[12] Roosevelt himself maintained a part-time residence in Warm Springs, Georgia, and was personally committed to addressing the economic woes of the South (deemed "the last holdout of the Great Depression"), but not even his personal attention helped: the South simply could not rise above its 250-year history of dependence on black slave labor.

Like a societal Janus, the South was immobilized by a divided vision, at once looking back with racist nostalgia to its old self and trying to look forward to develop and promote its new, more enlightened incarnation. This southern schizophrenia was poignantly revealed in 1939, when the film version of Margaret Mitchell's epic novel *Gone with the Wind* opened in Atlanta. Thousands of poverty-stricken southern whites flocked to the film premiere, wallowing in this woeful tale of the loss of a mythical plantation named Tara, reveling in a fantastic idyll of the Old South, when southern whites were rich and blacks were slaves, faithful servants who tended tresses and fields. The themes of *Gone with the Wind* allowed the southern white masses to dream and forget the harsh facts of life depicted in Erskine Caldwell's classic 1932 novel, *Tobacco Road,* about Georgia's landless and impoverished white majority. Only World War II would improve their reality.

Once again, war brought higher prices for cotton and other agricultural products, including peanuts for oil. There was even more economic investment and support from the military this time around: between 1940 and 1945, the federal government poured more than $10 billion into the South for war industries and military bases.[13] Only Texas could boast a greater number of wartime facilities than Georgia, all of whose big cities were granted military installations, from Fort Benning in Columbus to Warner Robins Air Field in Macon, Camp Gordon in Augusta, and Hunter Army Airfield in Savannah. Atlanta itself came to be encircled by military posts, including a resurrected Fort McPherson and the Atlanta General Depot. Most significantly the capital housed the massive Bell Bomber plant (forerunner of Lockheed), which produced B-29s and employed nearly thirty thousand people. For Atlanta, World War II ended the Depression.[14]

It was not merely the warm climate that attracted the military; there was the political clout that Atlanta's New South Democrats exerted in Washington. For example, Congressman Carl Vinson chaired the Naval Affairs Committee from 1931 through the war, and Senator Richard Russell was on the Appropriations and Naval Affairs committees.[15] Notably Russell would introduce legislation in 1949 to provide $4 billion to send southern blacks north and bring whites south. And in a later era, of course, U.S. senator Sam Nunn of Georgia, as chairman of the Armed Services Committee, would continue the tradition of boosting his home state's economy with billions of military dollars.

As the South began to climb out of the mud, a new southern dilemma arose, having to do with the disposition of its former slaves. Now that blacks were free, so to speak, they formed a dark cloud over the whites-only economy that had finally been achieved after the hard decades of the Civil War, Reconstruction, and the Depression. Most black Americans still lived in the South after World War II, and blacks in fact constituted a majority in many newly urbanized southern towns, including Atlanta. Maintaining black disfranchisement was critical to whites' retaining control of municipal resources and the booming postwar economy. (None of this was an issue in the North, where blacks were effectively disfranchised by their minority status and confined to industrial ghettos.) But southern blacks—especially veterans, home from fighting in the war and finding themselves and their families still suffering under Jim Crow—were now making demands for the equality that had never come with the resolution of the Civil War, demands concerning not only voting but also jobs and housing.

The southern black vote was quickly undermined and effectively dispatched by grandfather clauses, gerrymandering, poll taxes, and absurd literacy tests. Other disempowering tactics were employed as necessary. In Atlanta, white businessmen successfully pushed for a city bond issue to construct a north-south expressway through downtown, isolating poor blacks. These measures were insufficient, however, to halt the black quest for equality. The civil rights struggle that erupted in those postwar years, grounded in the 1954 Supreme Court decision in *Brown v. Board of Education* and in the 1955 Montgomery, Alabama, bus boycott, now directly threatened the newly resurgent, whites-only southern economy.

The Atlanta Spirit was desperately dusted off and wielded as a two-edged sword, to hold blacks at bay while hacking out a share of the postwar economic boom. Among other benefits, World War II had given Atlanta the opportunity to seize regional control of the air-passenger business. After the war and before leaving office, Atlanta mayor William Hartsfield had opened two air-passenger terminals and established headquarters for two major airlines, Eastern and Delta. Even as Atlanta's economy was taking flight, however, establishing the city's position as the capital of the New South, the movement for black civil rights was also gaining powerful momentum. Thus, in constructing a new economic initiative—the second Forward Atlanta campaign, in 1961—Atlanta's white entrepreneurs and newly elected mayor, Ivan Allen Jr., urged blacks as well as whites to embrace the business-oriented Atlanta Spirit.

Avoiding all mention of segregation and black disfranchisement, and despite the fact that 1961 was the year federal troops had to be called in to safeguard the integration of the University of Georgia by two black students, Allen promoted the city as one that fostered racial harmony. Indeed, this second Forward Atlanta campaign, like its predecessor and like the 1895 Cotton Exposition, set about soliciting business by depicting Atlanta as being not only pro-business but also "moderate" in terms of its racial climate. The campaign proved quite successful and was supported by Atlanta's benign black leadership, including "Daddy" King, father of Martin Luther Jr. Atlanta became known as a prime national-headquarters site; jobs increased by the tens of thousands, and the city began to be listed among the top ten in the nation in various economic rankings. In short order Allen succeeded in bringing the Milwaukee Braves to Atlanta, laying the foundation for a citywide rapid transit system (MARTA), establishing development of a new civic center, expanding the airport, constructing new skyscraper office buildings, and developing important art and cultural institutions. Soon Atlanta's population reached one million people.

By 1964, however, the year Martin Luther King Jr. won the Nobel Peace Prize, one year after the March on Washington, Georgia was still a Jim Crow state. Indeed, in a few years, in 1967, staunch segregationist and diner owner Lester Maddox would be elected governor. By 1970, however, blacks would dominate the Atlanta population, and there would be no doubt that a share of the political power could not be far behind. The only question, then, as posed by the Atlanta History Center's New Millennium promotional brochure, was "whether black politicians and white business leaders could coexist as partners." [16]

When Roy Barnes was sworn into office on January 12, 1999, as Georgia's new millennium governor, he rang the same New South themes. In his inaugural address, Barnes said, "One hundred years ago, life was very different in Georgia. Cotton was king and King Cotton was killing our economy. . . . Today . . . let us celebrate a New Georgia—a diverse population, a vibrant economy. . . . We can become not just the capital of the New South, but a capital for the New Century." [17]

The Old South was dying hard though. Despite everything, Georgia was still suffering from the final shock of the loss of King Cotton. Since the 1995 passage of the North American Free Trade Agreement, almost three hundred thousand jobs in the textile and apparel industries had been eliminated, the key to why the South led the nation in manufacturing job losses in the 1990s.[18] There was, too, the "black problem," now cast in the new light of a "crime problem." Now the crime problem represented a threat to Atlanta's upward economic thrust, riding on the wings of the Centennial Olympic Games. Like his predecessors, Barnes addressed this new problem by calling up the Atlanta Spirit, in which what was good for business was good for Atlanta, and, conversely, that Atlanta was always willing to do what was good for business. Barnes said, "And we will turn the tide on crime. . . . We must [not allow] crime [to] steal our strength and our future." [19]

In a word, and in Atlanta, *crime* was almost synonymous with *black*. In 1990, Atlanta had the highest crime rate in the nation.[20] It ranked third in murder, though the Georgia Bureau of Investigation (GBI) reported that the murder rate had increased nearly 15 percent in 1989 alone. Most of this was attributable to the outbreak of crack cocaine trafficking in the 1980s in the black community. Atlanta's first black mayor, Maynard Jackson, had attempted to repress this crime problem through reinstitution of an old nighttime curfew ordinance, which was primarily applied to young black males in the city's ghettos.[21] The crime rate had not, however, in any way been affected by any such measure by the time Atlanta hosted the Centennial Olympic Games.

On September 18, 1990, the International Olympics Committee awarded the right to host the 1996 Summer Olympic Games to Atlanta —over the sentimental favorite of Athens, Greece. This was certainly good for business, so the Atlanta Spirit exploded—no matter that crime in Atlanta was at an all-time high. The bid for the games had been orchestrated by private business corporation Atlanta Committee for the Olympic Games (ACOG), headed by Billy Payne. The Atlanta business community sprang into action to raise the necessary money to accommodate the Olympics. In a way, it had been waiting and preparing for this for more than a century. The games were projected to bring many millions of dollars into the city and to precipitate a tidal wave of future business billions.

While ACOG had either successfully suppressed the reality of Atlanta's high crime figures or found a partner in the International Olympics Committee to overcome the dark crime picture, it still had to promote the games so as to cleanse the city of its high-crime image. Moreover, it had to attend to the problems connected to Atlanta's burgeoning population of poor black people who had long been languishing in local ghettos that had now become "Olympic Ring Neighborhoods."

Indeed, despite Atlanta's rosy self-portrayals in its various propaganda efforts, 92 percent of the residents of all the newly named Olympic Ring Neighborhoods were black and poor.[22] Worse, Atlanta's overall poverty rate was 32 percent, higher than the national average.[23] Moreover, according to the U.S. Bureau of Economic Analysis, the city's salaries and wages at the time were much lower than the national average. Other documentation suggested other problems. Emory University urban historian Dana White said at the time, for example, that "Atlanta [was] 10 years behind Detroit in the disintegration of its downtown retail center."

Thus came the proverbial good news/bad news, in many ways a reflection filtering through the dark corridor of the last century. Another New South had to be born, one that had finally cleansed itself of the ashes of Tara, a shining Atlantis, found, in form if not in substance, to attract international billions. Thus, Payne, a "good ol' boy" if there ever was one, partnered with savvy civil rights icon Andy Young. Young had been the first black congressional representative of Georgia in a hundred years and the mayor of Atlanta for most of the 1980s. More important, his mayoral administration had been characterized as one that cemented the "alliance between city hall and business leaders."[24]

Now the slogan resounded, born of the old Forward Atlanta campaigns, that Atlanta was "a city too busy to hate." Atlanta, ACOG hawked far and wide, had done more than reckon with the dark past. It had spent the last century building itself not only as a transportation and regional business hub but as a model of social moderation, where blacks and whites together shared the burdens and benefits of this modern city and had made a home for *global* business.

The reality of Atlanta's high crime figures undermined this propaganda. While the city was armed to secure its boundaries during the weeks of the Olympic Games, in the meantime it had to overcome the fears of prospective tourists and, more important, investors. Thus, the new black mayor, Bill Campbell, a former city council representative and protégé of Maynard Jackson, elected during the pre-Olympics frenzy, announced that "reducing crime was the most important issue facing the city."[25] Cautioning early on that the problems of crime, violence, and drugs would take a long time to be resolved, Campbell let it be known that he would rise with full force to the urgency of the moment. In 1994, then, two years before the games, Campbell appointed a new police chief, Beverly Harvard. Harvard not only was the first black woman to head the police department of a major city, as was widely publicized, but also had absolute allegiance to Campbell. She took command of the Atlanta police department's seventeen hundred uniformed police and $100 million budget.

Though Harvard may not have, in fact, done anything to actually affect the crime rate in Atlanta, as a Campbell crony she knew what was required. Suddenly, it seemed, by 1995, Atlanta's crime statistics showed a sharp decline, almost as if timed for the Olympics. Indeed, during that same year *Fortune* magazine ranked Atlanta as the fourth-best city in America in which to do business, albeit *Fortune*'s managing editor, John Huey, was an Atlanta resident. In any case, the sudden drop in crime placed Atlanta second—and, proudly, not first—in the 1995 rankings of the nation's most violent cities.[26] This drop in crime was promoted to proffer a picture of security for Olympic Games visitors and to demonstrate to prospective investors that, while Atlanta, like other big cities, may have a crime problem, it was getting tough on its crime. Moreover, given that this stance was being maintained by a black police chief in a city administered by a black mayor, Atlanta could also assert— as in the past—that it represented a kind of balm for the national sores that had opened relating to charges of racism in police activity, from brutality, as exemplified by the Rodney King case, to racial profiling in arrest procedures, to the increasingly disproportionate percentage of blacks jailed and incarcerated. In 1981, Campbell's mentor, Maynard Jackson, had set the tone for such propaganda by blacks, announcing, "Atlanta has the best race relations of any city in the country."[27] Atlanta was now cast as a new model of urban success, no matter how cosmetic its approach to crime or how abysmal its refusal to even consider or discuss the underlying causes of such crimes.

Harvard would later challenge accusations that she had manipulated the city's crime figures for the games. Based on the allegations of a white deputy police chief, whom Harvard would demote and castigate, the GBI spent nearly a year reviewing the records reflecting Atlanta's incredible 70 percent increase in crime reports marked "unfounded," which accounted for the incredible decrease in crime figures for 1995 and 1996.[28] Its report concluded that nearly one-quarter of the cases marked unfounded, representing reports of rapes and robberies, were "erroneously dismissed."[29] Of course, all of this was years after the security success of the Olympic Games, which was marred only by the death of one black woman when a bomb exploded at one of the downtown venues, for which a poor white man was wrongfully charged and no one else was ever apprehended.

———

Most of Atlanta's crime figures represented what had come to be described, in the rise of the tough-on-crime era, as "black-on-black" crimes. Had business interests in Atlanta and elsewhere not begun a movement to reclaim the centrally located sections of the cities, initiating a kind of Reverse White Flight, such ghetto crime figures would never have become a national concern. In pre-Olympics Atlanta, ghetto crime was more than a matter of image for the city, or ACOG. ACOG needed those centrally located sites, and it needed them immediately. The Olympic Ring Neighborhoods, representing 13 percent of the city, were infested with not only crime but also poverty, or high concentrations of poor blacks. As their occupants had no stake in the games and loomed as an ugly detraction from them, a kind of emergency plan was devised to remove them from sight of the projected 2 million visitors and potential investors, investors not merely from "the North" but also from Europe and Asia. At the least, the games were slated to raise the gross state product by $5.1 billion.[30]

In the same year Campbell placed Harvard as chief of police, he supported the appointment of Renee Lewis Glover, who had been assistant finance director of his first mayoral campaign, to head the massive Atlanta Housing Authority (AHA). Atlanta ranked *second* in the nation in per capita public housing, and the agency that Glover took over was the *fifth* largest housing agency in the nation, with an annual budget of $500 million.[31]

By the time the Olympic Games began in July 1996, Glover had obtained $42 million in federal funding and had bulldozed the homes of all the poor black families from over a thousand units of the massive Techwood Homes (the first public housing project in the nation, built for whites only) as well as of the neighboring Clark Howell Homes, casting them from sight of the adjacent downtown "Olympic Village."[32] Residents were dispersed to alternative cheap housing, clinging to "Section 8" federal housing vouchers and promises to be returned to better facilities under newly devised "Further Assurances Agreements."[33] These resident agreements to move out, which facilitated their mass removal, were conceived by Glover, a former corporate attorney who would soon become one of the highest-paid public officials in the state and one of the highest-paid housing agency administrators in the nation.[34]

Residents remaining in the yet-to-be-redeveloped blighted housing projects, particularly those that would make up the AHA's "Olympic Legacy Program," suddenly became subject to Glover's harsh new policies. The most draconian was her "zero tolerance" drug policy, wielded in the pre-Olympics years to oust any and all residents and their entire families so much as suspected of drug dealing or, even, drug use. In conjunction with the Atlanta police and newly hired bands of private police, Glover began sweeping clean the housing projects of its poor residents, making way for more bulldozers. At the same time, the city passed an "urban camping" ordinance that permitted the arrest of homeless people, the number of whom, on any given night at the time in Atlanta, was estimated to be anywhere from 8,000 to 22,000, mostly black people.[35]

The first wave of Glover's plan, the removal of those housing projects—and the people in them—situated near the Olympic sites, was praised by the chief of the Department of Housing and Urban Development (HUD), Andrew Cuomo. Cuomo considered Glover a leader in the field, and she was given nearly carte blanche financial support from HUD.[36] Indeed, Glover, who would be credited with removing Atlanta's housing authority from HUD's "troubled" list, was in the vanguard of a national trend. In concert with her efforts and those of Cuomo, in December 1994, President Clinton identified thirty Atlanta neighborhoods—of which nineteen were, notably, Olympic Ring Neighborhoods—as "Empowerment Zones" and granted $100 million to Atlanta to make "improvements."[37]

Ultimately, in what was deemed a public relations success, the new Techwood Homes became the forerunner of a new model "mixed-income" urban community. Renamed Centennial Place, it was touted as a showcase of and cornerstone for the city's Olympic legacy. Now, Coca-Cola, Georgia Power, and the powerful Cousins Properties came to build Centennial Olympic Park near Centennial Place. Centennial Place and Centennial Park would be further developed and expanded, following the Olympics, by a business consortium formed for the games, operating as a nonprofit entity, called Centennial Olympic Park Area (COPA). With the financial support of the AHA and the political support of the city, COPA would soon orchestrate development of additional new housing, business parks, and other endeavors in the shadow of the Georgia Dome and would redevelop the blighted territories around it that were the prime real estate of new business dreams.

Ironically, even though the AHA needed resident approval to use HUD money for these various redevelopment projects, most of the people who were ousted have been unable, in the post-Olympics intoxication, to claim the promise of better housing, on which they had signed over their approval and rights. In the case of Techwood, 92 percent of the families who once lived there could not qualify for residency at Centennial Place.[38]

By the end of the twentieth century, Atlanta would show the second-highest increase in population of any city in America. Most migrants would be young white people from New York and Chicago. Furthermore, after the Olympics, Georgia would show a steady increase in tourism, providing, in the late 1990s, about 535,000 jobs and representing about $18 billion in annual income. Tourism would become second only to agriculture, still Georgia's largest industry. Atlanta would soon be ranked as the second-best place (behind Austin, Texas) for doing "high-tech business," ranking above Silicon Alley in New York, the high-tech corridor of Massachusetts, and the heart of northern California's powerful Silicon Valley, San Jose.[39]

In the meantime, Tom Cousins, who had built the CNN/Omni

complex downtown, among numerous other major projects in the city, would begin development of a new community in the still-occupied sections of the Eastlake Meadows housing projects, to accommodate refurbishment of the surrounding legendary Bobby Jones Golf Course and fulfill his dream of Atlanta's hosting a golf tournament. Georgia Power, a subsidiary of Atlanta-based Southern Company, the heaviest investor in the Centennial Olympic Park, had begun developing acres of downtown property for the business investors it hosted before and during the Olympic Games. Coca-Cola would secure the land in the blocks around Centennial Place for expansion of its headquarters. Turner Enterprises and its various subsidiaries and affiliates, which had inherited the Olympic Stadium, now called Turner Field, for Braves baseball, would complete development of the new Philips Arena downtown to accommodate Turner's Atlanta Hawks and new hockey team, the Thrashers, as well as major music concerts. In the post-Olympics years, Hartsfield Airport would become the busiest passenger airport in the world. Delta Airlines would expand its fleet in partnership with, among others, Air France. The various other big corporations and institutions based in Atlanta, including SunTrust Bank, United Parcel Service, Bell South, Home Depot, Georgia Pacific, Cox Enterprises, would undertake massive development plans for their share in this new economic boom. As the Hub of the New South, Atlanta would finally engage in big business, becoming a powerful partner in America's global economic dominance of the new millennium.

＝＝＝＝＝＝

By the time the Centennial Olympic Games arrived, there was really no place in Atlanta for Little B anymore. As a young black boy from a crack-infested community, he was the very demographic profile of what had come to be identified as the city's primary problem. He represented an impediment to development of the Olympic Ring Neighborhoods, from which his friends and family, as such, rather like roaches, refused to disappear. It was boys like him who created the high crime rate, either as victims or perpetrators, of whom the city had to be purged if it would claim its legacy.

Of course, this problem, as perceived, was not unique to Atlanta, or to the South. America as a whole, the majority of America, led by its corporate chiefs, had come to realize that America could not claim and hold its rightful place as global leader in the shadow of these problems of crime and poverty, black crime and poverty, sometimes referred to as inner-city problems. Incorporation of the blacks whose dominant presence blighted America's urban centers into the scheme of things was out of the question, as it had been out of the question since the rise of industrialization, since the end of the Civil War and the abolition of slavery. As Atlanta attorney Michael H. Trotter, president of Good Government Atlanta, forthrightly wrote not long after the Olympic Games were over, "We cannot solve the problems of Atlanta by helping the poor in our midst rise up from their poverty. . . . The problem is not that there are too many black people in Atlanta—there are too many poor people in Atlanta." [40] The problem was the same, in fact, a problem that had risen from the ashes of the Civil War: what to do with the blacks. And the answer had finally come, as pronounced clearly in the Reagan-Bush decade: "Get tough on crime!"

[5] The Bluff

In Atlanta the heat in summer, or even in late spring, can be oppressive, weighted with humidity and smog. Evenings, though, can be sweet, proverbially sultry with the scent of magnolias. And dawn can arrive with the singing of the thrasher or mockingbird, harmonizing with a colorful cardinal, complemented by the cooing of mourning doves seeking the loves of their lives. This land is the bastard beneficiary of the Cherokee and other native peoples who cherished and nurtured it for ten thousand years prior to English colonization and native removal.

In the Bluff the sounds and scents of life are different, of course, its singular bond with the other Atlanta being the oppressive summer heat. Its native beauty has been ravaged over the years in the losing battles for survival waged by its isolated population, ferociously competing for sustenance with nature itself. Nevertheless, the Bluff gave birth to Little B; it is where he grew. One wonders whether Valerie Morgan, his mother, ever smelled the magnolia's bloom in the night or arose to the song of the mourning dove.

The Bluff is black. No matter the euphemisms of late, it is a black ghetto. It is the Ghetto, whatever nuances might distinguish it from others elsewhere. It is not the conventional northern slum but a barracoon in the heart of the New South, where black people have been quartered since the end of slavery. The southern border of the Bluff is Simpson Street, called Simpson Road west of Ashby Street, which is its western border. Its northern border is Bankhead Highway, and to the east is Northside Drive. There are numerous neighborhood theories on how this section came to be called the Bluff—none of which makes reference to the few blocks of tiny Bluff Street not far away. Michael's explanation, as good as any, is that it is a place where no one can survive on a bluff, for life there is onerously stark. About twenty-three liquor stores line the five-mile east-west stretch of Simpson enveloping the Bluff, making up the highest concentration of alcohol outlets in the city, as licensed by the city.

Abandoned cars rust in the sun of Dalvigney Street and Echo Street and the other streets where Michael used to play. The red Georgia clay of the district's seemingly myriad vacant lots is obliterated by malignant growths of used condoms and used hypodermic needles and ordinary refuse. Vacated, dilapidated houses and apartments along Griffin Street are occupied by animal predators and scavengers, cohabiting often with the most desperate of crack addicts and, sometimes, adventurous neighborhood children. The inhabited houses are in general disrepair. Most are classified as being in violation of numerous city housing codes. No official from the city government comes to the Bluff about housing-code enforcement, however, any more than any other authority attends to other infrastructure matters, from maintenance of sewage, power, or telephone lines to delivery of ambulance, fire, or police services. The only concern attended to in the Bluff is the deadly business of drugs, their sales and distribution, involving dealers, users, and police.

No other neighborhood commerce thrives in or around the Bluff. There is no market selling fresh fruits or vegetables or meat or fish, no pharmacy or doctor's office, no bank branch or office complex, no dress shop or shoe store or bookstore, no ice cream parlor or movie theater or community theater. There is a church and, barely noticeable along the narrow streets, the occasional market like Henry's, where Darrell Woods was killed, where near-empty shelves offer potato chips and cookies, cigarettes and gum, pickles and pickled pigs' feet, sodas and milk, maybe popsicles and packaged lunch meat. Otherwise there are the liquor stores down on Simpson and, beyond, the proliferation of fast-food restaurants. This is the Ghetto, which is really not a community, in the sense of a collection of social, commercial, and cultural institutions owned and operated by, and offering goods and services to, the people living there.

A few blocks southeast of Simpson and Northside looms the Georgia Dome, which, as its advertising states, "is the largest cable-supported domed stadium in the world . . . home venue for the National

Football League's Atlanta Falcons . . . host to the gymnastics, basketball and the finals of team handball during the 1996 Centennial Olympic Games," and host to Super Bowl XXXIV in 2000 and, around the same time, a temporary home to the Atlanta Hawks.

Now, of course, the Hawks have Philips Arena, rising only a few blocks further east of the Bluff. A construct of Ted Turner's sports and entertainment corporation—named for the Dutch company Royal Philips Electronics, a major financing partner—the $213 million arena is situated so that Centennial Olympic Park is popularly considered its front lawn. Philips Arena has become one of the powerful anchors in Atlanta's downtown reclamation drive, which includes the $27 million renovation of Turner-owned CNN Center and Omni Hotel and Coca-Cola's "corporate campus" expansion.

Callously ironic in this business is the juxtaposition of the white-washed downtown and the Bluff. Philips Arena developers were "enticed" to build downtown by public money.[1] There were guaranteed revenues from an Atlanta-Fulton County Recreation Authority bond issue and a car rental tax, along with Empowerment Zone money and tax benefits. This same kind of financial finagling will provide for construction of (Tom) Cousins Properties' projected $150 million office tower on nearby Peachtree Street and the planned nine-block residential-business development of Centennial Olympic Park Area.[2] More ironic is the fact that not one dime of the millions and millions of dollars of local and federal government money used in these developments has been allocated to improve anything in the Bluff, even though this was the purpose for which such public money was, in the main, set aside.

This private theft of public money, while resembling the old urban renewal projects of the post–World War II decades, reflects an insidious change in public policy. It is strikingly similar to the 1965 construction of the Atlanta-Fulton County Stadium, for example. The stadium was built with millions of old Model Cities Program dollars set aside for improvements to the miserable Summerhill community where it would sit. Although this stadium construction and proposed attendant neighborhood renewal required elimination of hundreds of households, by 1990 Summerhill was a run-down community that had become, as it was said, little more than a "parking lot for Braves and Falcons fans." However, even though Summerhill, like other, earlier "urban renewal" projects nationwide, usurped public funds to the benefit of various private business ventures, it was underwritten by a public-spirited social philosophy that acknowledged the black ghetto and the role racism played in its existence.

In the late 1960s such endeavors had the stated goal of addressing the massive social problems related to the existence of the Bluff. This was powerfully articulated in the oft-quoted report of the National Advisory Commission on Civil Disorders—popularly known as the Kerner Commission Report. The report concluded that the massive black urban uprisings of the 1960s that were the subject of its investigation were an expression of black rage over the fact that America was "moving toward two societies, one black and one white—separate and unequal." Furthermore, the commission stated that "white racism" was the cause of the "explosive mixture" of poverty, discrimination, and resentment in the urban black ghettos, concluding, "What white Americans have never fully understood—but what the Negro can never forget—is that white society is deeply implicated in the ghetto. White institutions created it, white institutions maintain it, and white society condones it." [3]

Thus there came to be a national commitment of sorts incorporated into government and other programs to improve communities like the Bluff. Indeed, it was in this spirit that HUD itself was created as part of Lyndon Johnson's sweeping social program, the so-called War on Poverty. Now a new public policy would fix the "inner city" by criminalizing the poverty of its people and then bulldozing over them for the purpose of white reclamation.

The 1954 Supreme Court decision in *Brown v. Board of Education,* as it set about the desegregation of public schools and forced white Americans to integrate their schools via the invention of busing, undoubtedly triggered the urgent mass exodus of whites from urban America, commonly called White Flight. Whites able to flee blacks in the city invented lily-white middle-class suburban communities and school districts. In Atlanta the abandonment of the city by whites was so complete that blacks not only became the majority population but also, as in other big cities at the time, assumed power over local government. Unlike other big cities of today, Atlanta is still administered by blacks.

Now, though, a new generation of whites has been born, borne beyond busing on the wings of White Flight. This new generation of white suburbanites is enjoying a new, high-tech post–Cold War economic boom. They are the high-tech "instant-aires" (kids who have gone from middle-class boys to millionaire men through overnight sales of their computer programs) and other computer and wireless young entrepreneurs and workers, along with an accompanying legion of lawyers, accountants, stockbrokers, and other young professionals, all making more money than any previous such generation, and surely more than their intrinsic worth to society. In Atlanta they want to play where they work, among the gleaming office buildings of downtown. They are tired of living outside Atlanta's perimeter, the freeway system that creates a nongeographic circumference around the city. They are tired of being stuck in the amorphous life of Alpharetta or other Stepford-like suburban subdivisions, driving the freeways for hours a day back and forth to the office or to see the Hawks or Braves play. Older whites, too, have been suffering in the cultural vacuousness of suburban shopping malls. For them time outside the perimeter has created watercolored longings for a night on the town, at the theater or even the opera. The Atlanta opera and orchestra and theaters have longings of their own—for ticket sales—and the department stores long to relocate downtown, and the restaurants long to resume dinner service. In the wake of it all lies the Bluff.

The necessities of Reverse White Flight, then, have given rise to the new public policy. That policy is to make a place for old and new dreams of white urbanity not by acknowledging any social responsibility for or relationship to the Bluff, not by striving to uplift the Bluff, and not by integrating—or reintegrating—with the people of the Bluff. The aim is simply to get rid of the Bluff, by any means necessary.

The new public policy is to get rid of inner-city crime by getting rid of inner-city "criminals," to get rid of the scourge of the inner city and its poverty by getting rid of the people there, who are deemed too lazy to take care of the Bluff's precious blocks of real estate. This policy, it is touted, is neither race-based nor race-biased. Indeed, the new "conservatives" leading the effort would suggest, bastardizing the words of Martin Luther King Jr., that the new public policy is "color-blind." In Atlanta, as elsewhere, the goal has become a simple matter of cleaning up the inner city, creating the conditions for a new and better city, in order to bring back what Ronni French, founder and former director of the Atlanta Downtown Partnership, identified as "an upscale population."[4]

If the Bluff were only a few isolated blocks near the Georgia Dome, this new public policy would not be so heavy. In Atlanta, however, there are many Bluffs. They include, above all, the still-existing deteriorated units in the housing projects under the authority of the AHA, projects that contain almost fifty thousand people, nearly 100 percent of them black, and all, needless to say, poor. Noteworthy among them is Herndon Homes, situated off Simpson Road west of the Bluff, and the desolate downtown fringe communities of English Avenue and Vine City. And to the south of downtown Atlanta, in view of the golden dome of the state capitol, lies the Capitol Homes project, a stone's throw from two of the so-called highest crime districts in the city, Adair Park and Mechanicsville. In the hilly hinterlands northwest of the city, sprawl Hollywood Courts and Perry Homes. Farther west are the deplorable Bankhead Courts. On the city's eastern border lie the remnants of East Lake Meadows and its residents, attending the bulldozers of Tom Cousins' golfing fantasies.

Beyond the AHA domain are all the other all-black enclaves overcome by poor living conditions, deteriorating housing, few businesses, and so forth. In general, according to a 1998 *Atlanta Journal-Constitution* special report, of the 185,000 housing units in Atlanta, the city itself estimated that *one-fifth* were "substandard." Another 10,000 were deemed "serious hazards," either vacant, decrepit, or dangerous.[5] The majority of this run-down housing exists in Atlanta's black communities, most egregiously in the blocks incorporating the Bluff and adjacent communities.

Despite the popular psychobabble about the power of individual "affirmations," most people living in substandard housing in Atlanta's various Bluffs cannot afford decent housing, nor can they afford to make needed repairs to their existing residences. A study of Fulton County, Georgia, conducted by HUD in 1995, documented that between 1980 and 1990 the white population in the county increased 38 percent while the black population, most of whom live in southern Fulton County in "units [that] largely house low-income persons who cannot afford the necessary repairs," increased 100 percent.[6] Moreover, a significant percentage of blacks in Atlanta need the government's assistance to live anywhere at all, the Section 8 program recently having had a waiting list of more than seven thousand people. Beyond Atlanta, in twenty surrounding counties, nearly forty thousand families cannot afford adequate housing according to a 1998 HUD study.[7] The same HUD study acknowledged that over five million people in America, an overwhelming percentage of whom are black, need housing assistance. Notably, as HUD chief Andrew Cuomo admitted, most of the people who cannot afford decent housing or who need housing assistance are working every day.

The Bluff, then, is not merely a corridor in Atlanta at the turn of yet another century. If it were, the country's neoconservative pundits and policy wonks could rest on their assertion that responsibility for the Bluff falls squarely on the shoulders of its residents. Repairing the Bluff would turn, then, not on investment of money there, but on arresting its violent and perhaps violence-prone population, on repairing the breakdown of Bluff families by inculcating them with certain socially responsible values, and otherwise on developing a social policy to force the Bluff's overwhelmingly unemployed population to get a job.

The fact is, however, that Atlanta is overrun by Bluff communities, a proliferation that suggests a citywide social problem. Furthermore, the great masses of blacks in America, north and south, east and west, still live in communities that mirror the Bluff, in conditions of deterioration and disrepair, lacking needed services, with few community-based businesses, overwhelmed by the business of crack cocaine—communities that together make up a kind of national Empowerment Zone. The Bluff is East St. Louis, Illinois; Newark, New Jersey; Detroit and Cleveland and New Orleans and the nation's capital, Washington, D.C. These are the same ghetto cities innumerable studies over the years have identified as America's high-crime poverty pockets, communities whose names are so familiar that the identification of them as ghettos requires little further substantiation: from New York's Harlem to Chicago's West Side to Boston's Roxbury to nearly all of North Philadelphia to Baltimore's downtown Flag House Courts district to most of East and West Oakland to South-Central Los Angeles. The list is self-verifying.

There are, in addition, rural Bluffs. In the Mississippi counties that make up the Mississippi Delta region, for example, which represents the poorest section of the poorest state in America, approximately 80 percent of the poor are black people, people still tied to the land they have always worked.[8] Indeed, the entire Mississippi Delta region, including counties in Arkansas, Louisiana, and Mississippi, has "the most extensive black-majority area in the U.S. today."[9] Languishing in a two-hundred-mile stretch of catfish farms and cotton fields, where the economy has virtually collapsed, the Delta's blacks gasp for air in forsaken townships, dying off unnoticed.

That the masses of blacks in America live in the Bluff can be distinguished because housing and neighborhoods in America remain racially segregated. Of the more than eight million black families, over 50 percent reside in urban central cities.[10] Indeed, while Chicago has been cited as its most segregated city, America as a whole is more segregated today than ever.[11] If the Bluff is not a national social problem reflecting the persistence of racism, then, as the neoconservatives suggest, the thousands and thousands of black people in Atlanta, and millions and millions of blacks throughout the country, living in the Bluff, most of whom are working and not on drugs, are perhaps intrinsically socially dysfunctional and uncivilizable.

The only time life in the Bluff becomes the subject of national concern—and the Bluff does occupy a central place in the nation's daily discourse, via newspaper headlines and nightly television news reports—is in relation to "crime." Not only does crime in America have a color, which is "black"; crime also has a place: the Bluff, as it exists throughout the nation. According to a 2000 study of violence conducted by the Crimes against Persons Index, the highest crime district in Atlanta is composed of the all-black blocks within a half-mile radius of Turner Field. Furthermore, while the crime rate of Atlanta itself consistently ranked number one among large cities, the blocks surrounding Turner Field compose the highest crime district in America.[12] The particularly high crime rate of this area of Atlanta is followed closely by the poorest blocks of Chicago, New York, St. Louis, Baltimore, and so forth, all of which are black, further evidencing the plethora of black ghettos that remain in America.

The violence in the Bluff is not solely attributable to the crimes committed there. Black ghettos continue to suffer rampant police brutality.

Most of this police violence goes unheralded in the mainstream media, as it goes unredressed under the law. Increasing incidents of blatant and violent police abuses, though, have forced the issue, giving credence to the accusations by more and more blacks of unrelenting police repression in black communities across the nation.

Perhaps one of the most infamous of such incidents of abuse since the 1991 police beating of Rodney King in Los Angeles was the shooting death of Amadou Diallo in New York, during Black History Month of 1999. Even mainstream America wondered, in various newspaper and other media editorials, whether those four New York cops who killed Diallo in the Bronx had been slightly overzealous in their ongoing attempt to halt crime in the city. Even mainstream America was shocked over the swift acquittal of those cops for firing a total of forty-one bullets at this unarmed black man, nineteen of which penetrated Diallo's small body and took his life. Such mainstream sympathy seemed tempered, though, by the unabashed acceptance by the majority of white New Yorkers of the hard line on "crime" taken by their two-term mayor, Rudolph Giuliani. For, while Giuliani's policies may have provoked or provided the ambience for such a tragedy, had they not, in the end, cleaned up New York? Had Giuliani and the police not returned New York City to what was recollected widely as its once-and-former glory?

An incident like the Diallo murder is as common, though, as the very existence of the Bluff, rising to public scrutiny only on the level of egregiousness. During the year after Diallo was killed, a total of four unarmed black men were shot and killed by New York police, white police. The last victim in this rash of shootings was Patrick Dorismond, son of one of Haiti's best-known singers, shot in Manhattan by an "undercover" cop.[13] In between, in June 1999, three white New York policemen were acquitted on charges relating to the atrocious 1997 beating and sodomization of Abner Louima, inside their police precinct.

Elsewhere, in January 2000, a black Providence, Rhode Island, police officer was shot to death by two of his fellow officers, both white.[14] Officer Cornel Young Jr., whose father was a twenty-five-year veteran and the highest-ranking black officer of the Providence police force, was allegedly mistaken for a criminal suspect and killed by the other cops. Around the same time, a white policeman in Los Angeles was being "reprimanded" by the city's police commission for shooting an unarmed black woman to death. The victim, Margaret Mitchell, was fifty-four years old and had a college education; she had been rendered homeless on account of mental illness. The commission was divided as to whether the shooting was justified. Even though Mitchell weighed only 102 pounds, she was identified as a threat to the officers who approached her, because when they accused her of stealing the shopping cart she was pushing she fearfully retreated, brandishing a screwdriver.[15]

Statistically, the pervasiveness of unending police brutality against blacks in black communities is reflected best in the large and disparate percentage of blacks stopped and searched by police, both inside and outside ghetto areas. For example, while approximately 76 percent of people driving Maryland's I-95 expressway are white and 17 percent are black, only 20 percent of those stopped there by police were documented to have been white, while 73 percent were black. Indeed, in June 1999 the American Civil Liberties Union (ACLU) released its report on this stop-and-search issue, now euphemized as "racial profiling" by police, which has given rise to the popular phrase "driving while black." The forty-three-page ACLU report, citing police statistics and other data, concludes that overall law enforcement agencies "systematically" target blacks for searches, even strip searches, as pedestrians, motorists, and airline passengers, as a "crime-fighting tool." Albeit, 90 percent of whites polled in a Justice Department twelve-city survey in 1999 were "happy" with the police, their procedures, and the execution of their duties.[16]

Whether or not black people live in communities as wretched as the Bluff in which Michael Lewis was born, there remain two Americas, black and white, separate and unequal. This is reflected as much in the condition of black neighborhoods as in the condition of black people, represented by the devastating social and economic disparities under which the great majority of black people continue to live in America. In other words, the Bluff is more than a place. It is a condition.

In 1993, the United Nations issued a report on the quality of life in the world based on its study of the health, education, and purchasing power of the populations of 173 countries in the world. As a result of this study, the U.N. ranked countries in terms of "quality of life." The citizens of the United States ranked at the top—as might have been expected. Whites in the United States, considered separately, however, ranked number one in the entire world. Blacks in America, when viewed separately, ranked number thirty-one, along with Uruguay.[17]

In 1999 nearly one-quarter, 23.6 percent, of blacks in America lived *below* poverty, the poverty threshold for a family of four with two children under eighteen, for example, being $16,895 per year.[18] Black women heads of households earn around 40 percent less than white women heads of households, and more than half of black children under eighteen years old live in households headed by mothers only, among whom approximately 75 percent live in poverty.[19]

In the latest statistics for the United States, the unemployment rate for blacks remained more than twice as high as for whites; among young black males in central cities the unemployment rate is as high as 40 percent.[20] While by 2000 the percentage of blacks with high school diplomas was twice what it was in 1970, the percentage of whites with bachelor's degrees or higher remained twice that of blacks.[21] At the same time, the percentage of black engineers, physicians, and lawyers still hovered at approximately 2 percent.[22] Businesses owned by blacks, 90 percent of which are small, sole proprietorships, equal only 4 percent of all businesses in America and 0.4 percent of all business receipts.[23]

Finally, the rate of black infant mortality in the United States remains twice that of white infant mortality.[24] The maternal mortality rate for blacks is *four* times that of whites.[25] Of women with AIDS, 63 percent are black, and 65 percent of children with AIDS are black.[26] Black women have been dying of breast cancer at twice the rate of white women, as black men have been dying of prostate cancer at twice the rate of white men.[27] And because of the scourge of crack cocaine the black prison population has soared to a nationwide total of 42 percent, although blacks make up only 13 percent of the overall population.[28] In the end, in the main, it would seem that all black people in America live in the Bluff.

[6] Little B

*"**Naw. Naw.** I always had someplace to stay," Michael was saying, with defiance, apparently resenting the suggestion that he might ever have been homeless.*

    "But didn't you stay out all night on the street in the Bluff?"

    "Yeah. But I was makin' money."

    "Sellin' crack?"

    "All kinds of dope. Heroin, powder cocaine, weed."

    "You could sell all night? You had that many 'customers'?"

    "Yeah. All night long."

    "Mostly black? Mostly white?"

    "Both."

    "They drove through or what?"

    "On foot. In cars. You name it."

    "How old were you when you got out there?"

    "I was about ten, but I was still in school. I was just looking out. When I left Marilyn's house. . . ."

    "Marilyn Reed, the one who was your foster mother for a while?"

    "Yeah. When I ran away from her house, I quit school. I quit everything. You know. I was out there. Full time."

    "When was that? How old were you then?"

    "Eleven. Eleven years old."

His speech was rapid-fire now, not slow and southern. It seemed to reflect an inner urgency, the human survival instinct on full alert. From a very young age he was apprehensive, not being at home anywhere.

As he spoke, he was leaning far back on the rear metal legs of the plastic chair. It was a balancing act. We were alone in the huge hall that was the regular visiting room, but for the CERT (Correctional Emergency Response Team) guard, a young white the size of a football player whose role is to push and crush. The linoleum floor was prisoner-polished to a high gloss, and I instinctively feared Michael would fall, or I was anxious over the possibility of giving the guard the excuse to reprimand him. It was a boyish defiance. As soon as the guard moved, he flipped himself forward, with a kind of wink to me, and the world. He made me laugh and lose my superficial reserve as his legal investigator.

In those years called formative, Michael's life seemed to have been a vortex of treacheries to be survived or endured, never overcome, involving hunger, mostly, for food or a place to stay. He had taken on a gravity for which he was too young, too light, and too little. He had not been born a boy to be attended to and protected. Left to his own devices, he had become extraordinarily resourceful. By the third grade, when his home was the dope house, he knew how to ward off fear like hunger.

Bankhead Highway was really not that far from the apartments on Dalvigney Street (which everyone pronounced "Dal-veeny") that had become the local crack house where Michael lived. He thinks it was owned by his Big Mama, Jessie Mae Simpson, his sister's daddy's mama, not his biological relative, but family. He was eight then, and Tavia, his sister, called "Ta-Ta" (pronounced "Tay-Tay"), was five years old. They shared a room with twin beds in Big Mama's apartment complex on Dalvigney, a two-apartment nondescript edifice. He laughs when I ask whether there was a clothes washer or dryer there, though there were a television and telephone. He would put their clothes in the "buggy" and take them up to the washhouse on Bankhead.

"The buggy?"

"Yeah. You know, grocery cart."

"Oh. You walked?"

"It wasn't that far."

"What did you wash?"

"Mine and Ta-Ta's things."

"So, you know how to take care of your clothes?"

"Got to," he said, a sassy saying that would punctuate most of his responses to questions. "Got to roll with it."

Also living there on Dalvigney was Valerie, his mother, by then a full-fledged crack addict. She was coupled there with Thomas, Ta-Ta's daddy, also an addict. Jason, called J-Boy, Michael's and Ta-Ta's brother, was still living with them. The others came and went with the ebb of being high. There might be nine or ten each night, sleeping in the recesses of the small complex. Michael would tug Ta-Ta along past them in the morning to leave for school, after they had brushed their teeth and washed their faces and he had helped her get dressed. They ate breakfast, like lunch, at school, English Avenue Elementary.

"How did you feel about your house being the dope house?"

"Nothing to feel. Couldn't do nothing about it."

Michael finished the fourth grade at English Avenue; Ta-Ta stayed on until 1994 or 1995, when the school was closed down, boarded up as a hazard. By that time Michael had graduated from Capitol View Elementary and had started sixth grade at Ralph Bunche Middle School. When Jessie Mae Simpson was forced to move out of Dalvigney Street by the sheer tragedy of it all, she took them all—Michael, Ta-Ta, and Jason—with her to a house on Willis Mill Road. But soon, after her son Anthony was shot and killed right there in front of her house on Willis Mill, Big Mama herself died of cancer. That was when Michael and Ta-Ta were separated.

"You went to her funeral?"

"Yeah. At a church. But I didn't cry. I can't cry at funerals."

"You loved her?"

"I loved her, even though she wasn't my grandma."

"What did she look like?"

"I can't remember. That was a long time ago."

He ended up being placed in the group home on Springdale Road near Cleveland Avenue. He hated it. It was crowded with boys, thirty or maybe forty of them, mostly black boys, with the exception of two or three white boys who "acted black." That was when Marilyn Reed came to get him. Ta-Ta had moved in with her cousin, her father's niece. She was seven years old. Michael was ten.

That fifth-grade-year at Capitol View was memorable for Mr. Lovitt, Mr. Tommy Lovitt, one of Michael's teachers, a black man Michael characterized as "cool" because Lovitt was "raw and uncut"—meaning that he told a kid the truth, Michael explained. After school, at different periods during that post-Dalvigney period when he lived with Marilyn, he played basketball at the Kennedy Middle School Recreation Center, a block from Henry's, across from Beulah Baptist. He feels sure Marilyn still has his baseball trophies from the time he pitched for the Capitol View Tigers, a team of the Capitol View United Methodist Church near her home. But Marilyn's husband beat him with a closed hand. He said nothing to anyone, not even good-bye, not even to Ms. Al-Amin, his favorite teacher during the three months he spent in the sixth grade at Bunche, with whom he felt "comfortable." He put those months behind him, including the girls at Bunche, including Jennifer with whom he had been elected "unique couple." He ran back to the safety of familiarity, back to where Valerie stayed, back to the Bluff.

He was eleven, and Valerie, having been charged with gross negligence, had finally been declared an "unfit" mother in her third "deprivation hearing" in juvenile court. In those next two years, though, out on the streets in the Bluff, slinging dope in "the trap," he saw her a lot, tried to save her, he said.

"She always made sure we ate," he said of Valerie. "She called me her prodigal son. I never did know what she meant by that. . . . And she told me I was born on Echo Street, but I don't remember. . . .

"I knew she was on the pipe for a long time. I seen the pipe the first time on the bed, on Dalvigney. When I came back to the Bluff, she was strung out. We tried some of everything to help her. . . . When she would go to jail, Jason would pay her bond and tell the bail bondsman not to send her back to the Bluff. Send her to rehab."

"Where was that?"

"I don't know. All I know is she'd stay gone for two months or so, come back and chill out for another month, then be right back on it."

"What about your father? Did you know him or ever see him?"

"It was Jason didn't know who his daddy was. I knew my daddy. We didn't have no good relationship though. He might come through for something, or my grandma. . . ."

"Marian Scott, his mother?"

"Yeah. She might come get me and take me to him, or something. But it wasn't but every blue moon."

Michael came to stay on Holly Street with J-Boy. J-Boy's baby's mama, Shalance, and her two children lived there too. Michael had a bed there, but sometimes he stayed at Ebony's, deep in the Bluff. She was fine and brown and three years older. They would buy each other things. He was making real money. He could finally buy shoes. He had hated the other kids' new shoes, or the other kids for having new shoes. If he and J-Boy and Shalance did not buy groceries, they went out to eat, to the Red Lobster or even Houston's, a rather expensive chain restaurant. They had a car, which he swears he could and did drive. They went to the movies and the malls and Club Nikki over on Stewart Avenue.

"Every week J-Boy would pay me. I got around five hundred dollars a week."

"What did you do with it?"

"Bought clothes. For me and Ta-Ta. I might give her some money, too."

Government authorities inevitably identify a boy living like Little B did as having "fallen through the cracks," suggesting that American society has structured a network of safeguards, or "safety nets," to guarantee that its children do not go hungry, have decent housing, clothing, health care, and education, so children are not forced to resort to surviving by any means necessary, including by selling drugs. Alternatively there is the new conservative view, that the problems of Little B—or the problem of Little B—are attributable to the dysfunction of his family, rejecting any notion of societal responsibility for him, holding him accountable for himself. This latter idea has, in fact, found popular acceptance across the political spectrum. On one hand, there is the more liberal perspective, as infamously propounded some time ago by former New York senator Daniel Moynihan, wherein the Little B problem was deemed a result of the "matriarchal" structure of the black family, suggesting that the solution depended on a patriarchal restrengthening of the black family rather than on providing some sort of social safety net. The more right-leaning version, as advocated by former Georgia congressman Newt Gingrich, argues that the families and neighborhoods of the Little Bs are beyond repair, perhaps inherently so, and thus the problems he faces and presents can be remedied only if boys like him are removed from their families and communities and placed in reconstituted state-run orphanages. In any case, even the most conservative vision acknowledges that Michael is no aberration. That is, Little B is not one in a million. Little B is one *of* millions of children like him in America.

More than one in three black children in America are poor.[1] Indeed, Marian Wright Edelman, perhaps the single most respected authority on the state of children in America, founder and president of the Children's

Defense Fund (CDF), pointed out in a March 2000 statement that "one in five or 13.5 million children are living in poverty in America—5.8 million of them in *extreme* poverty of less than $6,500 a year for a family of three" (emphasis added).[2] Without respect for race, Edelman identified each of these poor children as "America's fifth child," referring to the one-in-five statistic. However, the profile that emerges of the "fifth child" is overwhelmingly a profile of America's black children, especially boys like Little B. "We neglect the fifth child, we don't feed him, we don't clothe him properly, we don't give him adequate shelter. We send him to school hungry, dirty, not dressed properly and expect him to compete with his wealthier peers for a quality education. We leave him to the violence of the streets and at risk of illness. He lives in fear and we expect him to abide by the rules. But there is one thing we promise to do for him. If he gets into trouble we guarantee him a prison cell."[3]

Similarly, in the *2000 Kids Count Data Book,* published by the highly respected nonpartisan Annie B. Casey Foundation, foundation president Douglas W. Nelson points out, "The number of children living in families that are extremely poor has remained virtually unchanged [since 1990]. This phenomenon can been seen most starkly in our major metropolitan areas, where there [are] . . . about 9.2 million children . . . particularly vulnerable. . . . A little more than half of these children live in neighborhoods where poverty rates are above 20 percent, and more than 1.1 million live in urban neighborhoods of extreme poverty, where more than 40 percent of the households live below the poverty line. . . . We now recognize that the majority of these families are not scattered randomly, but are concentrated in a relatively small number of specific neighborhoods in cities. . . . These families have been described as 'below poverty,' 'minority,' 'living in inner-city neighborhoods,' and [with] 'disproportionately single parents.' "[4]

In particular the state of Georgia, according to the report of Georgians for Children, an affiliate of the Casey Foundation, in its *Georgia Kids Count Factbook, 1998–99,* "remains one of the worst places in the United States for a child to live . . . rank[ing] . . . 43rd out of the 50 states and the District of Columbia in overall child well-being."[5]

At 712 Dalvigney Street, which became the drug house when Michael was eight years old, he and Ta-Ta lived on "the other side." That was how it was called by the permanent and transient adult residents. They slept in the upstairs of "the other side," which was the two-story apartment of the two-unit complex that had been made into one.

"Do you remember what color the building was?"

"Just white."

"Was it wood or what?"

"Sheet rock."

"Sheet rock? You know what that is when you see it? How?"

"I used to punch holes in the wall outside all the time. It was easy."

"Why did you punch out the walls?"

"I was mad all the time."

Michael had been moved out of Dalvigney, though, by his Big Mama, to Willis Mill, until she died. Then he had moved back into the Bluff with Valerie. She had a place on Griffin Street. He was nine years old then. Valerie's place was a rooming house next door to Henry's Market. Soon after he moved there, there was a police drug raid, he believes, or some kind of police raid. His mother and all the other users and addicts there were arrested. He was taken into custody by the Department of Family and Children Services (DFACS). That was when and why he came to stay in the group home on Springdale, from which Marilyn Reed was allowed to take him. He had lived a lot of different places by then.

"You used to live next door to the Suhs' market, where Woods was killed?"

"Yeah."

"How did the Suhs deal with all the dope dealing going on around their store?"

He laughs.

Notwithstanding the generally substandard condition of most of the housing in the Bluff, or that these living quarters were not supported by an adequate infrastructure, or that most residences lacked air-conditioning or washing machines or refrigerators, moving from one household to another, with short stays in each, in various neighborhoods, had to be a completely destabilizing living arrangement. The "fifth child," however, often changes residences more than once within the course of a year. According to the Casey Foundation's *Data Book,* in

1999 more than one-quarter of children living in "high-poverty" neigh-borhoods moved at least once that year.[6] Nearly half of them lived in a household without a car, adding isolation to instability. While most of these "inner-city" children lived in homes without computers (84 per-cent) or Internet access (94 percent), nearly one-fifth lived in house-holds without a telephone.[7]

In addition to such a stark absence of necessities in their homes, most inner-city children's neighborhoods lack the services and facilities that promote child well-being, such as parks and playgrounds, health clinics, child care centers, recreational and cultural centers, spaces for neighborhood celebrations, libraries, museums. According to the *Data Book*, "the absence of these critical links can compound the stress" ex-perienced by children living in impoverished neighborhoods.[8] Headed mostly by underemployed working poor single mothers, most of the families of these millions of children are not able to provide indepen-dently for such community services, any more than they can pay for summer camps or dance lessons or soccer teams.

One in ten children living in high-poverty central-city neighbor-hoods are living without either parent.[9]

"Ta-Ta, do you talk to your mom often?"

"Yes, ma'am," she says in her whisper of a voice, a little breeze that is still a little girl's voice at thirteen years old. She is tall, already taller than Michael, and lean, with the look and bearing of fashion model Na-omi Campbell. "I call my mom every morning."

"You do? How do you reach her?"

"She have a cell phone now."

"What do you talk about?"

"I ask her how she doing. If she had something to eat."

"You're happy when you talk to her."

"Oh, yes. When I couldn't see her before, I just cried and cried, every day."

"What about your father? Do you ever see him?"

"Yes. He be over in the Bluff. I took him a Father's Day card I made on the computer at school. I put a rose on it. It was real pretty. Then I put it in a frame."

"He was happy to get it?"

"Yes. He said, 'thank you.'"

What is perhaps most disconcerting for a child is either to be completely removed from her own family and neighborhood and entered into the foster care system or to be without any place to stay at all, homeless. According to the CDF, as of March 1999 there were "a record 547,000 children . . . in foster care." [10] In Georgia the number of children in foster care increased nearly 150 percent between 1982 and 1998 to twenty-two thousand children, a majority of whom are black. [11] Moreover, according to the CDF, there were 850,000 homeless children and youth in America. [12] A disproportionate percentage are from inner-city neighborhoods. While the exact number of homeless young children and teens is impossible to ascertain, some authoritative estimates suggest that, on any day and night, there may be as many as 2 million homeless children in America. Approximately twenty thousand of these children live on the streets of New York City. Various reports conclude that the increase in child homelessness is primarily attributable to the fact that these children are the first generation born of the 1980s "epidemics" of crack cocaine and AIDS. Nevertheless, in New York, as in other big cities, there are children sleeping on rooftops and in tunnels, mostly children of the inner city, not runaways from far away. Most are running, though, from abuse at home or in foster homes or in state-supported homes. Finally, an estimated 125,000 children in America have been orphaned because of AIDS, and "most of these children [are] poor and Black." [13]

"Why did you run away from Marilyn's house?" I ask Michael. "I thought it was a nice place."

"It was. She was living, all right."

"So why did you run?"

"Her husband used to beat me all the time. . . . I was gone."

"You'd never been beaten before, never given a spanking?"

"No, not no major whipping like that. . . . I don't think people should whip kids. I'm against it." He laughs.

The boarded-up windows of the English Avenue Elementary School are typical for schools in the Bluff communities across America. There is no money for repair and maintenance, either of the facility or of the curriculum. Charles Maxwell, principal of Wadsworth Elementary in the Atlanta area, said that he had an *annual* budget of $30 per child for "discretionary" funds, including for art supplies and field trips. He could not, therefore, afford to provide students at Wadsworth, nearly 100 percent of whom are black, with a trip to one of the most visited historic sites in America and located so nearby—the King Center for Nonviolent Social Change and the Martin Luther King Jr. National Historic Site. Most of the children never visit the King Center.

Almost fifty years after the Supreme Court's *Brown v. Board of Education* decision, America's schools are still segregated. Indeed, Kenneth Clark, the psychologist whose study was pivotal in *Brown*, stated on the occasion of the fortieth anniversary of the decision that in 1954, he "had not realized the depth of racism in America."[14] School segregation has had the deleterious effect blacks fought so hard to overcome by pressing for desegregation. It continues to render poor all-black public school districts so impoverished as to be unable to provide a proper education for its students. Atlanta's is such a school district, wherein 80 percent of its nearly all-black student population qualify for free or subsidized lunches.[15]

The correlation between investment of money and educational outcome is dramatically substantiated in the rankings of school districts in Georgia, as it is elsewhere in the country. Today the richest school districts, funded by local property taxes and rich parents, spend more than twice as many dollars per student as the poor districts.[16] Students from ghetto schools consistently score lower on every scholastic test than do students in the richest, predominantly white districts, even in the primary grades.[17] For example, the last data available from the National Assessment of Education Progress, a government reporting agency, indicate that 38 percent of white fourth graders in Georgia were rated "proficient readers," compared with only 9 percent of black fourth graders.[18] In the poor districts, children have few books, few supplies, and few qualified teachers, and classrooms are overcrowded. School buildings are deteriorated, with cracked paint, faltering air-conditioning systems, broken and missing furniture and windows, and nonfunctional science and sports equipment. And, as was recently revealed at Georgia's predominantly black North Clayton High School, they are infested with roaches and rats.[19]

But Michael was not attending any school at all. For two years he was absent from Ralph Bunche Middle School, where he was last registered, and nobody noticed.

Little B did not fall through the cracks. The statistics suggest that he is the rule rather than the exception. He is as predictably uneducated, and now incarcerated, as he is poor. He is a boy of the Bluff for whom, it seems, no bridge over troubled waters was ever constructed.

Incredibly, though, Sherekaa Osorio, director of public relations for DFACS, actually stated that he was "a boy who fell through the cracks."[20] She went on to acknowledge that, even though Michael had indeed been in the custody of DFACS when he was arrested, he had been considered in "runaway status" for more than a year before his arrest. He had come under the care of DFACS because of neglect and drug abuse in his household, she explained, adding, rather sympathetically, that boys like Michael really had "nobody to protect them . . . and nobody to go to." She would certainly not characterize him as a "thug." There really was little DFACS could have done, though, to take care of Michael, as its social workers and staff were "overburdened." Each child welfare caseworker was responsible, minimally, for about forty families, some with as many as three and four children. Moreover, as a caseworker's starting salary was twenty-two thousand dollars per year, it was difficult to find and keep qualified employees.

In late October 1998, in the frustrating process of trying to understand who had and who had had "custody" of Michael Lewis, now in jail, I contacted the office of Carmen Ferguson, program director of social services for DFACS. Ferguson told me that since Michael "had used several aliases" they had "lost track" of him until "he surfaced," when arrested.[21] As to the question of custody, she would look into the matter and call back. In November, Doris Carnes of Ferguson's office called and advised me, "We [DFACS] do not have custody of Michael Lewis. . . . His mother has custody."[22] To confirm this repudiation of Michael, Ferguson sent a letter in December 1998 to Michael's trial attorney, Patrice Grant Fulcher (she had gotten married), which in fact finally acknowledged that for some time before his arrest, as of November 27, 1995, Michael Lewis had indeed been in the "agency's custody." However, Ferguson's letter explained, the "Honorable Sanford J. Jones [juvenile court judge] later relinquished custody with Fulton County Department of Family and Children Services under a dismissal order . . . dated February 4, 1997."[23] This was less than a week after his arrest.

Ironically, a year later DFACS administrators themselves were thrust before the court of public opinion by an *Atlanta Journal-Constitution* reporter, Jane O. Hansen, in connection with the death of a child. Hansen, who had made a mission of unearthing the agency's abysmal failures, had discovered that a black boy named Terrell Peterson, who had died of abuse at the age of five, had also been written off by DFACS, another child who had "fallen through the cracks." Although his grandmother, aunt, and aunt's boyfriend were charged with killing this child, Hansen asserted that the boy's life could have been saved by DFACS. "Seven times between 1991 and 1995 . . . people called the Fulton County Department of Family and Children Services to report apparent neglect of Terrell," Hansen reported. While DFACS apparently placed the child with his grandmother, by 1996 he had been taken by ambulance to the hospital, yet again, again covered with bruises. Though a misdemeanor criminal charge was filed against the grandmother, as guardian, Atlanta municipal court judge Catherine Malicki dismissed the charge at a first hearing as "the victim was not in court." One year later Terrell Peterson arrived at the hospital in cardiac arrest and was soon pronounced dead. In light of the exposure given to this case, Sherekaa Osorio issued a statement on behalf of DFACS: "This case has been extensively reviewed since the child's death by county and state officials, and all policies and procedures were followed." [24]

Osorio told me, when I first interviewed her, that any number of public professionals, including police and school officials, were "mandated" by law to report to DFACS not only when they learned of a child's abuse or neglect, but also when children were absent from school, or truant.

Of the numerous appearances Michael made in juvenile court, however, none had been for truancy. Moreover, in those two years he stayed on the streets of the Bluff selling drugs, he was never once arrested by police—not for drugs, not for his obvious truancy from school. Other than encounters with members of the Atlanta police department's notorious special tactical team called the Red Dog Squad, Michael had only once been so much as approached by a police officer about not being in school. He went with this officer to the school he said he attended, and as soon as they arrived he ran back to the Bluff. Not even the Red Dogs arrested him, even though they, like regular Zone 1 Atlanta police officers, saw him all the time, alongside so many others, out on the corner, in broad daylight, selling drugs. Every so often, he reported, they would "swoop down." "Sometimes," he testified, "they would take me up to a liquor store on Bankhead at Northside." They would seize the dope and money, make idle threats, and then ride away.

What frequently put Michael in juvenile court, however, were mainly issues unrelated to any behavior or alleged wrongdoing on his part, his "runaway" charges, "ungovernability," the deprivation hearings, and so forth. Despite such appearances, and given that several of them were related to the charges leveled by DFACS against his mother, juvenile court judges never once questioned or investigated the issue of his residency or school enrollment. When contacted in this regard, the judges were silent. Judge Sanford Jones never returned telephone calls to him, nor did anyone from associate judge David Gettachew-Smith's office. The others were unreachable. Even if these judges had agreed to speak about what happened to Michael, the fact is that there is no place in the vast judicial network to which they might have referred or sent him except jail.

It seemed the school district had more options. So I continued to wonder why no one in the district seemed to have taken note of Michael's two-year absence. As he had last been enrolled in Bunche Middle School, I contacted Bunche. The assistant principal noted Michael's poor attendance record and mentioned that there were "disciplinary problems," though she did not have the files. She concluded the conversation by saying, "actually very few people remember him—even the counselors." [25] The response from Capitol View Elementary was even less forthcoming. Marcene Thornton, the principal, was extremely guarded, stating she "prefer[red] not to speak," that she had "no comment." [26]

Of course both Capitol View and Bunche have very dismal attendance rates in any event. The 1995–96 report of the Council for School Performance, prepared by the Applied Research Center, Georgia State University, shows Capitol View's absentee rate among the highest in the entire state and ranks the school in the lowest percentiles with respect to reading, science, and math. [27] Bunche, too, has one of the state's highest absentee rates and is ranked in the lowest percentiles in the state for reading, math, science, and social studies. [28] Once again, overcrowded, understaffed, and underfunded schools were failing their students, even failing to notice whether they showed up.

For black children like Michael, there has traditionally been the black church, at least as a last resort. Beulah Baptist sits in the area, near Griffin and Simpson, across from Kennedy Middle School, where Michael used to play basketball. I wondered how he had escaped the church's attention. When I contacted Beulah Baptist in June 2000, I spoke with Stephanie, who identified herself as "the pastor's administrative assistant." I had left a message previously for Rev. W. L. Cottrell and wondered whether he had received it. He had. He was, however, completely engaged for the next week, making it impossible for him to speak with me. She was sure he would contact me as soon as he could. I asked whether she remembered "the incident," occurring so close to the church, and asked whether the church had ever been in touch with Michael. Rather forcefully, she said, "We did not know him." [29]

[7] Superpredator or Outcast?

The autopsy report concluded that pieces of the cockroach trapped in her throat had blocked the airway to eight-month-old Tameka's lungs and asphyxiated her. Even though Shawntello Young's baby girl Tameka had died choking on a roach in Atlanta's Perry Homes housing project, it was assumed broadly that the actual cause of death was neglect or abuse.[1] Atlanta officials seemed in accord that, if Tameka had not died from ongoing neglect or abuse, then that day at the end of May 1996, at least, in the first light rising on the Olympic Games, Shawntello Young had surely left her baby alone at the mercy of the thousand dangers in her filthy apartment, as it came to be publicly characterized.

Indeed as the reports regarding the death of Shawntello Young's baby began dominating the local news, the focus quickly turned to Shawntello herself. In his postautopsy press conference Fulton County assistant medical examiner John Parker, who conducted the autopsy on Tameka's body, seemed to feel obliged to emphasize that "Tameka showed every sign of being well cared for." Furthermore Parker was quoted as saying that "the baby was clean. She had no diaper rash. The skin behind her ears was clean." Then, he added, apparently oblivious to the overtones, "This impresses me."[2]

Renee Lewis Glover, executive director of the Atlanta Housing Authority (AHA), was not impressed. Glover seemed to have spent most of her waking hours in those last two years in which she had been in office doing everything possible to rid the areas in her domain of criminal, unruly, and otherwise unseemly public housing tenants, all in preparation for the Olympic Games. Everyone had commended her for her work. Now, only a few months before the games, these headlines about

Young's baby's death in one of her public housing projects were threatening to taint her reputation and good work.

Hours after Shawntello and her family had concluded the memorial service for Tameka and had buried her little body in a white baby dress, Glover held a press conference meant to cure this problem. She accused Shawntello Young of having seen her daughter playing with a roach only minutes before the baby choked to death. She handed out to the press what she purported was a police report substantiating this accusation, wherein an Atlanta police investigator claimed that Shawntello had told her she had noticed her baby playing with a roach just before she choked, suggesting, among other things, that Shawntello had stood by and watched her baby choke to death. Finally Glover presented an AHA inspection report, dated October 10, 1995, in which the Young family had been given "failing and unsatisfactory housekeeping grades."[3] The point was, obviously, that the roach trapped in the baby's throat was in the home because Shawntello and her family had maintained a dirty apartment.

This theme resonated throughout the public discourse on Shawntello Young, a black unwed teen living on welfare in a public housing project who it was thought was probably to blame for her baby's death. Shawntello's apartment was inspected by the Fulton County Health Department and by the Department of Family and Children Services (DFACS). Reports of these inspections were published days after the baby's funeral under the banner headline "Child Safety Inspection."[4] The focus of the inspections, and the article, was whether or not, or perhaps to what degree, Shawntello had contributed to her baby's death through some kind of gross neglect, either in housekeeping or in caring for her child.

Even though there was no report or evidence that Shawntello had ever abused Tameka or her other young daughter, DFACS spokeswoman Sherekaa Osorio was quoted as saying, "We wanted to find out *also* if the mother's other child at the residence was being neglected or abused" (emphasis added). Osorio conceded that DFACS had "found . . . the other child was well cared for, well clothed, the house was reasonably straight and the mother was (an appropriate mother)."[5]

The newspaper nevertheless continued its reports, now focusing hard on Shawntello's personal history and persona. We learned that although Shawntello was "only a teenager" Tameka was not her first baby. "After her daughter Michelle was born [in 1993], Shawntello became pregnant again." This was part of a major feature, titled "Dreams of Faded Glory," about Shawntello's failures, which included being an Olympic Games spoiler because she was "a great swimmer who lost it all." [6] Her sinfulness now fully exposed, the feature's writers rather openly suggested that it was her own behavior, the bad choices she made, that ultimately led to the tragedy of her baby's death: "The teenage father [of Tameka], Antonio Tucker, was shot in the face and killed during an argument at Perry Homes before Tameka was born." The picture they painted was stunning. Incredibly, it ignored the heavy pain this young mother was surely suffering over the death of her baby daughter. At the same time, the writers castigated Shawntello as the implicitly "illegitimate" daughter of a welfare-dependent woman who had had ten children: "At 42, Roynell Young is already a grandmother and matriarch. Although all the [ten] children carry their mother's last name, they were fathered by two men." Finally Shawntello herself had become pregnant out of wedlock, not once but twice, and the second time by a "thug," and this after choosing to forfeit both her athletic promise and her education.

In a "related" article published on the same day, Glover announced initiation of "clean sweeps" of the AHA's more than fourteen thousand units. She explained that this new policy meant that tenants would have to pass "white-glove tests" for cleanliness inspections that would now be performed monthly, not annually. "Failure by a tenant to improve housekeeping after flunking an initial inspection could result in eviction." [7] The new policy was instituted in response to the fact that the Fulton County Health Department, in the wake of Tameka Young's death, had cited not Shawntello but the AHA itself for housing code violations at the baby's apartment.

Now the AHA's own citation was being foisted vicariously upon Shawntello Young's head. These pregames clean sweeps involved sudden unannounced inspections of people's apartments by a small, white-gloved army of Glover's AHA employees. Tenant resentment of the inspections turned to outrage, which was cleverly redirected onto Shawntello. In a newspaper interview, a resident who had been cited by one of the eighteen inspection teams for having "roaches throughout the kitchen" declared, "I didn't cause the roaches. I don't think they should make it hard for everybody because the baby died."[8] Glover, however, had advised tenants that, while the baby's death was a "terrible tragedy," the AHA maintenance and pest control records showed "no negligence" by her agency.[9] This was a matter of bad housekeeping, and she was going to make sure it never happened again.

Official Atlanta, in the anticipation of the coming games, was gratified that the city had dodged responsibility for the entire affair, all of which had been fully placed upon Shawntello Young herself. The next year Shawntello would sue the AHA and others for the gross negligence that had caused her baby's death.[10] Attorney Douglas R. Powell confirmed that the case of the *Estate of Tameka Young v. the Atlanta Housing Authority* had been quickly settled by the AHA for an undisclosed sum and, under its terms, sealed. And later there was a barely noticeable blurb in the *Atlanta Journal-Constitution* regarding the outcome of the lawsuit, wherein AHA spokesman Rick White acknowledged that the AHA had settled the lawsuit and had paid Shawntello Young for maintaining a "roach-infested apartment in Perry Homes."[11] Publicly, though, Shawntello Young would always remain the victim blamed for the crime.

The infant mortality rate for blacks in America is twice that for whites. Georgia has one of the highest infant mortality rates in the entire nation, ranking very near the bottom of the fifty states and Washington, D.C.[12] Lately some government agencies and private organizations have attempted to attribute this national shame to ignorance on the part of black mothers, ascribing the disparity to black infant "crib deaths" (known as SIDS, or Sudden Infant Death syndrome). It is now widely promulgated that black mothers have a sort of aberrant tendency to place their babies on their stomachs for sleeping and that this positioning is the primary cause of SIDS, which according to the American Academy of Pediatrics (AAP) "remains the highest cause of infant death beyond the neonatal period."[13] The AAP argues that strong evidence "in various well-designed epidemiologic studies" indicates that placing a baby on its stomach is "a major risk factor" for SIDS, but one that has "the greatest potential for modification." Thus a campaign, endorsed by the AAP, is being waged by the Consumer Product Safety Commission with advertising on black cable television shows to encourage black mothers to step out of their ignorance, turn their babies on their backs, and thus lower the black infant mortality rate. The AAP assertion that "black infants are twice as likely to be placed prone as white infants," on which this new campaign is centered, is primarily based on a single set of data collected from interviews conducted between 1995 and 1996 of less than four hundred "mother-infant dyads" in Washington, D.C., a study that concluded that among other things a "predictor" of the prone sleep position was "the black race." [14]

The first irony in all of this is that by definition SIDS means an infant's death by causes "unknown." According to the AAP, SIDS is "the sudden death of an infant under one year of age, which remains unexplained after a thorough case investigation, including performance of a complete autopsy, examination of the death scene, and review of the clinical history." Moreover, the AAP acknowledges that there are a host of other "risk factors" that may cause the unknown SIDS, including sharing beds with adults, overheating, loose bed clothes, preterm delivery and low birth weight, sleeping on soft surfaces (e.g., sofas), and maternal smoking. [15] Finally, notwithstanding the absence of data on the percentage of black infant deaths for which there has been the necessary "thorough case investigation, including performance of a complete autopsy, examination of the death scene, and review of the clinical history," the AAP has not proved a nexus between the alleged "black race" positioning of sleeping babies and the high black infant mortality rate. Indeed, according to the research conducted by Georgians for Children, the issue of SIDS and the high black infant mortality are completely separate, and if SIDS were taken out of the equation, the disparity between black and white infant mortality rates would remain the same. [16]

This implicit attribution of personal responsibility to black mothers themselves for the deaths of their babies, a variation on the themes raised in the death of Shawntello Young's baby, evades the more compelling objective realities. In the case of Shawntello Young, this evasion went not merely to the issue of the gross neglect on the part of the AHA with respect to maintenance of Perry Homes. It also had to do with the total environment of poverty and neglect to which Shawntello and Tameka and all the other Perry Homes' children had been subjected.

One point never raised in the public debate about Tameka's asphyxiation by a roach was that the Herman E. Perry Homes project, sitting between the notorious Gun Club Community Park and the Gun Club Public Sanitation Landfill, "posed serious health and safety hazards to the residents." Gun Club Park is known to be a haven for vermin, its once-useful outdoor pool holding only stagnant rainwater while its deteriorated community buildings and tennis courts are completely overgrown with vines. It has been the site of numerous rapes of neighborhood girls. As a result, Perry Homes ranks notoriously high among AHA properties for forcible rapes.[17]

The Gun Club Landfill, on the other side, is an environmental hazard, or as the Trust for Public Land environmental organization deemed it, "explosive."[18] It is a hill of waste two hundred feet high, one-half mile wide, and one-half mile long. Situated there since the 1970s and receiving the majority of the city's residential waste, it is so potentially dangerous that the city itself ordered it closed by October 1993.[19] For those nearly three years from that time to Tameka's death, however, nothing was done by any agency or entity to clean up the Gun Club Landfill's toxic compost.[20]

Moreover, Perry Homes is bordered on the west by Proctor Creek, which in 1996 was deemed by the city to be completely polluted.[21] According to the AHA's own report at the time, this pollution was primarily attributable to "storm water runoff from the steep embankments of the adjacent landfill." Along the southern boundary of Perry Homes is Rockdale Industrial Park, a forsaken property that came to be (and was at the time of Tameka's death) an unauthorized dump site.[22]

In its 1996 report regarding Perry Homes, submitted to the U.S. Department of Housing and Urban Development (HUD) in support of its application for a HOPE VI grant for $20 million, the AHA identified the housing project as a "physically depressed community" composed of "944 distressed housing units." The report revealed that by the time Tameka Young was choking to death on a roach Perry Homes, developed in the 1950s, had become so deteriorated that the AHA was now seeking approval for the demolition of all of its 184 buildings. Indeed, the report documented the fact that on June 3, 1996, only ten days after Tameka's death, HUD had already approved the total demolition of Perry Homes.[23]

In soliciting funding needed to demolish the existing units and to construct replacements, the AHA report noted first that 236 units of Perry Homes were already vacant by June 1996. Among those remaining, *all* were deemed "dilapidated structures" that posed "serious health and safety hazards to the residents." [24]

As it turned out, Perry Homes residents for years had been complaining to the AHA about the chronically wretched conditions in their homes, despite Glover's denials.[25] They had complained that their apartments, where more than 70 percent of the residents were children under seventeen years old, were being overrun by roaches, and also by rats and even snakes. But the horrific conditions at Perry Homes went unreported in all the major news accounts regarding the death of Tameka Young, as did Shawntello Young's love for her children. Worse, the AHA continued to promote the insidious insinuation that Shawntello Young's baby had died because of something Shawntello herself had done or not done as an unwed teen mother.

Not only had Glover publicly promoted this image of Shawntello, but also she actually exploited the tragedy of the baby's death in a last-minute addendum to her $20 million HOPE VI grant application to "redevelop" Perry Homes as "an example of the problems of public housing." "The tragedy of public housing, and particularly Perry Homes, can be seen in the death of Tameka Young, the 8-month-old daughter of an unwed teenage mother. . . . Perry Homes had the highest failure rate for public housing inspections. . . . This high failure rate may indicate an attitude of apathy and lack of pride in the community." [26] This malicious "spin" on Shawntello served to do more than exculpate Glover and the AHA from any responsibility in the baby's death. It served to satisfy the conditions of the Fulton County Superior Court consent decree that Glover and the AHA had been in violation of since February 1996 arising from two class action lawsuits that had been filed against the AHA for gross neglect and illegal activities in the maintenance of public housing in Atlanta.[27] Until Shawntello's baby's death exposed the AHA's failure of compliance to the most minimal requirements of the decree, Glover had been able to forestall court sanctions and community outrage.

The image of the black girl as seductive predator and bearer of "illegitimate" offspring dates, of course, from the slave era, evolving in the post-Emancipation decades into a number of mutations. By the 1960s she had come to be Daniel Moynihan's "black family matriarch," then Ronald Reagan's "welfare queen," and later Bill Clinton's "unwed teen mother." Indeed Clinton invoked this stereotype to wage his successful campaign to "reform," or virtually eliminate, the nation's welfare program for families with dependent children, targeting families headed by single mothers.[28] Thus this vilification of black girls has become so ingrained in the culture that it influences sweeping public policy. The new social drift to push millions of poor black girls and women further into poverty by cutting off all social welfare lifelines to them and their children and by uprooting them from public housing is rooted in this categorical castigation of them as socially dysfunctional and promiscuous.

Not only has there been *no* increase in the rate of teen pregnancies over the last forty years, but in fact the rate of teen pregnancies in the United States has dropped, as it has worldwide, according to reports of the Alan Guttmacher Institute, the National Center for Health Statistics, the Center for Population Research at the National Institutes of Health, and the U.S. Centers for Disease Control (CDC). Moreover, according to the 1997 report of the National Center for Health Statistics, the percentage of pregnant teens in 1995 was actually lower than in 1970 and even lower than in 1950. It is noteworthy that, like most teen girls' pregnancies, *most* of the pregnancies of women of *all* other ages are *unintended*, the result of unprotected sex or ineffective contraception. Nevertheless, a whole school of thought has arisen—and remains entrenched—suggesting the existence of a social scourge in a so-called rising rate of teen pregnancy—or black unwed teen mothers. Indeed the Atlanta-based CDC itself continues to identify teen pregnancy as a "paramount public health problem," without addressing or even making reference to the fact that many of these girls have been impregnated by older men, including rapists and relatives. With no basis in reality, then, the notion of rising promiscuity among teen girls—meaning primarily black girls —persists and has engendered studies, organizations, and legislation criminalizing and chastening them.[29]

Millions of tax and charity dollars are being used by agencies and nonprofit foundations to fund any number of so-called family planning programs targeting teens. Notwithstanding that black teens and other girls who become pregnant do not represent any extraordinary social danger per se, the unwed black teen girl, a girl like Shawntello Young, has become anathema in American society. A New York–based nonprofit organization called the Robin Hood Foundation actually issued a report the year Shawntello's baby died asserting the incredible conclusion that pregnant teens cost American society $29 billion a year "in expenses and lost productivity." What gave this dubious study significance was that it was issued through the White House by President Clinton with a view to developing a program to stopper this alleged social drain and to "combat teenage pregnancy," evidently in tandem with his "welfare reform" program, already in place.[30] Now, presumably, these girls might be forced not only out of their laziness and into minimum-wage employment but also to halt their evil ways.

Finally private charities have been organized around the immorality of teen girls' sexuality and their pregnancy without the benefit of marriage. As the referenced report of the Center for Population Research at the National Institutes of Health stated, the only difference between teen pregnancy figures at the end of the twentieth century and in the 1950s is that in the 1950s "pregnant teens got married."[31] Thus the only real issue these groups address is a "moral" one, or the "immorality" of "unwed" teen mothers. Prominent among them in Georgia is a group created and led by former actress and antiwar activist Jane Fonda. Her organization, Georgia Campaign for Adolescent Pregnancy Prevention (G-CAPP), has one primary agenda. At an annual luncheon hundreds of affluent predominantly white Atlanta socialites joined Fonda in applauding a theatrical piece Fonda had directed, in which young black boys and girls—and only black boys and girls—performed. In this one-act play the girls showed how and promised that they would "just say 'no' " to sex.[32] A G-CAPP board member then stood to remind everyone of how far they had come and how proud they ought to be of their work, now fully supported by Georgia governor Zell Miller. They still had, however, a long way to go, she urged, to realize their ultimate goal: "100% abstinence."[33]

Similarly, newly resurrected myths about the dark nature of black boys have found wide social acceptance, driving the implementation of new social and political policies rife with racism, particularly in relation to crime and punishment. These latter-day theories about black boys are rooted in the culture of American slavery, wherein the black male was identified as inherently savage, an immoral or amoral being possessing a bestial nature, and thus by nature inferior to whites and fit only to serve as a slave. As brutal as such a characterization seems in American hindsight, it has survived slavery itself.

This new groundswell of criminal accusations being hurled at black boys can find comparison only in the racist mob mood that prevailed in the 1930s. In March 1931, when millions—black and white—were suffering the ravages of the Great Depression, as America strained to change from an agrarian to an industrial society, the infamous Alabama case of the Scottsboro Boys came to the public's attention. Originally charged with fighting white boys in a railroad boxcar while traveling through Alabama, nine black boys ranging in age from thirteen to nineteen were, within weeks of their arrests, tried, convicted, and sentenced to death for the rape of two white women at a railway station. Historian and Harvard professor James Goodman described the mood of the country over this case in his critically acclaimed *Stories of Scottsboro:*

> Writers and editors all over the region agreed that it was the most atrocious crime ever recorded in that part of the country, perhaps in the whole United States, "a wholesale debauching of society . . . so horrible in its details that all the facts could never be printed," a "heinous and unspeakable crime" that "savored of the jungle, the way back dark ages of meanest African corruption." They were revolted by the story, but not surprised. Or if surprised, surprised only by the magnitude of the crime. They expected black men to rape white women. Blacks were savages, more savage, many argued (with scientific theories to support them), than they had been as slaves.[34]

While most of the boys spent more than ten years suffering in Alabama prisons for their "crime," all were eventually pardoned, paroled, or released, as the charges were eventually deemed false.[35]

Now, under the aegis of "urban crime," this old ascription of bestiality and criminality to black males—younger and younger ones—has found renewed acceptance in mainstream America.

In 1989, political and social turmoil erupted regarding what was referred to as the case of the Central Park Jogger, involving the old familiar criminal theme of the rape and beating of a young white woman allegedly by several black boys. What made this story sensational was how the police and the media cast it. It was said to represent a new wave of criminal activity, called a "wilding," perpetrated by a new and more vicious breed of criminal. This one word, *wilding,* arbitrarily attributed in most reports about the case to the accused boys themselves, evoked the old theme of the "criminal nature" of black males. This wilding was even more, it was being said. It was a "new thing," representing a new kind of youth gang activity, described as "savage gang rape."[36] This dark theme gripped many with terror and activated a repressed mass remembrance of racist feelings.

A major article, syndicated only weeks after the attack and the arrests of the young black *suspects,* demanded that "America's Black Leadership" denounce the attack of the white woman by these black boys, referring to them as "young savages who did the deed" and "remorseless monsters."[37] Another major newspaper article about "the savage attack" published sensationalist man-on-the-street opinions— notably of white males—about the attack and alleged attackers, though the suspects would not go on trial for another year. A "silver-moustached psychotherapist" interviewed while jogging through Central Park was quoted as saying, "I thought at the beginning it was drugs, but it's not drugs. As bad as crack is, at least it would be some sort of excuse. But there's no excuse for that type of bestiality." Another interviewee said, "They should be tried as animals. . . . What does the Humane Society do with animals like that? Puts 'em to sleep."[38] The next day another piece unabashedly identified the incident as reflecting a "race" problem: "The jogger, in a coma now after being left to bleed to death after the rape and beating, is white. Her accused attackers are blacks, some as young as 13 years old." This piece went on to opine, "There was no apparent motive for the attack. The boys, now in jail, said they were just looking for some 'fun.'" Then the piece quoted an anonymous radio talk show caller to sum up the national mood: "Don't call them animals. . . . Call them savages, black savages."[39]

Now the reports became frenzied, predicting the possibility of more such attacks, auguring the coming of gangs of black boys descending on Central Park to commit more "savage" acts. New York police were reported to state that while the term *wilding* was new to them, the activity was not. "For years, loosely organized packs of marauding youths have roamed the streets and parks bullying, robbing and attacking victims at random." [40] The mayor, Ed Koch, cautioned that the mere act of jogging in "some parts" of New York meant "you're endangering your physical well-being." The head of the New York Road Runners Club warned joggers to avoid the northern area of Central Park, "that area bordering on Harlem." [41]

These frightening random attacks were said to target white victims. Even though the Central Park Jogger herself remained unconscious, the *Atlanta Journal-Constitution* reported that New York police records indicated that "the assailants . . . discussed 'getting whitey' or getting a 'white jogger.'" The reportage was rife with suggestive imagery, that the assailants were "wolf packs" of black boys out on the prowl from their ghetto enclaves. Even a black female psychologist, Lisa Whitten, of the Association of Black Psychologists, encouraged this predator fable, saying of the *suspected* boys, "They're human beings who went berserk . . . macho, aggressive, strong." [42]

The reports continued to fuel public hysteria and rage. With no substantiation whatsoever and in blatant disregard of reporting only verifiable facts, newspapers like the *Atlanta Journal-Constitution* reported that the woman's rape had been perpetrated by "a pack of teenagers . . . a pack of 33 . . . [who] went 'wilding' through Central Park." [43] The sensationalized reports of thirty-three unmistakably black boys obliterated the fact that only eight boys were actually arrested, and some of the eight were charged with other alleged assaults in the same time period. Of those eight, only three would stand trial. Nevertheless, even a week after the arrests, the *New York Times* quoted New York police spokesman Lt. Stephen P. Davis as saying, "This is a large group of kids from the projects, running around in bands, jumping people." Moreover, the article continued, "the attacks grew out of a pastime called wilding, in which friends from three neighboring housing projects gathered in packs and set out to attack people for fun, especially joggers and bicyclists in the northern reaches of the park." [44]

In the end, the three boys actually tried for the assault on the woman jogger, tried for rape and attempted murder, were convicted of the rape, even though "*no* physical evidence, including blood, semen, DNA samples and hair, was found to link the defendants to the crime." This was so despite the announcement at the posttrial press conference by two of the jurors that they "did not believe the 3 defendants [had] committed the rape." It was so even though "the only semen identified on the jogger the night of the attack was that of her boyfriend." All three were acquitted of attempted murder.[45]

In the aftermath, though, what remained was mass acceptance of the notion of a new criminal breed of black boy. This idea conformed with New York prosecutor Elizabeth Lederer's description of those boys she had prosecuted for the rape of the Central Park Jogger, whom she had deemed predators, who solely "out of boredom and disaffection . . . set upon the park after sundown to harm whoever got in their way." And despite the reality of the outcome of the trial, this incident triggered more than a revival of racism in the mass mind—as the *Atlanta Journal-Constitution* reported, the case became "a national symbol of urban violence and racial tension." [46] It supplied fodder for a political agenda that gained momentum over the next five years and culminated in the 1994 juvenile crime legislation of the Clinton administration.

At the time, however, in 1989, Republicans in Congress began clamoring for tougher juvenile crime laws in response to this case. New Hampshire Republican congressman Chuck Douglas specifically referred to the Central Park Jogger and the concept of "wilding" in beginning to lobby for the tougher juvenile crime laws. Indeed, Douglas cited this case as he and the other members of the Republican Research Committee Task Force on Crime shaped the focus of what would become a body of new harsh juvenile crime laws, whereby kids could be tried as adults, announcing, in street vernacular, "If you're going to do big-boy crime, you're going to do big-boy time." [47]

Resurrected racist myths have reduced the problem of crime in America to the problem of blacks in America, particularly poor, black inner-city boys. This is evidenced in many ways, most particularly in the passage and application of the invidious new juvenile crime laws, as well as in the new notion of police racial profiling and in the intensification of old police brutality directed at blacks. The results are devastating for blacks. In 1998 the international secretariat of Amnesty International issued a scathing report regarding human rights violations of children in the U.S. justice system, stating that "at every stage of the justice system, racial and ethnic minority children are present in numbers greatly out of proportion to their numbers in the community. 'The evidence strongly indicates that one reason for this is discrimination on the part of law enforcement and justice system personnel.' " [48]

In Georgia, since the 1994 passage of the state's tough juvenile crime law, about 75 percent of all children arrested and over 90 percent of all children tried and convicted as adults have been black.[49] When asked why it was that nearly all of the children he had prosecuted as adults in DeKalb County, Georgia, had been black, District Attorney J. Tom Morgan responded, "They're the ones committing all the crimes." [50] In a late 1999 television interview with Katie Couric of the *To-day* show, Morgan refined this point. Couric's interview was occasioned by the case of Nathaniel Abraham, a black boy from Michigan who was eleven years old when he was arrested. Nathaniel had come to be known as "the youngest person in America to stand trial for murder," or the youngest to be tried as an adult. Morgan explained that the criminal justice system served two great societal interests: to punish wrongdoers and to protect society from them. The latter was why he maintained Nathaniel had to be tried as an adult. Morgan asserted that Nathaniel's behavior "over the years of his life had proven his effective unfitness to live in civilized society." Even though Nathaniel had not gone to trial at that point, Morgan concluded by saying that the protection of society was paramount in this case because Nathaniel Abraham was a "predator." [51]

This shadowy image of the black boy as predator has now been imprinted on the public mind beyond the traditional southern strongholds of racism. It has given rise to a new lexicon of racism and created a new national myth to validate an old and deep American racism. This new myth has achieved credibility through a collection of pseudointellectual works produced by a group of prominent ideologues of the far Right. Leading the pack is John J. DiIulio Jr. DiIulio, a former professor of politics and public affairs at Princeton University and the University of Pennsylvania, is almost singularly responsible for the invention and promulgation of the myth of the black boy as criminal "superpredator."

While DiIulio professes to be nonpartisan, he is primarily affiliated with the most extreme Right—Republican individuals, organizations, and so-called think tanks. He is the former director of the Center for Public Management at the Brookings Institution, the think tank of the ruling circle. He receives significant funding from the ultra-Right John M. Olin

Foundation. He is or has been a member or affiliate of the far-Right Heritage Foundation, the Council on Crime, and the Ethics and Public Policy Center—of which, notably, Elliott Abrams, one of the memorable players in the Iran-contra scandal, is president. He is most closely affiliated with the Manhattan Institute for Public Policy Research and is the director of its affiliate, the strange right-wing religious entity called the Jeremiah Project.

It was under the banner of a newly launched journal, the *Weekly Standard,* that DiIulio introduced his "superpredator" treatise, in November 1995, in an article entitled "The Coming of the Super-Predators." Today the *Standard* advertises itself as the "most influential magazine in Washington" and boasts of DiIulio as a contributing editor and of contributions from a "Who's Who" of politics and journalism, including William Bennett, Robert Bork, William F. Buckley Jr., Dinesh D'Souza, Newt Gingrich, Jesse Helms, Daniel Patrick Moynihan, Charles Murray, Antonin Scalia, Clarence Thomas, James Q. Wilson, and Tom Wolfe. The superpredators DiIulio warned America were "coming" in ever-increasing numbers were identified as "at-risk juvenile males . . . who are basically unsupervised, not in homes where they are given the most rudimentary education . . . who are simply surrounded by deviant, delinquent criminal adults, in fatherless, godless, and jobless settings. . . . They are remorseless . . . they lack empathetic impulses; they kill or maim or get involved in other forms of serious crime." [52]

He sounded the alarm again in the spring 1996 issue of *City Journal,* the organ of the Manhattan Institute. This article was more specific as to the color of the superpredators; its title was "My Black Crime Problem, and Ours." In it DiIulio cried out that there would be "an estimated 270,000 more young predators on the streets than in 1990, coming at us in waves over the next two decades. . . . Half of these juvenile superpredators could be young black males." Although DiIulio would actually promote himself and his theories as racially unbiased, his words and work reveal him to be an entrenched racist: "If blacks are overrepresented in the ranks of the imprisoned, it is because blacks are overrepresented in the criminal ranks—and the violent criminal ranks, at that." While this article disclosed that DiIulio had invented the notion of the black superpredator based on his personal adolescent fears growing up a lone "white ethnic" in a Philadelphia area "surrounded by black teen-agers from adjacent neighborhoods," he has glorified and grafted his fears into a racist movement: "My black crime problem, and ours, is that for most Americans, especially for average white Americans, the dis-tance [between whites and the black superpredators] is not merely great but almost unfathomable, the fear is enormous and largely justifiable, and the black kids who inspire the fear seem not merely unrecognizable but alien." [53]

Rather incredibly this alarm soon rang out in other, more estab-lished journals, as *City Journal* itself found its way into established cir-cles, endorsed by the likes of New York mayor Rudolph Giuliani, author Tom Wolfe, and commentator George Will. *Time* magazine, crediting Di-Iulio as a primary source and carrying an accompanying photograph of him captioned "Princeton's John DiIulio warns of 'superpredators,'" published the news that "a teenage time bomb" was about to explode. *Time* warned that the new superpredators represented the birth of a new breed of human being: "They are just four, five and six years old right now, but already they are making criminologists nervous." "They" are black boys, described without specific racial referents, though sugges-tively, as young males "growing up . . . in abusive or broken homes, with little adult supervision and few positive role models . . . [who] spend too much of their time hanging out on the streets." And as North-eastern University criminologist James Alan Fox warned apocalypti-cally, "This is the calm before the crime storm. . . . We may be blind-sided by this bloodbath of teenage violence that is lurking in the future." [54]

At the end of the same year, DiIulio's *Body Count: Moral Poverty . . . and How to Win America's War against Crime and Drugs* was published by Simon & Schuster. It was cowritten by John P. Walters and William J. Bennett. The lesser-known Walters was identified by the titles executive director of the Council on Crime in America and former deputy director for Supply Reduction in the Office of National Drug Control Policy. Ben-nett, of course, was a stalwart of the Reagan-Bush era, as secretary of ed-ucation in the administration of Ronald Reagan and director of the Office of National Drug Control Policy under George Bush. Moreover, he was a fellow of the Heritage Foundation. A major contributor to *Body Count* was James Q. Wilson, professor emeritus at the University of California,

Los Angeles, identified here as a criminologist. Wilson was also the co-author, with late Harvard professor Richard Herrnstein, of a thematically related volume entitled *Crime and Human Nature* (Simon & Schuster, 1985), the subject matter of which was the "root causes" of crime, social and *biological*. Herrnstein is best known posthumously for his best-selling book, with Charles Murray, *The Bell Curve: Intelligence and Class Structure in American Life.*

Body Count was written, according to its authors, in an "attempt to explain America's violent crime plague." They warn, "As high as America's body count is today, a rising tide of youth crime and violence is about to lift it higher." This plague, they predicted, was being and would be visited upon the nation by "a new generation of street criminals . . . the youngest, biggest and baddest generation any society has ever known." They were the "superpredators," the product of "places that may best be called criminogenic [*sic*] communities—places where the social forces that create predatory criminals are far more numerous than the social forces that create decent, law-abiding citizens." [55]

If there was any doubt that the superpredators they warned America about were, singularly, young black men, they clarified this at every opportunity: "The black-white differences in rates of criminal offending reflect the fact that, on average, black children are more likely than white children to grow up without two parents or other adults who supervise, nurture, and provide for them." Furthermore, they vehemently argued that the racial disparity in the U.S. incarceration rate is a function of this black "moral poverty": "These statistics originate largely in the fact that young black males commit crime at higher rates than young white males. . . . Racism does not even begin to explain it." This is why, they conclude, "We are terrified by the prospect of innocent people being gunned down at random, without warning and almost without a motive, by youngsters who afterwards show us the black, unremorseful face of a feral, pre-social being." [56]

These "criminogenic" communities—a term apparently invented by Wilson—of which they speak are black ghettos: "Most inner-city children grow up surrounded by teenagers and adults who are themselves deviant, delinquent or criminal." This is why, they explain, "so many inner-city children grow up . . . almost completely unmoralized [*sic*]." They elaborate: "A good deal of the violence, chaos, and dysfunction in these crime-infested settings is related to drug and alcohol abuse. Studies show that alcohol abuse is a major public health problem in inner-city black neighborhoods." [57]

Thus the superpredator emerges as an animal, a "vicious unrepentant predatory street criminal," with a "violent, hair-trigger mentality . . . [, who] will do what comes naturally: murder, rape, rob, assault, burglarize, deal deadly drugs and get high." Furthermore, "to these mean-street youngsters, the words 'right' and 'wrong' have no fixed moral meaning." [58]

What makes this bestial syndrome dangerous to America is that it is no longer confined to the inner-city haunts of the superpredator. DiIulio's prowling black boy criminal focuses attacks on white America: "The superpredators place no value on the lives of their victims, whom they reflexively dehumanize as just so much worthless white trash." Even more terrifying for America is their apocalyptic prediction: "With the coming of the superpredators, many pieces of numerical data . . . suggest to us that today's baddest boys do at least three times as much serious harm and gratuitous violence as did their crime-prone cousins and uncles of the 1950s or 1970s." Worse, this was an explosive problem, for they estimated that by the year 2000 "there will be . . . thirty thousand more. . . . Get ready!" [59]

The power in DiIulio's word is that he is not a lone wolf crying unheeded. Besides his own academic affiliations, his connections to William Bennett and the Brookings Institution and Olin Foundation began to elevate him to a sphere of influence that affected and altered public policy. Indeed the Clinton administration's harsh 1994 amendments to the federal juvenile crime laws, carried under slogans like "three strikes you're out" and "do the crime, do the time," were the direct product of the superpredator theories postulated and promulgated by DiIulio and his cohorts.

This new wave of laws washed over the nation. In 1995 the right-wing then-governor of California, Pete Wilson, focused much of his second-term inaugural address on this racist criminalization of ghettoized black boys, urging passage of laws for their long-term incarceration: "Now the teen predator who does violence to his victim will be prosecuted not as a juvenile but as an adult." [60] Wilson's way would prevail, though it would not come until he left office, after the election of a new

Democratic governor of California. In early 2000, California passed its version of the juvenile predator laws, in which children as young as fourteen years old could be prosecuted and incarcerated as adults.

At the same time as Wilson's speech, in January of 1995, Oregon congressman Republican Ron Wyden was introducing the national Consequences in Sentencing for Young Offenders Act, to increase penalties for juvenile crime offenders and permit adjudication of juveniles in adult courts. Wyden's proposals would come to be incorporated into the Juvenile Crime Control and Delinquency Prevention Act of 1998. In his Congressional argument for his bill, Wyden stated his legislation would "address the glaring shortcomings [and] . . . adopt a new philosophy of juvenile justice—one built on meaningful sanctions. This concept has been endorsed by the likes of James Q. Wilson from the University of California at Los Angeles. . . . Dr. Wilson has been good enough to counsel me with respect to the legislation." [61]

By 1996, the year *Body Count* was published, Republican representative Bill McCollum of Florida was introducing a bill in the House to try kids as adults in order to "put a finger in the dike" of a juvenile crime wave.[62] McCollum's bill was initially titled the Superpredator Incapacitation Act. That was soon changed to the Violent Youth Predator Act, supported by Newt Gingrich and Bob Dole. While House Democrats opposed this name and changed it, they, along with their Republican counterparts, carried the bill and its sentiments into law, as the Juvenile Crime Control Act of 1997, with the full support of the Clinton administration. In fact, a companion bill was introduced by Democrat Robert Scott of Virginia, with California Republican Frank Riggs, to allow states to incarcerate children in adult prisons. In the Senate, Utah Republican archconservative Orrin Hatch introduced another version of the same legislation, echoing the same sentiments. McCollum founded the argument for his bill on the DiIulio philosophy, warning America of "a coming generation of super-predators." [63] Endorsing McCollum's harsh legislation, Clinton stated: "We know we've got about six years to turn this juvenile crime thing around or our country is going to be living in chaos." [64]

DiIulio is not merely a Right ideologue and not merely influential in the arena of criminal justice. He has gathered allies in several arenas, including a number of blacks. While the wife of Boston-based black minister Eugene Rivers might characterize DiIulio and Rivers as "very odd soulmates," DiIulio has clearly found a collaborator in Rivers. Indeed, Rivers's wife concluded, "they really think alike." Part of the superpredator theory is that these black boys are "godless" in their immorality and *feral* existence. Like a Christian missionary, DiIulio would, as others before him, bring Christian morality to the savage superpredators and presumably transform them. Or, like others before him, he would offer them the alternative of hellish punishment and incarceration forever. In this, he has found a brother in Rivers. Rivers, touted in a June 1, 1998, *Newsweek* cover story as "unwilling to make liberal excuses for urban pathologies," has given DiIulio's mission a home in his small Boston parish.[65] Furthermore, Rivers, who claims to have been a one-time gang member in Philadelphia and believes his embrace of holiness via Pentecostal Christianity saved him from the harsh streets, has come to embrace DiIulio's argument that these boys are predators who are not so much economically as *morally* impoverished. They simply need to change their evil ways. DiIulio has said, "When everything is said and done, we believe that, as Christians, we should feel convicted [sic] by the fact that we are dealing with this problem of moral poverty and so-called super-predators. Our response can't be simply to lock these kids up, even though that's something we must do in far too many cases."[66] DiIulio's blessing by a black like Rivers runs over in his participation in the organization Campaign for Effective Criminal Justice, where he is in league with Reverend Calvin Butts, the famed black pastor of Harlem's massive Abyssinian Baptist Church, and Reverend Floyd Flake, a black former New York congressman who is further closely aligned with DiIulio as an Adjunct Fellow of the Manhattan Institute.[67]

Inculcation of the myth of the black boy as a superpredator has provided absolution for racism. It has lifted the burden of black suffering, or suffering blacks, from white shoulders, permitting the shrug. It has lightened the heaviness of wrestling with the riddle of the highly disproportionate incarceration rate of young black males. It has validated white flight as it accommodates the ruthlessness of the new urban gentrification. It has become more than myth. Unlike the fables of the black male as rebellious slave murderer or rapist of white women, the fabulist tale of the superpredator resists repudiation as racist, for it has been baptized by certain blacks and alchemized as scientific conclusion.

―――――――――

Indeed the superpredator myth has been propelled into popular acceptance by a proliferation of treatises and theories purporting to be new scientific discoveries. Dressing racism in scientific garb is not, however, new. This recent version only represents an inversion of emphasis, from white supremacy to black inferiority, an inferiority further identified as *inherent*, or "genetic." In the superpredator's case, this includes "moral" inferiority. However, these latest scientifically clad claims invoked to prove the inherence of black inferiority—moral, intellectual, and otherwise—are mere restatements of the fallacious old doctrines of hereditarianism and biodeterminism previously employed to advance the notion of white supremacy. Nevertheless, the scientism surrounding the myth of the black boy as superpredator—like that of the black girl as slothful, immoral child-bearer—has reestablished acceptance of racist dogma in American life.

The genetic connection to this resurrected racism was most clearly set forth in *The Bell Curve*, published in 1994. Despite the controversy and opposition raised by the book, it remained on the *New York Times* best-seller list for quite a while. Coauthor Charles Murray had previously written *Losing Ground: American Social Policy, 1950–1980*, in which he made an argument for the dismantling of the welfare system so as to stop the wasting of tax dollars on "welfare queens," whom he deemed as draining the American economy with their inherent laziness and immorality. *Losing Ground* came to be identified by the *New York Times* as "the [Reagan] administration's new 'bible.' " [68]

In *The Bell Curve*, Murray and Herrnstein propound the same racialist theory, here claiming to prove black *intellectual* inferiority. To do this they first asserted that intelligence could be quantified and that the so-called Intelligence Quotient (IQ) test, in any of its variations, is a scientific measure of intelligence. Murray and Herrnstein concluded that, as the scores of blacks on standard academic tests in the United States have been consistently lower than those of whites, blacks as a race have an overall lower IQ than whites as a race—and this without reference to blacks elsewhere in the African diaspora, or to whites elsewhere, or to the fact that race itself has no biological definition or distinction at all. Moreover, they argue that this lower IQ reflects an intellectual inferiority that is inherent, making the absurd assertion that IQ is "somewhere between 40% and 60% hereditary." [69]

Notwithstanding Murray's failure of credentials, as a political science professor now operating out of the rightist American Enterprise Institute, with respect to any claim to expertise regarding intelligence there is absolutely no biological or other scientific definition of intelligence. Moreover, even though coauthor Herrnstein was a psychology professor at Harvard until his death, and studies regarding the elusive concept of intelligence have generally been relegated to the purview of psychologists, his and Murray's eight-hundred-plus-page so-called bell-curve study represents the antithesis of any definition of scientific inquiry. Finally, the very foundation of their conclusions has been discredited by established academicians. In early 2001 Richard C. Atkinson, president and regent of the University of California, publicly recommended that the university "no longer require the SAT I for students applying to UC," stating, "This recommendation has significant implications for the University of California since we are one of the principal users of the SAT." Atkinson, who as director of the National Science Foundation developed theories and formulas regarding memory and the learning process that remain influential in the field, explained that he had come to the realization that those students who had achieved high SAT scores had done so primarily because their instructors had "spent time not aimed at developing the students' reading and writing abilities but rather their test-taking skills." His conclusion was that "America's overemphasis on the SAT is compromising our educational system." [70]

Nevertheless, there are adherents to the Murray and Herrnstein theories, and race-based questions raised as to *why* blacks have had lower "standard" test scores than whites—or, more accurately, what is wrong with blacks. *The Bell Curve* premise that the asserted lower IQ scores of blacks as compared with whites is "probably attributable to genetic factors" continues to drive public policy. [71] This is so notwithstanding the effective irrelevance of the SAT, the test on which their thesis primarily rests, or the fact that their ipse dixit of inherent black intellectual inferiority is in direct contradiction to the principles attending the very development of the IQ test, in 1905, by French psychologist Alfred Binet. Though *The Bell Curve* asserts that an IQ score has a *"physiological* basis," Binet vehemently rejected any hereditary connection to his test or to the question of intelligence.[72]

The ultimate fallacy of *The Bell Curve,* and the ultimate proof of the intrinsic racism in propositions like those of Murray and Herrnstein, lies, however, in the conclusions of the investigations of biologists and geneticsts, including those of the Human Genome Project, to whom the study of heredity rightly belongs. In February 2001, Celera Genomics of Rockville, Maryland, and the International Human Genome Sequencing Consortium, a group primarily supported by the National Institutes of Health and the Wellcome Trust of London, published joint findings in the journals *Science* and *Nature* regarding the genetic composition of human beings. In announcing the project's results, Celera's president, J. Craig Venter, made the following statement:

> Today we are announcing the publication in *Science* of our initial (first look) at the human genetic code, while our colleagues are announcing the simultaneous publication of their analysis. . . . These independent, often competitive efforts produced agreements on the broad themes. . . . There are many surprises from this first look at our genetic code that have important implications for humanity. . . . The small number of genes— 30,000 instead of 140,000—supports the notion that we are not hard wired. . . . One gene leads to many different products and those products—proteins—can change dramatically after they are produced. . . . *We now know that the environment acting on these biological steps may be key in making us what we are. Likewise the remarkably small number of genetic variations that occur in genes again suggest a significant role for environmental influences in developing each of our uniqueness.* . . . The *Science* cover and the Celera genome sequence from five individuals . . . of *self-identified ethnicity* . . . represent some of the diversity of human kind. We are confident that our sequence will help to demonstrate that the human genome will not aid those who want to perpetuate racial prejudice. . . . On this, Charles Darwin's birthday, it is fitting to recall his words in *The Descent of Man.* He said: "False facts are highly injurious to the progress of science, for they often endure long." [emphasis added][73]

The real and only point Murray and Herrnstein raised was that because this black intellectual inferiority they identified was hereditary, it was immutable. Thus social and public policy had to be adjusted accordingly. They proffered, therefore, proposals for policies regarding public education in light of such asserted inherent black intellectual inferiority, arguing, for example, that it was useless to continue to spend public money on programs to improve educational opportunities for black children. They argued for an end to affirmative action college entrance programs, a halt to any additional spending on inner-city public schools, and the elimination of any remaining school desegregation plans. They went further and claimed that there was, in fact, a *causal* relationship between low black IQ and black poverty and, most of all, crime figures for black youth: "Virtually all of the difference in the prevalence of black and white juvenile delinquents is explained by the IQ difference." [74] Thus, Nature itself had placed blacks at the bottom of life in America.

The reappearance of the notion of the genetic inferiority of the black, as argued by Murray and Herrnstein and complemented by DiIulio's "black crime problem," has become the pretext for making the very question of crime in America synonymous with being black in America. This idea is bolstered by more and more academics and publications, whose significant credentials would seem to cleanse the issue of prejudice.

In 1996, for example, the American Academy of Psychiatry and the Law published an article asserting that "there is now substantial evidence that heritable factors play a role in the genesis of repetitive antisocial behavior." Thus grounded, the article would examine "the implications that current research in behavioral genetics [sic] may have for assigning unlawful behavior." [75]

A 1995 conference funded by the National Institute of Health and sponsored by the University of Maryland was called "Research on Genetics and Criminal Behavior: Scientific Issues, Social and Political Implications." As Katheryn K. Russell of the Department of Criminology and Criminal Justice at the University of Maryland reported in her book *The Color of Crime*, this conference had previously been titled "Genetic Factors in Crime: Findings, Uses and Implications." However, as there was so much criticism of the first conference as "a thinly veiled attempt at promoting racial eugenics," it was abandoned. It was soon reconstituted under the new title by the same sponsors, funded by the federal government.[76]

As Russell also reported, at the 1995 annual meeting of the Behavior Genetics Association, Florida State University professor Glayde Whitney gave a keynote address in which he stated that there was a "high correlation" between the high murder rate in American cities and the high percentage of blacks living in them. Specifically Whitney, a past president of the academic organization, stated, "Like it or not, it is a reasonable scientific hypothesis that some, perhaps much, of the race difference in murder rate is caused by genetic differences."[77]

That same year Frederick Goodwin, former administrator of the Alcohol, Drug Abuse, and Mental Health Administration and, according to Russell, "one of the leading *federal* researchers on genetics and violence," gave a speech at a meeting of the National Institute of Mental Health Advisory Council. Later, Goodwin would be a keynote speaker, appearing with William Bennett and Steven Hyman, director of the National Institute of Mental Health, at the September 1998 conference of one of DiIulio's affiliate organizations, the Ethics and Public Policy Center.[78] At the 1995 conference, Goodwin, according to Russell, "compared the inner city to a jungle and described Black men as predatory and hypersexual, like rhesus monkeys." Then Goodwin elaborated: "Now, one could say that if some of the loss of social structure in this society, and particularly within the high impact inner city areas, has removed some of the civilizing evolutionary things we have built up . . . maybe it isn't just the careless use of the word when people call certain areas of certain cities jungles."[79]

The pseudoscientism surrounding the superpredator theory has apparently provided a socially acceptable legitimacy to new "research" that hauntingly echoes the infamous Tuskegee Syphilis Experiment. A number of such "studies" unabashedly investigate an alleged genetic relationship between black males and crime—focusing on young black males in urban environments. One example is the "Violence Initiative" of the National Institute of Mental Health (NIMH), a division of the National Institute of Health, a proposal exposed in the 1994 book *The War against Children of Color,* intended to "identify and treat one hundred thousand inner-city children who have been labeled as genetically predisposed to commit crime."[80] With this book, the authors, Peter Breggin and Ginger Ross Breggin, inspired a national campaign against the proposal. However, presently the NIMH continues such research into the notion of genetic predisposition to crime, particularly among black youth, based on the hypothesis that "tragic events like the shootings at Columbine High School capture public attention and concern, but are not typical of youth violence. Most adolescent homicides are committed in inner cities." [81]

Another "experiment" was conducted by the New York State Psychiatric Institute, in affiliation with Columbia University and the Mount Sinai School of Medicine, wherein fenfluramine, the core component of Fen-Phen, the diet drug marketed to reduce obesity, was injected into one hundred healthy, mostly black boys, ages six to ten. According to the documents, these Fen-Phen injections would somehow determine whether there were "biochemical roots of violence." Even when Fen-Phen was deemed dangerous for dieters and was pulled from the market in 1997, the "experiment" on the boys continued, lasting from 1992 through 1997. The cochair of the Columbia University review board that approved the experiment, B. Timothy Walsh, acknowledged that the black boys who were the subjects were "obtained from the New York City probation department." All of the boys seemed to have had older brothers on probation, and parents of the boys reported that they allowed their young sons to participate in the experiment because they were led to believe this would bode well for their older brothers.[82] Their mothers were paid $125 for their participation. After the experiment was exposed by a complaint filed by Disability Advocates, the study was suspended in early 1998. Predictably, no connection was found between the genetic composition of the boys and crime in the city. The director of the Psychiatric Institute, John Oldham, defended the "study," stating, "Is there or is there not a correlation between certain biological markers and conduct disorders or antisocial behavior?" [83] The effect on the boys' health as a result of these Fen-Phen injections, however, remains to be determined.

At the end of The Bell Curve, Murray and Herrnstein propose that there is only one ultimate solution for the "growing underclass" of young black criminals and their families, mired in the "sloth" of their low IQs, who cannot be allowed to overtake the city centers of America. They must be placed in a "custodial state": "In short, by custodial state, we have in mind a high-tech and more lavish version of the Indian reservation for some substantial minority of the nation's population, while the rest of America tries to go about its business." [84]

Despite the propagation of the idea of the black as a criminal, as a superpredator, crime in America is really not a "black thing." As Katheryn Russell documents, this propaganda about blacks and crime "would not be so odd if Whites were not responsible, in raw numbers, for most of the crime that is committed. Each year, Whites account for almost 70% of the total arrests." However, as she astutely points out, "phrases such a 'White crime' and 'White-on-White crime' are not part of our public lexicon on crime." [85]

Ingrained racism has obscured the reality about black boys and girls in America and has precluded investigations and studies into their real lives. It is really no secret, for example, that the suicide rate for young black males has *tripled* over the last fifteen years, reflecting not rising criminality but increased depression among them.[86] This depression has real roots, in overwhelming black child poverty, infant mortality, ghettoization.

───────────

In that first year of his incarceration at Lee Arrendale State Prison, often referred to as "Alto" after the small town of its locale, Michael's voice remained too young to resonate the squeaky approach of manhood. His first Christmas list, like his still smooth face, reflected this lingering prepubescence, pregnant with candy and cookie requests.

By then, he had already been classified by prison officials as a "predator."

"I really like that candy," he says over the telephone.

"Yes, but you need to eat some vegetables," I respond, automatic alma mater.

It's not a serious conversation. We laugh.

"No, I'm serious," I insist. "You'd better get used to it, 'cause when you get out, you will eat some broccoli."

"Oh, no-o-o-o. . . . Okay, okay. If I have to, I'll eat some greens. Crumble up some of that cornbread into 'em, put some hot sauce on 'em, mix it up, and eat it all with my fingers."

"Not in my house."

"Yeah, but that's the ghetto way. . . . Say," he continues, this being, I've learned, his introduction to a new subject, "say, you don't really know much about the ghetto."

"What're you talking about? I was born in the ghetto. Raised in the ghetto."

"Yeah, but that was back in your day," he argues, becoming the teacher. "Did y'all have crack or AIDS back then? . . . Say! I think I might have been one of those crack babies."

What is most dangerous about the new promulgation of racist hereditarian theories about black children is that they have found their way to the very pinnacle of America's public policy. Just as Murray and Herrnstein had specifically suggested that such efforts were a waste of public money—assuming inherent black intellectual inferiority—the new Bush administration would abandon a commitment of public funds to improve inner-city schools, identified as "failing." Instead, finally closing the chapter on busing, the Bush administration would offer vouchers, or coupons, for those few who can find their way out of the ghetto to pay for transportation and tuition at "private" schools that may or may not have the ability, but certainly would have no legal obligation, to accommodate them. The rest, the students and their schools, will be left behind—or perhaps worse.

Snidely exploiting the words of the great black educator Mary McLeod Bethune, as adopted as the motto of the Children's Defense Fund, to "leave no child behind," to sloganize his education plan Bush would institute *The Bell Curve* dictum. First, his plan identified its theory, the core of which is to address the problem, as Murray and Herrnstein identified it, of black academic "failure," mockingly calling it the problem of "the soft bigotry of low expectations": "The academic achievement gap between rich and poor, Anglo and minority is not only wide, but in some cases is growing wider still." The Bush solution would strip schools in poor "minority" communities of support, offering, instead, individual coupons of questionable value: "Without consequences for failure, there is no pressure to succeed. For that reason, an 'accountability principle' requires that federal reward funds should flow to states and schools that improve student achievement, and consequences should be imposed on those whose performance stagnates or declines. . . . Funding will be withdrawn from states that permit student performance to decline. . . . Parents of students trapped in chronically failing schools will have the option of transferring to another public school . . . or private school alternatives." [87]

Although Bush expediently sidestepped use of the word "vouchers," the National Education Association (NEA) provided a translation in its attack on the plan: "NEA opposes proposals that undermine Title I and a commitment to level the playing field for low-income children: Title I vouchers . . . proposed in the Bush plan . . . would seriously undermine a commitment to help schools with the greatest need." [88] The fact is that the Bush program would strip the majority of black children trapped in the ghettos of America of the last possibility of education and break down the very idea of mass public education in America.

The last section of the Bush education proposal portended something even more destructive, relating to an "initiative" to "triple Federal character education funding, and expand the role of faith-based and community organizations in after-school programs." To accomplish this end, Bush created a strange new so-called faith-based social services operation: "In every instance where this administration sees a responsibility to help people, it will look first to faith-based organizations. . . . These neighborhood healers will not replace government, but partner with it to make life better for those in need. With this budget, the president commits our nation to mobilizing the armies of compassion . . . to transform lives. . . . This is the next bold step of Welfare Reform." The Bush budget proposed funding for this faith-based program of $8 billion. [89]

What made this initiative so ominous was not merely that Bush's attorney general, far-Right ideologue John Ashcroft, former governor and senator from the Missouri Ozarks, closely affiliated with Pat Robertson and the Christian Coalition, not only endorsed it but previously proposed such "faith-based" crusades in connection with the 1996 welfare law. It was not merely that when asked for proof that these programs could achieve the desired ends, the Bush administration's response was to cite the "successful" work of the Texas-based Prison Fellowship Ministries, headed by Chuck Colson, former Watergate "hatchet man." [90] What has made this program really dangerous, particularly for black youth, is that it was initiated by the man Bush named to head the $8 billion mobilization of "armies of compassion," the first director of the White House Office of Faith-Based and Community Initiatives, John DiIulio.

In this capacity DiIulio became directly responsible to the president to carry out the directive, under Executive Order, among other things to "eliminate unnecessary legislative, regulatory, and other bureaucratic barriers that impede effective faith-based and other community efforts to solve social problems."[91] Having become a self-proclaimed born-again Christian since inventing his racist superpredator theory, which fostered the institution of the iniquitous public policies still in place to-day that target black children, particularly boys, DiIulio now offered his belief that the boys he had identified only moments before as inherently evil superpredators were now redeemable through his own faith-based, and particularly "Christ-centered," programs. It is a notion tainted with the same racist tenet, however, that something is fundamentally wrong with inner-city black boys.

Based on the hypotheses that "studies indicate that religious in-volvement reduces teen pregnancy, suicide, drug addiction, abuse, alco-holism, and crime," and that "grassroots inner-city outreach ministries have been credited by numerous leading socials scientists with playing a major role in helping at-risk youth to avoid violence," the Bush plan became the very expression of DiIulio himself.[92] Armed with his new po-litical powers, DiIulio came to have access to billions of dollars in public funds to launch a program to reform the superpredators by exorcising the evil he saw in them.

———

In the introduction to *The Mismeasure of Man,* Stephen Jay Gould recalls what Charles Darwin, the English naturalist and father of organic evolu-tion, argued in his seminal work on the theory of evolution, *Voyage of the Beagle,* in denouncing slavery. Darwin stated, "If the misery of our poor be caused not by the laws of nature, but by our institutions, great is our sin."[93]

This "great sin" is precisely what is being promulgated and prac-ticed, once again. In an interview in an obscure journal called *Skeptic,* published in connection with the publication of *The Bell Curve,* author

Charles Murray provided unabashed articulation as to how deep are the roots of this great sin: "Our vision is Jeffersonian. . . . We say that people bring different things to the table. The important thing is that everyone be given the opportunity to go as far as their . . . intelligence will take them. The crucial factor . . . is not equal outcomes. . . . Thomas Jefferson would read *The Bell Curve* . . . nodding his head in approval. He believed there was a natural aristocracy." [94]

III
THE ROOT OF THIS EVIL

[8] Monticello Revisited

On April 20, 1994, *Paul Touvier became the first Frenchman to be convicted of "war crimes against humanity." Touvier had been known as "the hangman of Lyon," serving in the French Nazi collaborationist Vichy government under the infamous Gestapo chief Klaus Barbie. The Vichy government had sent seventy-six thousand Jews to the German concentration camps, including four thousand children who were gassed at Auschwitz. Touvier had evaded capture since the end of World War II, primarily because of protection by the hierarchy of the French Catholic Church. Though he was guilty of much more, Touvier was tried for the murders of seven Jews at Rillieux-la-Pape in 1944. He was sentenced to life in prison at the age of seventy-nine. (He died two years later in a prison hospital near Paris.)*

The French government prosecutors of Touvier were widely criticized for trying such an old case. Many French cried out, "Why?!" Vichy had long been "forgotten or swept under the rug." Touvier was old. The war was long over. They begged the prosecutors to let France turn this ignominious page of history. At trial, one of the government lawyers revealed why they had gone forward with prosecution of this old man, stating, "At the Arc de Triomph, there is a place for everyone but the 76,000 Jews who disappeared. We have waited 30 years for the vise to be loosened, so that we can speak; and, 20 years for justice. It has taken fifty years to bare the shame and the pain experienced by our ancestors; 50 years to break the taboo, to look Vichy in the face, without hatred and without fear." Another prosecutor spoke of why this trial was important for the French people: "It was a plan of the Nazis, but the complicity was

*French." "Touvier's crimes are written in the history of France," they ar-
gued passionately. And, finally, "a page of history cannot be turned until
it is written."*[1]

─────────────

Racism is deeply rooted in the American way of life. Founding father
Thomas Jefferson wrote: "I advance it . . . that the blacks, whether originally a distinct race, or made distinct by time and circumstances, are inferior to the white in the endowments both of body and mind."[2]

This Jeffersonian concept of race, about white superiority and black
inferiority, laid the foundation for American scientific racism. It came to
be as indelibly written into the social structure and cultural fabric of
America as Jefferson's articulation of human freedom in the Declaration
of Independence, and as carved into the American design as Jefferson's
visage on Mount Rushmore.

Jefferson is undoubtedly the very personification of America and
also of America's rhetorical duplicity. Jefferson was at once the architect
of a social scheme based on the ideal of the equality of all men and one
of the largest slaveholders of his time. Jefferson's theories about black
inferiority that balance this seeming incongruity were fully articulated
in the only book he ever authored, *Notes on the State of Virginia,* first
published in Paris in 1784, dated 1782. The *Notes* have been republished
in various volumes ever since. One of the more recent editions, in *The
Life and Selected Writings of Thomas Jefferson,* edited by Adrienne Koch
and William Peden, refers to the *Notes* as having been "praised by repu-
table twentieth-century historians of *science* as the *most influential scientific book* written by an American . . . [which] continue[s] to be of interest for the clarity, vigor and occasional beauty of Jefferson's prose"
(emphasis added).[3]

It is in this manifesto that Jefferson establishes the "scientific" justification for American slavery and racism, and it is here that Jefferson
would cure the national schizophrenia of juxtaposing freedom with oppression and resolve the American dilemma of simultaneously advocating the freedom of *all* men and the enslavement of *black* men. Jefferson's *Notes* provides the clearest articulation of his true social philos-
ophies, concepts that formed and remain the very cornerstones of the
national psyche and the rationale for why, in America, the black was not

and could not ever be included in the canon that all men are created equal. Jefferson simply contended that the black was *not—*by *nature—* like other men.

In *Notes* Jefferson articulates a legal plan for the new republic, particularly the new commonwealth of Virginia where he resided. He advocates retaining English common law as the foundation of the new world's law, and he discusses the ultimate, inevitable "emancipation" of black slaves. He proposes a program to accommodate this inevitability, which was simply that the blacks could be "colonized to such place as circumstances of the time should render most proper," assuming, however, that there had been the "inducement" of "an equal number of white inhabitants" from Europe to "migrate hither." [4] At that point, Jefferson set forth his central arguments on black inferiority.

"*It will probably be asked, Why not retain and incorporate the blacks in the State . . . ?*

"*. . . To [the] objections, which are political, may be added others, which are physical and moral. The first difference which strikes us is that of color. Whether the black of the negro resides in the reticular membrane between the skin and scarf-skin, or in the scarf-skin itself; whether it proceeds from the color of the blood, the color of the bile, or from that of some other secretion, the difference is fixed in nature.*" [5]

Jefferson then explored what he deemed to be the intrinsic value of this color difference:

"*And is this difference of no importance? Is it not the foundation of a greater or less share of beauty in the two races? Are not the fine mixtures of red and white . . . preferable to that eternal monotony, which reigns in the countenances, that immovable veil of black which covers the emotions of the other race?*" [6]

So powerful was this articulation that it has survived the centuries and become a belief that is now commonly maintained by many whites as fact: that white skin and, therefore, white people are, first of all, *aesthetically* superior to black people.

Jefferson continued:

"*Add to these, flowing hair, a more elegant symmetry of form, their own judgment in favor of the whites, declared by their preference of them, as uniformly as is the preference of the Oran-utan for the black woman over those of his own species.*" [7]

Jefferson bolstered his theory of this physiological inferiority of blacks by offering a "biological" analysis:

"Besides those of color, figure, and hair, there are other physical distinctions proving a difference of race. They [blacks] have less hair on the face and body. They secrete less by the kidneys, and more by the glands of the skin, which gives them a very strong and disagreeable odor."[8]

Jefferson extended his theory on the racial inferiority of blacks to include *character*. He proposed, for example, what became a widely accepted belief among American whites, and even some blacks, that blacks are foolish, puerile, irresponsible.

"A black after hard labor through the day, will be induced by the slightest amusements to sit up till midnight, or later, though knowing he must be out with the first dawn of the morning."[9]

Jefferson crafted numerous other stereotypes in order to prove how inferior he deemed the basic character of blacks to be. One was his declaration that blacks are fundamentally foolhardy.

"They are at least as brave [as whites], and more adventuresome. But this may perhaps proceed from a want of forethought, which prevents their seeing a danger till it be present."[10]

Now Jefferson constructed the myth of the black man as a sexual predator.

"They are more ardent after their female; but love seems with them to be more an eager desire, than a tender delicate mixture of sentiment and sensation."[11]

And he painted blacks as slothful, bestial.

"In general, their existence appears to participate more of sensation than reflection. To this must be ascribed their disposition to sleep when abstracted from their diversions, and unemployed in labor. An animal whose body is at rest, and who does not reflect must be disposed to sleep of course."[12]

In his determined pursuit to validate his own and his country's enslavement of blacks, Jefferson devised a pseudoacademic theory, by which he claimed that blacks were *intellectually* inferior to whites, uneducable, and therefore incapable of functioning in society as full and equal partners with whites.

"Comparing them by their faculties of memory, reason, and imagination, it appears to me that in memory they are equal to the whites; in rea-

son much inferior, as I think one could scarcely be found capable of tracing and comprehending the investigations of Euclid; and that in imagination they are dull, tasteless, and anomalous. . . . It will be right to make great allowances for the difference of condition, of education, of conversation, of the sphere in which they move. Many millions of them have been brought to, and born in America. Most of them, indeed, have been confined to tillage. . . . Yet many have been so situated, that they might have availed themselves of the conversation of their masters. . . . Some have been liberally educated . . . and all have had before their eyes samples of the best works from abroad. . . . But never yet could I find that a black had uttered a thought above the level of plain narration."[13]

This theme of the intellectual inferiority of blacks applied equally, Jefferson postulated, to the *arts.*

"[I] never saw even an elementary trait of painting or sculpture [in a black]. In music they are more generally gifted than the whites with accurate ears for tune and time. . . . Whether they will be equal to the composition of a more extensive run of melody, or of complicated harmony, is yet to be proved. Misery is often the parent of the most affecting touches in poetry. Among the blacks is misery enough, God knows, but no poetry. . . . Religion, indeed, has produced a Phyllis Whately [Wheatley]; but it could not produce a poet. The compositions published under her name are below the dignity of criticism."[14]

Finally Jefferson summarized his contentions about blacks in a proposition that is the very rampart for racism in America today: that the foundation of this black inferiority he conceived and advanced is *genetic.* First he stated that the simple admixture of "white blood" to the black evidenced an "improvement." With this, he also gave birth to the contemporary notion that lighter-skinned blacks are superior to darker-skinned blacks.

"The improvement of the blacks in body and mind, in the first instance of their mixture with the whites, has been observed by every one, and proves that their inferiority is not the effect merely of their condition of life."[15]

His sinister summation:

"Notwithstanding [the] discouraging circumstances among the Romans, their slaves were often their rarest artists. They excelled too in science, insomuch as to be usually employed as tutors to their master's chil-

dren. . . . *But they were of the race of whites. It is not their [the blacks']
condition then, but nature, which has produced the distinction."*[16]

His conclusion bears repeating:

*"I advance it, therefore, that the blacks, whether originally a distinct
race, or made distinct by time and circumstances, are inferior to the
white in the endowments both of body and mind."*[17]

Slavery of the black was right:

"What further is to be done with them?"[18]

Jefferson's racist theories, like his expressions of independence and
freedom, represented an Americanization of the theories of the Enlightenment. As he had borrowed liberally from the "natural law" speculations and writings of the prominent Enlightenment philosophers for his
Declaration of Independence, Jefferson similarly employed prominent
Enlightenment notions about blacks to shape a racist culture in America. Jefferson considered himself, and remains deemed, a participant in
the eighteenth-century Western trend known as the Enlightenment, or
Age of Reason, fostered by seventeenth-century scientific discovery.

Among the most influential so-called rational, humanitarian, liberal new men of the Enlightenment were French philosophers François
Voltaire and Jean-Jacques Rousseau, Scottish philosopher David Hume,
and German philosopher Immanuel Kant. As Bucknell University professor Emmanuel Chukwedi Eze pointed out in his book *Race and the
Enlightenment: A Reader,* prominent Enlightenment philosophers espoused the same notions of the inherent intellectual inferiority of blacks
Jefferson espoused. For example, as Eze points out, Hume wrote, "I am
apt to suspect the Negroes . . . to be naturally inferior to the whites.
There never was a civilized nation of any other complexion than
white. . . . No ingenious manufactures among them [Negroes], no arts,
no sciences." [19] Immanuel Kant, whom Jefferson seems to have plagia-
ristically restated in his *Notes,* wrote in his "On the Different Races of
Man," "The superabundance of the iron particles . . . precipitated in the
reticular substance through evaporation of the acids of phosphorous
(which makes all Negroes stink) cause the blackness . . . in short, the
Negro is produced, well suited to his climate . . . lazy, soft and daw-
dling." [20] Moreover, in "Observations on the Feeling of the Beautiful and
the Sublime," Kant stated that "the Negroes of Africa have by nature no
feeling that rises above the trifling." [21]

Whatever these racist notions may have meant to the men of the Enlightenment, for Jefferson and his English colonial brothers the propagation of black inferiority served a very useful purpose: the justification for black slavery in the land of the free. Moreover, it served the interest of maintaining the institution of slavery and its enormous profitability through control of the increasingly significant black slave population. Jefferson so understood the threat a growing black slave labor force represented that he not only proposed colonization but also issued a warning to his brother slaveholders: "The spirit of the master is abating, that of the slave rising from the dust, his condition mollifying, the way I hope preparing, under the auspices of heaven, for a total emancipation, and [I hope] that this is disposed, in the order of events, to be with the consent of the masters rather than by their extirpation." [22]

Indeed, early American colonial slaveholders were confronted with the Sisyphean challenge of satisfying the need for more slave labor, to increase tobacco, cotton, and other labor-intensive agricultural production, and at the same time contending with the threat, and the fear, posed by the increasingly large black slave population. By 1750 there were over 235,000 blacks in the thirteen colonies and a total population of only 1 million whites. [23] The only way to manage this business was to completely control the slaves, generation upon generation.

Every available means came to be exploited to do so. As noted historian Howard Zinn points out in A People's History of the United States, quoting Kenneth Stampp, author of the definitive The Peculiar Institution: "A wise master did not take seriously the belief that Negroes were natural-born slaves. He knew better. He knew that Negroes freshly imported from Africa had to be broken into bondage; that each succeeding generation had to be carefully trained. This was no easy task, for the bondsman rarely submitted willingly. Moreover, he rarely submitted completely. . . . There was no end to the need for control." [24]

Zinn then writes, "The system was psychological and physical. . . . The slaves were taught discipline, were impressed again and again with the idea of their own inferiority to 'know their place,' to see blackness as a sign of subordination. . . . To accomplish this there was the discipline of hard labor, the breakup of the slave family . . . the creation of disunity among slaves . . . and finally the power of law and the immediate power of the overseer to invoke whipping, burning, mutilation, and death." [25]

In addition, appealing to the mass white population with the old myths of Anglo-Saxon superiority promulgated by early English Protestant colonists served to break down European tribalistic tendencies and unite all whites against the threat of black slave insurrection, as well as Native (Indian) rebellion. As Yale University political science professor Rogers M. Smith cites in *Civic Ideals: Conflicting Visions of Citizenship in U.S. History,* "To flourish, most British colonists felt that they had to dispel the tribes [of Native Americans] and enslave Africans. Any suggestion of political equality was therefore anathema to them. Instead, they needed myths of their own superiority." [26]

The significance of maintaining the slave institution lay not merely in the profitability arising from the sales and distribution of the products produced by slave labor, and the growing, international market economy. Slavery also provided ordinary white Americans and their descendants the dreamed-of life of the old European royalty they at once abhorred and coveted, albeit that it came more by might than by divine right.

Monticello is the quintessential metaphor for this uniquely American monarchy. Monticello was the family seat of Thomas Jefferson, his five-thousand-acre plantation in Albemarle County, Virginia, atop a magnificent hill nestled between the mighty Alleghenies and the Blue Ridge Mountains of the powerful Appalachian chain, where Jefferson harbored his slave mistress and forcibly fathered her slave children. Monticello was both Jefferson's Arcadia, the refuge where he contemplated life and his place in it, and the rugged reserve of misery and suffering for the hundreds of black human beings who lived and died there as his slaves. Monticello was Jefferson's empire, where he wrote and thought about freedom and democracy and allegedly agonized over the immorality of slavery—though through two terms as president and as an elder statesman for the remainder of his life he never renounced the institution of slavery and never endorsed the emancipation of black slaves in America. Although some Jeffersonian scholars make the debatable assertion that Jefferson freed, or "bequeathed" freedom, to a handful of his slave artisans, the reality is that Jefferson never—not in his life or in any bequest—"freed" his slaves, including his own slave children.

Slaves built the main mansion at Monticello, its Roman neoclassic structure, all of its thirty-three rooms, containing eleven thousand square feet of living space, its thirteen skylights, its three indoor toilets, its brick-lined air shafts that ventilated Jefferson's interior rooms. As one of Monticello's modern tour brochures explains, if one were to

> look down Mulberry Row [Monticello's slave quarters] to the northeast, [there is] a stable. . . . Here Jefferson's slave Wormley looked after his carriage and saddle horses. . . . [Further down is] 'Weaver's Cottage' . . . the site of Monticello textile manufacture. . . . A dozen slave women and younger girls worked at Hargreaves spinning jennies . . . [making] cloth for the slave laborers from wool and hemp produced on the plantation and cotton bought by the bale. . . . The Mulberry Row cabins were occupied mainly by household servants—women who did the cooking, washing, house cleaning, sewing, and child tending. . . . [The] Blacksmith Shop/Nailery . . . was built . . . about 1793. Here Jefferson's slaves Little George, Moses, and Joseph Fossett shoed horses, repaired the metal parts of plows and hoes, replaced gun parts, and made the iron portions of the carriages. . . . Nailrod was hammered into nails by as many as fourteen young male slaves, aged ten to sixteen.[27]

Inside the mansion, the most significant area is a massive room that composed Jefferson's private library and study and sleeping quarters. Monticello tour guides now acknowledge that Jefferson allowed *no one* into this area who had not first obtained his express permission to enter. Situated in the center of his rich library and study, Jefferson had constructed an exotic sleeping arrangement, where his unique bed was at once a kind of alcove and room divider. Above Jefferson's bed is an enclosed room, forming a stone canopy over it. This upper room is approximately equal in dimensions to his sleeping alcove below and is a kind of small inaccessible mausoleum, its only apparent opening being a set of three large fenestrae, on one side only, trimmed with neoclassic borders. There is, however, a door perpendicular and connected to the head of the bed, behind which is a small passageway, a kind of vestibule, the ceiling of which extends to the floor of the upper room. There had originally been an opening at the *top* of this vestibule and a "tiny stairway" inside it that allowed entry to the upper room. This room above Jefferson's bed was where Sally Hemings was kept.[28]

In 1764 Jefferson inherited about twenty slaves from his father. However, when he married Martha Wayles, he inherited an additional 135 slaves. Among Martha's slaves was Sally Hemings, who was also Martha's half sister, daughter of the slave Betty Hemings and Martha's father, John Wayles, an international slave trader. Sally, considered an "octoroon," or a black with only one-eighth black blood, born in 1773, was only fourteen years old when she accompanied the younger of Jefferson's two surviving children by the deceased Martha, his daughter Mary, to join him in Paris. When Sally Hemings returned with Jefferson, she was pregnant with his child.[29] Jefferson never again married, and Sally Hemings bore eight of his children. She lived at Monticello as his slave until he died in 1826, and she died a slave, in 1835. After Jefferson's death, Sally Hemings, over fifty years old, and the rest of his slaves were sold at auction by his heirs to pay down his incredible debts:

> "Notice from Richmond *Enquirer* 7 Nov. 1826: 'Executor's Sale': On the fifteenth of January, at Monticello . . . the whole of the residue of the personal property of Thomas Jefferson, dec., consisting of valuable Negroes, stock, crops, etc., household and kitchen furniture. The attention of the public is earnestly invited to this property. The Negroes are believed to be the most valuable for their number ever offered in the state of Virginia. . . . Thomas Jefferson Randolph, Executor of Th. Jefferson dec'd."
>
> The Inventory: "Barnaby, $400; Hannard, $450; Betty old woman, no value . . . Jenny, $200 . . . James, $500 . . . Amy, $150 . . . Wormsley, $200 . . . Peter Hemings, $100 . . . Sally Hemings, $50."
>
> "What do I have, whatdo I have, whatdoihave for this lot number thirty-four, three prime male field hands, twenty-six to twenty-nine, broken here at Monticello, in perfect health, no scars, bruises, defects *of any kind*. . . . What am I bid, whatamibid, three hundred, four, four fifty . . . ladies and gentlemen, three prime Monticello slaves. . . . Do I hear nine? . . . A female, twenty-nine years old, breeder, light-skinned, seamstress and cook, perfect for a housekeeper for a young gentleman; may I start at four hundred . . . female slave, fifteen, guaranteed virgin, healthy . . . trained as a house servant. . . . Do I hear three hundred? . . . Ursala. Twenty years old, ladies and gentlemen, look at that body. Born to breed. Look at those breasts. Ladies and gentlemen, do I hear four fifty?"[30]

The institution of black slavery was, first and foremost, essential to the very survival and existence of the American colonies. Thus the issue of slave control was written into the country's earliest legal codes. As Rogers M. Smith points out, "The fears about black uprising expressed in these repressive laws were certainly not ill-founded; blacks acted repeatedly to resist their oppression. . . . In 1713, 1722, 1730, and especially 1739–41, slave uprisings or conspiracies occurred in Virginia, South Carolina, New Jersey, and New York." [31]

By the 1700s, Virginia had developed a slave code that read, "If the [runaway] slave does not immediately return, anyone whatsoever may kill or destroy such slaves. . . . If the slave is apprehended . . . it shall be lawful [to punish] said slave, either by dismembering, or in any other way . . . as [the court] in their discretion shall think fit, for the reclaiming any such incorrigible slave and terrifying others from the like practices." [32] Similarly Maryland passed a law in 1723 providing for "cutting off the ears of blacks who struck whites" and allowing for hanging and quartering of slaves deemed "criminals." [33] These laws were executed with brutal exactitude. In 1712, as a result of a large-scale revolt, twenty-five New York slaves, including women and Native Americans, were "hanged, burned or broken on a wheel." [34]

As black slaves were considered chattel, or personal property, under the various colonial laws, an owner or master could exact whatever punishment he deemed necessary for failure to work or other disobedience. The daily brutality perpetrated against blacks as slaves, the lashings, beatings, rapes, mutilations, is well documented, most poignantly in the various slave narratives that came to be published. That of the great black abolitionist ex-slave Frederick Douglass provides powerful testimony:

> My first master . . . was called Captain Anthony. . . . He owned two or three farms and about thirty slaves. His farms and slaves were under the care of an overseer . . . a miserable drunkard, a profane swearer, and a savage monster. He always went armed with a cowskin and a heavy cudgel. I have known him to cut and slash the women's heads. . . . Master was a cruel man. . . . I have often been awakened at the dawn of day by the most heart-rending shrieks of an own aunt of mine, whom he used to tie up to a joist, and whip upon her naked back till she was literally covered with blood. . . . He would whip her to make her scream, and whip her to make her hush. [35]

More intricate and perhaps more effective as to the control of slaves was the institutionalization of a slave social and cultural structure that divested each enslaved human being of every vestige of his or her personality and humanity and of any relationship to family or any community, slave or free. Indeed, most social scientists and psychologists writing on the subject concur that, notwithstanding the effects of separation of blacks from their native Africa, from their homelands, families, languages, religions, cuisine, treatments, songs, dances, customs and mores, the American slave institution's proscription of black family life and its constant destruction of attempts to form family life may have been the most brutally forceful means of controlling the black slave population. "The slave family had no standing in law and was the focus of some of the strongest pressures of the slave regime. In all slave states, the wife or husband or children could be separated and sold to other slaveholders in other counties and regions." [36]

The biography of the extraordinary feminist and abolitionist who came to call herself Sojourner Truth, *Narrative of Sojourner Truth, a Northern Slave,* dictated to writer Olive Gilbert, compellingly attests to this family destruction:

> Isabella's father was very tall and straight . . . which gave him the name of "Bomefree"—low Dutch for tree. . . . The most familiar appellation of her mother was "Mau-mau Bett." She was the mother of some ten or twelve children; though Sojourner is far from knowing the exact number of her brothers or sisters. . . . Of the two that immediately preceded her in age, a boy of five years, and a girl of three, who were sold when she was an infant, she heard much. . . . At length, the never-to-be-forgotten day of the terrible auction arrived, when the "slaves, horses, and other cattle" of Charles Ardinburgh, deceased, were to be put under the hammer, and again change masters. Not only Isabella and Peter, but their mother, was now destined to the auction block.[37]

Just as powerful was the psychological control imposed by the promulgation of black inferiority and the parallel notion of white superiority, the Enlightenment invention of the concept of a "natural aristocracy." The inherent inferiority of the black and superiority of the white, which served to validate the "rightness" of slavery, came to be widely accepted. By the time Andrew Jackson became president in 1829, the country had established itself and its citizens as a "white republic." As historian Rogers M. Smith explains, "More emphatically than the Jeffersonians, Jacksonian Democrats presented America as a state-centric, commercial, *white* republic, and they now defended that claim chiefly in terms of racial superiority rather than strained doctrines of consent . . . present[ing] the purpose of America as the advancement of Protestant Anglo-American civilization." [38]

The doctrine of white supremacy became so much a part of the American fabric that by 1857 the Supreme Court, ruling in the case of *Dred Scott,* the transplanted slave who sued for his freedom, wherein Chief Justice Roger Taney inscribed Jacksonian racism into the law, held that *no* black *could* be a citizen "within the meaning of the Constitution"—including so-called free blacks—and, in obiter dictum, stated infamously, "A black man has no rights a white man is bound to respect." [39]

Even white abolitionists and antislavery proponents adhered to notions of black inferiority and white superiority. Although white writer Harriet Beecher Stowe's best-selling novel *Uncle Tom's Cabin,* published in 1852, assailed the Fugitive Slave Act of 1850 as immoral, Stowe herself did not believe that blacks were equals with whites. As Rogers Smith points out, "Stowe did not question the reality of racial differences. She presented blacks not as true equals. . . . Stowe favored educating blacks and then sending them to Liberia." [40] Stephen Douglas, hated by the South for advocating excluding slavery in the new territories of the country, argued that any decision regarding slavery "should be made by white men alone, because: 'this government of ours . . . was made by the white man, for the benefit of the white man, to be administered by white men.' [And] each 'inferior race' should receive only the rights that white men thought proper, and 'equality they never should have.' " [41]

Despite this oppressive history, blacks resisted slavery, and struggled, however unsuccessfully, to find freedom in America. Even despite the immediate threat of beating and death, slave men and women refused to work, ran away, committed suicide, even killed their oppressive masters. Noted historian Herbert Aptheker identifies at least 250 organized slave revolts, uprisings, and conspiracies involving ten or more slaves in the 250 years chattel slavery existed in America.[42]

The question of black slavery would be decided, in the end, by warfare, though it was not the central issue of the Civil War. As Abraham Lincoln himself noted in rejecting black enlistees for the Union army after the surrender of Fort Sumter, the Civil War was "the white man's business."[43]

Lincoln, while hated in the South for opposing the extension of slavery into the vast new territories of the West, always equivocated on the question of the abolition of slavery and never embraced the ideal of the equality of blacks and whites.[44] He advocated, instead, colonization for blacks and supported enforcement of the vicious Fugitive Slave Act, which facilitated capture of runaway slaves in the new territories.[45] Indeed, Lincoln's support, as a congressman, of the Wilmot Proviso to ban slavery in the territories presumed to be acquired after the Mexican-American war went not to slavery but to the question of protecting and serving the interests of "free white laborers."[46] Moreover, in his famous debates with Stephen Douglas, Lincoln stated, "There is a physical difference between the white and black races which I believe will forever forbid the two races living together on terms of social and political equality . . . and I as much as any other man am in favor of having the superior position assigned to the white race. . . . I am not, nor ever have been, in favor of bringing about in any way the social and political equality of the white and black races."[47]

The elite and rich northern whites Lincoln mostly represented wanted a new, industrial America. Members of the southern planter class opposed that, not merely as an infringement on their way of life, but also because the new construct of paying white—and perhaps even black—laborers to work in and build up the vast new Western territories threatened to diminish their incredible economic and political power. Thus, when Lincoln was elected president in 1860, seven southern states seceded from the Union. Lincoln responded harshly in April 1861 by trying to take back the federal base at Fort Sumter, South Carolina, with military force. Four more states seceded, effectively setting off the war. Nevertheless, Lincoln had been, and remained, accommodating to the southern planters. In his inaugural address in March 1861 he told them, along with the rest of the country, "I have no purpose, directly or indirectly, to interfere with the institution of slavery in the States where it exists. I believe I have no lawful right to do so, and I have no inclination to do so." [48]

Moreover, even as the war dragged on and Lincoln issued his preliminary Emancipation Proclamation in September 1862, he let it be known that he was threatening to free southern slaves only to force southern states to return to the Union. That is, Lincoln promised he would leave slavery intact in states that would return to the Union, and he gave them four months to make a decision. [49]

When the proclamation was actually issued in January 1893, it did, however, encourage black rebellion, even though Lincoln had clearly stated therein that this proclamation was a "fit and necessary war measure for suppressing said rebellion." Blacks, however, in light of the war and the proclamation, seized the moment and began abandoning southern plantations in the hundreds of thousands, cutting the labor backbone that had supported the South in its efforts to fight this "white man's war." As W. E. B. DuBois explained, "These slaves had enormous power in their hands. Simply by stopping work, they could threaten the Confederacy with starvation. . . . It was this plain alternative that brought Lee's sudden surrender." [50] This, indeed, turned the tide of war.

Still Lincoln did not allow blacks to fight in the Union army for what had become the issue of black freedom, or the abolition of slavery. He had written a letter to Horace Greeley, editor of the New York *Tribune,* explaining his position: "Dear Sir . . . I have not meant to leave any one in doubt. My paramount object in this struggle is to save the Union, and is not either to save or destroy Slavery. If I could save the Union without freeing any slave, I would do it." [51]

[9] Post-Emancipation Fight for Freedom

We have pioneered civilization here; we have built up your country; we have worked in your fields, and garnered your harvests, for two hundred and fifty years! And what do we ask of you in return? Do we ask you for compensation for the sweat our fathers bore for you—for the tears you have caused, and the hearts you have broken, and the lives you have curtailed, and the blood you have spilled? Do we ask retaliation? We ask it not. We are willing to let the dead past bury its dead; but we ask you now for our *rights*.

> Henry McNeal Turner, 1868, on the occasion of being forced to resign, along with all his other black colleagues, from the Georgia state legislature.[1]

American apartheid was the immediate answer to Turner's question. Like black enfranchisement and economic empowerment, social and political equality for blacks was out of the question, post-emancipation.

The Civil War, independent of the resulting passage of the Thirteenth Amendment to the Constitution abolishing slavery, had been not only "white men's business," as Lincoln had stated, but *rich* white men's business. Lincoln's northern industrial capitalists had won. In his *People's History*, Howard Zinn mounts this point convincingly, quoting from *The Age of Enterprise* by Thomas Cochran and William Miller: "Webster was the hero of the North—not Emerson, Parker, Garrison, or Phillips; Webster the tariff man, the land speculator, the corporation lawyer, politician for the Boston Associates, inheritor of Hamilton's coronet. 'The great object of government' said he 'is the protection of property at home, and respect and renown abroad.' For these he preached union; for these he surrendered the fugitive slave."[2]

Even before the war, in 1861, Lincoln had brought about passage of the Morrill Tariff, allowing manufacturers to raise prices of consumer goods, a law benefiting the northern industrial class. Under the 1862 Homestead Act, the federal government would grant 160-acre plots of "unoccupied" land in the new territories of the West to anyone—anyone white—who could cultivate it for five years. The price of $1.25 per acre, or two hundred dollars, was prohibitive to most whites. However, during the Civil War Lincoln *gave* one hundred million of those Homestead Act acres to various northern railroad developers—for free.[3] Finally Lincoln and Congress set up a national bank in partnership with private banks and bankers.

Lincoln's assassination days after Lee's surrender at Appomattox, Virginia, which had ended the Civil War, was irrelevant revenge for the South. The southern planters, the rich white men whose war it had been, struggled to rebuild "Tara," while their northern industrial counterparts began consolidating their war profits and expanding westward with their steam and trains and boats along their new railroads and canals.

The majority of America's whites were poor, however. The 1850 census showed that in the South there were one thousand families who had a total income of $50 million a year. The collective income of the rest, 660,000 white families, was $60 million. More than half a million of these poor whites, on both sides of the war, conscripted to fight, had been killed.[4] (Notably, despite Lincoln's resistance to arming blacks to fight in the Union army, 185,000 blacks had fought for their freedom in what eventually became a Union army subdivision, the "United States Colored Troops.") The poor white tenant farmers of the South, struggling harder than before the war, moved to the cities. In the southern cities, though, they found themselves literally living on the streets.

Poor white workers in the North fared no better from the war. In 1840, 11 million Americans lived in cities; by 1860 New York City alone had a population of 1 million people. According to Howard Zinn, these northern whites had not been "enthusiastic about a war which seemed to be fought for the black slave, or for the capitalist, for anyone but them."[5] The Irish immigrant workers in New York, particularly, had no concern over the status of blacks competing with them for jobs as longshoremen or barbers or domestic servants.

In effect, the vast majority of whites in America, North and South, after the Civil War, were in the streets looking for work. In the South, these streets were suddenly overcome with America's black, ex-slave population. At the end of the war, there were 4 million blacks in America—who were neither slave nor free. Nobody seemed to know what to do with them. According to the 1860 census, the black population, nearly all concentrated in the South, was, in the former Confederate states, nearly equal to or, in Alabama, Florida, Louisiana, Mississippi, and South Carolina, even greater than the white population.[6]

Union army general William T. Sherman had developed a plan, however, early in 1865, for what to do with the blacks after the war, a war he knew, by then, he was winning. Not necessarily opposed to slavery, more to secession, Sherman agreed with black spokesmen with whom he met in Savannah that blacks needed their own land on which to live and work.[7] Although a group of whites had formed the American Colonization Society to encourage and finance blacks to go to and settle homesteads in their invented country of Liberia in West Africa, Sherman used the power of his position to issue Special Field Order No. 15, granting lands seized by the Union forces to ex-slaves. This order designated the entire southern coastline, "from Charleston, south" and thirty miles inland for a black settlement, wherein each black family could possess and occupy no more than "40 acres of tillable land."[8]

Soon Congress created the Freedmen's Bureau to administer the transition from slavery, to provide for distribution of and resettlement onto the forty-acre plots. When the Freedmen's Bureau was slow in allocating theses plots, blacks began to seize the lands. By June 1865, only months after the war's end, over forty thousand free black families had moved onto these lands.[9]

Months later, however, in August, Lincoln's vice president, now President Andrew Johnson, stripped blacks of such landholding in defiance of Sherman's order and the institution of the Freedmen's Bureau. In May, Johnson had granted "amnesty" to thousands of Confederate leaders. Now he "restored" their lands, at the point of a bayonet, as it were. He commanded the U.S. Army to push blacks off these "white" lands by the end of the year, offering blacks the option to stay only upon signing "labor contracts" with the "rightful" white owners.[10]

We are given no straw, yet they keep telling us to make bricks.

Israelites to Pharoah, Exodus, 5:15, 16

Post-emancipation, most blacks literally did not know where to go. There was no place to go. Many thousands of newly freed slaves spent the next decade wandering the territories of the South on foot looking for food or work, looking for their lost mothers, fathers, siblings, or children who had been sold off to unknown places.

The testimonies of former slaves of the time, particularly those collected under the Federal Writers' Project of the 1930s, bear rich witness to this terrible struggle to survive in post-emancipation America. In *Before Freedom: When I Just Can Remember,* several such testimonies were published, including that of eighty-two-year-old Violet Guntharpe, who had been a teenager at the end of the Civil War:

> "Honey, us wasn't ready for the big change that come. Us had no education, no land, no mule, no cow, not a pig, nor a chicken, to set up house-keeping. The birds had nests in the air, the foxes had holes in the ground, and the fishes had beds under the great falls, but us colored folks was left without any place to lay our heads. . . . Lots of the chillun die, as did the old folks, while the rest of us scour the woods for hickory nuts, acorns, cane roots, and artichokes, and seine the river for fish." [11]

While the Thirteenth Amendment abolishing slavery had passed in the Congress, it would not be ratified until December 1865. In the meantime, most southern states passed laws specifically related to the rights and governance of former slaves, which collectively came to be called the Black Codes.

The most common issue the Black Codes addressed was "black crime," and the most common "crime" identified in various Black Codes was "vagrancy," for which blacks could be fined and/or jailed, in violation of the "unemployment" prohibition under the codes. These codes also criminalized black gun possession, voting, assembly after dark, and desertion from work, all of which, as University of Maryland law professor Katheryn K. Russell describes in *The Color of Crime,* congealed to create "a new system of involuntary servitude." [12]

Pre-emancipation, there had been the Slave Codes, under which every black person was deemed a slave, with the limited exclusion of "mulattoes," resulting in punishments under the law being meted out by "degree of Blackness." The "mulatto" exclusion became too dangerous, though, since it provided a means for slaves to "pass" into freedom and was superseded by the "one-drop rule," whereby anyone with one drop of African ancestry was deemed "black," or a slave. There were also the northern Black Laws, wherein the rights and freedom of movement of "free" blacks were severely restricted. Under the new Black Codes, though, many of which permitted *any* white to arrest *any* black, "blackness itself was a crime." [13]

The variations on these themes were insignificant. In Georgia, for example, the 1865 legislature, adulterating the Thirteenth Amendment itself with the passage of Black Codes to regulate black labor, defined "a black" as anyone with "one-eighth black blood," or with a black great-grandparent. Thus all blacks were subject to the codes. The labor-contract provisions of Georgia's codes reduced black laborers either to the ruthless sharecropping system or to the brutal peonage system—which would continue in Georgia for nearly a century. Furthermore, white "employers" could fire blacks without paying them. Like most other states' codes, while permitting blacks to marry—though not inter-marry or miscegenate—and "legitimizing" black children, Georgia's codes restricted all other movements of blacks. Thus "jobless" blacks were generally deemed "vagrants," for which they could be arrested, convicted, and sentenced to serve in the exploding black convict-labor force.[14]

Blacks fled to the cities. Between April and December of 1865 the black population of Macon, Georgia, doubled, to six thousand. Unable to pay rents and otherwise denied housing, blacks built shanty towns and rummaged through white garbage for food. The result was devastating. In December 1865 five hundred blacks in Macon fell dead from malnutrition or disease. The rest, according to historian Donald L. Grant, were rounded up and transported back to "their former masters." [15]

Last desperate attempts were still being made to provide blacks the means to survive post-emancipation—without consideration for the meaning of freedom. The most significant was that made by white U.S. congressman Thaddeus Stevens. In 1867 Stevens introduced legislation in Congress to permanently grant and distribute to each black family fifty dollars and forty acres of the same southern lands confiscated by President Johnson on behalf of the southern planters. This bill was soundly defeated, crushing Stevens, who died the next year and willed his body be buried in a black cemetery. Thus the passage of the Fourteenth Amendment later that year, granting blacks citizenship as persons "born or naturalized" in the United States and prohibiting states from denying blacks due process, under the Fifth Amendment, or equal protection under the law, was effectively meaningless.

The Black Codes would have been insufficient in themselves to deny blacks all vestiges of freedom. It was the white terrorism that underwrote the codes that forcefully foreclosed freedom to blacks in America for the next century.

In 1867, the first national meeting of the Klu Klux Klan was held in Nashville.[16] The same year, the terrorist organization Knights of the White Camelia was formed in Louisiana. Other groups would soon organize elsewhere, including the Red Shirts and the White League. In Georgia the various white militia bands, typically composed of former Confederate soldiers, organized under the names Black Horse Cavalry, the Jayhawkers, the Regulators.[17] In general, these armed whites would ride the South to murder, maim, repress, and intimidate "unruly" blacks, blacks deemed in violation of any of the Black Codes and blacks who managed to acquire land, with the goal of returning the black population to its former state of slavery.

Newspaper records indicate that sixty blacks were killed in 1873 in what was known as the Colfax Massacre, on Easter Sunday in Grant Parish, Louisiana. In 1874, sixteen blacks were reported to have been lynched in Tennessee. So many blacks were killed in 1875 in Vicksburg, Mississippi, that federal troops were sent in to restore order, and in the same year nearly thirty blacks were killed in the Clinton, Mississippi, Massacre. The next year so many blacks were killed in South Carolina that federal troops were sent there to halt a massacre.[18] These activities muted, and essentially nullified, the ratification of the Fifteenth Amendment in 1870, which guaranteed the right to vote to all citizens regardless of "race, color or previous condition of servitude." With the complete withdrawal of federal troops from the South at the official end of Reconstruction in 1877, blacks recognized the absolute untenability of living free in America.

By 1893, the United States faced its biggest economic crisis ever. Hundreds of banks collapsed. Thousands upon thousands of small manufacturing and retail businesses failed. Millions of workers suddenly became unemployed, all triggered by the unchecked speculations and machinations of the winners of the Civil War. At this point even the most progressive whites were willing to deny blacks inclusion in favor of their own kind. In the 1894 organizing effort of the American Railway Union, for example, the leadership of which included the great socialist Eugene V. Debs, the new union voted to exclude blacks from membership as it made a thrust to organize for better wages from the new Pullman Palace Car Company.[19]

Ironically, exploitation of this national desperation created even greater wealth for the new class of northern industrial robber barons. In 1890 a mere 1 percent of the population of the United States controlled more wealth than all the rest. In the 1880s and early 1890s, using a Jeffersonian model and under the authority of Lincoln's 1864 Contract Labor Law, they imported whites from Europe as cheap labor for their new industries—cheap *white* labor, as immigration laws prevented " 'inferior races' from acquiring U.S. citizenship."[20] By the 1890s, nearly 10 million Italians, Jews, Greeks, and Russians had been brought to America to work in their new factories, crowding the Irish immigrants who had arrived in previous waves. Moreover, thousands of Chinese immigrants were imported by railroad companies to cheaply build the railroad tracks for ongoing westward industrial expansion. So it was that the Astors and Vanderbilts and Rockefellers and Carnegies and Morgans and Mellons increased their wealth astronomically, fantastically, beyond anything since Rome itself.

The slavery that had built the foundation for this new wealth, and this new wealthy class, was all but forgotten, as the freed slaves were pushed from sight, back to virtual slavery, by domestic and immigrant whites scrambling for a place, now indistinct and united in their hatred of blacks. Therefore, in 1896, when Homer Plessy attempted to assert what he believed the modest citizenship right to ride a Louisiana train in the same car as whites, having paid the same price, the Supreme Court spoke for White America, ousting Plessy from that metaphorical freedom train. There would be no place for blacks in America. That is, the Court, in *Plessy v. Ferguson,* established the rule of "separate but equal." [21]

Plessy was a light-skinned black, referred to as an octoroon. He had boarded a railway carriage with whites and had been ejected under a Louisiana statute requiring "equal but *separate*" accommodations for blacks and whites on all railroad trains operating within the state, providing segregated or partitioned cars. Plessy's lawyer, Albion Tourgée, sued, stating his removal, like the Louisiana law, was in violation of the Thirteenth and Fourteenth Amendments.

The case reached the Supreme Court. Plessy's case was complicated by the fact that it required the court to rule on Louisiana's statutory definition of who was black. This was quickly ruled a "state's right." Then, writing for the majority, Justice Henry Billings Brown dismissed the issue of the Thirteenth Amendment and focused on the Fourteenth Amendment, on the definition of citizenship and its rights and privileges. Brown, a Massachusetts Republican, used the so-called antiregulatory (now "government intervention") argument employed by racists of the day to justify his ruling. [22]

The *Plessy* Court held that "social prejudices" and "racial instincts" could not be "overcome by legislation." Furthermore, the question of citizenship under the Fourteenth Amendment went to states' actions, not *private social* matters. Riding on a railroad car alongside whites was a social matter, not a right of citizenship. The railroad company had a right, and the state could protect that right, to separate whites from blacks in its cars, assuming the accommodations were "equal":

"The object of the [Fourteenth] Amendment was undoubtedly to enforce the absolute equality of the two races before the law, but in the nature of things, it could not have been intended to abolish distinctions based on color, or to enforce social, as distinguished from political equality" (emphasis added).

This ruling opened the floodgates of injustice and inequity, condemning blacks to life in a hostile white-dominated world in which blacks had no stake or interest or power. The Court in *Plessy* had established and legalized American apartheid.

Institutionalizing Jim Crow segregation came to define life in America, as the term "Jim Crow" had become, by 1838, a crude synonym for a black.[23] State after state passed more and more laws under the rule of *Plessy*. In the South, Jim Crow laws dominated everyday life. More often than not, there were "white only" accommodations and no separate ones for blacks, equal or otherwise. In effect, blacks could not use public toilets, drink from public water fountains, eat in public restaurants, stay in hotels or boardinghouses, use parks or other recreational facilities, shop in retail stores, go to theaters, attend schools, use libraries, be treated in hospitals, rent or buy property or houses, be fairly employed or equally paid for labor, own businesses, or be buried in cemeteries, and they certainly could not take a seat in a public train.

The denial to blacks of life, liberty, and the pursuit of happiness was complete, enforced by the rule of *Plessy* and of the mob and the gun. Named for Charles Lynch, a Virginia farmer of the Revolutionary period who was known to orchestrate and carry out brutal extralegal punishments to those he deemed transgressors, the so-called lynch laws became the source of the violent oppression of blacks through the end of the nineteenth and well into the twentieth centuries. It became a common practice to lynch and murder blacks to terrorize them in order to accomplish numerous goals, primary among which were relinquishment of land or jobs. While the most common excuse for the hangings or mob murders of blacks was rape, or attempted rape, official records show that less than one-third of lynchings related to allegations of sexual assault against white women.[24] Moreover, in the preceding years, during slavery, "white rape of black women was far more common than black rape of white women."[25] The known record of black lynchings is compelling:

    1882—49 blacks lynched in America
    1883—53 blacks lynched in America
    1884—51 blacks lynched in America
    1885—74 blacks lynched in America
    1886—74 blacks lynched in America
    1887—70 blacks lynched in America

1888—69 blacks lynched in America
1889—[no record]
1890—85 blacks lynched in America
1891—113 blacks lynched in America
1892—161 blacks lynched in America
1893—118 blacks lynched in America
1894—[no record]
1895—113 blacks lynched in America
1896—78 blacks lynched in America
1897—123 blacks lynched in America
1898—101 blacks lynched in America[26]

Overall, from 1882 until 1968, the U.S. Census Bureau counted the lynchings of 4,742 blacks in America.[27] Between 1889 and 1918, Georgia had more lynchings of blacks than any other state.[28] The great historian and antilynching crusader Ida B. Wells-Barnett, who documented lynching reports contemporaneously, recorded the number of lynchings of blacks in America between 1878 and 1898 at ten thousand.[29]

═══════════

Blacks fought back and fought to survive, to overcome the devastation of life after *Plessy*. Over the next decades, blacks organized, first against lynching and all other manifestations of white racist terrorism and violence, repression, and exploitation. Blacks organized against Jim Crow discrimination, toward inclusion in the American scheme, to achieve social and political equality, to be employed and own businesses, to be educated, to live in decent housing, to have access to medical care, to enjoy public accommodations, to have freedom of movement. Also, blacks organized for economic independence, to develop independent social and political structures. Blacks used violence and nonviolence to protest civil wrongs and gain civil rights and human rights, to be free from exploitation and oppression and to realize self-determination. Blacks became nationalists and separatists and internationalists and integrationists. Every single effort was made to find freedom. And every single step taken was made with bloodshed.

Over the next eighty years blacks struggled for freedom: the early post-emancipation efforts to define the black agenda, from Booker T.

Washington's so-called accommodationist strike for black economic autonomy to Du Bois's and the NAACP's thrust for social and political equality, to the efforts of Marcus Garvey toward black independence and nationhood; the movement of black workers to organize for black employment and fair and equal pay, as the nation shifted completely to urban industrialization; the protests against lynchings and the resistance to white violence; mass marches and the voices raised in the prose and poetry of the Harlem Renaissance, the voices of Langston Hughes and Claude McKay and Zora Neal Hurston, supported by the strains of the blues and of jazz, Billie Holiday writing and singing about lynching in "Strange Fruit"; the powerful effort by the NAACP that resulted in the Supreme Court's 1954 decision in *Brown v. Board of Education of Topeka, Kansas* that overturned *Plessy*, at least regarding public education; resistance to the violent backlash after *Brown* and busing by white America, from the attacks on the Little Rock Nine and six-year-old Ruby Bridges and Autherine Lucy to the Boston bus burnings, as north and south of the Mason-Dixon Line whites violently resisted public school integration.

In 1955, a turning point was reached in the Montgomery, Alabama, bus boycott against segregated public transportation, set off by the dynamic Rosa Parks, which thrust Martin Luther King Jr. center stage in history. Over the next intense decade of the struggle, civil rights workers were murdered in Mississippi and elsewhere, hundreds of thousands marched on Washington, and four little girls were killed in a Birmingham church by a white terrorist bomb. Organizations like CORE (Congress of Racial Equality) and SNCC (Student Non-Violent Coordinating Committee) struggled to enforce voting rights and other civil rights.

Despite the too-little, too-late passage of the 1964 and 1965 Civil Rights Acts, accompanied by the American assault on the Gulf of Tonkin, the opening salvo of the Vietnam War, black rage was rising. It burst forth in Watts, California, in 1965, the haunting voice of Malcolm X calling for black unity from the grave. A new youthful drumbeat called for "Black Power!" Efforts were made to establish a new agenda for blacks, a liberation agenda, brought on by revolution, in the vanguard of which was the newly formed Black Panther Party.

Black urban uprisings now exploded all over America, triggering government investigations that concluded, in the words of the Kerner

Commission report, that America remained a nation divided, black and white, "separate and *un*equal." Nevertheless, now the national government, while fighting a war against the Vietnamese, waged war on its own citizens, its black citizens. Under the leadership of FBI director J. Edgar Hoover and the aegis of the government's dormant anticommunist counterintelligence (COINTELPRO) operations, Hoover promised to eliminate the rise of a potentially dangerous "Black Messiah" who could threaten the peace at home. Martin Luther King was assassinated, and nonviolence was dead.

A few years later, Black Panther Party leader and imprisoned author George Jackson would also be assassinated. Before his death, he would write, in his internationally acclaimed book *Soledad Brother,* of the assassination of Dr. King and prophetically of what soon came to be the death of the very will of blacks to continue to fight for freedom: "M.L.K. . . . was indeed a devout pacifist. It is very odd, almost unbelievable, that so violent and tumultuous a setting as this can still produce such men. He was out of place, out of season, too naive, too innocent, too cultured, too civil for these times. That is why his end was so predictable." [30]

In that same year that King was killed, 1968, Hoover declared the Black Panther Party "the greatest threat to the internal security of the United States" and promised all-out war to eliminate the party and any other black organizations or individuals with similar "communist" agendas. The next year, 1969, began with the assassinations of southern California party leaders John Huggins and Bunchy Carter, and ended, in December, with the largest, most violent police assault on citizens in the nation's history, a five-and-one-half-hour raid on the party's headquarters in Los Angeles and with the FBI assassination of Chicago party leaders Mark Clark and Fred Hampton.

In 1977 the great freedom fighter Fannie Lou Hamer died, suffering and relatively alone. In many ways, she had been the voice of that last powerful effort by blacks for civil and human rights in the sixties that came to be known as the Movement. Up from the Mississippi Delta, she used to sing the freedom songs, saying, "Singing is one of the main things that can keep us going. When you're in a brick cell, locked up, and haven't done anything to anybody but still you're locked up there and sometimes words just begin to come to you and you begin to sing. Like one of my favorite songs. . . ."[31]

> *This little light of mine*
> *I'm gonna let it shine*
> *This little light of mine*
> *I'm gonna let it shine*
> *This little light of mine*
> *I'm gonna let it shine*
> *Let it shine, oh, let it shine, oh, let it shine.*

[10] This Little Light Extinguished

By the time Little B was born in 1983 it was the Age of Reagan. Like the millions of black girls and boys born in the generations before and since emancipation, he stumbled into life along a precipice abutting unabating poverty and oppression. Now, though, nothing lighted the way; no dream stood between him and the nigthmarish fall into the abyss of black life in America, which suddenly included crack cocaine.

"That's 'cause you the crack baby," she hurled at him so playfully that it was almost lost in her usual repartee.

"What did you say?" I interrupted, too forcefully.

"She's always tryin' to tell me I'm the crack baby, when she knows she is," Michael responds, looking at Ta-Ta, laughing, batting back the ball in this game.

The prison video cameras are overhead, and I wonder if they can capture the conversation. It would be illegal, and irrelevant. There are no secrets at Alto. This was no secret.

They were giggling, lost in play, beyond the barbed wire and walls, romping along a beach, splashing water at each other, playing their games.

"Naw, you the crack baby."

"No, you!"

"No, you!"

"You."

Now Ta-Ta must guess the colors of the M&M candies in his hand. There are four. No peeking.

Now they remember some rap song they used to sing together. They

repeat the words in unison, fast, eyes holding the gaze of the other's, re-
membering.

Now they rapidly recite a hand-clapping rhyme, hands flashing
like Flamenco castanets, hand-to-hand, hands-to-knees, hands across
hearts.

Suddenly, an announcement, a southern drawl: "It is now three
o'clock. Visitin' hours are now over. All visitors must leave immediately.
Inmates, remain in place."

The Age of Reagan produced an America in which one-quarter of
the nation's children, 12 million children, lived in poverty. The poverty
rate among blacks soared to 33 percent, and nearly 90 percent of black
women heads of households under twenty-five years old and their children lived *below* the poverty level. In fact, black children were growing
up on welfare at a rate four times that of white children.[1]

Under the Reagan economic agenda, referred to as Reaganomics or
supply-side economics, billions were cut from social welfare programs.
In 1981, $25 billion was cut from welfare programs for women and chil-
dren, particularly Aid to Families with Dependent Children, child nutri-
tion programs and food stamps; another $20 billion was cut from them
in 1982, and another $20 billion in 1983. By 1984, $140 billion had been
cut from social programs.[2]

It was an America in which millions of schoolchildren were disqualified from the free school lunch program, the only meal for many, while
the Agriculture Department declared ketchup a sufficient substitute for
a vegetable in those lunches.[3] Breadlines, nonexistent since the Great
Depression, began appearing in America's cities, as the new phenomenon of "homelessness" spread, *most* of which hundreds of thousands of
people were unemployed workers and many of whom were children.[4]
Nevertheless, Reagan's attorney general, Edwin Meese III, before being
driven from office by scandal, would say not only that there were "no
authoritative figures that there [were] hungry children [in America],"
but also that "some people go to soup kitchens voluntarily . . . because
the food is free and that's easier than paying for it." And the President's
Task Force on Food Assistance actually issued the statement that there
was "no massive hunger problem" in America and that in fact "black
children [on Welfare] were probably the best-nourished group in the
United States."[5]

At the same time, unemployment grew rapidly. By 1982, 30 million Americans were unemployed. The next year the unemployment rate in America reached 9.5 percent, the highest rate since 1941. Black unemployment rose to two-and-one-half times that of whites, with unemployment among young blacks reaching 40 percent. Unemployed millions of people permanently lost medical insurance and therefore access to medical treatment.[6]

Simultaneously, while $181 billion was added to the so-called defense budget, Reagan cut taxes for the very rich. The Reagan era produced the end of the "progressive" income tax structure, based on greater income tax rates for those with greater income. Taxes for the very rich were lowered 50 percent, and by 1986 income tax for the top earners was down to 28 percent. While corporate chiefs eliminated workers en masse in the new "downsizing" programs, engendered and engineered by a new wave of brutal corporate takeovers, and the number of low-wage service jobs increased, the net worth of the *Forbes* magazine "400" tripled. Despite the 1987 stock market crash, the greatest failure since 1929, and although approximately $70 billion a year was lost in tax revenues, at the end of the Reagan era, not only had the rich gotten richer, but the richest 1 percent of the country had gained one trillion dollars.[7]

Because civil rights laws had opened windows of opportunity for some blacks, an increasing number of blacks were deemed part of the middle and even upper classes. However, the Reagan administration, with the support of a Democratic Congress, did everything but completely overturn those laws, as it abandoned all commitment to their enforcement.[8] Still, the majority of blacks made up the so-called underclass. And life for the mass of poor blacks in America's inner cities became worse than ever, wretched, accounting for the fact that the overall life expectancy of blacks was ten years lower than that of whites and that the black infant mortality rate was rising, higher in some cities than in Bangladesh, Jamaica, or Costa Rica.[9]

The use and distribution of a new drug, "crack" cocaine, began to devastate life in the black ghettos of America during the Reagan era. At the same time, a new plague struck. In 1981, the Centers for Disease Control began reporting sudden deaths by a little-known pneumonia and soon by a rare skin cancer, Kaposi's sarcoma, both seemingly striking and killing only homosexual men. Soon identified as AIDS, this was a disease the Christian Right began calling "God's Revenge," with the Rev. Jerry Falwell specifically naming it the "gay plague." [10] Cases of this new disease began to overtake the black ghettos of America as destructively as did crack cocaine —with its attendant violence.

The legacy of officially sanctioned violence against blacks found new incarnations in urban police forces. In 1982 Los Angeles police chief Daryl Gates blithely announced that the highly disproportionate number of blacks dying at the hands of L. A. cops under the "choke hold" arrest procedure was because something was wrong with blacks: "Their veins or arteries do not open up as fast they do with normal people." [11]

Finally, during those same years, the "white flight" resistance to the desegregation of public schools, after the 1954 Supreme Court decision in *Brown* and its progeny, transformed America. The last of the majority white population of the country settled into lily-white suburban subdivisions. Businesses big and small were following white flight, building suburban executive parks and office complexes and completely uprooting urban industrial bases. America's cities came to be dominated by blacks and black poverty. In some cases entire cities, like Detroit and East St. Louis, became black ghettos.

———

It had taken one hundred years, from 1865 to 1965, for blacks to be guaranteed meager citizenship rights, one hundred years of struggle, involving lynchings, bombings, bloodshed, and the marches of the Civil Rights movement. Finally the Johnson administration had scripted the 1964 and 1965 Civil Rights Acts, prohibiting segregation in restrooms, parks, restaurants, public transportation, and the like and protecting black voting rights. It was under this same administration, however, that the Dream for anything more began to die.

Martin Luther King Jr. was assassinated on the march to developing a Poor People's Campaign, organizing black and white and Native American and all other poor people in the country to come to and occupy Washington, D.C., until there were *human* rights guarantees for everyone, guarantees for jobs and housing and an equal share in the wealth of the nation. He said of the Poor People's Campaign,

The policy of the federal government is to play Russian roulette with riots; it is prepared to gamble with another summer of disaster. Despite two consecutive summers of violence, not a single basic cause of riots has been corrected. All of the misery that stoked the flames of rage and rebellion remains undiminished. With unemployment, intolerable housing, and discriminatory education, a scourge in Negro ghettos, Congress and the administration still tinker with trivial, halfhearted measures. . . . The time has come for a return to mass nonviolent protest. Accordingly, we are planning a series of such demonstrations this spring and summer, to begin in Washington, D.C. They will have Negro and white participation, and they will seek to benefit the poor of both races.[12]

Whether or not King was assassinated under orders of Johnson confidant J. Edgar Hoover, director of the FBI, who unabashedly hated and harassed King, after King's death the mass movement King was singularly capable of galvanizing began to draw its last breaths. Though fifty thousand marched on Washington as planned, they did not stay but were driven out by the National Guard. All that seemed to be left was the rage, as expressed for days after King's murder in April 1968 in the violent, responsive uprisings by blacks in over a hundred cities, which were contained only by the deployment of twenty thousand federal troops and thirty-four thousand National Guards.[13]

Just before Malcolm X was assassinated in February 1965, he met with Coretta King in Selma, Alabama. Martin Luther King was in jail. Malcolm had moved away from the Nation of Islam, had formed the Organization of Afro-American Unity, and was seeking to unite his efforts with those of King. After King was shot down, Coretta King would say that, had they not been killed, "at some point the two would have come closer together and would have been a very strong force in the total struggle for liberation and self-determination of black people in our society."[14]

In the aftermath, ghettoized blacks rose up in violent frustration over the manifestations of racism in America—in Cleveland, Gary, Miami, Hartford, Chicago, Springfield, Jacksonville, Augusta, and elsewhere. Black students militantly protested racism and forced universities and colleges to admit more black students and to include black studies courses—at Boston University, Trinity College, Columbia University, Ohio State, Northwestern University, San Francisco State, Cornell University, and elsewhere. The Black Panther Party stepped into the leadership of the Movement, with an agenda for black liberation through revolutionary change, opening chapters in every major city in America. This militant wave yielded the first black mayors in numerous cities that blacks now dominated. At the end of 1968, nine blacks took seats in the U.S. Congress, the largest number of blacks elected to Congress since 1875. After the November 1970 election, twelve blacks went to Congress.[15]

With the election of Richard Nixon in 1968, though, the dynamic changed. When Nixon ran against Kennedy in 1960, had only white votes counted, he would have been president.[16] Now Nixon, the anticommunist McCarthy era prosecutor, had easily won office as the voice of what he called the "Silent Majority," the white majority, the suburbanized whites who had fled blacks in the cities, who were tired of antiwar protests, counterculture antics, and "black power." Now, while Nixon stepped up the war in Vietnam, he gave Hoover full sway to do the same at home. Law-and-order legislation was passed, loosing local and national police forces. Thousands of antiwar demonstrators were arrested and in some cases, as at Ohio's Kent State University in 1970, killed. Black Panther offices and homes were targeted for relentless police and FBI raids, as members were arrested and jailed and killed. National Guards were mobilized to put down uprisings of blacks all over America, in Cairo, Illinois, Baton Rouge, Fort Lauderdale, and elsewhere. Only one year after Nixon's election, even the moderate NAACP, which had challenged Dr. King's opposition to the Vietnam War, announced that it considered Nixon "anti-Negro."[17] The newly formed Congressional Black Caucus boycotted Nixon's 1971 State of the Union address. In September of that year, fifteen hundred New York state troopers stormed Attica State Correctional Facility, which had been seized by prisoners, nearly all of them black, demanding minimum wages for labor and better food and other conditions. The state troopers shot and killed thirty-two inmates and nine guards.[18]

In 1972, the NAACP announced that "unemployment of urban blacks was worse than at anytime since the Great Depression of the 1930s."[19] Despite the black outcry, Nixon was reelected. That same year, the California courts were wrestling with the case of *University of California Regents v. Bakke*, which would only make matters for blacks worse, introducing into the American lexicon the language, and the harsh reality to which it spoke, of "reverse discrimination."

Nixon was eventually ignominiously driven from office in the 1974 Watergate scandal. Hoover had died in 1972. However, the damage was done. While a 1974 report of the Joint Center for Political Studies documented that there were 108 black mayors in America, they were, in effect mayors of the ghetto.[20] Black child poverty had increased, black unemployment remained high, and the number and percentage of blacks in prison was steadily escalating. By the time Nixon left office, the post-emancipation dream about freedom and equality and human rights for blacks, like the plan to start life over on "40 acres of tillable land," had all but died.

———

Nixon left a powerful legacy. He had established the absolute power of the presidency and sealed the link between the presidency and big corporate interests. The Watergate Senate investigations had, of course, centered on the so-called illegal corporate contributions to Nixon's re-election campaign. No future president could be elected without them. The subsequent Carter presidency confirmed this shift.

While some viewed Carter as a kind of champion of blacks, Carter had a solid base in the most racist enclaves of his native Georgia. A millionaire peanut farmer, Carter had first been elected to office in the early 1960s as a state senator representing Sumter County. Sumter was considered the most conservative—or racist—district in the entire state at the time.[21] Moreover, Carter, a fifth-generation Georgia cotton grower, was the son of an avowed segregationist father and could trace his inheritance back to a great-great-grandfather, who, killed as a Confederate soldier, had willed his heirs not only the Carter farmland but also the Carter slaves. Furthermore, when Carter was elected governor of Georgia in 1970, his running mate for lieutenant governor was staunch segregationist Lester Maddox, Georgia's previous governor. While Carter would later claim a dislike for Maddox and would irritate Maddox by hanging a portrait of Martin Luther King Jr. in the state capitol and by appointing blacks to judgeships, at the time he stated that he was "proud" to have Maddox as his running mate.[22]

The Nixon legacy was indeed intact under Carter. This was true

even though Carter became president by easily defeating Nixon successor Gerald Ford, who had "pardoned" Nixon and under whom the war
in Vietnam had ended, in 1975, with American defeat. Despite claims
that he "sympathized" with the antiwar movement, Carter was a strong
supporter of the Vietnam War to the bitter end, and appointed as secretary of energy James Schlesinger, who had been the Nixon secretary of
defense. Furthermore, his first budget proposal increased the military
budget by $10 billion. Despite the appointment of civil rights veteran
Andy Young as ambassador to the United Nations, Carter continued to
support the regimes of brutal dictators around the world, including that
of Marcos in the Philippines, Pinochet in Chile, the Shah in Iran, and Somoza in Nicaragua. Domestically, Carter maintained the Nixon agenda
of corporate influence over the presidency; American "multinational"
corporations as a group now constituted the third largest economy in the
world, after the Soviet Union and the United States itself. Moreover, Carter did little to improve benefits to the poor, favoring increases to the military budget, actually proposing at one point the elimination of second
helpings of milk in free school lunches to add $25 million to the Depart-
ment of Agriculture budget. By 1979, Children's Defense Fund president
Marian Wright Edelman was compelled to announce that one in every
seven children, nearly 10 million, had no source of health care. At the
same time, Edelman pointed out, the government, under Carter, had
"found $275 million to bail out Litton Industries and handed the Navy
two destroyers ordered by the Shah of Iran."[23]

Iranian oil was important. That was why the United States had originally propped up Mohammad Reza Shah Pahlavi to rule Iran. By 1979,
though, the Shah was driven out of office by the Iranian people. He fled
to the United States with the help and protection of President Carter.
When Iranian protesters demanded the Shah's return and Carter firmly
refused, they took over the U.S. embassy in Teheran and held fifty-two
embassy workers as hostages. Carter's failure to secure a quick release
of the Iranian-held hostages opened the door for the Age of Reagan.

At the time of the Reagan election, despite the number of blacks
now occupying elective office, the majority of blacks lived in urban ghettos. Unemployment among blacks was nearing 15 percent.[24] Increasingly, underpaid black women were becoming the sole supporters of the
black family. Moreover, blacks were still fighting tooth and nail to en-

force school desegregation, to bolster black schools suffering the economic consequences of white flight, to maintain affirmative action programs, to overcome bank "redlining" and other new-age discrimination practices, and to otherwise develop a survival agenda.

While Reagan was rising to power on Carter's "weakness" in handling the Iranian hostage business, U.S.-supported Nicaraguan president Anastasio Somoza Debayle was being overthrown by a left-leaning organization allied with Castro, the Sandinistas (the Sandinist National Liberation Front), which was forming a government and nationalizing the country's industries. These events congealed to create conditions that would bring about worse suffering to American blacks than anything since the Emancipation Proclamation. That is, the Reagan election and the U.S. efforts to oust the Sandinistas would trigger the trafficking and mass use in the urban ghettos of America of the new, cheap, smokable, highly addictive drug "crack" cocaine.

In 1996 journalist Gary Webb produced a series of articles in the *San Jose Mercury News* about a connection between crack cocaine in black America and covert operations of the CIA that should have triggered congressional investigations on the scale of Watergate. There was, instead, a haunting silence, even on the part of the Congressional Black Caucus—notwithstanding its idle threats or empty promises to "hold hearings," as echoed by Los Angeles congresswoman Maxine Waters and California senator Barbara Boxer, or the promise of then-director of the CIA John Deutch to order "investigations." Though Webb himself soon went into relative obscurity, his *unrefuted* exposé documented the delivery of a death blow to blacks underwritten by the government.

Webb revealed that from the early 1980s the CIA facilitated, instigated, or was otherwise involved in the trafficking of crack cocaine to finance the group of Nicaraguan anticommunist guerrillas collectively known as the contras.[25] (It is noteworthy that George Bush was director of the CIA, under Gerald Ford, from 1976 to 1977.) This program was set in place primarily by Juan Norwin Meneses Cantarero, a leader of the largest of the contra guerrilla groups, the Fuerza Democratica Nicaraguenese (FDN).

Before the fall of Somoza, Meneses had been known in Nicaragua as

"Rey de la Droga" (King of the Drugs), and he had been under investigation for some time by the U.S. Drug Enforcement Agency (DEA). He was closely affiliated with Somoza, two of his brothers having been generals in Somoza's defeated army. His FDN superior was Colonel Enrique Bermudez.[26]

Arming and otherwise assisting the contras was a national security priority for Reagan from the outset of his presidency. The 1979 Sandinista ouster of Somoza was intolerable. The CIA could remember the fiasco of its 1961 Bay of Pigs invasion. That Castro was still in place only exacerbated the sting of it all. Furthermore, Carter had made the mistake of resolving the buildup of anti-American tension in Panama at the time by signing an agreement with left-leaning Panamanian leader Omar Torrijos Herrera to turn over the Panama Canal to Panama at the end of 1999. Torrijos had threatened to blow up the canal, which he had described as a "colonialist tumor." Thus U.S. interests in the important interoceanic region of the Caribbean were falling apart when Reagan took office. Any means necessary had to be and were employed to "take back" Nicaragua. Reagan would liken the contras to "America's Founding Fathers."[27]

Although Reagan authorized the CIA to "begin covert paramilitary operations against the Sandinista government" in December 1981, the $19.9 million funding allocation was considered insufficient to mount a successful campaign. Worse, there was growing sentiment in Congress against providing any funding to the overthrow of other governments, which would result in the prohibition of all support for the contras between 1984 and 1986.

Exiled Nicaraugans were desperate to return the Somoza government to power. These exiles included Oscar Danilo Blandon Reyes, selling cars in East Los Angeles, and Meneses, who was living in the northern California Bay Area. The two met and traveled to Honduras to meet FDN military chief Bermudez, who reminded them that their cause was so important that, in terms of raising funds, "the ends justif[ied] the means." Meneses and Blandon began trying to raise money by selling cocaine.

While Bermudez, subsequently mysteriously killed, would deny he was speaking of drug dealing and turning over the profits to the contras, he knew Meneses well, and the business of Meneses was well known. Furthermore, the Los Angeles sheriff's affidavit under which Blandon would come to be arrested in 1986 stated, "Danilo Blandon is in charge of a sophisticated cocaine smuggling and distribution organization operating in southern California. The monies gained from the sales of cocaine are transported to Florida and laundered through . . . a chain of banks . . . [and] filtered to the *contra* rebels to buy arms in the war in Nicaragua." [28]

Blandon who eventually became a DEA informant could not sell the first two kilograms of cocaine Meneses supplied him, however, at a rate the DEA stated was $5,200 per ounce at the time. Around the same time, drug dealers on the street were becoming aware of the potential market to blacks of this expensive drug, particularly as it was being cooked into freebase and condensed, or cracked into hard nuggets with ten times the potency of powder cocaine.

One of those street-level dealers in Los Angeles was Ricky Donnell Ross, who with a friend had begun a small distribution business supplied by a Nicaraguan named Henry Corrales. Corrales introduced Ross to Blandon, who considered Ross the perfect distributor for all the cocaine Meneses could supply. Ross developed a network through members of the local street gang, the "Crips," whose members he knew or whose acquaintance he cultivated. Millions of dollars per week in cheap "rocks" of crack would be distributed through this gang network— more money than Ross or any of the young blacks to whom he wholesaled had ever imagined being in possession of, money for which they would and did steal, die, and kill. Ross, who came to be known as "Freeway Rick," made millions of dollars and dominated the crack trade, as other wholesale dealers could never compete with him and his inexhaustible supply of cocaine from Blandon. [29]

It is worth noting that before that, in the late 1960s and early 1970s, during the time the Black Panther Party existed in southern California, there was *no* gang activity in Los Angeles. Once the party chapter was effectively wiped out or driven underground, rather typical neighborhood gang rivalries were renewed. A few years later, however, these south-central Los Angeles neighborhood gangs—primarily the Crips, eventually the Bloods, and their various subsets—became embroiled in increasingly violent conflicts over distribution of crack cocaine. Before that time, poor blacks did not use cocaine, as it was either too expensive or unavailable.

Meneses himself was never arrested or prosecuted by any U.S. agency, though he eventually trafficked millions of dollars in cocaine and at least forty-five DEA indictments were filed against him. He remained free to set up numerous "legitimate" businesses and buy various homes in Oakland, San Francisco, Hayward, and elsewhere in northern California. He became so emboldened that in 1984 he posed for a photograph with FDN political boss Adolfo Calero, published by the *Mercury News* with the Webb articles. Calero had been a CIA operative for a long time and became, as Webb characterized it, "the public face of the contras in the United States."[30] Calero would later testify at the 1989 trial of Oliver North in relation to the Iran-contra affair that North was a "sort of savior" for the contras: "We're going to erect a monument to him when we free Nicaragua."[31]

Early in Reagan's first term, Oliver North, then a relatively low ranking Marine Corps major, was assigned to the National Security Council. North would become the most visibly important link to developing the military and financial support for the contras. By 1987, the House Foreign Affairs Committee began an investigation into the activities of North, by then a lieutenant colonel, as well as others, about suspected illegal government arms sales to Iran. In the end, it was determined that North, Admiral John Poindexter, and others had violated the law and arranged arms sales to Iran, not only in exchange for American hostages held in Lebanon but also to finance the contras. Moreover, they had done so not as rogues but as operatives of officials at the highest level of government, unquestionably including secretary of defense Caspar Weinberger. The final report of the whole Iran-contra Affair would not be issued for seven years. In it, independent counsel Lawrence Walsh charged Reagan with "setting the stage" for the illegal Iran-contra deals, with giving North "an invitation to break the law" and having "knowingly participated or at least acquiesced in the efforts" of North and other top aides in covering up those illegal activities.[32]

Back in 1987, however, in the early days of the Iran-contra investigations, there had been a congressional investigation into the connection between funding for the contras and drug dealing, conducted by a Senate Foreign Relations subcommittee chaired by John Kerry. As a result of testimony from several CIA operatives, including that of Alan Fiers, the CIA's chief in Central America, Senator Kerry concluded, "Individuals who provided support for the *contras* were involved in drug trafficking . . . [and] the U.S. government had information regarding the involvement either while it was occurring or immediately thereafter." [33]

Earlier that year, the National Urban League's "State of Black America" report had stated, "Black Americans enter 1987 besieged by the resurgence of raw racism, persistent economic depression and the continued erosion of past gains." By 1988 the overall black unemployment rate was over 12 percent. The poverty rate among blacks was more than 33 percent, and the poverty rate among black children was 45 percent. [34] Worse, by then the inundation of America's black communities with cheap, highly addictive crack cocaine was filling the vacuum of this despair and poverty.

Crack cocaine had elevated the Crips and Bloods into ghetto drug cartels, whose territorial wars for distribution markets in California had invented the "drive-by" shooting and, spreading beyond the state and all over the country, had escalated the murders in the black ghettos to numbers never seen in the history of blacks in America. Crack cocaine had fostered a "gangsta" culture and become the primary economy of black America. In that cancerous decade or so, the use and distribution of crack cocaine in the black communities of America had come to destroy the lives of millions of black people and their children, as it would their children's children.

The flagrant drug trafficking operations of Panama's leader General Manuel Noriega were an embarrassment to the new administration of George Bush. Not so long after Reagan became president, Panama's leader, Omar Torrijos Herrera, who had forced Carter to turn over the canal to the Panamanians by 1999, was killed in an airplane accident. Rising as his replacement was Noriega, acknowledged to have been on the CIA payroll since 1955. The United States finally had a friend in power in this important region. Noriega had opened Panama as a base for contra operations and had even met with North about those operations. There were even photographs of him with Bush, who had, as director of the CIA, protected Noriega.[35]

Running on a platform that included advocating the death penalty for "major drug traffickers" and the eradication of "welfare fraud," George Bush took office in 1989 after defeating Democrat Michael Dukakis, governor of Massachusetts, by attacking him for being "soft on crime." Bush had made much of how Massachusetts had furloughed black convicted murderer Willie Horton, who had escaped on furlough and raped a woman and stabbed her fiancé. Horton's darkened image had emblazened the television screens of America in oft-repeated last-minute Bush campaign advertisements that many blacks denounced as "racist." This would be revelatory of the climate in America for blacks under Bush.

Not long after the Bush inauguration, the Supreme Court banned a Richmond, Virginia, program setting aside a percentage of the city's public works contracts for minority-owned construction companies. Sandra Day O'Connor, a Reagan-appointee, writing for the majority, called the set-asides "reverse discrimination." The strong dissent to the decision was made by an aging Thurgood Marshall, stating the decision represented "a full-scale retreat from . . . remedial efforts directed toward deliverance of the *century-old* promise of equality of economic opportunity" (emphasis added). Later that year, the Court ruled that white workers claiming "reverse discrimination" could seek redress and remedy under the civil rights laws. The National Urban League denounced these decisions as "threats to the vital interests of American blacks."[36]

At the same time, the black poverty rate rose to three times that of whites, and soon one of the country's largest black-owned banks, New York City's Freedom National Bank, would be declared insolvent. Before the first year of the Bush presidency was over, the Centers for Disease Control declared that 27 percent of all AIDS cases were among blacks, as the black infant mortality rate remained at double that of whites.[37]

At the end of that first year, Bush invaded Panama. Though Panama had been the primary way station for the cocaine traffic headed from Colombia to the United States, it also had housed U.S. military bases. It contributed millions of dollars a year to the United States in the tolls it collected. It had flown the U.S. flag since 1903. That Noriega had profited a little from providing safe passage to drug traffickers from Colombia, with which Panama shares a 135-mile rain forest border, traveling to the United States in planes and boats through Panama's seventeen hundred miles of waterways, inlets, and bays, in and out of its fifteen hundred islands, had seemed a small price to pay. Noriega, though, had apparently begun double-dealing, openly talking with Castro and other regional brothers not friendly to the United States, and openly trafficking drugs. Bush *ordered* Noriega to step down. When he refused, Bush sent thousands of U.S. armed forces into Panama to "arrest" him. Thousands of Panamanian civilians were killed before Noriega surrendered. He was shipped off to Miami to stand trial.

Bush legitimized this attack on Panama as an effort not only to arrest Noriega but to "crush the cocaine trade." Ironically, after Noriega's capture, and even as he was about to stand trial, the DEA reported an *increase* in drug trafficking through Panama.[38]

More interesting was the appearance of convicted Colombian drug kingpin Carlos Lehder as a *key prosecution* witness at Noriega's trial in late 1991. Lehder, a founder of the infamous Medellin drug cartel then sentenced to life in prison for drug smuggling, testified that he had done business with Noriega. He also testified that the Medellin cartel had given $10 million to the contras.[39] This had been facilitated by a contra leader named Felix Rodriguez. While Rodriguez and contra chief Adolpho Calero immediately denounced and denied the testimony, Lehder's credibility as a witness had been vouched for by Noriega's federal prosecutors. Moreover, in the Iran-contra investigations, Rodriguez, a former CIA agent, had been confirmed as an "operative in Oliver L. North's secret network to resupply the Nicaraguan contra rebels."[40] And in the 1987 Kerry hearings regarding Iran-contra, Senator Kerry had concluded: "Elements of the contras themselves knowingly received financial and material assistance from drug traffickers."[41]

All of this was silenced by the din of the time. At the beginning of 1991, Bush had invaded Iraq. It was a short war that had resulted in the deaths of hundreds of thousands of Iraqi people, a combination of "tens of thousands" killed during the forty-two days of bombing and troop invasions and the thousands upon thousands of casualties of the devastating aftermath, including an estimated 5 percent of Iraqi children under five years old.[42]

Moreover, America seemed on the brink of a new era of violent uprisings in the urban streets, a la sixties. The streets of black Los Angeles, indeed those all over black America, were hot with bated breath awaiting the outcome of the trial of four white Los Angeles cops for the March 1991 brutal beating of black motorist Rodney King. The acquittal of the cops would trigger mass black rage and the most powerful uprising of blacks since the sixties.

What was even more distracting, though, was the Bush nomination of Clarence Thomas in July 1991 to fill the vacancy on the Supreme Court left by Thurgood Marshall. In many ways, this nomination constructed a stage in the theater of the absurd on which the country could play out its return to a "simpler time." Marshall, architect of the NAACP's legal challenge that resulted in the 1954 Supreme Court decision in *Brown*, the last liberal voice on the Court, now eighty-two years old, would be replaced by another black man. Yet it would be this black man who would put an end to what was left of the civil rights gains Marshall had been able to force through the Court, purchased with black blood.

After the smoke cleared on the Anita Hill controversy and Thomas was confirmed, what was clear to everyone was that the Supreme Court of the United States was not the pinnacle of an impartial and independent judicial system. It was another arm of the men in power, as it always had been. What was new was that now a black man could do for a white man what a white man had always done for himself. That is, now a black man, Clarence Thomas, had become part of the powerful tide of Supreme Court decisions that would sweep blacks back, back toward the days of *Plessy v. Ferguson*.

In that year, 1991, Little B came to live in a crack house in Atlanta, sometimes called Black Mecca. He was not yet ten years old.

IV
NEW AGE RACISM

[11] Marching from Monticello

The symbolism seemed lost in the celebrations on Pennsylvania Avenue, or it was overshadowed by the bright azure of inaugural day and the
apparent changing of the guard, from the old to the new.

On January 17, 1993, three days before that day he was officially
sworn in as the forty-second president of the United States, William Jefferson Clinton launched his first term in office in the same manner as
had Thomas Jefferson in 1801. Indeed, it began at Monticello. After rev-
erently touring the mansion, Clinton stopped in Jefferson's private study
to comment to his entourage on how particularly honored he felt to be
assuming office in the year that marked the 250th anniversary of Jefferson's birth. Reviewing the study, he explained why he wanted to "begin
at Monticello." Like Jefferson, Clinton said, he "believe[d] in the power
of the ideas which [had] made this country great." Then, like Jefferson,
Clinton led a caravan—of chartered buses, as opposed to horse-drawn
carriages—over the exact 121-mile route Jefferson had taken from his
beloved Monticello, in Virginia, up to Washington, D.C., for his inauguration.[1]

This presidential tradition of Jefferson had been lost in time until
that moment. Clinton was resurrecting it. Following in the footsteps of
his hero and professed namesake, he was symbolically singing America.
The black poet Maya Angelou would celebrate this auspicious occasion
in her inaugural day poem as a kind of new "morning in America."[2] But
for the black vote, more than 80 percent of which was cast for Clinton,
George Bush would have won the presidency again.[3] Indeed, as Clinton
became one of only 16 presidents in the history of the country up until

that time to have been elected with less than 50 percent of the popular vote, Clinton's election turned on the black vote.[4]

It was not simply that he was a Democrat. It was not even the vigor with which he pursued the black vote. It was certainly not his well-promoted, sensitive sixties style and image—which would inspire a number of black personalities to actually refer to him as America's "first black president." For many blacks, Clinton seemed to hold out new hope. Primarily, though, Clinton would be, more than anything, *Not Bush.*

He would *not* be simultaneously insulting and setting blacks back with Clarence Thomas appointments. He would *not* be holding forth the Reagan-Bush Welfare Queen to justify eliminating the government's meager handouts to the poor, especially the black and poor, especially women and children. He would *not* be raising up Willie Hortons to solicit support for passage of so-called tougher crime laws, aimed at erasing the young black male population. He would *not* be a friend to Panamanian dictators-cum-drug traffickers to maintain the deal that had been flooding the black communities of America with more cheap cocaine than all the heroin the Mafia had ever dreamed of floating in the ghettos of another time. He would *not* oppose health care plans that might finally afford black and poor people access to the available antidotes to the diseases of poverty. He would *not* support public school cutbacks and private-school tax breaks for the rich, worsening the country's failing public school systems, particularly those in inner cities, where most students were black and poor. He would *not* support the end of affirmative action in employment or higher education. He would *not* tax black and other poor people to death in order to infinitely increase the so-called defense budget, so as to provide "subsidies" to the big corporations of the postindustrial military-technological complex. He would *not* allow these same subsidies to be used to "downsize" black and other poor working people into the oblivion of unemployability, while developing international markets through the exploitation of other people of color in the Third World. He would *not* be protecting the oil and other business interests of U.S. corporations by invading underdeveloped countries, particularly in the African diaspora, using an army of black cannon fodder to do so.

Clinton may not have been some great white champion come to res-

cue the suffering black mass from centuries of oppression. He was, however, *Not Bush*. He had indeed promised he was *Not Bush*. Thus blacks
overwhelmed the voting places of America in record numbers, in the
largest black voter turnout since the sixties, to use the ballot, for which
so much blood had been shed, to vote for William Jefferson Clinton.

As inaugural day approached, it seemed black people were even
slated to be center stage in the Clinton administration. Among the new
presidential best friends were one-time civil rights activists Vernon Jordan and Ron Brown. Maya Angelou would be the first poet to read at a
presidential inauguration since Robert Frost did so at Kennedy's inauguration. Bill Cosby was organizing an all-star jazz band to play for the
president at one of the inaugural balls. The Queen of Soul and other
soul-stirring blacks would entertain at others. A new man was coming
to live in the White House, a man whose very presence seemed to signal
a new day for blacks. Then the president-elect baptized his new administration at Monticello, where Thomas Jefferson lay resting in peace, carried even to his grave by his slaves.

The black celebrations of Clinton's inauguration obscured this symbolism, however, and all its dark ironies. Indeed, soon, this symbolism
revealed a sinister similitude, and something else, something that came
not merely with Clinton's march from Monticello, or with the White
House dinner celebration of Jefferson's birthday, which Clinton hosted
for other Jeffersonians.[5]

It was not long before William Jefferson Clinton began to show himself not only to have never been "Not Bush," but to be more-than-Bush,
worse-than-Bush, even a pretender to the mantle of Jefferson, a New
Age Jefferson, a racist charlatan who would sell bane to blacks as balm
for centuries of wounds.

━━━━━━━━━

Even after eight years in office, Clinton, like Jefferson in his waning
years, continued to feign confusion over the fact that the American institution of slavery, as the source of America's deep-seated racism, was
also the source of the miserable social conditions under which the black
masses continued to suffer. For eight years, he vacillated on addressing the failure of school desegregation efforts and the dismantling of affirmative action programs. He hoped that race discrimination might, in

time, resolve itself. For eight years, he repelled requests, even by his black friends, to deliver a presidential apology for slavery, ultimately proclaiming that "the question of race is, in the end, still an affair of the heart."[6] Instead he set up a paper Presidential Advisory Board to "study" and have "dialogue" about race "relations."[7] He repudiated even the legitimacy of making any official gesture of atonement to blacks for the crime of slavery and its unrelenting ramifications, arguing that a White House apology would encourage demands for reparations and that time had rendered the question of reparations to blacks for slavery moot: "It's been so long, and we're so many generations removed."[8]

Within less than a year of assuming the presidency, Clinton began to lay the foundation for the rise of a new kind of racism in America, a kinder, more palatable racism, which was effectively a recasting of the Jeffersonian justification for slavery. As Jefferson had reasoned that the Roman slave could rise out of slavery on account of his "whiteness" whereas the black was doomed to slavery because of his inherent inferiority to whites, Clinton now promulgated the idea that the fault for the continuum of black misery lay not in the scheme of things in America but in some flaw in blacks themselves, filtering this recast racism through the crystals of New Age rhetoric relating to the power of introspection and self-healing.

In an insightful analytical piece, published in the January 25, 1993, issue of *Newsweek,* writer Howard Fineman captured this unique side of Clinton, stating, "America gets a New Age president this week." Fineman observed that while Clinton's favorite book was *Gone with the Wind* (his copy "bound in leather in his library") Clinton could "speak in the rhythms and rhetoric of pop psychology and self-actualization . . . [and] from time to time in the lingo of 'centering' the personality and 'channeling' creative personal energy."[9]

In his November 13, 1993, speech in Memphis, Tennessee, Clinton set forth in full his New Age Racist doctrine. Standing in the very pulpit of the Church of God in Christ where Dr. Martin Luther King Jr. had delivered his last sermon, Clinton audaciously admonished the blacks there, and across the nation, for creating the deplorable state of black America.

Beginning with what could be said to be paternalistic pleasantries, Clinton thanked the black congregation and praised the meal prepared for him by one of the church stalwarts: "Now, if you haven't had Bishop Lindsey's barbecue, you haven't had barbecue." Moving to the meat and potatoes of his message to the blacks, he first acknowledged the significance of the black vote, stating, "By the grace of God and your help, last year I was elected president of this great country." Then he announced how he had reciprocated for all that: "There are five African-Americans in the cabinet of the United States, $2\frac{1}{2}$ times as many as have ever served in the history of this great land." [10] His relationship to the blacks thus established, Clinton outlined his agenda for blacks, founded on the philosophy that he could not help those who would not help themselves.

Invoking the name of Dr. King, Clinton began to hammer home this message: "Unless we do something about crime and violence and drugs that is [sic] ravaging the community, we will not be able to repair this country." With unabashed hubris, Clinton spoke for Dr. King: "If Martin Luther King . . . were to reappear by my side today and give us a report card on the last 25 years, what would he say?" As though issuing such a report, Clinton dared to say, assuming the very voice of Dr. King, "He would say: 'I did not live and die to see the [black] American family destroyed. I did not live and die to see 13-year-old [black] boys get automatic weapons and gun down nine-year olds just for the kick of it. I did not live and die to see young [black] people destroy their own lives with drugs and then build fortunes destroying the lives of others. . . . I fought for freedom . . . but not for the freedom of [black] people to kill each other with reckless abandon . . . not for the freedom of [black] children to have children and the fathers of the children to walk away. . . . I did not fight for black people to murder other black people.' " [11] Then, mimicking the dramatic final flourish of a black Baptist preacher, and with astonishing arrogance, Clinton demanded the blacks take a pledge to "honor the life and the work of Martin Luther King" as defined.

Thus Clinton introduced a theme for the whole country to adopt, tenets of a New Age Racism that would come to be established over the next eight years of his presidency, not only in the national culture but in presidential policies that would slam shut the last legal doors of opportunity to blacks in America. There, in Memphis, Clinton denied history and reality and assailed blacks for wasting their "freedom": "How could we explain [to Martin Luther King] that we gave people the freedom to succeed, and . . . millions abuse that freedom [by destroying] the things that make life worth living and life itself?"[12] He chastised blacks for responding to this unseen freedom with incivility, stepping on elusive opportunity and fostering black misery, for fathering the "breakdown" of the black family, harboring the monster of "black-on-black" crime, permitting the promiscuity that had led to so many unwed teen mothers. This was the black affliction, which could be remedied only through acknowledgment of the problem and development of *self-healing* changes in blacks themselves, not by government or social programs.

There in Memphis, Clinton condemned blacks for being unable to overcome the thousand blows dealt during centuries of slavery. In Memphis, Clinton reprimanded blacks for being unable to overcome a postemancipation America that spawned and nurtured the scourge of the Black Codes, the atrocities of the Ku Klux Klan, the strangulation of Jim Crow, and a long train of racist abuses that had sent blacks running from South to North and back again, outnumbered and outgunned in a thousand bloody struggles, including that in which Dr. King himself had been brutally assassinated.

——————

The Clinton era began with the breach of his preelection promise to institute a national health program slated to serve the underserved, particularly poor blacks. The health care system in the United States remained the same for the duration of his presidency, the most expensive in the world, one under which black and other poor people live and often die according to their ability to pay.[13] At the end of the Clinton era, 35 million people, over 10 million of them children, were still without health insurance, and therefore without access to medical care.[14]

Within a year of his election, though, Clinton made his first real strike against blacks: his "Three Strikes" crime bill, providing for life imprisonment for a third criminal conviction, including for minor parole violations and drug addiction. This was tragically brought to light by the grandfather of Polly Klaas, the California girl snatched from her bedroom and violently murdered by a convicted kidnapper out on parole, whose family had supported the Clinton "Three Strikes" crime bill, as Clinton had invoked the name of Polly Klaas in vehemently arguing for it: "When they sought our votes, the sponsors of three-strikes promised the public that their bill would remove dangerous criminals from our streets. Today [five years later], only a fraction of those serving 25-life sentences fit that profile, while a staggering 78% of second-strikers and 50% of third strikers were convicted for nonviolent offenses." [15] This led to the explosion in America's prison population to over 2 million by the end of the millennium, 1 million of whom, by 1998, were incarcerated for nonviolent crimes, and a highly disproportionate number of whom were black males, particularly young black males.[16] Indeed, under Clinton, more people were imprisoned than under the Bush and Reagan administrations *combined.*[17]

Clinton's crime bill not only increased the number of blacks in prison but also inspired a booming new industry. His 1994 crime bill's allocation of $9.7 billion for prison construction was deemed "very favorable" to private prison operators and other business executives, as it provided for the establishment of what the *Wall Street Journal* identified as America's new "prison-industrial complex." The ever-increasing incarceration rate of blacks created a wellspring of profits for businesses, private companies and investors, unlocking the floodgates to billions of federal and state government dollars to construct and operate private prisons to accommodate this burgeoning population. Other profits were realized in the manufacture of products and delivery of services utilized in prison construction and operations, in the purchase of products and services needed in prisons, in the sale of products and services to prisoners, in the exploitation of cheap prisoner labor to manufacture goods and provide services sold to the general public. This new industry soon held a significant place in the trade on the stock exchange. By 1996, as Clinton began a second term, America was opening around three new prisons per week.[18]

In addition, Clinton shelled out even more millions of tax dollars to enlarge local police departments, despite the fact that a highly respected urban policy organization like the Milton S. Eisenhower Foundation determined that such an increase would be ineffectual in reducing crime. Ultimately the foundation, created as an outgrowth of the 1960s Kerner Commission to continue the study of the causes of crime and violence in the inner cities, originally headed by President Dwight D. Eisenhower's brother, came to issue a scathing commentary on the entire "get-tough" crime agenda that would become a legacy of the Clinton era, an agenda that resulted in increased police arrests of nonviolent offenders and "racial profiling," in harsh mandatory sentences and soaring rates of incarceration, particularly of young black males, as a means to reduce crime or address its underlying causes:

> It is immoral for the states to spend more on prison building than on higher education. It is immoral for white corporations in the prison-industrial complex to profit from incarcerating minorities sentenced with racially biased drug laws. It is immoral for the rate of incarceration of African-American men in America today to be four times higher than the rate of incarceration of Black men in pre-Mandela, apartheid South Africa.[19]

"Lewis!" the white CERT guard shouted at Michael, appearing as though from thin air, combat boots pounding the linoleum floor of the visiting room as he marched, exceptionally tall and well built, marched over to where we were sitting, alongside the vending machines, filled with candy and potato chips and the remaining sausage and biscuit sandwiches Michael liked and microwave popcorn and sodas. The guard gestured with his finger. Everyone was startled, except Michael. He followed the guard to the restroom used by inmates, the door of which was visible from nearly all angles in the spacious visiting room. The time was interminable.

The other ladies looked, the black mothers nearby, mumbling, not daring more, watching their sons, watching the restroom door. One told me she could see the guard's hands patting, feeling. She could not see Michael, naked now.

Had I seen the slave auction block? Was the auctioneer's call, "look at 'im now, young and strong, turn around now, make a fine field hand, what am I bid," familiar, really? It was a nightmare recollection that swelling tears could not wash away. I was dizzied by time.

He emerged and walked down the few steps from the restroom to our space, determined steps, not fearful.

"What happened?" I asked breathless, as if it were a reasonable question.

"Aw, he just said he had to do it. Said the female guard at the entrance thought I had taken some quarters from you," speaking of his touching the plastic sandwich bag in which money for the vending machines was transported inside.

The vision of him being searched, strip-searched, spread-eagle, young, tender nudity violated by unauthorized hands, overcame me. The tears came.

"Say! Come on, now. Don't do that. I can handle this."

_____

While the prison ranks swelled, in eight years, Clinton was silent about the irrefutable nexus between the startling rise in black crime figures and the flooding of black communities with crack cocaine that began in the Reagan era. Despite the DEA's post-Noriega assessment that drug trafficking through Panama, for example, had increased, in 1994 the Clinton administration announced that the new drug policy was to "scrap" *all* efforts to stop the flow of narcotics into the United States, since that program had been "unsuccessful." This announcement was made by Timothy E. Wirth, whom Clinton had appointed to head the newly funded global affairs unit of the State Department, nicknamed "the G Group," a subdivision of which was a bureau named International Narcotics Matters. Wirth, named Undersecretary of State for Global Affairs, went on to say, "We have to be realistic about the fact that we're going to have cocaine and heroin on the streets of the United States." Thus, Wirth continued, the Clinton administration policy was, as it remained from that point forward, to "concentrate on eradicating drug-yielding crops" and "discouraging drug use," a policy, in effect, of benign neglect.[20]

Similarly, even though Clinton had identified himself as the education president, in eight years he did nearly nothing to address the question of the failure of public education in general and the disastrous effect it had had on black children in particular. This nothing included encouraging passage of the Goals 2000 Educate America Act in 1994, promoted to set "world-class education standards."[21] This had, in fact, been a Bush plan to fund certain academic achievement goals while avoiding funding improvements to poor schools or supporting school desegregation. While Clinton augmented the original plan with funding for programs that made schools "safer," the funding for its meager education goals was so questionable that it prompted New York senator Patrick Moynihan to ask, "Are we in fact legislating an official lie?" [22] In any case, with respect to improving the educational opportunities for ghettoized black children, the National Urban League deemed such goal-setting as setting up "an unconscionable trap between lofty standards and lousy schools." [23] This nothing also included authorizing the Department of Education to cut off federal funds to schools that did not adopt the policy of expelling students charged with bringing guns to school. [24] In running for reelection, however, Clinton proposed a fifteen-hundred-dollar college tuition tax credit for students who maintained a B average. [25] At the same time, the Perkins loan program for poor college students was being cut, along with the overall education budget. [26] Under Clinton, education as a share of the gross domestic product came to be 40 percent less than it had been during the 1970s. [27]

In the end, while Clinton promoted the mandatory training of schoolchildren on the Internet as a priority education goal, he did nothing at all with respect to improving educational opportunities for black and other poor children in America. [28] The Children's Defense Fund would conclude, "Equal educational opportunity is a myth in millennial America. The richest school districts spend 56 percent more per student than do the poorest." [29] Moreover, Head Start programs served only one in three eligible children. The states continued to spend more on prisons than on schools. And by the end of the millennium, as black children became more and more isolated in impoverished school districts, the Eisenhower Foundation would report that "government [had] abandoned the policy goal of school desegregation." [30]

What William Jefferson Clinton did achieve with respect to black and other poor children was to cut off their lifelines to food and medical care by bringing about the "end of welfare as we know it." Trading on his accusations of the "crime" of the "breakdown" of the black family and the "sins" of unwed teen mothers, he argued, "To strengthen the family we must do everything we can to keep the teen pregnancy rate going down." Now criminalizing the poverty of black mothers and their children, he threatened them in his 1996 State of the Union address: "The era of big government is over." Promising to end welfare by the end of the year, he stated, "For too long our welfare system has undermined the values of family and work"; then, with incredible sardonicism, "I challenge people on welfare to make the most of this opportunity for independence." [31] Having inculcated the themes of his Memphis speech, by which he had effectively resurrected the popular image of Ronald Reagan's Welfare Queen, that lazy trifling black woman either having babies or "cheating the system" to obtain a welfare check, Clinton successfully led a campaign to end sixty years of government assistance to poor women and their children with the 1996 passage of the Personal Responsibility and Work Opportunity Reconciliation Act.

The era of big government may have ended for poor black women and their children, but not for rich corporations and their executives. Clinton successfully spearheaded the most comprehensive trade agreement in history under the General Agreement on Tariffs and Trade (GATT) accord, and pushed through the North American Free Trade Agreement (NAFTA), which effectively paved the way for black and other poor working people in the United States to be replaced by the cheap labor of starving people in the Third World and Eastern Europe. [32]

Sensing criticism, Clinton decided to formally address the miserable status of the black masses by organizing a spectacular of stars, including George Bush in a starring role, in Philadelphia in April 1997. A cavalcade of such political and entertainment greats converged on the city to launch an illusory program that made a mockery of black poverty. Referred to as the President's Volunteer Summit for the Future, the program was an idea of late Republican governor of Michigan George W. Romney, and it was to be headed by Gulf War general Colin Powell. Not a program at all, it was a star-studded stroll through the ghettos of Philadelphia, the point of which was to inaugurate the final abdication of any duty on the part of government to resolve the problems of poor blacks, which Powell stated was "beside the point of the three-day summit." [33] That responsibility was now to be tossed to the winds of the nebulous universe of volunteerism.

Essentially, William Jefferson Clinton did nothing to elevate the economic status of blacks and other poor people in America. In fact, the Clinton era was in many ways more detrimental to blacks than the Reagan and Bush years had been. The June 1996 U.S. Census Bureau report showed that the gap between the richest 20 percent of Americans and the rest of the population had become *wider* than at any time since

World War II. In fact, the income gap in America had grown *faster* during the first two years of the Clinton administration than in all eight years of Ronald Reagan's presidency.[34] At the same time, the median family income for whites remained double of that for blacks, while the black poverty rate remained double of that for whites. Regarding this ongoing disparity, the National Urban League stated, "The origins of the racial wealth gap are found in the long-term effects of slavery and Jim Crow practices in the U.S. South, which impeded black acquisition of property." [35]

Although the "Republican Revolution" of 1994, arriving on the heels of Clinton's assumption of the presidency, was widely considered a reactionary thrust to undermine and overcome the Clinton agenda, it was Clinton himself who accommodated the Republicans. In the vanguard of this Right revolution was Georgia congressman Newt Gingrich, who, despite using student deferment to avoid service in the Vietnam War, was a "hawk" who had been a strong supporter of Reagan's "Star Wars" defense budget increases and of massive aid to the contras.[36] After his first election to Congress, representing that district in Georgia that included Atlanta's Hartsfield Airport, Gingrich showed himself to be more Right than Reagan. Indeed, at the 1984 Republican convention, Gingrich led a move to have a platform adopted that was considered more "conservative" than the one proposed by Reagan himself. By then, Gingrich was also promising to lead a Republican charge to "win back" the majority in Congress. Though he became House minority whip in 1989, during the Bush presidency, Gingrich was able to find the success he had been seeking only under Clinton.

History has documented that whatever differences may have existed between Clinton and Gingrich, they were superficial, stylistic perhaps. Substantively the two operated in tandem in a world in which racism was deemed dead so that any lingering manifestations of it, such as unrelenting and overwhelming black poverty, could be said to represent failures in blacks: the breakdown of black families, black crime, unwed black mothers. As former Clinton secretary of labor Robert Reich, considered one of the most liberal members of the Clinton White House, would come to acknowledge: "The point of least resistance was to move toward the way Newt Gingrich looked at the world." [37]

There was, in fact, no resistance. In September 1994, Gingrich had orchestrated a flag-waving rally on the grounds of the Capitol building in Washington of over three hundred Republican candidates for House seats in the coming November elections. There Gingrich and the majority white candidates announced their execution of a "Republican Contract with America." Days before, the minority leader of the Senate, Bob Dole, along with Senator Phil Gramm, had conducted a similar, smaller rally on Capitol grounds of Republican challengers to incumbent Democrats in the Senate, endorsing a similar plan. Together, they pledged to introduce, within the first one hundred days of the 104th Congress, a ten-point platform of proposed laws to accomplish goals that would effectively legislate blacks back to the era before the 1964 civil rights bill, back even before *Brown v. Board of Education.*

As a result of that election, Bob Dole became Senate majority leader and Gingrich became Speaker of the House, having secured majority status for the Republicans in Congress, which was the first time in forty years. Finding a place of comfort for the Republican agenda under Clinton, within one hundred days of their takeover, Gingrich and his Republicans would force nine of their ten manifesto proposals through the House of Representatives.[38]

Most of their proposed legislation would be enacted, supported, and shepherded into law by Bill Clinton. Politically preemptively, as it were, Clinton had already signed his 1994 "Three Strikes" crime bill, which was the full expression of the "Contract's" proposal no. 2., "The Taking Back Our Streets Act." The Contract's proposal no. 3, "The Personal Responsibility Act" would become Clinton's 1996 Welfare Reform Bill: "The Personal Responsibility and Work Opportunity Reconciliation Act." Not insignificantly, fulfillment of the Contract's proposal no. 1, "The Fiscal Responsibility Act" to balance the national budget, became the primary legacy Clinton would claim for himself. Moreover, proposal no. 6, "The National Security Restoration Act," to restore "the essential parts of [the country's] national security *funding,*" which called for a $60 billion increase in defense spending, was executed by Clinton in 1999, the first defense department budget increase since Reagan.[39]

All of this inspired a regressive, reactionary political and social land-scape in the country, inciting a new rush of age-old racism, as repre-sented in the popular culture, where any effort to redress or express concern over racism or black poverty was now openly maligned as "po-litical correctness."

Among those Republicans who rose to power in the Gingrich Revo-lution was Georgia's notorious congressman Bob Barr. Barr, who would go on to become assistant majority whip in the House, had long been closely affiliated with the Christian Coalition, from which he had re-ceived several awards, and, more recently, with the overtly racist Coun-cil of Conservative Citizens.[40] Mississippi's Trent Lott, who became Sen-ate majority leader under Clinton, unabashedly advocated the country's return to embrace the "fundamental principles" of the Confederacy. In 1984, Lott, as a U.S. congressman, stated in an interview in the *Southern Partisan* magazine that "the fundamental principles that Jefferson Davis believ[ed] in [were] very important to people across the country, and they appl[ied] to the Republican Party."[41] Lott, too, was aligned with the Council of Conservative Citizens.

The Council of Conservative Citizens, like the Christian Coalition, might have been viewed as a fringe group of zealots that represented the last gasps of white supremacists in America if it were not so solidly linked, like the coalition, to such powerful politicos as Barr and Lott. Al-though Lott and Barr both denied knowledge of the council's racist te-nets, which include a denunciation of Martin Luther King Jr., referring to him as a "depraved miscreant," and a belief in maintaining "the pu-rity of the white race," both had appeared as keynote speakers at council gatherings. Moreover, Lott's column appeared regularly in the council's newsletter, the *Citizens Informer,* and Lott had once declared that the council stood for "the right principles and the right philosophy."[42]

Interestingly, the council hosted a 1999 stump speech by David Duke, seeking election to the congressional seat vacated by Louisiana representative Robert Livingston, who had succeeded Gingrich as House Speaker until revelations of his extramarital affairs triggered his resignation. Duke, Grand Wizard of the Knights of the Ku Klux Klan in the 1970s, who subsequently had significant plastic surgery performed on his face reportedly to ameliorate his old image, had reemerged as a Republican. The new Duke promised the council gathering that if elected he would become the first person "to stand up openly and proudly to defend the rights of white Christians." [43] Duke, who even criticized George W. Bush as a "renegade Republican," referred to himself as "the best known spokesman for white rights in this country." [44]

In fact, a more powerful spokesman for white rights was the behind-the-scenes architect of the 1994 Republican Revolution, Ralph Reed. Reed, who became head of the Christian Coalition founded by televangelist Pat Robertson, started out as the leader of the College Republicans at the University of Georgia. It was Reed's design, relating particularly to "tough" crime bills and "welfare reform," that Gingrich took to Congress. Reed stated, "You had darn better get used to religious conservatives in the political arena because we are here to stay." [45]

Indeed, Reed was right. While Gingrich himself stepped down in relative ignominy in 1998, the reactionary movement he fostered, with the accommodation of Clinton, remains fully entrenched. In the same year as Gingrich's Republican Revolution, 1994, George W. Bush ousted Democrat Ann Richards to become governor of Texas. Despite a Democratic majority in the Texas legislature, Bush was able to run a government responsible for more executions than any other state, with Houston soon having the distinction of being deemed "the capital of capital punishment." Texas maintained "the largest prison population in the United States," in which blacks came to be imprisoned at seven times the rate of whites, and passed legislation providing for some of the harshest "welfare reform" cutbacks and toughest juvenile crime penalties in the nation. [46] More significantly, in 1999 Ralph Reed became an adviser for Bush's presidential campaign, helping ensure that Bush would get the Christian Coalition's endorsement. [47]

It was Clinton, however, who seized the day from them all. In the very year of the Republican Right mobilization, Clinton usurped their claims of conservative toughness on crime with the passage of his crime bill. This bill was so reactionary that it was denounced by one of Clinton's own primary crime legislation policy makers, deputy attorney general Philip B. Heymann, upon his resignation from the Justice Department. Heymann, a lawyer and professor highly respected in law enforcement circles, announced his opposition to even the key tenet of the Clinton crime bill, stating the "three strikes and you're out" provision was an "empty solution" that would have a "negligible effect on crime" reduction. Heymann further noted that the proposed third-strike lifetime penalty would cost taxpayers between six hundred thousand and seven hundred thousand dollars to incarcerate *each* person so convicted for the years of the rest of his life after fifty, an age at which studies showed criminal activity to be virtually nonexistent.[48] In other words, the only value in supporting such a bill was political expediency.

One of the cornerstones of what was now popularly known as the Clinton Crime Bill was the creation and funding of state "boot camps" for "youthful offenders," a highly disproportionate number of whom would be, of course, black children.[49] The treatment children received in these boot camps was so brutal that the camps were not only denounced by the nation's child advocacy groups as violating the rights of children as defined by the United Nations, but also had to be shut down on the orders of various official agencies, including the U.S. Justice Department itself. In 1998 the entire juvenile justice system in Georgia was indicted by the U.S. Justice Department, which issued the opinion that "the paramilitary boot camp . . . [was] harmful to . . . youths" in Georgia and ordered the state to shut down the camps and completely reform the entire juvenile justice incarceration system on account of "widespread neglect and abuses."[50] This was particularly startling since Georgia's boot camps, funded under the Clinton Crime Bill, had been initiated at the personal urging of Clinton ally Georgia governor Zell Miller.[51] In 2000, boot camps in South Dakota, where children were placed for "offenses" as light as truancy, were placed under investigation by the Justice Department for abuses of children, which included being "handcuffed spread-eagled to beds."[52] These investigations revealed among other things that in 1999 a fourteen-year-old girl in one camp had collapsed and died after being forced to run a grueling course and left lying in the sun. Investigations for similar abuses were simultaneously under way in Delaware, Texas, Illinois, California, Louisiana, Virginia, and Florida.[53] Like Georgia, by the end of 1999 Colorado, North Dakota, and Arizona were forced on account of unchecked abuses to eliminate the camps.[54] In Maryland boot camps, where children were "slapped, punched or knocked to the ground by guards," discovery of abuses led to the ouster of the head of the state's juvenile justice system and an FBI investigation. Lt. Governor Kathleen Kennedy Townsend, in charge of overseeing the state's juvenile justice system, issued a report describing the barbaric treatment of children in the state's boot camps as "an abuse of power and an unconscionable abuse of authority."[55] Significantly, while Clinton had traveled the country encouraging institution of these boot camps as a means of addressing juvenile crime, the boot camps have proved to be completely ineffective as a crime deterrent.[56]

Second, the Clinton Crime Bill provided for life in prison and even the death penalty for certain drug offenses. Moreover, the bill directed the U.S. Sentencing Commission, empowered by Congress to establish sentencing standards, to review and "enhance" the guidelines of the 1988 law relating to mandatory prison sentences for drug use and sales.[57] The mandatory sentences courts were directed to impose, regardless of statutory limits, incorporated into the 1994 crime bill from the 1988 law passed in the height of the Reagan-era crack wars, were harsh. A person convicted of possession of only five grams of crack with the intent to sell it would receive a five-year mandatory prison sentence. Worse, the only drug for which *simple* possession carried a mandatory sentence for a first offense was crack cocaine, which was five years. On the other hand, simple possession of five grams of powder cocaine generally resulted in probation, and for any other drug, a maximum of one year. More egregious was that people convicted of possession of *five hundred* grams of powder cocaine with the intent to distribute it received the same five-year mandatory sentence as for five grams of crack. This meant that the ratio of the quantity of drugs for which a person was sentenced to the five-year mandatory minimum years in prison as between crack and powder cocaine was one hundred to one. By the end of 1994, nearly 85 percent of defendants convicted of crack possession were black, even though two-thirds of crack users were found to be white or Hispanic.[58]

In 1995, as directed by the Clinton Crime Bill, the Sentencing Commission made its recommendation. Seeing the inequity in the sentencing rules for crack and powder cocaine and the disparity in their application, the commission recommended equalizing the quantity ratio for the mandatory sentence. Clinton rejected its recommendation; it was the first time the commission's recommendations had been rejected since its establishment.[59] In 1997 the Sentencing Commission again tried to reduce the disparity, to a compromise of a five-to-one ratio. The Clinton administration overruled that with a ten-to-one ratio. Law enforcement agencies all over the country now continued to target inner cities in a vicious cycle of the disparate application of the law, as courts continued to impose the disparate sentences mandated under the Crime Bill. Thus this part of the Clinton Crime Bill alone, and as replicated in the states, was almost singularly responsible for the phenomenal increase in America's prison population, an increase dominated by hundreds of thousands of drug addicts and users and small-time dealers, disproportionately composed of black men and women. By 1996, 86 percent of federal crack defendants were black, and nearly 75 percent of all state prisoners incarcerated for simple drug possession were black.[60] As the Clinton Crime Bill was adopted by the states, twelve states and the District of Columbia were imprisoning blacks at a rate more than ten times that of whites.[61] In Georgia, adoption of this legislative model resulted not only in an increase in the state's prison population but, in nearly 70 percent of the prison population being black.[62]

One of the main features of the Clinton Crime Bill was, of course, the "Three Strikes and You're Out" section, *requiring* a federal court to sentence a convicted felon to life in prison for a third offense.[63] While the law was touted as able to rid the nation's streets of "career criminals" who habitually committed "violent" crimes, the reality was far different. Under the "Three Strikes" provision, the determination of what offenses would be considered second and third "strikes" to trigger *automatic life imprisonment* was open to broad interpretation, and it has been broadly and selectively interpreted and applied by police, prosecutors, and courts, with demonstrable difference along race lines. It has swept people convicted of a third offense that was neither violent nor predatory in with violent offenders—for whom there was already *no* "early release" under the law. This included third-time drug offenders.[64]

Under the Clinton Crime Bill, and as adopted in state after state, people were sentenced to life in prison for "third strike" convictions, not only for serious crimes but also for nonviolent crimes such as burglary or petty theft, for selling ten dollars' worth of crack, for writing bad checks, and, in one notorious case, for stealing three steaks.[65] One of the most infamously iniquitous examples of the abuses arising from this section of the Clinton Crime Bill, as adopted, came in the 1995 California case of a black man, previously convicted for robbery and drug possession, who was sentenced to life in prison for snatching a single slice of

pizza from people eating lunch along a pier, a petty theft deemed a felony only because of his record. Two years later, on account of national
and even international protests, a judge found a legal technicality enabling him to reduce the "third strike" sentence of life in prison to four
years in prison.[66] In its adoption of this federal legislative model, Georgia, under the leadership of Democratic governor Zell Miller, became a
"two strike" state.

Finally, the Clinton Crime Bill introduced the nation to the dismantling of the country's one-hundred-year-old juvenile justice system, undermining the very principles on which it was founded.[67] The primary
theory guiding the creation and maintenance of the country's juvenile
justice system, in which children would not be held to the same standard as adults, was that an irresponsible or criminal act of a child was
attributable to the failure of adults—parents or others—to properly educate and guide the child. Thus the system was founded on the ideal that
at that point, society or the state would remove the child from the parent and assume the role of *parens patriae,* to correct—and protect—the
child.[68] The second great principle guiding the system was that a child
was deemed more likely than an adult to be able to be rehabilitated, and
that rehabilitation, not merely punishment, was a goal. Under this system, as under every other definition in international law, a "child" was
a person under eighteen years of age. Indeed, this definition of a child is
widely applied in the United States. Outside of the new crime legislation,
children under eighteen years old—and in many cases people under
twenty-one years old—cannot, except in extraordinary circumstances,
vote, work, buy alcohol or cigarettes, or enter into legal contracts, and
those under sixteen cannot drive or join the armed forces. Children thirteen and fourteen years old have almost *no relationship under the law
equal to adults,* except, now, to be tried in criminal courts as adults.

The 1994 Clinton Crime Bill, however, provided for adult prosecutions of children young as thirteen years old for certain violent crimes,
for certain drug offenses, and for membership in street gangs. While the
1994 law did not require *automatic* adjudication of children as adults, it
provided for discretion by courts, upon review of each case, to do so.[69]
The important thing this federal law did was to provide a model for
states. In 1998 Clinton further encouraged state replication of this law by
making relevant federal grants to states contingent on states permitting

prosecution of children as adults.[70] Georgia's governor Zell Miller, a strong Clinton ally, immediately followed through, however, with sponsorship of Georgia's notorious S.B. 440 law, also passed in 1994. As Miller had brokered a move further to the right of the federal law with respect to "three strikes," making Georgia a "two strikes" state, he vigorously promoted passage of a juvenile crime bill that was harsher than the federal model. Under the Georgia juvenile crime law Miller maneuvered through the legislature, judicial discretion to review each case for prosecution as an adult was abandoned in favor of discretion of prosecutors *not* to prosecute children as adults. This opened the floodgates to the prosecution of children in the state. It was under this law that over 94 percent of the children prosecuted in the Atlanta counties of Fulton and DeKalb have been black boys and girls.[71] This would soon include Little B.

=====

The Personal Responsibility and Work Opportunity Reconciliation Act of 1996, which Clinton pushed through and signed into law, cut off federal assistance to poor families, a program that had been in place for sixty years. Upon signing the Act, Clinton announced he had finally done what he had promised: "Today we are ending welfare as we know it."[72] The target of this bill was the primary program of "welfare," Aid to Families with Dependent Children (AFDC), most of whose recipients were poor, disproportionately black, single mothers and their children. At the time, there were 4 million single mothers on the program, and, it was noted, half were unmarried.[73] AFDC assistance was ended by the act. For the time being, transitional aid was to be provided by funding to states under a federal granting plan called Temporary Assistance for Needy Families (TANF). TANF, replacing not only AFDC but also Emergency Assistance to Families with Children and JOBS (a welfare job-training program), mandated that poor mothers get a job within two years or lose all government assistance to them and their children. While the budget for food stamps was not cut to families with children, entitlement to food stamps was "tightened," effectively cutting the average benefit, according to studies, from eighty to sixty-five cents per person per meal.[74] At the same time, the act reallocated the money that had assisted poor women on welfare to private employers as "incentives" to hire them.[75] Precisely as the "Republican Contract" had promised, Clinton's act was projected to "save" $60 billion in government spending, over six years, mostly coming from cuts in food stamps.[76]

As TANF was implemented in Georgia, it completely ended entitlement to benefits to the 124,000 families receiving assistance and created instead, in the spirit of the act, a "temporary" cash assistance program called Georgia Temporary Support Grants. This limited the *lifetime* benefits mothers and their children could receive to four years—even lower than the limit under the federal statute, which was five years. Moreover, no additional benefits payments would be made for a child born within ten months of an application for welfare. At the same time, Georgia allocated over $5 million of its federal grant to make state grants to organizations with programs designed to reduce teen pregnancy and, particularly, unmarried teen pregnancies.[77]

Finally, the Georgia law required eligible recipients to sign "personal responsibility and work participation agreements," immediately cutting benefits 25 percent for the "first violation" of such agreements. Such violations included failure to attend a parent-teacher conference, failure to attend family planning sessions, nonparticipation in substance abuse treatment, quitting a job, and failure to cooperate with child support enforcement efforts, typically for collection of money from missing or absent fathers. In addition, benefits could be reduced for mothers whose children dropped out of school and teens who left school or did not receive passing grades. All assistance would be cut forever for a second violation of the agreements, under a "two strikes and you're off" provision.[78]

Nationwide, by 1999, many thousands of women and children and other poor people had been tossed into a hopeless poverty by Clinton's welfare reform because of violations of draconian rules. In Kentucky, for example, 58 percent of people receiving benefits were cut off on account of rules violations. In California and Illinois, almost half of those eligible were removed as a punishment. In Iowa, 47 percent were penalized for violations by being disqualified for assistance.[79] Moreover, by then nearly seven hundred thousand mothers and children and other former recipients who had found jobs had lost health insurance for their families, adding to the nearly 40 million Americans who were uninsured.[80] And the poorest families, including those who found work and relinquished welfare, were driven deeper into poverty.[81]

It was a new day in America. California's then-governor Pete Wilson, in announcing his early support of the Clinton welfare reform plan and promoting its adoption in California in his second inaugural address in 1995, spoke with an unleashed vitriol against poor—especially black—women:

> We must choose whether California will be the Golden State—or a welfare state. . . . We will demand that all citizens . . . pull their own weight and meet the test of personal responsibility. We will make it clear that welfare is a safety net not a hammock. . . . We will correct our laws to make clear that . . . the costs are simply too high for society to continue tolerating the promiscuity and irresponsibility that have produced generations of unwed teen mothers. . . . We will insist that those who receive public assistance earn it . . . vowing to keep faith with California's favorite son Ronald Reagan's vision for America.[82]

An even more vicious voice was raised in New York City by Mayor Rudolph Giuliani, elected the same year Clinton took office, 1993. In New York City, one in every seven residents had been poor enough to qualify for welfare.[83] As the spirit of Clinton's welfare reform spread to New York, Giuliani promised to "end welfare by the end of this century completely." Toward this end, by 1998 he had created the nation's largest "workfare" force, under which he commanded over thirty thousand poor New Yorkers, including *disabled* mothers, to work for their welfare checks, for well below the minimum wage, cleaning city streets and parks. By then he had cut more than four hundred thousand women and children from the welfare rolls. Giuliani came to consider this program to be "a cornerstone of his legacy," which he deemed "much more significant than the reduction in crime" for which he was so notorious.[84]

═══════════

While the Clinton bill had "ended welfare as we [knew] it," cutting off poor mothers and their children from meager assistance payments, the surpluses from welfare cuts increased *"corporate welfare"* as few knew it.[85] This corporate welfare included government subsidies, grants, no-

interest loans, and tax deductions to pay or provide for real estate acqui-
sitions, goods and services, advertising, construction of plants and offices and stores, training of workers, and, in the case of some corporations, as a primary or even sole source of revenue.

The corollary relationship between the cutoff of assistance to poor
women and the increase in corporate subsidization by government is
most striking in the benefits that were bestowed on corporations *on
account* of welfare reform, managing welfare-to-work job training programs, increasing child-support collections, even taking over management of social services casework. According to *Time* magazine, Lehman
Brothers considered this phenomenon a "welfare-management gold
rush" and concluded that the "welfare-management business" had become a "huge revenue target" with a "potential market at more than
$20 billion a year." [86]

Even though Virginia-based Maximus, Inc.'s annual income of $127
million arises solely from "welfare administration work," making it the
largest company specializing in this "work," other, bigger corporations
have profited more. One of the most stunning examples is that of defense
and aerospace giant Lockheed Martin. Its "government services division" soared to become the corporation's fastest-growing sector because of the millions it receives annually from the government to maintain computer programs to track down so-called deadbeat parents of
children slated to be removed from the welfare rolls. [87] In 1998, Citicorp,
the world's largest credit card issuer, rushed to pay $11.5 million to ac-
quire Gtech Holdings Corporation's state contracts for Electronic Benefits Transfers, under which plastic electronic cards were used to distribute food stamps and monthly cash benefits allowances. This acquisition
was carried out with Citicorp's expectation of realizing millions more
government dollars in profits via payments for each food stamp card
issued, each cash benefit check processed, and each cash withdrawal
from ATMs. [88] EDS, in 1998 alone, received a $45 million grant to com-
puterize the state of Virginia's Medicaid system. [89]

More significant, however, is the fact that, between 1992 and 1998,
40 percent of the *$5 billion* federal endowment to the Export-Import
Bank of the United States intended to support "companies that sell
goods abroad" went to only five "beneficiaries": AT&T, Bechtel, Boeing, McDonell Douglas (which merged into Boeing), and General Elec-

tric. Boeing was the largest beneficiary, receiving $11 billion in bank guarantees for worldwide aircraft sales financing. All these corporations received many millions of government dollars through the bank under the theory that they would create more jobs for Americans through a buildup of global sales. However, while General Electric, for example, with 1997 profits at $8.2 billion, continued to receive bank funds as well as other federal "corporate welfare benefits" in the form of export subsidies and loan guarantees, in eleven years, it eliminated more than 120,000 jobs. Overall employment among these five corporations dropped 38 percent. According to a 1998 investigative report by *Philadelphia Inquirer* journalists Donald L. Barlett and James B. Steele, published in *Time* magazine, the federal government "shells out $125 billion a year in corporate welfare." [90]

At the local level, Barlett and Steele documented any number of examples of corporate welfare, citing, for example, how the state of Illinois gave $240 million in tax dollars to Sears, Roebuck to keep its corporate headquarters and fifty-four hundred jobs there, in which case *each* job had cost taxpayers forty-four thousand dollars. Similarly Indiana gave $451 million to United Airlines for a facility that would employ sixty-three hundred people at seventy-two thousand dollars per job. Barlett and Steele concluded, "*Fortune* 500 companies . . . have erased more jobs than they have created this past decade, and yet they are the biggest beneficiaries of corporate welfare." [91]

At the same time, Clinton courted the African "market" for the benefit of private corporations, with Coca-Cola in the lead and Jesse Jackson in tow. In 1998, Clinton, his wife, Jackson, as Clinton's "special envoy," and various American business executives traveled eleven days on the continent to promote Clinton's African Growth and Opportunities Act, a trade bill—or, as Clinton quipped, trade instead of aid.[92] This trade bill would do more than offer economic opportunity as opposed to charity. It would right wrongs Africa had suffered, Clinton said: America "received the fruits of the slave trade. And we were wrong in that . . . [b]ut perhaps the worst sin America ever committed about Africa was the sin of neglect and ignorance." [93]

The act, strongly supported by the Coca-Cola Company, would set up financial aid to African countries to develop infrastructures and governments to accommodate the prospect of trade with the United States, contingent on certain strict U.S.-imposed and -monitored guidelines. Among those contingencies was agreeing to use any U.S. assistance to establish market-based economic structures, as defined by the International Monetary Fund, to join the World Trade Organization, and to minimize funding public education, health, and transportation. In other words, as author and activist Randall Robinson of the TransAfrica organization identified it, the act, sponsored by Indiana Republican senator Richard Lugar, would place African countries in the untenable position of accepting an investment of so-called trade dollars in exchange for sovereignty.[94]

Those countries that could and would comply would benefit not only with direct funding but also with the lowering or waiving of tariffs and quotas on African-made goods exported into the United States.[95] The most contentious section of the law, though, related to clothing manufacture in Africa, the import of which into the U.S. would be contingent on the use of U.S. raw materials.[96] Strongly supported by Fruit of the Loom, this would open up a new market for American manufacturers while threatening the jobs of the remaining garment workers in the country via exploitation of so much available cheap African labor. More important, as the forty-eight countries of Sub-Sarahan Africa had a total population of 700 million people, these millions of people loomed as a powerful new market that now provided "enormous commercial potential for U.S. exporters."[97] In May 2000, the African Growth and Opportunities Act, incorporated into the Trade and Development Act of 2000, along with the similar U.S.-Caribbean Basin Trade Partnership Act, was signed into law by Clinton, launching what Clinton actually referred to as a "New Africa."[98]

In fact, there was nothing new about this policy toward Africa. It was merely a kind of new-age reflection of the long-established neocolonialist policy of the U.S.-controlled World Bank in its virtual post–World War II domination of Africa. Clinton himself had already sent U.S. armed forces to Somalia to restore order to the country engaged in civil strife in order to protect American oil interests.

Though Major General Muhammad Siyad Barre had established Somalia as a socialist state in 1969 after leading the effort to oust the last European colonialists, in 1980 he signed an agreement with President Jimmy Carter. Carter had promoted and supported Barre's unsuccessful

invasion of the Ogaden desert region controlled by Ethiopia, which Somalia had long claimed. Though driven from the Ogaden by his former
Soviet allies and the Ethiopians, Barre was now an ally of sorts of the
United States, allowing the United States to set up air and naval facilities
along Somalia's significant coastline touching the Gulf of Aden and the
Indian Ocean, as fed by the Arabian Sea, the Gulf of Oman, and significantly, the Persian Gulf.

Barre continued to receive CIA support and U.S. funding under the
Reagan and Bush administrations. During that period, he literally sold
two-thirds of Somalia to four U.S. oil companies: Conoco, Amoco, Chev-
ron, and Phillips. While this report was officially denied, Conoco was
the only major corporation to maintain a headquarters in the Somalian
capital of Mogadishu through the years of warfare conducted by the
U.S., first under Bush's "Operation Restore Hope" and then under Clinton. Moreover, the Conoco Somalia Ltd. offices had become a de facto
American embassy by the time the first U.S. Marines landed under the
Bush invasion in 1992. These oil companies had invested millions of
dollars into the exploration and exploitation of untapped oil deposits
there, based on a 1991 World Bank study.[99] This was, however, before
Barre was ousted and hacked to death by his own people in 1991. After
that, Somalia was on the verge of finding its way—however seemingly
chaotically—to independence and, perhaps, to rejecting the oil companies' claims on most of its land. Bush had intervened to recoup what
losses he could by restoring order, as part of what he referred to the
"New World Order." Clinton, however, established New Age order. After
sending thousands of troops back into Somalia in June 1993 and augmenting that troop presence later on, Clinton brokered deals with the
toughest of the factional leaders, called "warlords" by the CIA. Eventually he was able to withdraw the troops, leaving in place, by 2000, a
"provisional" government led by men educated in the United States and
friendly to U.S. interests.[100]

First, Africans were abducted and exported to America by European
colonialists for slave labor. Centuries later, under the Truman doctrine of
"stopping the spread of communism," the United States returned to Africa to kidnap the continent's bounty of natural resources by setting up
neocolonialist chieftains, like Sese Seko Mobutu in the former "Zaire"
and Barre in Somalia. The "Clinton Doctrine" was to seize on Africa as

a massive new marketplace and cheap labor base for American corporations under the theory that what was good for corporate America was good for Africa.

_____

In this new sociopolitical climate settled by Clinton, the wretched status of the majority of blacks became, at best, completely marginalized, as black oppression under slavery and Jim Crow were recalled as historical footnotes. This was made clear when Clinton appeared in 1997 at the fortieth-anniversary memorial service for the "Little Rock Nine." The Nine were blacks who had, forty years earlier, survived savage racist assaults attempting to integrate Central High School in Little Rock, Arkansas—which was fifty miles from Clinton's own house at the time, in Hot Springs. In that infamous moment, over one thousand federal troops were sent to the school to repel the violence being meted out against the Nine. As to the ongoing school segregation that bore down so hard on black children in ghetto schools, that was being maintained even as he spoke forty years later, even as he acknowledged, with unabashed understatement, that "there [was] still discrimination in America," Clinton offered "reconciliation" in lieu of remedy: "Reconciliation is important, not only for those who practice bigotry, but to those whose resentment of it lingers." He concluded with the insidious suggestion that "the question of race is, in the end, still an affair of the heart." [101]

Earlier that same year Clinton had made it crystal clear that he did not consider it to be "government's role," or his, to redress past wrongs committed against blacks during slavery or post-emancipation. Pressed to speak to this issue by any number of moderate blacks, many of whom considered themselves presidential friends, by his recent creation of the Presidential Advisory Board on Race to promote dialogue on race relations, and by the promotion by several white Congressmen of legislation that would state that "Congress apologizes to African Americans whose ancestors suffered as slaves," Clinton responded. In a CNN radio interview on June 15, 1997, Clinton said, "Just to say that it's wrong and that we're sorry about it is not a bad thing. That doesn't weaken us." [102] However, as to the related question of reparations for slavery, Clinton announced his opposition to the idea, saying, "It's been so long, and we're so many generations removed." [103]

This sentiment was echoed, around the same time, by the chairman of the newly formed Presidential Advisory Board on Race, the venerated black historian John Hope Franklin. Asked in the board's first press briefing whether the president of the United States should "formally apologize for slavery," Franklin replied, "I think every person in the United States ought to recognize the fact that [slavery] was a despicable, terrible act on the part of our founding fathers. . . . Whether it can be subsumed under an apology by anybody, one person, I don't know, I'm not prepared to say." [104] Not much later, however, in August 1997, Clinton clarified the matter. Concerned that an apology would trigger demands for reparations, Clinton announced, through an Associated Press wire release issued by White House spokesman Mike McCurry, that he had "scuttled the idea of a national apology for slavery." [105]

While slavery had received a presidential pardon by Clinton, dismissed as having occurred "too long ago" and "too many generations removed," this question apparently posed no problem for the official recognition and remembrance of slaveholders and slaveholding. By the year 2000, South Carolina was still flying the Confederate flag atop its statehouse, although strong protest had been initiated by the NAACP, which called for a tourist boycott of the state. George W. Bush, as a presidential candidate, took the position that the question was for the state to determine and that the NAACP should "butt out" of the state's business.[106] In July 2000, however, in the wake of the loss of millions of dollars in tourist revenues, the state ceremoniously took down the Confederate battle flag from the top of the statehouse dome, only to fly it thirty feet high in front of the statehouse at the Confederate soldier monument.[107]

In the year 2000, Georgia, too, was still proudly waving its state banner at its statehouse, emblazoned with the "stars and bars" of the Confederacy. As the success of the South Carolina flag controversy spilled over into Georgia, a strong challenge to the flag was renewed. In light of the economic losses to South Carolina, Georgia's governor, Roy Barnes, who as a legislator in 1993 had actually cosponsored an unsuccessful bill to withhold funds from local governments that would not fly the state flag, now championed a compromise with black legislators. In January 2001, the Georgia legislature accepted a new state flag design, one in which the Confederate battle symbol was present but considerably reduced in significance. The state flags of Florida, Mississippi, Alabama, and Arkansas continue to fly strong symbols of the Confederacy, however, while Confederate Memorial Day is officially celebrated throughout the South. In Georgia it is a paid holiday for state workers, on April 26, whereupon the Sons of Confederate Veterans and United Daughters of the Confederacy and the like hold parades and conduct other official memorial ceremonies. And in the year 2000 the state of Georgia allocated $2.36 million tax dollars to purchase and preserve the 505 acres of "the last remaining undisturbed Civil War battlefield," where Confederate soldiers fought the Battle of Resaca against General Sherman, a place deemed by proponents of the preservation to be "the highest priority site in the South." [108]

By 1995, the ideal of affirmative action as a means of remedying past discrimination against blacks was effectively abandoned in America. Under the law, it began to be virtually dismantled by the Supreme Court ruling that year in the Colorado case of *Adarand Constructors Inc. v. Pena,* whereby a white company owner sued because he had lost a government guardrail contract to a Hispanic, given priority consideration under applicable guidelines as "socially disadvantaged." Justice Sandra Day O'Connor, speaking for the majority, stated that the equal protection clause of the Constitution applied to "persons" not "groups," refusing to uphold, thereby, the affirmative action policy that had permitted Pena the contract. Denouncing all distinctions based on race—not, however, on gender—with respect to doing business with the federal government, the Court left open the slim possibility, under the rigorous "strict scrutiny" judicial standard, that some preferential policy might apply where: (1) there was a *compelling* government interest, and (2) where there was an *identifiable* showing by an *individual* of past discrimination. In other words, the Court overturned federal government affirmative action policies.

One irony in this ruling the Court had rendered to accommodate the rising racism in the political mood was that it related to government business, not private business, where racism could continue to run its natural course. Indeed, the Glass Ceiling Commission report of that year documented that among the Fortune 1,000 industrial and 500 companies, 97 percent of senior managers were white, and 95 to 97 percent were male.[109] The other irony was the Court's willingness to rescind what were merely meager opportunities for blacks and other nonwhites, a giant snatching up crumbs from the table.

Some policies, for example, had simply promoted affirmative action, such as that of the Agriculture Department requiring that rural housing grantees be "encouraged to use minority banks." On the other hand, the specified percentages of other programs were typically very small, such as that of a 1991 transportation act requiring that "not less than 10 percent" of contracts go to *small* minority *and* women companies, or the Defense Department's 5 percent goal; only 15 percent of all the affirmative action programs even specified percentages. Moreover, companies that qualified for "set-aside" contracts were not all black or all nonwhite, or even black or nonwhite at all. Under the Small Business Administration rules, which were the model for other federal programs, companies had to be simply 51 percent owned and operated by people classified as "economically disadvantaged"—though equally qualified to do the work. In the end, by 1995 thirty-two of the one hundred highest-ranked black-owned businesses had or were participants in such government programs, indicating how paltry was the black share of business in America and foreshadowing how abysmal that reality would become without affirmative action.[110] About a month after the *Adarand* ruling, Clinton, in what was cast as a "solemn speech" at the National Archives, while stating that the country should "reaffirm the principle of affirmative action," endorsed the Court's ruling. Indeed, earlier in 1995, Clinton had essentially signaled the Court and the country to cast off such an affirmation, declaring, "We shouldn't be defending things that we can't defend." Now, he stated, in acquiescence to the Court's ruling on affirmative action programs, the country should embrace "a simple slogan: mend it, but don't end it." Saying nothing more, proposing nothing more, this activist president, who had personally pushed through passage of his 1994 crime bill, as he would his 1996 welfare reform legislation, simply issued an executive order directing his cabinet to review all programs and conform them to the Court's dictum. He ordered them to immediately reform or eliminate any program that created a quota, or created "preferences," or created "reverse discrimination," or had already satisfied the goal of equal opportunity.[111]

The floodgates were open for the states. In California that same year then-governor Pete Wilson issued his own executive order, by which he abolished as many affirmative action programs relating to state hiring and contracting as his power permitted and eliminated 118 relevant boards and commissions. At the time, of the state's 150,000 regular employees, only 12 percent were black, and, interestingly, by then California no longer had a majority white population. With that order, not only did Wilson become the first governor to cut back affirmative action programs, he also had the distinction of having overturned the affirmative action orders issued by three previous governors, Jerry Brown, George Deukmejian, and Ronald Reagan.[112]

With that, Wilson began to wage a campaign to accomplish the rest of this antiaffirmative agenda not swept up in his order. That campaign was mounted through the state's infamous 1996 ballot initiative Proposition 209, snidely named the California Civil Rights Initiative. The proposition was to ban "preferential treatment" based on race or gender in public employment, public education, and public contracting, applicable to state and local governments, higher education, community colleges, and elementary and secondary schools. Ironically headed by a black businessman, Wilson disciple Ward Connerly, and supported actively by former Klansman David Duke, Proposition 209 passed in the November 1996 election. It paved the way for other states. Similar initiatives were proposed in Washington, Florida, Illinois, Oregon, Colorado, and Nevada.[113]

California had for some time been in the vanguard of the anti–affirmative action movement. The 1978 Supreme Court ruling in *University of California Regents v. Bakke,* while allowing race to be used to diversify a university student body had eliminated the notion of "quotas" to do so and had created the concept of "reverse discrimination." In 1995 Ward Connerly, as a Wilson appointee to the Board of Regents, had led a successful crusade to forbid university officials from employing any "race-based" factors for student admissions. Notwithstanding that there was no prohibition for special admissions for numerous other categories of students, such as for children of alumni and sports, what made this effort so absurd was that at the time only 4 percent of the 162,000 students on the system's nine campuses were black.[114]

This example was soon followed by others. Significant among them was the dismantling of the University of Texas affirmative action admissions program in 1997. Like California's, this effort, too, exposed the depth of racist policies in the country, in that a massive campaign had been conducted to attack the university's admissions programs, resulting in the reduction of the number of blacks students in the undergraduate freshman class from 300 to 150, among 6,500, and in the first-year law school class, from 40 the previous year to only 4, among 488. Likewise, in 1998 the University of California's Boalt Hall Law School in Berkeley, under a similar ban of affirmative action, reduced the law school population of blacks from twenty to one student.[115] And, in July 1999, on a court challenge by a white female student resulting in a complicated judgment, the University of Georgia was compelled to review and "justify" its affirmative action use of race in admissions. As in the other examples, while this challenge was mounted by a white student not academically qualified for automatic admission, it was effectively successful even given that only 6.2 percent of the University of Georgia student population was black.[116]

At the end of the millennium, finally, even the powerful decision in the 1954 case of *Brown v. Board of Education of Topeka* to desegregate America's public schools was reversed. The country had embraced what Harvard professor Gary Orfield, coauthor (with Susan E. Eaton and Elaine R. Jones) of the definitive *Dismantling Desegregation: The Quiet Reversal of Brown v. Board of Education,* has identified as *resegregation.* Worse, at the highest levels, there was no challenge to this shameful reversal. As Orfield pointed out, "Although the Clinton Administration [had] seen the largest increases in segregation in the last half century, it . . . proposed no policies to offset the trend and [did] not include the issue among its priorities for education policy."[117]

This had been effected through a series of Supreme Court decisions, from the 1974 Michigan case of *Milliken v. Bradley,* confining desegregation to cities, to the 1991 *Dowell* case, putting time limits on desegregation programs, to *Freeman v. Pitts,* in 1992, dismantling desegregation plans, to *Missouri v. Jenkins,* in 1995, disallowing even financial improvements to segregated schools to make them "equal" though "separate." As Orfield analyzed, these rulings "freed" school districts of the taint of discrimination, permitting the resurrection of racist segregationist policies. They have allowed white parents to sue to stop efforts to desegregate schools. Indeed, they have actually forbidden school districts, like those in Boston, where so much blood was spilled over busing, to voluntarily desegregate schools.[118]

In a country in which "all the major institutions are controlled by whites," as Orfield has noted, school desegregation is critical for blacks. The irony is that most white children in America attend schools that are mostly white. At the same time, black and other nonwhite students more than likely attend schools that are not only racially segregated but also overwhelmed by deep poverty. Among white school districts, 92 percent are not burdened by such levels of poverty. Still, states have fought tooth and nail, armed by Supreme Court decisions, to resegregate America's schools. Since 1980 all states with significant black enrollment have resegregated, the highest increases having been in Rhode Island, Wisconsin, Florida, Oklahoma, Maryland, Delaware, and Massachusetts. The most segregated states for black children are Michigan, Illinois, and New York. Black students in Connecticut and New Jersey attend highly segregated schools in very poor districts surrounded by wealthy suburban districts. California has become one of the most segregated states in terms of black children, resegregating its schools along with a number of the Old South states of Mississippi, Alabama, Louisiana, and Texas. Even states with few blacks have resegregated, including Minnesota, Arizona, Colorado, and New Mexico, as well as Oregon, with less than 3 percent black students and Washington with less than 5 percent.[119]

In effect, something worse than the overturning of *Brown* has occurred. As to public education, particularly, the country has returned to the "separate but equal" era of *Plessy v. Ferguson.*

———

The era of big government being over, as Clinton promised, there remained nothing to dike the deluge of racism descending on black children seeking education in their crumbling ghetto public schools.

It made Michael's attendance at the dilapidated English Avenue or Capitol View Elementary School or Bunche Middle School as irrelevant as his two-year absence from any school in the Bluff. It reduced the notion of equal opportunity for a boy like him to a Dickensian absurdity.

Imprisoned since thirteen years old, impoverished since birth, Little

B's whole life is a reflection of the racism in America that came full circle in the Clinton era.

One could speculate what Clinton might have said to Little B if he'd ever stood by his side or noticed him, as Clinton imagined what Dr. King might have said to black families assembled in Memphis not so long ago:

"Little B, the era of big government is over for you. If you're in prison, it's not government's fault. If you want to blame somebody other than yourself, blame your mother, a crack addict. Blame your absent father, also a crack addict. Blame your community, rampant with violence, failing in education, refusing to work for a living, depending on welfare and wanting special treatment to get a job.

"The history of black slavery and oppression under Jim Crow and de facto discrimination is sad. But that's over now, and it has nothing to do with why you are where you are. And, anyway, I can't fix all that with a check, not a welfare check or a reparations check. This is not the business of government anymore. You and your people will have to grow up and take responsibility for yourselves.

"So if you, like the millions of black children languishing in the concrete fields of Chocolate City surrounding the White House, or in the projects of Detroit or the West Side of Chicago, or in the streets of New York or New Orleans, or in the shacks of Mississippi, or walking in the gangs of Los Angeles, or selling crack in Oakland have nothing more, this is not the fault of slavery or Jim Crow or government or anything else or anybody else. America offered you the opportunity to make the right choices and you made the wrong ones. Little B, this is your fault!"

[12] The Abandonment

Michael was in the hole, again. It was almost that time of year deemed the most sacred. He would be ineligible for the last Christmas package of the old millennium. This year there would be no books or music cassettes, no candy canes or Gummi Bears, no cashew nuts or cookies, no new underwear or pajamas or socks. It was the end of his second year at Lee Arrendale State Prison, known as Alto. He was sixteen years old now.

It was a black woman who had put him there this time. Michelle Carter was a counselor for the boys there under seventeen years old. The first counselor, two years before, had been a white man who Michael told me called him a "nigger." The counselor had been responsible for his first DR (disciplinary report), for which he had gone to the hole the first time, a case of "insubordination." Now it was Michelle Carter's time.

It was not really "the hole" of the imagination, some dark sensory-deprivation cell. It was an isolation cell, however, where, Michael reported, he stayed all day, a small space of bare furnishings, a toilet and sink, a bed, a shelf, where he was allowed to listen to the radio he had had to buy. This was his twenty-fifth or twenty-sixth time in an isolated cell in the SMU (special management unit). Though he had been classified a "predator" from the beginning—forecast by the disembodied voice that spoke to him on his arrival in the 4:00 A.M. dark of early December 1997, saying, "So you're the little motherfucker that killed that man in front of his kids"—the DRs that had resulted in his being sent to isolation were for nonviolent infractions, usually for "failure to follow" and "insubordination." It was Kafkaesque.

Before the Civil Rights and Black Power movements of the sixties, the last mass effort by blacks for human rights, there would never have been a Michelle Carter at Lee Arrendale State Prison. Affirmative action had opened the doors to this job for Carter, though she did not seem to have an appreciation of this. "I'm just as intelligent as you are," she had told me during that period at the end of the millennium when she cut off my visits to Michael. She did this because of my insubordination to her.

As Michael had not been regularly involved in any type of education program—routine though that was for kids at Alto—I had questioned her about this. She did not like that. Moreover, earlier I had questioned her about Michael's being sent to the hole, as she had been the one who had "written up" that infraction. She had not liked that either. On another occasion she had, impermissibly, intruded on a visit and, running her hand across Michael's head, had advised him to get a haircut. I had not liked that.

Now Carter and the warden's assistant, Donna Wilson, had stripped me of any standing to visit Michael, effectively depriving him of any visits. Other than the sporadic visits he had with his father's mother, Marian Scott, who had limited transportation, I had been Michael's only regular visitor. My visits had been as a "legal investigator" for his appeal, under the auspices of his trial attorney, Patrice Fulcher. It was our scheme to use me—on a volunteer basis—to keep Michael in communication with the world, in the absence of funding for such visits and any real appeal effort being mounted by the Conflict Defender's office, and in the absence of family able and willing to visit. In that "legal" capacity, however, I could not accompany Michael's sister, Ta-Ta, for visits.

At thirteen years old, Ta-Ta could not visit him alone and had to be accompanied by an "authorized adult visitor," which I was not. Shalance Battle could visit, as Michael's "sister-in-law," mother of his brother's children, but she had no car. Shalance had been the only person ever interviewed by the press in all the articles written about Michael who had said something positive about him, who had adamantly refuted the charge that he was a "thug." She was a fireball of energy, with a brown and delicate face, a true wisp of a girl, strong and wildly loving of her children, who possessed a deep sweetness that was in conflict with the veneer of toughness she presented to her boys, though they never seemed to mind her as she commanded them, rapid fire. As a working single mother, however, Shalance could rarely visit. Thus it was necessary to alter my status to "significant other," a status reserved for one or two people who were not family members. Michelle Carter's denial of my new status and thus my right to visit, on grounds that I had "lied" about my "legal" relationship to Michael, would be overcome in time. In the meantime, for this holiday season, she had prevailed, not only in limiting the visiting possibilities for Michael but in sending him back to the hole for the arrival of the new millennium.

From a distance it was hard to see the weight of it all on Ta-Ta's face. She and the girls we took to celebrate her fourteenth birthday that November 1999 all carried bigger burdens than their girlishness seemed capable of. Sometimes it was evident. It was not, however, when they all squeezed into the car with girlish giggles. Their laughter fogged up the car windows; their music blared from the radio. I resigned myself to an afternoon in adolescence. It was not at the Red Lobster restaurant, five girls drinking "virgin" strawberry daiquiris, filled with the hope that lives in the House of Tomorrow, as Khalil Gibran so poetically painted. It burst forth at the Sparkle skating rink, even as Ta-Ta and the girls twirled around the rink to her favorite song, played especially for her birthday, a tender song called "We Can't Be Friends" by Deborah Cox and R.L. from Next, even as the colored lights and eyes of adolescent boys "from the 'hood" sparkled on the girls. Ta-Ta suddenly stopped and fell against the roller rink railing, tears flowing. They gathered around her, this gaggle of brown girls who knew, their rollers skates scraping up the nap of the red carpet that encircled the rink as they escorted her to the sidelines.

"What's the matter, Ta-Ta?" "What is it?" they cried out together, holding her up, bending low with her. "Why're you crying, Ta-Ta?" so softly, sweetly.

"I'm havin' my birthday and my brother can't even be here," she sobbed. There was the collective response of silent commiseration. "I miss my brother!"

If Jefferson's Monticello served as more than a metaphor for Clinton in the White House, because *no fundamental* change in the status of blacks had occurred in all the intervening years, this plantation model symbolizes, too, an enduring culture of slavery in America.

During the height of his popularity in the early sixties, Malcolm X broadly explored and explained how a culture of slavery had indeed survived and was still wedded to the socioeconomic structure in America at the time. Malcolm's raw and powerful imagery related to the two primary roles blacks served in the slave structure: the Field Slave and the House Slave. Noting that blacks in either capacity were slaves, Malcolm cited how critical differences in their roles and relationship to their Masters affected the institution of slavery and its continuation.

The Field Slave, representing the great majority of blacks, was the backbone of the plantation labor force, working in the field from sunup to sundown, sleeping in shacks constructed there. The House Slave worked in the bosom of the Master's house, as cook or butler or maid or manservant or artisan, and lived in or near the House. Generally, the House Slave suffered a less brutal life than the Field Slave, a back less lashed, hands less hardened, a stomach less starved. Thus, like a hostage who suffers the Stockholm syndrome, the House Slave came to identify with the Master and the Master's needs, capable of crying out, as Malcolm suggested, "Massah! Massah! *Our* house on fire!"

Although the House Slave might, on the one hand, poison the Master's food or steal food from the house for the Field Slave, the House Slave was mostly terrified of being forced into the brutalities of the Field. Thus the House Slave could become the obedient slave, the obsequious slave, the slave collaborator, willing to turn on his slave brothers and sisters in the Field or in the House, to inform the Master of any plans of resistance or uprising. This is considered the root cause of the failures of the great nineteenth-century slave revolts led by Nat Turner and Denmark Vesey and Gabriel Prosser. The colluding House Slave was willing to forfeit a chance at freedom itself to remain in the Master's House.

The only slave more accommodating to the institution was the Black Slave Overseer, sometimes called the Nigger Driver. The Nigger Driver worked the Field Slaves and whipped them as soundly as any white overseer for laziness and other infractions that might slow down crop production and threaten profits. The Black Slave Overseer might even kill another slave to maintain the Master's plan.

Finally, the old plantation structure was further accommodated by the mistress of the House, commonly referred to as "Miss Ann," glamorized by Margaret Mitchell in the person of Scarlett O'Hara. Miss Ann was the woman of the house, a staunch defender and supporter of the patriarch who was the master of all, including her. Miss Ann was capable of whipping the House Slaves she managed in order to maintain the House of the Master. Miss Ann realized an otherwise unrealizable lifestyle of relative comfort by willingly acting as a partner in the crime of slavery.

What Malcolm X pointed out was how this cultural model was maintained into the twentieth century. Blacks not only remained in the same oppressive relationship to the new industrial economic structure as under slavery, but also remained trapped in the same inferior role in the social and cultural scheme under American apartheid. Now the Field Slaves were the black masses, sharecropping or cleaning the factories of an urbanized America, cordoned off in their southern shanty towns or new northern ghettos. The House Slave now owned a funeral home or barbershop or catering business or, having miraculously managed an education at one of the land-grant or turn-of-the-century colleges built for blacks, was a teacher, a doctor, or a lawyer, mostly attending other blacks. Though he was, like the post-emancipation Field Slave, suffering under social segregation and discrimination, the industrial House Slave often harbored the mentality of the old House Slave, particularly in fear and hatred of the Field Slave and in obsequiousness toward the Master, who was now an industrial Robber Baron.

Employing this powerful symbolism and the parables he constructed around it, Malcolm X pounded home the message to blacks to throw off the yoke of the mentality of slavery, which at once divided and contained blacks, and unite in a single struggle toward freedom.

As a culture of slavery facilitated maintenance of the black slave labor force that developed the country's powerful agrarian economic base, the rise of industrialization based on black, as well as white immigrant, labor exploitation was accommodated by the institutionalization and the inculcation of racism, wherein Jim Crow came to be served by Uncle Tom. Now, with the astronomical global profit projections from America's new economic shift to a base of high-speed technological production, America's new Masters, presiding over a New World Order, have fashioned a new domestic social Darwinist agenda justifying the continued exploitation of the poor, especially those eternally poor black masses. It is this paradigm that gave birth to what might be called New Age Racism in America.

Still owning nothing of significance, blacks as a people have little significance in postindustrial America except as unskilled labor and a potential consumer market. Beaten down in the losing battle for equality, in employment, education, and social standing, forty acres forgotten, the black masses languish underemployed and unemployed, undereducated and uneducated, and poor in the nation's ghettos. Thus the centerpiece of the New Age Racist agenda has been to forge blacks into a viable market by forcing those millions of ghettoized blacks back to their "natural" role as cheap labor, so as to supply them with an income in order to build up the black consumer market. If they cannot assume this cheap labor/consumer role, blacks have no real value or place in the New World Order.

The exception, of course, is the New Age House Negro. Also owning nothing of significance in postindustrial America, the New Age House Negro, though elevated to the house on the back of black struggle, finds his significance in his ability and willingness to serve the New Age Racist agenda. Indeed, his very livelihood is dependent on this willingness, a willingness to do even more than his historical counterpart. The New Age House Negro must round up the lazy black Field Slaves, the unwed welfare mothers and their children, the criminal predators and the rest of the postindustrial black residue, and himself open the dikes of social Darwinism that will drown this black riffraff, those who will not or cannot swim in the new economic tide—including, and especially, the Little Bs.

It was this kind of commitment that lifted black Harvard University professor William Julius Wilson, among others, above the ranks. Indeed, Wilson wrote part of the script that Clinton used to successfully enact the Republican "Contract." This gave Wilson, among other things, regular invitations to dinner at the Clinton White House.[1]

In Memphis, Clinton acknowledged Wilson specifically, stating, "The famous African-American sociologist William Julius Wilson has written a stunning book called *The Truly Disadvantaged,* in which he chronicles in breathtaking terms how the inner cities of our country have crumbled as work has disappeared. . . . We cannot . . . repair the [African] American community and restore the [African] American family until we provide the structure, the values, the discipline and the reward that work gives." Thus selling his welfare reform legislation to blacks, Clinton added, "Work organizes life. It gives meaning and self-esteem to people who are parents [*sic*]. It gives a role model to children." [2]

Thus the draconian welfare reform plan that criminalized and targeted and further impoverished so many black mothers and their children was gilded with a moral justification, founded in the alleged immorality of "welfare dependency" and the purported morality of "work."

Left, like the majority of black academics, to the ghetto of black studies, originally at the University of Chicago, Wilson rose above the fray on his theories relating to the social dysfunction of blacks, particularly those in the housing projects and ghettoized blocks of the South Side of Chicago, as set forth in *The Truly Disadvantaged*. Although his theories amounted to no more than the recycled notions from Daniel Patrick Moynihan—Wilson has been called "a black reincarnation of Moynihan" [3]—Wilson's theories are more closely aligned with those presented in *The Bell Curve* by Herrnstein and Murray (despite Wilson's weak criticism of Murray as "dishonest"). Wilson's articulation is distinct, then, primarily because he is black.

Wilson has been central to providing the fodder for the inculcation of New Age Racism, which has transported him beyond the field of ordinary black life. Here was the very president of the United States using Wilson's own words to establish national policy, relating not only to welfare reform but also to affirmative action, criminal law reform, and race relations. As Wilson asserted that Clinton "had vision" with respect to welfare reform, Clinton quoted Wilson almost verbatim in Memphis. [4] In his defining theoretical work, *When Work Disappears*, referred to by Daniel Patrick Moynihan as a "masterwork," Wilson said this regarding the value of "work" as a means to an end for the black underclass: "Regular employment provides the anchor for the spatial and temporal aspects of daily life. It determines where you are going to be and when you are going to be there. In the absence of regular employment, life, including family life, becomes less coherent." [5]

Wilson's promotion of this ethos for poor blacks in America is a treachery, even without regard for the fact that he bolsters it with reference to renowned French sociologist Pierre Bourdieu, who denounces the very neoliberalism Wilson seems to embrace.[6] That is, Wilson, while calling for public policies like welfare reform to force seemingly unemployable blacks into his utopian workforce, asserting at the same time that "private" employers are "reluctant" to hire inner-city blacks because they lack "work readiness," Wilson claims that with proper training these blacks could be employed, even without affirmative action, because of "corporate liberalism."[7] It seems impossible that Wilson could be so identifiably black—having had a mother who cleaned houses for a living, having gone to college by benefit of a church scholarship, having laid claim to academic credentials built on studying the blacks of South Side Chicago for more than twenty-five years—and still seriously conclude that the problems of the poor urban black masses and their solutions should or could center on the ideal, abstract or otherwise, of "work" in the globalized American "labor market" as dominated by domestic racism.

After more than twenty-five years of study, Wilson cannot possibly believe poor urban blacks suffer unemployment and underemployment because they do not *want* to work, as he implies—referring to the "decision to act in ghetto-related ways"[8]—that is, that they do not *want* to earn enough money to live in decent housing, eat healthy food, have adequate medical care, get a good education, and provide a brighter future for their children. As a sociologist, he cannot possibly have missed how, despite years of bleeding to enforce *Brown,* the great majority of blacks remain confined to their inferior places in the workforce, if any place at all. Wilson cannot possibly have missed that despite the bleeding of blacks under Jim Crow to get a job and all the efforts of black activists to enforce affirmative action in employment, blacks still suffer discrimination in employment opportunities. Mostly, however, after more than twenty-five years, Wilson cannot possibly have missed that most poor blacks *do* work, work at two, and sometimes three, low-level minimum-wage jobs, as cooks and clerks in fast-food restaurants, as maids in hotels, as janitors in office buildings, or performing a host of repetitive tasks in light-industry factories, even as he acknowledges a "class" of black "working poor" living "just above the poverty line," slipping down into the black "underclass."

The historical context in which blacks came to reside in Chicago's ghettos has been well documented, perhaps most popularly in Nicholas Lemann's work on the subject, *The Promised Land*. Blacks migrated to Chicago looking for *work*. They came there only to find work, because they were not being paid for their work sharecropping in Mississippi or because they could no longer fend off KKK and other white terrorists' attacks while trying to find other work. Surely Wilson has read about the 250 years of slavery in America in which blacks worked, from sunup to sundown, for which they were not and have never been paid. Surely this is not the work he would have blacks perform, the work that "provides the anchor for the spatial and temporal aspects of daily life." As a sociologist, Wilson is surely aware of the struggle under the Civil Rights and Black Power movements, particularly in the latter half of the twentieth century, for full employment for blacks, a full and equal employment that was denied blacks all through the twentieth century.

The question arises, then, what is the *work* Wilson idealizes that would provide the black underclass an "anchor" for a "coherent" life? Is it the bare-minimum-wage work that hardly affords survival, yet enough to enable participation as a consumer in the scheme of things? Should this work be meaningful either to the individual or to society? Wilson's analysis fails to fully incorporate the role of racism in black unemployment and underemployment, as he speaks of cases where there is a "tendency to discriminate" in hiring, as well as cases where "employers' perceptions [about the work readiness of inner-city blacks] reflect some aspect of reality." [9] Moreover, his analysis skirts the issue of the *meaning* and the reality of work in a high-tech economy, and with uncaring understatement he concludes, "In short, economic growth today does not necessarily produce good jobs." [10]

Should blacks enroll in the military, then, to serve as low-level cannon fodder for the wars of America's oil men, as in the Gulf and Somalia—and now Afghanistan? Should blacks strive to find worth in work for American corporations that make products that pollute and poison the earth and the people in it, including themselves? Should blacks seek worth in work in the ranks of police and prison guards who practice racial profiling and brutality against other blacks? What work is it to which Wilson would consign the black masses in the New World Order?

Indeed, he has a vision, a "broader vision," as he names it—that notably does not include any program of economic independence or self-determination for blacks or black communities. It is field work. For the long run, Wilson advocates development of a "public/private partnership" to "raise the performance standards" of public schools and provide other programs to prepare ghetto students for "technical training" to make them "job ready," while, in the short run, he would employ the otherwise unemployable blacks in "public sector employment": that is, "infrastructure maintenance jobs . . . public service jobs . . . and . . . neo-WPA jobs . . . at slightly below the minimum wage." [11] To clarify this, Wilson outlines several examples: "the cleaning of streets twice a week instead of once a week; the opening of libraries on weekends and in the evenings; the cleaning of municipal parks, playgrounds, and other public facilities." [12]

Wilson now resides in Harvard Square, far, far away from the world of those in the black underclass, the study of which has been his work. Sitting in the shadow of W. E. B. Du Bois, Wilson has become a member of a clique of like black men, black men who likewise were propelled to residency at Harvard by the black student uprisings and other protests of the sixties, a clique led by Henry Louis Gates Jr.

Indeed, it is not Wilson but Gates who is the Head New Age Negro at Harvard, and presumably in American academe. Gates, W. E. B. Du Bois Professor of the Humanities, is chair of the Afro-American Studies department and director of the W. E. B. Du Bois Institute for Afro-American Research. Over the last several years, he has successfully entrenched himself into new quarters and recruited to his fiefdom the small clique of blacks that have appointed themselves the voice of the black experience in America, "public intellectuals," whose sole endeavor seems to be the profitable packaging of the black experience in magazine articles, CD-ROMS, books, and popular television documentaries in ways that make it inoffensive and palatable for white consumption.

Much of Gates's work is a bastardization of the Talented Tenth theory espoused at one time and later renounced by Du Bois, considered the preeminent black intellectual of the twentieth century and architect of the Civil Rights movement. Arising from his German studies relating to the notion of a "natural aristocracy" and his admiration for the ideas of a black Episcopal priest named Alexander Crummell, Du Bois came to promote a theory that "the Negro race, like all races, [would] be saved by its exceptional men." Going further, in his essay "The Talented Tenth," part of a collection entitled *The Negro Problem: A Series of Articles by Representative American Negroes of Today,* Du Bois asserted, "Was there ever a nation on God's fair earth civilized from the bottom upward? Never; it is, ever was, and ever will be from the top downward that culture filters." [13] It was Du Bois's idea at the time, therefore, that blacks were generally "uncivilized" and that only a "natural aristocracy" among them, composed of "exceptional men," could elevate the race so as to be worthy of inclusion and equal participation in the American society.

This is Gates's theory now, even as he aspires to the mantle of Du Bois, who by the time of his death in 1963 had become a Pan-African anticapitalist militant.[14] There is another glaring difference. Gates seems to have little if any interest, as Du Bois did throughout his life and in the evolution of his philosophy, in elevating the race. Indeed Gates has said, "I'm sure that there are some African-Americans who wake up every day and think about the socioeconomic evils affecting our community, when they first look in the mirror, but I'm not one of them." [15] Thus, as Gates occupies the Du Bois chair, he misinterprets and misuses the man and his work, suggestively identifying himself, and those of his clique, as members of the illusory Talented Tenth, described in another day as "quality folks" and "representative Negroes," all toward serving the same interests as those of the individuals who pay him to sit there.

Gates clings to the ideal of a civilized, primarily white America, to which the black underclass remains unworthy or incapable of inclusion, reflecting darkly the historical debate that arose between and divided Du Bois and Booker T. Washington and their respective followers. David Levering Lewis, the definitive biographer of Du Bois, wrote (in reference to Du Bois's essay on his conflict with Washington entitled "Of the Wings of Atalanta [Atlanta]") how Du Bois spoke to "the deepest concerns of his class, protesting Washington's turning the black world upside down so that the starring roles went to peasant farmers, skilled mechanics, and domestics, forcing The Talented Tenth off stage." [16] Still, Du Bois organized the vanguard of the Talented Tenth—the educators, lawyers, publishers, physicians—to come together for the 1905 meeting in Niagra Falls, Ontario, Canada, that was the embryonic formation of the National Association for the Advancement of Colored People (NAACP), committing his talents and education (he was the first black to win a Ph.D. from Harvard) and very life to the elevation of the status of black people, including those peasants and domestics who followed Washington.[17]

Gates's convolution of the ideas of Du Bois was best revealed in his own "documentary" film *The Two Nations of Black America,* broadcast during Black History Month of 1998, produced by Frontline for PBS, with Gates as narrator. As the camera pans over a number of poor, seemingly homeless blacks sitting in the streets of Boston outside Harvard University and follows the footsteps of Gates passing them by, Gates begins his narration with an ominous statement: "I wonder sometimes if all of us were even meant to reach the promised land." [18] After a scene involving black "rappers" on the street, he interviews his colleague William Julius Wilson, querying him as to whether there was any meaningful bond between black academics like themselves and those "boys in the 'hood." Wilson coolly responds, "To think that our situation is comparable to that of the inner-city black is ridiculous." Gates reflects on this and states, "I find it hard to concede that these hoodlums are part of the same community I belong to. . . . This guy from the street seemed like a Martian to me." [19]

Toward the end of the film, the camera sweeps the Massachusetts Bay as Gates concludes with a certain sentimentality: "Now when I'm seeking that haven of like-minded black people, I go to Martha's Vineyard off the coast of Massachusetts. . . . In August, few places in America are more integrated than the Vineyard." Finally, though, surrounded by members of his clique, including Wilson and Orlando Patterson and Cornel West, Gates, as chief spokesman for the New Age House Negro and new crop of black Public Intellectuals in American academia, reveals the heart and soul of his race theory: "Home for me is Harvard Square. . . . Our community of black professors has more in common with our white colleagues than with our brothers and sisters still in the ghetto." [20]

Gates has, in fact, molded himself into a new model House Negro, one that is even more subservient than the old House Slave of Malcolm X or the early twentieth century's Uncle Tom. While the old House Slaves might have snitched on other slaves deemed disobedient, they still saw themselves in relation to the Field Slaves and were capable of slipping pieces of chicken out the back door of the House from time to time to their sisters and brothers in the Field. The Gates model, however, severs all ties with his brother in the Field, hates his brother for failing to imitate him, a dark imitation of his "white colleagues," and would do more than snitch on his underclass brother but would, by disavowing him, join forces with racists to destroy him: "We have two nations; and they are both black . . . [but] there is nothing natural about feeling compassion toward those people who look like you, but who have not been as successful as you. . . . You see, the causes of [black] poverty . . . are both structural and behavioral. . . . Deciding to get pregnant or not to have protected sex. Deciding to do drugs. Deciding not to study. Deciding, deciding, deciding. . . . Thirty-five million [black] people are not all going to be in one economic class, and we need to begin to understand that." [21]

Because of the fragility of the foundation of New Age Racism, in its subtleties and deviousness and newness, without the support of the New Age House Negro, the whole structure might collapse. It is this complicity of blacks that has enabled the New Age Racist agenda. Ward (Wardell) Connerly, for example, leading the charge toward the complete dismantling of affirmative action programs in the country, did for "Massah," one could say, what "Massah" could not do for himself. That is, had a white man been deemed the architect of California's Proposition 209, it would have been summarily discredited as racist. Connerly's spearheading the Proposition 209 anti–affirmative action initiative deflected charges of racism.

Although Connerly claimed his commitment to the anti–affirmative action campaign to halt the use of "racial preferences" programs in employment and higher education was based on the obtuse theory that such programs stigmatize blacks as "inferior," he was, rather disingenuously, still registering his own business as "black-owned" to qualify for state consulting contracts amounting to more than $1 million.[22] Indeed, his career as a businessman rose on account of "special treatment" he received as a black. His first real job, for example, was at a Sacramento redevelopment agency, one of many such government agencies that dotted the country at the time, an outgrowth of the Johnson administration War on Poverty. In 1966 he started working with the California Department of Housing and Community Development, another government program. In 1968 he met then-assemblyman Pete Wilson and was hired by Wilson to work in his assembly office. With the help of Wilson, Connerly was eventually able to open his own business, Connerly & Associates, which provides consultation to local governments and others on how to comply with state land-use, housing, and building regulations—notably, a business dependent on government contracts. While Connerly asserts that "Wilson is the reason [he is] a success," the growth of his business is primarily attributable to the "set-aside" contracts he has received over the years.

On the other hand, Connerly continues to exploit and misappropriate Dr. Martin Luther King's name and image and words, relating to King's famous reference to a "color-blind society" in his ongoing pursuit to overturn affirmative action policies nationwide, now under the aegis of the organization he formed after the success of Proposition 209, the American Civil Rights Institute. Unimaginably, as head of this organization, Connerly met with Clinton in 1997 to ask the president of the United States to urge his Race Relations Board to consider ending affirmative action and racial preference programs.[23] Earlier that year, however, Connerly had announced his opposition to Clinton's alleged consideration of making an official apology for slavery, stating, "Apologizing for slavery is probably one of the dumbest things anyone could do."[24]

———

More than merely advocating and sanctioning government policies that contributed to and maintained the wretched state of ghettoized and millions of other poor blacks, there had now come to be a new crop of Negroes who, positioned to actually influence the outcome of government activity, were actively undermining the cause of improving the lot of blacks in America. Although their positions had been purchased with black blood in more than one hundred years of struggle, these new Negroes had become collaborators in a scheme that was imprisoning and further impoverishing more and more blacks. Given the moribund state of independent efforts by blacks for freedom, government policies and programs still represented the sole resort of blacks for redress and remedy for past harm, the sole relief and hope for the millions of Little Bs.

Singular among those that could be deemed New Age House Negresses, as among House Negroes in the history of blacks in America, is Condoleezza Rice, the first woman named Assistant to the President for National Security Affairs. Without the benefit of being "Miss Ann," Rice is still wedded to George W. Bush, as she served his father. Upon his election in 1989, the elder Bush engaged Rice as director of Soviet and East European Affairs in the National Security Council and, later, as his special assistant for national security affairs. She was well credentialed for these posts, with a Ph.D. in political science, having been a Fellow in the Arms Control and Disarmament Program and a National Fellow at the right-wing Hoover Institution, both at Stanford University. Moreover, as Rice has stated, "I'm really a Europeanist." [25]

Her commitment to the Bush men borders on sycophancy and reaches beyond academic interests and Europeanism to a surrendering of self and soul. This was exhibited in her speech in support of George W. Bush for president at the 2000 Republican National Convention. After giving honor and praise to "those great Republican presidents who sustained American leadership," Gerald Ford, Ronald Reagan, and George Herbert Walker Bush, Rice became ebullient over the nominee: "George W. Bush challenges us all to call upon our better selves, to be compassionate toward those who are less fortunate, to cherish and educate every child, descendants of slaves and immigrants alike, and to thereby affirm the American dream for us all." [26]

Therein lay the point of her discourse and, indeed, of her very presence there, as in the lives of the Bush men. Rice would emblematize their truth, found in the philosophy of New Age Racism, wherein racism is declared ended, with the purpose of dissolving blacks' unity of purpose, a unity that represents the greatest potential threat to the New World Order, wherein each, black and white alike, is reduced to the powerlessness of one, struggling alone to survive in a global social-Darwinist game Bush and his brothers control. Thus Rice shamefully exploits her very heritage to serve Bush: "George W. Bush would have liked Granddaddy Rice. He was the son of a farmer in rural Alabama, but he recognized the importance of education. . . . Granddaddy saved up his cotton for [college] tuition. . . . And my family has been . . . college-educated ever since." [27]

Rice's reward for her unprecedented servility to racists has been, of course, a place at the Bush table and unprecedented personal participation in the affairs of the House, not to be confused, however, by power, personal or otherwise. While Rice assumes the position held by Henry Kissinger under Nixon, Colin Powell under Reagan, Brent Scowcroft under the first Bush, her seat at the National Security Council table is secure contingent on her commitment, and commensurate with her compliance, to serving the interests of those who ruthlessly usurp the interests of people of color around the world and her own people at home. Rice serves with fervor, showing a willingness to wield a global gun against not only Africans throughout the diaspora but any and all other people seeking independence from the global extension of American corporate capitalism.

Rice unabashedly makes clear the ruthlessness of her commitment to the Bush agenda at every opportunity. In one speech, she stated, "I am a major supporter of the role of private capital. . . . I think it's a good thing that markets dominate. . . . With no Soviet Union to support the socialist alternative, it's now very clear: there is one international economy. You'd better find your place within it, you'd better succeed, or you're going to lose and you're going to lose big-time."[28] At another time, she stated; "Power matters. . . . Yet, many in the United States are . . . uncomfortable with [it]. . . . This discomfort leads to . . . the belief that the support of . . . institutions like the United Nations is essential to the legitimate exercise of power. The 'national interest' is replaced with 'humanitarian interests' or the interests of 'the international community.' . . . Foreign policy in a Republican administration will most certainly be internationalist. . . . But it will also proceed from the firm ground of the national interest, not from the interests of an illusory international community."[29]

Rice's callous commitment to Bush extends to the domestic field. On one hand, she recalls her race as a palliative for Bush's brand of racism and an exculpation for a history of racist oppression of blacks: "In many ways, I'm a typical American story. . . . I lost a little friend in that church bombing in 1964, at Sixteenth Street Baptist Church. But our parents really did have us convinced that you couldn't have a hamburger at Woolworth's but you could be president of the United States."[30] On the other hand, she rationalizes racism, stating with respect to a program of diversity at Stanford University, while she was Provost there, "I'm the chief academic officer now. I say in principle that I don't believe in and in fact will not apply affirmative action." [31]

Rice's consort with Bush and his pernicious program of market expansion worldwide is criminally conscious, as she is one of the very few Negro neoliberals in America: "Outside of security, for the most part I think you can step back and let things happen. . . . The sheer number of transatlantic mergers suggest that business is not having any difficulty, almost treating the boundaries as non-boundaries." [32] As for those "security" questions, Rice asserted, "George W. Bush is a man of his word, friend and foe will know that he keeps his word and tells the truth. . . . George W. Bush believes that America has a special responsibility to keep the peace. And I want to assure you, if the time ever comes to use military force, President George W. Bush will do so to win, because for him, victory is not a dirty word." [33] Globally, in the post–Cold War era, that use of military force supports the work of unelected entities like the Trilateral Commission, the Council on Foreign Relations, and the World Bank in the promotion and protection of American corporate interests around the world, counter to the best interests of the majority of people around the world. It defends the price-gouging activities of pharmaceutical companies with respect to AIDS treatments in Africa, kills tens of thousands of people in Somalia and the Persian Gulf for oil company profits, maintains corrupt and vicious government regimes, imposes trade deals that have reduced more and more countries, particularly in the Third World, to extreme poverty, and serves the exploitation and spoiling of the world's wetlands and rivers and soil for harvesting more corporate profits.

As for the millions of Little Bs in America, Rice recognizes that so many are "trapped in a bad school in the country's big cities." Attributing this to the Democratic Party, she offers, first, the "new approaches" of the Republican Party: "For African Americans in particular, what I've been saying is just take another look." However, Rice warns blacks about trying to usurp the Bush power: "Just like I'm always telling people in the Balkans . . . 'Get over it, don't fight last century's wars and hatreds,' . . . African Americans [have to] look at what's happening today." [34] Today, Rice states, suspending reality itself, all the Little Bs have to do is follow the "Republican principles," that "in America, with education and hard work, it really does not matter where you are from, only where you are going." [35] In the ultimate gesture of betrayal, Rice holds herself out to black children as the exemplar of the rightness of the agenda of Bush and the Republicans.

George Bush understood the nature of the New Age House Negro. If no one else, Clarence Thomas had shown him the way, had shown him how far afield a black might go to serve and be included in the status quo and how useful that could be in preserving it. Although Bush had been unable to sweep the country to the Right, as did Clinton, whose execution of the end of welfare and the rest of the Republican program had come solely through his successful engineering of black support, with Thomas, Bush had erected the framework for Clinton—and for his own son.

The jolt of the Bush nomination of Clarence Thomas for the Supreme Court was powerful. Proverbially, it killed two birds for Bush. Thomas's very blackness allowed him to confound and destabilize black and liberal opposition to his nomination as to his policies in general, while ironically Thomas's own affiliations restored to Bush the support he needed from the Extreme Right. Indeed, Bush did not consider Thomas for nomination until he was recommended by New Right activist ideologues Thomas Jipping of the Free Congress Foundation and the organization's president, Paul Weyrich, also founder of the Heritage Foundation. Soon the Thomas nomination was further supported by notorious archconservatives and racists like Senators Strom Thurmond of South Carolina, Orrin Hatch of Utah, and Jesse Helms of North Carolina. In the background was Ralph Reed of the Christian Coalition, which would spend at least $1 million, on an advertising campaign in support of Thomas.[36]

Certainly no one conscious at the time thought that Thomas was a great legal mind that had overcome color with content—not even the large percentage of blacks who initially supported him, most of whom had never heard of him but were just happy to see a black face. Not only had Thomas gone to Holy Cross as a "King scholar," an affirmative action program, he had also been entered into Yale Law School in 1971 at the height of black student uprisings around the country, when Yale was aggressively recruiting blacks. Though he has had most of his Yale record sealed, one unsealed record showed he was near the bottom of that class. Moreover, as he has bemoaned, "No one would hire me after law school." [37] He made up for it from the beginning with a character of boot-licking deference to the white establishment.

Up from the obscurity of the Field of Pin Point, Georgia, and now clutching his new credential, Thomas found government jobs. Interestingly, even his first government job came under the patronage of a rich white Republican, John Danforth, who was at the time the attorney general of Missouri. While visiting his alma mater, Yale Law School, Danforth had inquired about for a "qualified" black to work in his office. Thomas worked a few years in Danforth's Missouri office. When Danforth went on to become a U.S. senator (replaced by John Ashcroft, now the U.S. attorney general), he eventually brought Thomas to Washington as his legislative assistant. Through a series of opportunist machinations, Thomas obtained a job as assistant secretary for civil rights in the new Reagan administration's Department of Education.[38] In a short time, he became head of the Reagan Equal Employment Opportunity Office (EEOC), the court of last resort for blacks and others seeking justice in job discrimination cases. Thomas went further than even Reagan could have imagined, nearly imploding the whole EEOC structure, dismissing case after case, and finally reducing to nil the conditions on which grievances could be redressed, sending blacks back to seek employment without even the veneer of equal opportunity.[39]

Thomas had become a kind of Volunteer Overseer, a New Age "Nigger Driver," keeping blacks in check, willing to do for Reagan what Reagan could never have really done for himself. In 1990 Reagan's successor, Bush, rewarded Thomas with a federal judgeship at the United States Court of Appeals for the D.C. Circuit.

Before Thomas was nominated for the Supreme Court, blacks, feminists, and liberals had been ready for Bush, ready to rally the nation to reject the prospective nominee, as they had been with Robert Bork, the previous nominee. They knew what another conservative vote in the Court forecast. Now, though, Bush was ready, too. He paraded out his Negro, Clarence Thomas, announcing he was the "best qualified," wielding the whip of racism against whites who might challenge his credentials, carrying a paddle for spanking feminists with accusations of a "high-tech lynching," and bitch-slapping blacks who did not like it.

Freed by Bush of self-loathing from alleged taunts by other blacks as

"America's Blackest Child," Thomas did everything to show his gratitude for his individual inclusion in the American scheme, and at its
pinnacle. From the day of his nomination, teary-eyed, Thomas gushed,
"Only in America could this have been possible. As a child I could not
dare dream that I would ever see the Supreme Court, not to mention be
nominated to it." [40] Thomas has done more than show his gratitude, of
course, sliding into place to the right of Antonin Scalia, where there was
barely room, voting over and over for the dismantling of affirmative action and school integration programs, doing his best to shred the tattered
black agenda. Ultimately he paid his debt to Bush with a critical vote,
along with Rehnquist and Scalia and Kennedy and O'Connor, in the Supreme Court decision that overturned the popular vote in the 2000 presidential election and situated Bush's son—who received 8 percent of the
black vote—in the White House. [41]

As Thomas became only the second black in the history of the country to sit on the Supreme Court, Colin Powell became the first black to
hold the nation's highest military post, as chairman of the Joint Chiefs
of Staff, appointed by Bush in 1989. In effect, Powell became Clarence
Thomas with a gun.

Though it was never quite clear—until he received the *Essence*
magazine award for "Man of the Year" and appeared on the cover of
Ebony magazine—that Powell even identified himself as a black, what
was clear, from the time Bush thrust him into the forefront of the Gulf
War public relations campaign, was his readiness to kill for American oil
companies and a Texas oilman who was now president of the United
States. Of the Bush administration's campaign of all-out war against Iraq
after Iraq's occupation of Kuwait, Powell stated that Kuwait "was worth
fighting a war over" because it "measured up" as a "regime, as a nation,
and, frankly, as the source of 20 percent of the world's oil." [42] (More accurately, Kuwait was believed to hold 10 percent of the world's oil reserves at the time.) [43] Also clear was Powell's commitment to oversee the
thousands of his black brothers and sisters, now represented in a larger
percentage in the rank and file of the military than in the population, and
send them off to kill people who were not their enemies and die for oil
interests that were not their own. [44]

The child of poor Jamaican immigrants, Powell found that serving
in the military of his family's adopted country was the one career avenue

available that could be rewarding in terms of both income and inclusion. This was particularly so for an immigrant black boy with average academic competence. Only his enthusiastic participation and success in the ROTC program at City College of New York lifted his grade point average to a C by graduation.[45] From there Powell embarked upon a lifetime of unparalleled obedience and devotion to the U.S. Army, an ambitious partisan in vicious and unconscionable programs of warfare that brought death and destruction to people of color around the world.

In 1962 Powell went to Saigon as one of thousands of military "advisers" under the Kennedy administration's effort to establish an illegitimate "noncommunist" government in South Vietnam, the failure of which would lead to the Vietnam War. Powell returned to Vietnam in 1968 as Deputy Assistant Chief of Staff for Operations at Americal Division headquarters in Chu Lai. Only months before, the First Platoon of the C Company of Americal Division had committed the infamous massacre at My Lai, in which hundreds of unarmed Vietnamese civilians, mostly women and children, were raped and slaughtered. Powell was commanded by Americal's adjutant general to investigate reports of the massacre. His report said the "charges were false," and he closed the investigation. Years later Powell would defend his participation in the cover-up of the well-documented massacre by stating that he was "mystified" by those early investigations and knew nothing of My Lai until years later.[46]

It was this kind of absolute commitment that delivered Powell to the highest ranks of a Republican, white-dominated national security establishment in Washington. Obtaining an MBA through an army program, he soon became a prestigious White House Fellow and protégé of two important players in that establishment, Frank Carlucci and Caspar Weinberger. Moved up in rank to a lieutenant colonel, Powell's first post-Vietnam assignment, in 1973, was to take over the Second Infantry Division in Korea, where black soldiers had been declared "black militants" for protesting racism in the ranks. His assignment was to "crack down" on them, which he did with a certain keenness, later describing that year he spent "whipping his Korean battalion into shape" as the "most satisfying ever." [47]

When Reagan appointed Weinberger as secretary of defense, Weinberger employed Powell, by then a brigadier general, as his military assistant. Even though Weinberger was notoriously charged in the Iran-contra affair in connection with illegal arms sales to Iran to illegally finance the Nicaraguan contras (he was later pardoned by Bush), Powell himself escaped prosecution and public scrutiny. It is widely believed, however, that as Weinberger's chief of staff Powell was certainly aware of Weinberger's activities and that in fact Powell was probably directly involved in the illegal shipments of missiles to Iran. This suspected involvement was further supported by Powell's close friendship with Prince Bandar bin Sultan, then Saudi Arabian ambassador to the United States and one of the known key figures in the affair, whom Powell still identifies as a "dear friend" and tennis partner.[48] Furthermore, Powell had been the main cohort of Dick Cheney, the future secretary of defense under Bush, in the Reagan administration's efforts to lobby Congress for funding for the contras.[49]

After the Iran-contra scandal, Frank Carlucci became national security adviser and made Powell his deputy. Soon Powell positioned himself to be appointed national security adviser by Reagan, and finally, in 1989, Bush installed him as chairman of the Joint Chiefs of Staff, charged with executing the Bush military agenda. The Bush military plan, as it came to be enacted, engaged more troops and involved the country in more military action than at any time since the Vietnam War. That same first year of his presidency, 1989, Bush had Powell invade Panama.

Although neither Reagan nor Bush used the mighty, multibillion dollar military machine they commanded to interdict and halt the tonnage of cocaine and other drugs trafficked through Panama into the United States, Bush directed Powell to invade Panama to "arrest" one man, Manuel Noriega, for "drug trafficking." Powell attacked Panama with unwarranted force, including twenty-four thousand U.S. troops accompanied by stealth bombers, gunships, and special forces. When "Operation Just Cause" was finished, the Nicaraguan embassy had been mistakenly assaulted by U.S. armored personnel carriers, a U.S.-supported president had been secretly sworn in, and thousands of Panamanian civilians had been killed. Although the official death toll was three hundred Panamanian military personnel, two hundred Panamanian civilians, and twenty-three U.S. troops, later reports, including one by CBS's *60 Minutes,* documented that approximately four thousand

Panamanians, unarmed civilians in the main, had been killed in the invasion. Moreover, Noriega, whom Powell had brutishly referred to as "a dope-sniffing, voodoo-loving thug," lived through the invasion, walked out of the residence of the Papal Nuncio where he had been hiding, and surrendered.[50] Powell would say, "The loss of innocent lives was tragic." [51]

Soon Powell directed the Bush war against Iraq. After its attack on Kuwait, Iraq had come to control 20 percent of the world's known oil reserves, envisioned by Bush as enabling Iraq, under the leadership of Saddam Hussein, to manipulate the prices of the world's oil. If Saddam Hussein somehow came to seize control of Saudi Arabia, as the highly publicized reports of the CIA were suggesting was imminent, he would control 40 percent of the world's oil reserves.[52] Bush declared Hussein to be Hitler.[53] Powell promised he would end this economic nightmare.

The assault on Iraq lasted forty-two days, during which time over five hundred thousand U.S. troops were deployed, supported by aircraft carriers, new stealth fighter planes, and B-52 bombers, which dropped eighty-eight thousand tons of bombs, many times more powerful that the atomic bomb dropped on Hiroshima, along with napalm, cluster bombs, and fragmentation bombs.[54] The massive air invasion pounded and destroyed civilian facilities, schools, hospitals, mosques, government offices, and private homes, though it was met with almost no aircraft or antiaircraft resistance.[55] According to the U.S. government count, "tens of thousands" of Iraqis were killed, along with an unclear number of U.S. soldiers.[56] However, subsequent independent investigations, including that of former U.S. attorney general Ramsey Clark, have documented that nearly *three hundred thousand* Iraqi people, soldiers and civilians alike, were killed in the invasion, including hundreds of women and children huddled in the Al-Ameriyah air-raid shelter who were incinerated.[57] In response to press inquiries about these alarming statistics of the number of dead, Powell said, "It's really not a number I'm terribly interested in." [58] Even after the cease-fire, however, U.S. airplanes continued to strafe the area, killing thousands more, including surrendering Iraqi soldiers and civilians fleeing Kuwait on foot along a seven-mile stretch of highway that led to Iraq, which came to be called the Highway of Death. Powell coolly commented on this years later, stating that it was an "unpleasant" scene, "where people were just being slaughtered as our planes went up and down." Then, when Bush decided the war's objectives had been sufficiently accomplished, Powell said, "If that's the case, why not stop the killing." [59]

It was his ruthlessness in winning this oilman's war and his savage willingness to kill anything standing that affected American corporate interests that secured for Powell a place next to Bush for life. Moreover, like that of Clarence Thomas, Powell's presence, as a black man, seemed to repel black and liberal criticism of Bush's bloody policies. Most blacks opposed the Gulf War. [60]

At the 2000 Republican convention in Philadelphia, Powell made a powerful endorsement of the new Bush. By then Powell had reinvented himself as a charity fund-raiser, head of the Clinton-created America's Promise organization, whereby he solicited corporations to support superficial self-help programs for "the nation's at-risk kids," to "transform them from potential delinquents and dependents into good citizens," stating, "to a large extent, this is an African-American problem." [61] Keeping in step with this theme, Powell observed at the convention that "the issue of race still casts a shadow over our society." However, he said, Bush had made a commitment to "reaching out to minority communities and particularly the African-American community."

As he hailed the man who would become the new chief of the armed forces, Powell seemed to hold forth a different promise with respect to "the nation's at-risk kids." "If you want young people to become contributing citizens and not convicts," he told the convention, America had to "give minorities a choice," a choice that seemed reflected in his own "choices" and in the disproportionately high percentage of blacks in the rank and file of the nation's armed services and in the nation's prisons. It seemed black youth, too, had to make a "choice"—between fighting and dying for America's corporate interests or spending the rest of their lives incarcerated:

> "If we give them that choice, it will be good for our party. But above all, it will be good for America. . . . Good for America—that must be the measure for all that we do. . . . Whether it's economic policy or military strategy or seeing what we can do to make our American family more inclusive, [George W. Bush] will always try to do that which is good and right for America." Then more to the point: "He will not repeat the mis-

takes of the past and let our insurance policy, our armed forces fall into disrepair. . . . Ronald Reagan and George Bush didn't let that happen, and I know that President George W. Bush will not let that happen either.[62]

Finally Powell returned to the core issue: "We defeated communism. . . . The sick nations that still pursue the fool's gold of tyranny . . . are investing in their own demise as surely as the Soviet Union did. . . . Count on it. Today, we are the most powerful nation on earth—militarily, economically, by any measure."[63] And, as the new Bush slipped into office, Powell took his place beside him as the nation's first black secretary of state.

Less brutal but as complicit in the New Age Racist agenda was Clinton "First Buddy" Vernon Jordan. While an aura of secrecy surrounded Jordan's role in the Clinton White House, there was no question of his well-touted extraordinary access to the president and, presumably, to presidential power, access no other black had had. If, as Jordan apologists would argue, he "quietly work[ed] in the background and weigh[ed] in on critical issues such as affirmative action,"[64] in light of the breakdown of affirmative action programs under Clinton, the further impoverishment of black mothers and children under his "welfare reform" program, and the exceptional number of blacks incarcerated under Clinton's "Three Strikes" crime bill, what was evident was that Jordan's "quiet work" did nothing to overcome the Clinton agenda that set blacks back in America. This was particularly reprehensible given Jordan's own history in the Civil Rights movement as one-time director of the National Urban League, a history that was at once his personal stepping-stone to vicarious power and, as in the case of the other highly placed black functionaries, a weapon against black criticism of the president. In exchange, as First Buddy, Jordan "golf[ed] with Clinton and vacation[ed] with him on Martha's Vineyard."[65] Indeed, Jordan, who came to sit on at least ten corporate boards, once asked rhetorically, "Has my life been enhanced and enriched by my relationship with the president?" and answered, "Absolutely."[66]

Similarly Alexis Herman stood for Clinton. As a black woman appointed labor secretary, after Robert Reich, Herman's very presence sanitized the just-passed Clinton welfare reform program, not only on account of the propaganda criminalizing unwed black mothers that attended the legislation but also given that black women and their children indeed represented a significant percentage of the nearly 13 million people receiving welfare.[67] Given that Herman had a background in social work, originally with Catholic Charities, her wholehearted support of Clinton's welfare reform program—as contrasted with Marian Wright Edelman's denunciation of it—only exacerbated this disgrace. Indeed, in overseeing the "welfare-to-work" component of the new law as it evolved into vicious state "workfare" programs, particularly outrageous in New York, Herman stated, "I've made welfare-to-work one of my top priorities."[68]

State workfare programs forced people to take "public sector" jobs, including street cleaning and the like, at less than the minimum wage. As one New York labor lawyer stated it, "It is a novel paradox of our time that at the very time both private and public sectors are 'downsizing' . . . this new 'Workfare' approach is being put forward—a doomed elixir."[69] Even though Herman's department eventually assessed that "workfare" jobs qualified under the Fair Labor Standards Act as minimum wage work and began requiring that states guarantee minimum wages be paid for welfare-to-work jobs, this set up antagonistic competition for jobs between workers paid at higher union-negotiated wages and unrepresented minimum-wage welfare workers, forced to take jobs or lose necessary supplementary benefits like food stamps or Medicaid.[70]

Herman justified the ignominy. Sworn into office in May 1997, by June Herman was selling "welfare-to-work" programs at the 1997 Conference of Mayors in Chicago. Outrageously, she started her speech there by thanking Mayor Richard Daley "for [his] fine leadership of the City of Chicago"—where 99 percent of the children automatically transferred to adult court in the Cook County criminal justice system were African American or Latino, the worst such record in the nation, denounced by the Children's Defense Fund and the Catholic Conference of Illinois.[71] Pledging to bring jobs to cities like Chicago, where, Herman stated, "as the sociologist William Julius Wilson has written, 'work ha[d] disappeared,'" Herman gave her blessing to the malicious "welfare-to-work" program, which would further impoverish the families of most of those black children sitting in the Cook County jail even as she spoke.

A few years later, Herman would actually speak of the success of the welfare-to-work program, even despite acknowledgment that the nation's minimum wage, adjusted for inflation, was "still 25% lower than it was in 1979," and that "someone who works full-time, year-round, at the minimum wage earns less than $11,000 a year . . . [which was] below the poverty line for a family of three in this country." Nevertheless, showcasing her "mentee," a former welfare recipient, she touted welfare reform, stating, "today, the percentage of Americans on welfare is the lowest in more than thirty years." She proudly attributed this "success" to the Clinton administration and her work in it: "They underestimated . . . the willingness of this administration to make tough choices." [72]

The activity of high-ranking black academics and political functionaries in advancing the New Age Racist agenda is powerfully reinforced by black voices in the media. A leader of this pack is syndicated columnist Armstrong Williams, of Washington, D.C., onetime "confidential assistant" to Clarence Thomas, when Thomas was chairman of the EEOC.[73] A professed political pundit who spreads the message of the dysfunction of ghettoized blacks, Williams refers to himself as a "proud conservative." He lambastes blacks for "welfare dependency" and "behavioral poverty" relating to "illegitimate" black children and black joblessness. A would-be "spook who sat by the door," Williams denounces black activists as "poverty pimps [who] exploit those who are marginalized by focusing on their problems." [74]

At the *Washington Post*, Courtland Milloy would dismiss racism and blame black men for their own high incarceration rate: "So many of us have lost the right to vote because we are convicted felons. . . . Just because someone builds a prison does not mean that we have to go there . . . enough of this begging others to save us from ourselves." [75] Similarly, nationally syndicated columnist Leonard Pitts has focused much in his opinion pieces on the denunciation of young black men. Also silent on the role of racism, Pitts used up one of his columns in the *Atlanta Journal-Constitution* to denounce "rap music" as the "music of thug values." To Pitts, this music is not a voice—and the only voice—speaking of and for young people locked in the hard life in the ghetto, but a representation of "the self-destructiveness of too many black males." [76]

On the other hand, *Washington Post* columnist Juan Williams would discredit the work and image of the man who dedicated and lost his very life in the effort to elevate the condition of blacks. On the occasion of the 2000 celebration of Martin Luther King's birthday, Williams publicly assailed the King family for trying to reopen the James Earl Ray case in an effort to uncover what role the U.S. government might have played in King's assassination—a presumption maintained by nearly all blacks, as borne out by a preponderance of the known facts. Stating that their attempts threatened to "tarnish the family's image—and King's," Williams himself would whitewash the question of who really killed the Dreamer, as the Dream. Using sophistic reasoning, resounding that of the FBI itself, Williams stated, "We [?] can't find anything that says that James Earl Ray didn't commit the murder or that he was aided in a large conspiracy." [77] During the Gulf War, Williams had similarly snidely assailed Coretta Scott King, and vicariously, again, King himself. Using his position at the *Washington Post*, Williams editorialized his anger with blacks for not being supportive and proud of Colin Powell, whom Williams characterized as leading the nation's military with "warmth, strength and competence." He specifically attacked Mrs. King for announcing her opposition to the Gulf War as she said her husband would. Pleading the case for warmongering on behalf of American oil companies, Williams contended, "Coretta Scott King has . . . phrased her opposition to the war solely in terms of the U.S. final response to Saddam's aggressions . . . as if the United States had suddenly begun war without provocation." [78]

While these journalists justify racism in their denunciation of blacks, author Ellis Cose would palliate racism by obfuscating the black reality, as he did in a massive article *Newsweek* magazine made into a 1999 cover story, incredibly entitled "The Good News about Black America." In it, Cose asserted that it was "the best time ever to be black in America." [79]

Cose's analysis was, at best, narrow, defining his good times in terms of what was less "bad" for and about blacks in America, an improved state he attributed to "the transformative power of America": "Murders and other violent crimes are down. Reading and math proficiencies are climbing. Out of wedlock births are at their lowest rate. . . . Fewer blacks are on welfare. . . . And the percentage of black families living *below* the poverty line is the lowest since . . . 1967." Filtering the black reality through the lens of cheery Census Bureau press releases, Cose failed to reflect, for example, that that "lowest" percentage of blacks living below poverty represented over 8 million people, further reflected in a sample family of one parent and two children under sixteen trying to live on around thirteen thousand dollars per year—or less. And while dismissively acknowledging that not *all* blacks were experiencing "today's good times," Cose discounted the millions of other working blacks living at or close to the poverty line.

More significantly, in a mountain of minutiae Cose chose to bury the reality that blacks, considered either collectively or individually, neither own nor control anything at all in the economic structure of America, not any significant part of manufacturing, banking, energy, transportation, communications, telecommunications, or any other core industry or enterprise. At the time of his report, black business revenues represented less than one-half percent of all business revenues in America.[80] Moreover, the median net worth (assets less debt) of whites at the time was around forty-nine thousand dollars, as compared with that of blacks, around seven thousand dollars.[81] Cose's measure of black success seemed rather like Gershwin's Porgy, who said, "I've got plenty of nothin' and nothin's plenty for me."

Cose declared, nevertheless, that "the black middle class [was] booming," a claim presumably propped up by the article's accompanying full-page color photograph of young black couples sitting at an upscale bar. It was a picture truly worth a thousand words, for black "buying power," or black consumerism, seemed to have been used as the definition of black "middle class," a term lacking precise socioeconomic definition. It is noteworthy, however, that in 1999 only 5 percent of those earning more than seventy-five thousand dollars a year were black, as compared with 85 percent white. Moreover, the greatest number of blacks earned between fifteen thousand and twenty-five thousand dollars.[82] Among occupations, blacks were a little over 7 percent of the total of managers and executives, less than 9 percent of the professions, while representing around 18 percent of service workers.[83]

Left to the resort of black consumerism, then, the centerpiece of Cose's "boom" was the development of an "urban reclamation" project where a Chicago ghetto used to be. There, he reported, a white developer had built new housing that white-owned banks lent blacks money to buy, and a white-owned supermarket sold blacks white-manufactured groceries, and the white-owned (Loews Corporation) Cineplex Odeon movie theater sold tickets and popcorn to blacks to see white-produced movies.

As additional support for his assertion of a black middle-class boom, Cose offered a collection of strange and nonrepresentative statistics, none of which reflected his "boom": a small percentage increase in college graduation among black women over *twenty* years, from 14.5 percent to 18.5 percent, although there was a decline in the numbers for black men; a reduction in the number of births among unmarried black women; a decline in black infant mortality over thirty years, although the rate remained more than double the white infant mortality rate; a decrease in the total number of black homicide victims over a fifteen-year period, although the number remained four times higher than for whites; an increase in the median annual income for a black family of *four* over nearly twenty years, from thirty-thousand to thirty-five thousand dollars, although the income of a similar white family during the same period went from fifty thousand to sixty thousand dollars. Oddly Cose also offered as an index of black success the increase in the black-white intermarriage rate, which rose, between 1990 and 1998, from 0.4 percent to 0.6 percent of all marriages, and finally that 69 percent of whites polled by *Newsweek* responded that they "personally admired" Michael Jordan, though even more, 72 percent, personally admired Colin Powell.[84]

This is the kind of propaganda that proclaims the end of racism in America, which would foreclose forever any social commitment to remedy the wrongs of racism as it exists in America, with an offer of proof that blacks would be well in America if they would simply rise to the occasion, stop depending on welfare and drugs, stop having babies out of wedlock, stop committing so much crime, and just get a job.

Making this argument far more aggressively than Cose, however, or indeed than any of the others, are the ruthless academic writers Thomas Sowell and Shelby Steele. Churning out a seemingly infinite sea of mean-spirited denunciations of blacks, in book after book and article after article, Sowell and Steele have earned incomparable endearment among the most racist and reactionary elements in America, rewarded with fellowships at Stanford University's right-wing Hoover Institution and the illusion of membership in the American mainstream.

Ironically, or perhaps not, each claims some undocumented history in leftist or civil rights or black power causes, on which each would, presumably, claim a right to speak so viciously against every possible social construct that might elevate blacks from what is unquestionably an oppressed state. Steele's opposition to affirmative action, for example, is his raison d'être and is so fierce that he even condemned attempts in the aftermath of the success of California's sweeping anti–affirmative action Proposition 209 to reserve a few small opportunities for blacks against a long history of injustice: "We are seeing a new generation of engineering schemes that achieve 'inclusion' by extending the tolerance for mediocrity . . . 'X percent plans' [for university admission] . . . mak[ing] 20 percent of the students in inner-city schools eligible where previously only a small percentage were eligible." Evidently, this would be an outcome Steele would find abhorrent: "Absent a hard-earned parity of skills and abilities between the races, 'inclusion,' is necessarily a corruption." [85]

Sowell blames the Democrats for this "corruption." Unlike the Republican Party, he has said, the Democratic Party "cuddles up with race hustlers . . . who promote this paranoid tribalism" of coddling inner-city black students, resulting in their failure to get into colleges and in the need for desegregation programs: "Another factor in the decline of . . . education in low-income minority communities . . . is the difficulty of either punishing or expelling disruptive and violent students who destroy the education of other students. Liberal judges have made it literally a federal case when schools crack down on disruptive and violent students." [86]

Both these men snidely claim affirmative action, busing, and other "liberal" programs of "social engineering" that might benefit blacks— arising, in any case, Steele has said, from "white good will"—actually work to the detriment of blacks by making blacks "passive," by "perpetuating dependency." Offering nothing in the place of something, it is Sowell and Steele who are dependent. They are dependent on white ill will for their jobs as academic "Nigger Drivers," who would whip their own people with their words, drive other blacks back to keep a place for themselves in the American mainstream of which they sing. According to Steele, "If my benefits come to me primarily as a black and not as an

American, then the effect over time is to undermine common society . . . this kind of thinking causes me not to move into the American mainstream." [87]

———————

The assassination of Dr. King left a gaping hole in the black body, and a broken heart. It was a deep cut to the continuum of black struggle. Dr. King, almost alone, had been able to keep blacks' eyes on the prize, toward realizing not only civil but human rights in America, which was freedom. King, alone, could at once galvanize the masses of blacks and rein in the privileged blacks. Coming from them, he was able to speak their language, could make them remember whence their privilege came, persuade them to refrain from wallowing in privilege, remind them of their reality as black people, compel their commitment to uplift their less-privileged brothers and sisters from their wretched state and mobilize their important participation in the movement for social change that would set free all black people, including themselves.

After King, the Black Panther Party stood as the sole bulwark for the black masses, as it organized the last great effort of blacks in America for liberation. Like King, the party, as an organization, was targeted for destruction by the FBI, as evidenced by Hoover's infamous announcement that the party was "the greatest threat to the internal security of the United States." With the collapse of the party, crushed by the FBI's COINTELPRO operations and overwhelmed by battle fatigue, came the death rattle for the cooperative effort of blacks for total liberation, leaving blacks immobilized in a vertiginous void.

Now, year after year, the privileged blacks were distancing themselves more and more from the rest, erasing even King's voice from memory. Too many blacks who had come to occupy places of power in the American scheme, no matter how limited, no matter how vicarious, were beginning to feel no obligation to align themselves with the struggle of the black masses, were doing nothing for the black community, and doing nothing with impunity, were doing nothing to use their limited powers to elevate the Race. Now, they seemed to rise guiltless above the underclass, even renouncing their ties to the black underclass.

Loosed, they celebrated themselves, celebrated "getting paid," not worried about the price. They celebrated even as Little B went from poverty to prison, even as the fathers of all the other Little Bs languished in prison, as their mothers struggled in poverty, as their communities still tried to survive, to overcome institutional racism and its ravages, and to battle the scourges of crack and AIDS. These blacks celebrated their place in the scheme, becoming as minstrels in the slave quarters, dancin' and singin' for "Massah."

Appearing in circuslike clown makeup on the cover of *Vanity Fair* magazine, in August 1998 comedian Chris Rock was heralded as a black success story, compared on the pages inside to the fictional television family the Jeffersons. Inside were two full-page photographs of Rock in "white face," his entire face blanched with stark-white pancake makeup, Rock wearing a black top hat and tuxedo. Rock was identified by his close friend Bill Stephney as "old-school": "If Nixon's supporters were the silent majority, then Chris's black audience sort of mirrors that—without saying Chris is Nixon." However, in response to the assertion by the piece's white author, *Vanity Fair* contributing editor David Kamp, that he had "sometimes been labeled a voice of young black conservatism," Rock somewhat defensively announced that he was really a "fan" of President Clinton. "I view Bill Clinton as the first black president," Rock added.[88]

Rock had no retort, however, for the message of his well-promoted comedic routine "Niggas vs. Black People," characterized by Kamp as "the forbidden truths of African Americanness." In it, Rock divides blacks into two classes, the low class being the "Niggas," whom Rock hates, saying, "I *love* black people, but I hate niggas! Boy, I wish they'd let me join the Ku Klux Klan."

In another part of the world of black entertainment, actor Samuel L. Jackson was assailing black director Spike Lee for Lee's outrage over white director-writer Quentin Tarantino's brazen and abundant use of the word "nigger" in his films, particularly *Jackie Brown*. Lee claimed Tarantino used the word "nigger" thirty-eight times in that screenplay: "Quentin is infatuated with that word. What does he want to be made— an honorary Black man?"[89] Jackson, whose role as a crack addict in Lee's acclaimed 1991 film *Jungle Fever* was pivotal to his Hollywood success but who rose to fame in Tarantino's *Pulp Fiction*, publicly attacked

Lee, declaring sarcastically that Lee did not speak for black people: "I didn't get a chance to vote in that election [of Lee as a black spokesman]."[90] Saying that *Jackie Brown* was a "good film" and that Lee hadn't "made one of those in a few years," Jackson supported Tarantino's argument that he used the word "nigger" so often in his script because it authenticated the story of *Jackie Brown*. Moreover, Jackson actually defended Tarantino's "right" to write "nigger" into his scripts, saying, "Black artists think they are the only ones allowed to use the word. Well, that's bull. . . . If I say the word, it's cool, but because Quentin wrote it, it ain't? Come on!"[91]

In the music industry, hip-hop and rap "godfather" Russell Simmons, primarily responsible for exploitation of the genre, had thrust this ghetto beat into the mainstream culture not only to the benefit of himself and a few of his artists but also—and mostly—to the tremendous financial benefit of the white men who own the record industry, the owners of Time-Warner, Sony, and Arista. Indeed, under Simmons and his various business partners the whole culture of rap and hip-hop music came to focus away from hard social commentary on the black condition to the "ideal" of "getting paid." In a 1999 *New York* magazine interview, Simmons explained, "I want the *money*. If you want to push bigger buttons, you have to get inside the building."[92]

Simmons is indeed "inside" the House, as such, having moved on up from the ghetto of rap. Investing his rap millions elsewhere, Simmons parties in the Hamptons, flies around on Tommy Hilfiger's private jet, dines with close friends like Donald Trump. One exception, apparently, is his first creative partner, a black man named Andre Harrell, with whom Simmons remains close. Harrell discovered Sean "Puffy" Combs, who became, of course, the notorious "Puff Daddy," recently reinvented as Sean "P. Diddy" Combs.[93] Combs's last rap message, which would override that of "gangsta rap," related to a presumed conflict between the "player"—a ghetto black who has gotten rich—and the resentment of the "player-hater"—the black still stuck in the ghetto. Using the form, though not the content, of Public Enemy's messages to the grassroots of black America, Combs elevated this "playa" and "playa-hata" theme in his New Age record release "P.E. [Public Enemy] 2000." In it he urged the brothers in the 'hood to identify not with their other brothers and sisters but with the "man in the silver Bentley."[94]

Of course, Combs, like Simmons, never really lived in the 'hood. Perhaps this was why it was so easy for Simmons to shrug off the idea of any commitment to using his new power to changing anything in the scheme of things for other blacks, such as those black kids who invented rap but who are still stuck, as it were, in the ghetto as "player haters." In the *New York* magazine interview, Simmons summed up his feelings in this regard: "Rappers are spokespeople for the people who have nothing. We can't empower them all." [95]

Even as he hosted his 2001 "Hip-Hop Summit," sounding a non-commercial theme in the ill-defined goal of getting "hip-hop artists and the entertainment industry to take back responsibility," Simmons was merely shoring up his own economic base in rap and hip-hop music. [96] Surrounding himself at the summit with the likes of NAACP president Kwesi Mfume, the Nation of Islam's minister Louis Farrakhan, self-described "original" Crips gang member Michael Concepcion, and Recording Industry Association of America president Hilary Rosen, Simmons laid a foundation to repulse rising legislative attacks on the content of rap and hip-hop music, threatening his interests. This was evidenced in the summit's hollow final agreements, to enhance "parental advisory labeling" on records, develop "mentoring programs" for *artists* and form ongoing committees to address "issues important to the Hip Hop community such as freedom of speech." [97] There was no commitment of an investment in the ghettos of the origins of rap and hip-hop of any of the millions and millions of dollars Simmons and the record industry had realized from this music. There was not even a recognition of duty to the Bluffs across the nation or the millions of Little Bs living in them, whose nickels and dimes supported Simmons and this billion-dollar-industry, as their words of rage over their depressed condition had invented this music that had become what Simmons enthused was "the most powerful cultural influence in America and probably in the entire history of the music culture." [98]

The culture of New Age Racism also brought blacks to the age of Oprah. Despite the number of black women journalists who dot the television landscape as local news anchors, with the exception of Winfrey the voice of black women is silenced in this medium that so influences life itself in America. And Winfrey does not use her powerful voice to speak out on behalf of black women, or men. This has been, apparently, a conscious decision: "The other kids were all into black power and I wasn't a dashiki kind of woman. . . . Excellence was the best deterrent to racism and that became my philosophy." [99]

Winfrey, who has managed to become a cultural icon in mainstream America, wedged herself into place by ousting all contenders and competition with vulgar, sensationalist programming, including topics such as "satanic abuse" and "women who've killed," along with guests that included white supremacists. [100] Indeed, the very first show Winfrey broadcast from outside her Chicago base was in Forsyth County, Georgia, where, during Black History Month in 1987, she devoted one hour of national television time to interviewing local members of the Ku Klux Klan. [101]

Forsyth had been the scene of recent unrest relating to its history as a "racist bastion," where almost no blacks had been able to reside in seventy-five years. Following the alleged rape of a white woman in 1912, for which two black men were "legally" hanged and another lynched, blacks had been driven from Forsyth by violence and threats of violence, which had reduced the black population over time from over one thousand in 1910 to only one resident by 1980. A small "brotherhood walk" of blacks and whites a week or so before Winfrey came to town had been met with such violence that the organizer moved out of state. Days later, twenty thousand predominantly black demonstrators marched through the county in protest. This was soon followed by a "white power rally." [102]

Capitalizing on the controversy, Winfrey brought her cameras to the Dinner Deck restaurant in the county's heart to give "the beleaguered people of Forsyth County a public forum." [103] Winfrey was the only black in the room of a selected all-white audience of one hundred people. Boosting her ratings by giving comfort to the complaints of Klan members and their brothers, Winfrey listened to leaders of the committee to "Keep Forsyth and Dawson Counties White" tell her why they resisted any form of racial integration in the area: "You have blacks and you have niggers. . . . If niggers move into Forsyth . . . it's going to be like . . . Atlanta, nothing but a slum area." Outside the restaurant, blacks protesting the show were being hauled off to jail. Led by Hosea Williams and Rev. C. T. Vivian, stalwarts of the Civil Rights movement, the protesters charged Winfrey with "scheming" to "exclude all blacks" from the show and carried signs that read "Like Forsyth, Oprah goes all white." [104]

Although one audience member told Winfrey she herself was "welcome in [his] home any time," she returned to Chicago to prepare for her next show, about "men who dress as women." While the Forsyth "event" certainly provided a building block for Winfrey's celebrity, over the next months civil rights organizers in Atlanta continued the struggle to stop the violence and threats against blacks in Forsyth. Now, however, this struggle included defending Williams and Vivian and the others. At a rally at Ebenezer Baptist Church, Martin Luther King Jr.'s old church, Rev. Joseph Lowery and Coretta Scott King and others denounced the criminal charges leveled against the protesters. Winfrey would say she was "disappointed" by Williams's arrest. At the same time, she explained, "there [were] members of [Forsyth] who [were] God-fearing but because they'[d] been raised to exclude blacks from their lives, racism [was] a hard thing to erase from the heart. And there [were] people who wanted to try." [105]

It was this kind of programming that brought fame and fortune to Winfrey, eventually ranked by *Forbes* magazine among the four-hundred richest people in the United States. While this programming came to be sanitized over time, as Winfrey shifted to providing another kind of comfort to what became her core audience of white women, in the form of "lifestyle" and glamour "makeovers," diets, and New Age self-healing readings and practices and endless self-deprecating discourse over her own weight and "nappy" hair, Winfrey carefully avoided using her unparalleled power and voice on behalf of black women, even as the political agenda pounded poor black women and their children into deeper poverty and degradation. What Winfrey did do, once, in 1996, was to contribute about eight hundred thousand dollars—publicized as "millions"—to a paternalistic program dubbed "Families for a Better Life." As Clinton launched his welfare reform program, Winfrey publicly promised herself to "move 100 families out of public housing, off public aid and into better lives." Receiving over thirty thousand calls from poor Chicago area families, the agency Winfrey employed to administer this experiment honed the number down to five families, four of which were headed by single black mothers. Winfrey halted the program in its first year, however, because the women

had been designated by the administrators as incurably "welfare dependent." The fact was that the program's managers were found to have
used nearly all the money for personnel and administrative budget ex-
penses, a public relations fiasco Winfrey would not abide.[106]

Winfrey has abandoned any further forays into the business of the
black community and has returned to an intensification of programming
about her failings and fears and the like in what she calls "Change Your
Life TV." Winfrey conducts ad nauseam examinations of her pain over
being in her skin with the assistance of a "team of experts," a group of
whites possessing curious credentials. She acts as a conduit for viewer
contributions to her "Use Your Life Awards" to small charitable efforts
through an "Angel Network," and with Gary Zukav, a former Green Be-
ret turned New Age writer, she takes "personal voyages" that never take
her back to the black community.

In what is now broadly called the "postfeminist" era, a New Age Miss
Ann has slipped into place. Like the New Age House Negro, she occupies
an old place in which new clothing is worn. More than on account of the
so-called feminist movement, the white women who have come to in-
habit lofty places in the American scheme have done so as beneficiaries
of affirmative action programs, bought with black blood. Indeed, every
study on the subject indicates that more than any other group it is white
women who have benefited from affirmative action, especially in employment.[107]

Thus settled into these positions of power, and power held less vicariously than before, divorcing themselves from the coalition of the disfranchised that propelled them into higher places, these New Age Miss
Anns have become, as before, collaborators in a racist design. The New
Age Miss Ann has moved back into the bedroom to share power with her
man and join him in the exploitation of other women to maintain her
place, willing even to hurl black women back to a place in her kitchen.

If newly elected New York State senator Hillary Rodham Clinton
ever had a commitment to equality for women in America, if she ever
had a concern over the plight of poor and working people who had no
health insurance and therefore, no health care, if she ever had a commitment to the "Village" that was to take care of the children of the poor

and powerless, it is hard to remember it. She has clearly forgotten it. What she came to remember, it seems, was her place as an upper-class white woman, daughter of Republicans, wife of the president, the First Lady. What she did in her place was a powerful nothing by the side of her man, as he erased the idea of universal health care, as he further impoverished black mothers and their children and imprisoned black men.

In that, her duplicity was certainly equal to his. In that, she is the prototype of the New Age Miss Ann. Rising, Scarlett-like, from the ashes of White House foibles and folly and scandal, renouncing her momentary loss of memory, when she had pronounced that she was no poor white girl who would "stand by her man," she not only swallowed the Monica Lewinsky business whole, as she sealed her lips on the summary dismissals of Lani Guinier and Joyceyln Elders, but also whipped all her husband's opponents back into place herself and maintained order in the White House.[108]

Also standing by Clinton's side, seizing power under the umbrella of feminist progress, Janet Reno became the first woman U.S. attorney general. Carrying out the agenda of racist men better than any man, Reno, former attorney general of Florida, lobbied hardest for incorporation of the "boot camp" program for youth offenders into the Clinton crime bill, actually stating that "our single greatest crime problem is youth violence."[109] This program was, of course, so vicious that it came to be denounced by child advocates and human rights organizations across the nation and was in many cases disbanded. Abiding by Clinton through all the years as his legal enforcer, aiding and abetting his agenda, it was Reno who powerfully oversaw the "three strikes" prosecutions and the imprisonment of the disparate number of black men who now fill the nation's jails and prisons.

Indeed, a virtual gang of New Age Miss Anns has come into being inside the American government, sharing power with men in maintaining the wretched status quo for blacks. In the Supreme Court, Justice Sandra Day O'Connor has played a pivotal role in the breakdown of affirmative action, writing the devastating decision in the definitive 1995 case of *Adarand* and setting into stone the "racialization" of affirmative action. There are, too, the few women in the august body of the U.S. Senate, joined now by Hillary Clinton, whose presence has been meaningless, at best, to the interests of blacks. This includes even the two liberal senators from California, Diane Feinstein and Barbara Boxer, who enthusiastically supported the 1994 "Three Strikes" crime bill.

Ultraconservative former New Jersey governor Christine Todd Whitman is now head of the Environmental Protection Agency—an incredible irony, given that in the aftermath of her two terms as governor New Jersey ranks among states with the dirtiest water.[110] Whitman gained real notoriety, however, for the brazen racial profiling practiced by New Jersey state police when she was governor, whereby black men driving along the New Jersey Turnpike were targeted for arrest as suspected drug dealers. While Whitman was forced to apologize for the rampant use of this practice and fire the state police chief, it was only after federal and grand jury investigations of New Jersey police practices were under way, after the state police chief unabashedly revealed his race-based procedures in a sensational newspaper article, and after a photograph surfaced of Whitman herself, in 2000, standing behind a black man who was bent over spread-eagle, having been stopped by state police. Whitman was "patting him down." [111]

Journalism has seen a similar rise of New Age Miss Anns. In 1999, the *New York Times Magazine* devoted a special issue to the evolution of women over the centuries of the closing millennium, entitled "The Shadow Story of the Millennium: Women," the writers of which were predominantly white women. The cover art, described as a "millennial convergence," was a fusion of portraits of three white women representative of women in the fourteenth, nineteenth, and twentieth centuries. The lead article was written by Gail Collins, whose piece set the tone and defined the meaning of the special issue: "A Social Glacier Roars: After centuries of submission and subordination, *women around the world* are achieving critical mass" (emphasis added). This piece was accompanied by a full-page color photograph of a woman offered as the image of the "Millennial Woman." She was a purported anthropological prototype of women in the beginning of the millennium, who was, in a word, and in a world in which the majority of women, as men, are nonwhite, a white woman: "The millennial woman was not that different from today's inhabitants of central France, Switzerland, southern Germany, northern Italy and the Balkans." [112]

In the 164-plus pages of this special issue of the magazine about the status and stories of women in the *world* during the ten centuries just

passed, only two black women were noted to have existed, both identified in a section called "Irritating Women," presumably to men: nineteenth-century antilynching crusader Ida B. Wells-Barnett and blues
singer Ethel Waters. Waters was further identified in the one-quarter column devoted to her as having been "born illegitimate," whose "highest
aspiration was to be a lady's maid," and who was a "lesbian . . . who
could swear like a stevedore." [113]

There was no other reference to black women from the United
States, nothing about Harriet Tubman or Sojourner Truth or Mary
McLeod Bethune or Fannie Lou Hamer or Marian Wright Edelman or
Angela Davis or any other black women warriors who affected the
course and status of blacks as well as women in the less than half mille-
narian history of the country. There was nothing about women of Africa, or the Caribbean, or South America. Even among the anonymous
women of the millennium depicted therein, there were no black models
or exemplars.

These New Age Miss Anns, now positioned powerfully in the Fourth
Estate, had, like their men, written black women, all the women of the
African diaspora, out of one thousand years of history, had reduced
black women to invisibility in the panoramic pantheon they painted,
even as they decried the "shadow" status of women and celebrated the
emergence of white women from that shadow.

No one, however, could more personify the New Age Miss Ann than
Atlanta's Mary Rose Taylor. Taylor, former wife of television journalist
Charlie Rose, wife of Atlanta real estate developer Mack Taylor, and best
friend of author Tom Wolfe, is the spirit and driving force behind the restoration and establishment as a historical site of the Margaret Mitchell
House. Considered "the patron saint of Margaret Mitchell's legacy," Taylor has not only promoted Mitchell's work and history as a writer but has
put forth an image of Mitchell, as of Mitchell's fictional alter ego, Scarlett
O'Hara, as a feminist hero.[114]

Of her virtual obsession with institutionalizing Mitchell-O'Hara,
Taylor, a one-time journalist, explained in an *Atlanta* magazine interview in 1998 that it came to her after she married a millionaire: "I
couldn't have children. I really felt I needed to do something that had socially redeeming value." That "something" was the restoration of Margaret Mitchell's house in Atlanta, Margaret Mitchell's image, and that of

her slaveholding mirror image, Scarlett O'Hara, and the racist culture that attended it all. Like Mitchell's Scarlett, Taylor fought the fires, the literal fires, that burned much of Mitchell's House at the onset of the restoration effort, two fires—one in 1994 and one in 1996. Finally, however, Taylor opened the door to the house in 1997, soliciting her friend Tom Wolfe to make the "inaugural address," as it was touted. Thus Taylor established one of the new tourist sites in Atlanta.

Soon, in 1999, she had raised enough money to add a new wing, a fifteen-hundred-square-foot museum, featuring numerous exhibits from the film of *Gone with the Wind*, the entrance dominated by a larger-than-life portrait of Vivian Leigh as Scarlett O'Hara. The new wing opened with a gala on the day that marked the sixtieth anniversary of the premiere of the film in Atlanta. Film memorabilia are in abundance, clothing and mementos of the characters, Rhett Butler, Scarlett and even "Mammy," the only name of Hattie McDaniel's character, a character and name still fondly recalled by racists. Thousands of visitors to Atlanta have now traipsed through this lore, this house that would celebrate southern "antebellum" white life, a culture of slavery to which Taylor has built a small monument in the heart of the "Black Mecca." [115]

We've had a special plight for 350 years. You thought you was more because you was a white woman, you had this kind of angel feeling that you were untouchable. There's nothing under the sun that made you believe that you was just like me. . . . It is certainly not my purpose to replace or supplement a white, male, middle-class elite with a white, female, middle-class elite. I believe very deeply that the hope of an effective women's political movement lies in reaching out to include those who have been double and triply disfranchised—reaching out to working women, to young women, to black women, to women on welfare. [116]

Fannie Lou Hamer

The question arises: where have all the feminists gone? Where were Patricia Ireland and the National Organization of Women (NOW) women when Clinton was hurling black and other poor women and their children into the abyss of his welfare-reform program? Reportedly, Ireland herself, then president of NOW, was standing outside the White House the day the legislation was signed, crying out with a few others,

"Shame! Shame!" after which she fasted several days in protest. Where, however, was the effort of Ireland and the other NOW leadership in bringing to bear the power of their organization against welfare reform, the power of those thousands of white women they had organized to march and stand up and fight for women's reproductive rights and deliver *Roe v. Wade*, who stand still on a platform that pledges to fight against violence against women? Where were they when Clinton violated and assaulted inner-city black women and Latina women in America's barrios and poor white women trudging the hills of Appalachia? According to writer Barbara Ehrenreich, this betrayal was "American feminism's darkest hour since Eleanor Roosevelt took a stand against the equal rights amendment." [117]

NOW cofounder Gloria Steinem, for one, was busy writing articles in support of Clinton as he faced impeachment for violating another woman: "President Clinton may be a candidate for sex addiction therapy. But feminists will still have been right to resist pressure by the right wing and the media to call for his resignation or impeachment." [118] The year after Clinton signed his welfare reform legislation, NOW's other cofounder, Betty Friedan, was "terribly pleased to be invited" to participate in Clinton's inaugural festivities. [119] And while author-feminist Susan Faludi had once indicted Friedan as a "neoconservative," she made a case for Clinton in the *Nation*, saying women now possessed "the power to forgive men." [120] Indeed, Ireland, Steinem, and even Carol Moseley-Braun, who had voted against the welfare legislation, were among the celebrants at Clinton's second presidential inauguration in 1997. [121]

Silence and mealymouthing over welfare reform abounded among women's organizations committed, or once committed, to securing women's rights and humanity. Among the mealymouthed was even the National Council of Negro Women, whose president, Jane Smith, said, "We talked about two things that were important to us about women and welfare reform. One comes from the motto of Mary McLeod Bethune, which is, 'Leave no one behind.' That is our response in working in our states. We have sections in different states to make sure that we understand the state plans." [122] There was silence from the women of EMILY's List, an organization founded for the very purposes of electing to political office men and women who pledged to serve the interests of women and of opposing those who did not. The fact was that the dominant so-called feminist movement of the late sixties and seventies had surrendered to some ideal of "postfeminism," former feminist leaders having mostly slipped back into the comfort of being white women in America.

As the late Jerry Rubin and his brothers had returned to Wall Street, literally, going from "Yippies" to "Yuppies" as Rubin coined it, who could support the likes of Rudolph Giuliani, sometime feminists had come to wallow in the "choices" their new personal power afforded, relegating issues of racism and welfare reform to obsolescence.

Similarly when the Clinton Crime Bill was passed, ushering in an era of an unleashed and unbounded racism in the criminal justice system, the American Civil Liberties Union (ACLU) was conspicuously silent, issuing a position paper a few years later opposing the law.[123] There was a searing silence on the startling rise of the black incarceration rate on account of the Clinton "Three Strikes" law by the National Bar Association (NBA), the organization of black lawyers formed because of discrimination in the American Bar Association. On the other hand, the NBA became embroiled in a highly public debate over the controversial invitation members of the organization had extended to Clarence Thomas to give a keynote speech at its 1998 annual convention—which, in any case, Thomas did.

While some professed liberals and radicals have simply abandoned their commitments to progressive principles and activity, a number of erstwhile radicals and liberals have actually joined the ranks of racists and reactionaries. Chief among them is New Right ideologue David Horowitz.

At the root of Horowitz's shift from a self-professed radical editor of the old *Ramparts* magazine and supporter of the Black Panther Party to one of the most reactionary voices in America is racism. Back in the sixties, Horowitz, with typical paternalism, attempted to exceed his role as a party supporter and define and manipulate its agenda and members, including founder and leader Huey P. Newton. Expelled from all affiliation with the party, Horowitz mounted a lifelong campaign of hatred against the party. As one commentator stated, "This sense of acting out of personal injury permeates everything Horowitz writes today." [124] He has indeed spent decades since the party's demise, and particularly after the death of Newton, obsessively struggling to write himself into historical significance by at once associating himself with and demonizing Huey P. Newton and the Black Panther Party. In article after article over the years, though, in which Horowitz denounced the party as "Murder Inc." and a gang of "thugs" and Newton as a "cop killer," Horowitz began to extend his hatred to blacks in general, wedging a place for himself in the ranks of the American Right.

Exploiting and exploding his claim as a veteran of the American Left with ties to the party, Horowitz offered the Right a way to sanitize racism, as he invented for them a kind of New Age racist patois. Brazenly stating, for example, that Newton possessed a "crazy nigger persona" and that the dissolution of the party was attributable to "crazy niggers killing crazy niggers," Horowitz supplied racists with a stratagem for again saying "nigger" out loud. [125]

Heavily funded for some time by right-wing entities like the Olin Foundation and the Bradley Foundation, Horowitz finally launched himself into notoriety by publishing, as an advertisement in a number of college newspapers, a position paper originally entitled "Ten Reasons Why Reparations for Slavery Is a Bad Idea—and Racist Too." Asserting, among other "reasons," that blacks had already been paid reparations "in the form of welfare benefits and racial preferences," Horowitz finally fully exposed himself to be a piece of the fleshy underside of the sixties who had survived to become just another racist in America.

Likewise, Jerry Brown, former California governor, now mayor of Oakland, California, has been born again as a racist. Even when Brown announced his candidacy for mayor of Oakland in 1998, he still seemed committed to a progressive ideal. As head of his We the People organization, he had been denouncing corporate greed while promoting social justice. Moreover, he was still criticizing the agenda of Clinton, against whom Brown had once run for the Democratic Party presidential candidacy. He was reaching out to blacks, the majority population in Oakland, for support, with a promise to serve the forgotten black agenda if he became mayor. Despite blacks having come to dominate Oakland politics, the emptiness of their offices and most of their commitments had not improved the situation in decades. Brown's candidacy represented a breath of fresh air.

In the months before election day, however, Brown began to unmask himself as a potential Bay Area Rudolph Giuliani, developing a new rhetoric about "urban restoration." Still able to exploit the hope he had held forth to Oakland's massive population of poor and working blacks, however, Jerry Brown slid into office as the city's first white mayor since 1977. Immediately he began to promote one of the most radically racist and reactionary agendas in urban America.

In his inaugural address, Brown's stated priority for Oakland was to "reduce crime." Even acknowledging the dramatic drop in crime, he pledged to *"rid* [Oakland's] neighborhoods of *criminals,"* based on the malicious "broken windows" policing theory of criminologist James Q. Wilson.[126] Ruthlessly employed by Giuliani in New York, this tactic related to eliminating the "fear" of crime by rounding up what even Wilson acknowledged may not be criminals but "disreputable or obstreperous or unpredictable people: panhandlers, drunks, addicts, rowdy teenagers, prostitutes, loiterers, the mentally disturbed"—who theoretically created, like "broken windows," an ambience for crime.[127] This is but the rallying cry of New Age Racists, employed to abandon any social commitment to investing in improving America's black ghettos and, worse, to justify purging blacks from these rich urban centers to make them once more lily-white. It is a kind of final solution, whereby inner-city blacks are criminalized and imprisoned.

This accommodates Brown's next priority, to bring ten thousand "new" people into downtown Oakland. It is clear his intent is new *white* people as, in his inaugural address, he spoke of bringing back ten thousand of those who were among the "millions [who had] joined the great exodus outward"[128]—an obvious euphemism for "white flight"—and later stating, "The only way to get more retail downtown is to get more shoppers downtown. That means people with disposable income."[129] Brown would call them back with the promise that they would not have to be confronted by or live in proximity to the impoverished and undesirable blacks from whom they had fled.

Brown has emerged as a New Age "Massah." Having centralized political power in his own hands as mayor (via City Charter changes), he would use it as a whip to lash blacks for the impoverished state of Oakland and strip blacks of the last vestiges of power there. The fact is, however, that Brown has cohorts who have vested financial interests in downtown and port development, and Oakland's massive port is anchored in predominantly black West Oakland, contiguous to downtown. Less than a year after his election, Brown appointed his former campaign treasurer, John Protopappas, one of the major developers of downtown and port properties, to the Port Board.[130] As the Rightist *City Journal* glowingly characterized it, "beneath his left-wing rhetoric, Brown has a realistic, even conservative streak." [131]

The last hope for ghettoized black children like Little B, as embodied in blacks elected to public office, was also eroding and slipping away. The absolute abandonment seemed to come during the 1998 Clinton impeachment process, when the Congressional Black Caucus (CBC) rose up, as they never had in the nearly thirty-year history of the CBC, to defend Clinton. CBC chair, California congresswoman Maxine Waters, passionately stated in a meeting of the House Rules Committee, "The Congressional Black Caucus has made the decision to be the fairness cop [on the impeachment issue.]. . . . We've been in this struggle for fairness for so long." Former civil rights activist and leader Georgia congressman John Lewis, who had marched with Dr. King and had suffered so many blows in the infamous bloody assault on blacks marching across the Edmund Pettus Bridge in 1965, said, "The CBC understands more than others how this system can discriminate. As minorities, we're very sympathetic to someone who has not been treated fairly by the system." Longtime congressional representative of Harlem, Charles B. Rangel, a founding member of the CBC, stated, "Black communities around the country want us to protect this president." Representative Earl Hilliard of Alabama actually compared the prospective impeachment of Clinton to racism in the criminal justice system: "We see this process as being unfair to the president, just as it's unfair to African-Americans and other minorities accused of crimes." Numerous others issued public statements of support, including Elijah Cummings of Maryland, Sheila Jackson of Texas, and William J. Jefferson of Louisiana.[132] Added to this chorus was the voice of civil rights activist and popular personality Jesse Jackson, who stated, on the occasion of Martin Luther King's birthday commemoration in 1999, "Dr. King would be suspect of the impeachment process because he would be suspect of the impeachers." [133]

The CBC, referring to itself as "the conscience of Congress," went further.[134] Even in the aftermath of Clinton's welfare reform and crime bills, and at the height of the Clinton-Lewinsky scandal, which some labeled Zippergate, the CBC honored Clinton at its annual dinner. In his keynote speech there, Clinton acknowledged the CBC's strong support for him: "I want to thank you for standing up for me and understanding the true meaning of repentance and atonement." [135]

This was the height of irony. Not only had Clinton rejected the idea of America's "atonement" for slavery, the CBC had never pressed him to do so. The original vision of the CBC, when it was formed thirty years before, "to promote the public welfare through legislation designed to meet the needs of millions of *neglected citizens*" (emphasis added), was now blurred if not blinded. In thirty years the CBC had been, more than anything, self-perpetuating.

Indeed, it was only when Newt Gingrich became Speaker of the House and stripped the CBC, along with the other so-called legislative service organizations, of funding for its offices and programs, kicking the caucus to the curb, so to speak, that the caucus can be recalled to have spoken out vehemently for "black rights." Then-chair Kweisi Mfume challenged Gingrich over this defunding, stating, with unprecedented indignation, "They have created forty-one pit bulls [members of the caucus] that will chase this [Republican] elephant day in and day out." [136] This black militancy on the part of the caucus was startling, particularly coming from Mfume, who not only had voted for Clinton's "Three Strikes" crime bill but had been praised by the White House for manipulating the majority of his CBC colleagues to support the bill and, indeed for "bringing the bill through." [137]

Moreover, the CBC as a group had not demonstrated such militant support for Michigan representative John Conyers's *annual* battle, since 1989, to pass legislation (H.R. 40) that would simply establish congressional hearings on the issue of slave reparations: The "Commission to Study Reparation Proposals for African Americans Act." Although most members had voted against Clinton's welfare reform bill, the CBC had been soft-spoken on the law's devastating effects on the lives of women and children in their districts. And even though CBC leader Maxine Waters once forcefully demanded "investigations," albeit by the CIA and the Justice Department, into the suspected connection between the contras and the sudden influx of crack cocaine in the inner cities, based on the facts revealed in *San Jose Mercury News* journalist Gary Webb's articles, no such probe was vigorously pursued.[138]

This is what made the CBC plea for Clinton ultimately insidious. There had been no such militancy for black mothers and children when Clinton forced through welfare reform, no such militancy for the crack addicts who had become the main victims of the contra cocaine deluge *and* the Clinton "Three Strikes" law, no such militancy over reparations. There had been no passionate or militant stance in the Congress on behalf of the plight of black girls and boys like Little B.

Blacks claiming leadership, even in the bastion of the Black church, were now casting out the Little Bs, like biblical idol worshipers. In 1994, a consortium of prominent black church leaders, Baptists and others representing churches in some of the most depressed communities in America, issued a statement through the White House supporting Clinton's crime bill, stating, "We believe there is no more important responsibility of society than to raise its children to be come upstanding adults. . . . That is why we support the president's crime bill." [139]

In addition, there is the Rev. Jesse Jackson. Jackson has done more than give abiding support to the Clinton agenda, having defended Clinton's refusal to issue an official apology for slavery, for example, by saying of such an apology, "It's not a good thing. It has no substantive value to it." [140] Worse, however, he has provided fodder for the racist theories at the foundation of the Clinton Crime Bill (as promulgated by John DiIulio, who cited Jackson in one of his articles): "There is nothing more painful for me at this stage of my life than to walk down the street and hear footsteps and start to think about robbery and then look around and see it's somebody white and feel relieved. How humiliating." [141]

Finally, ascending with the new Bush presidency's "faith-based initiatives" program, administered by DiIulio, is Rev. Eugene Rivers. Unlike blacks in vogue during the Clinton presidency, Rivers assumes a "black militant" stance in his embrace of the reactionary political agenda of DiIulio and Bush, and particularly as it relates to the Little Bs of America.

Wielding self-promoted "street credentials," as an erstwhile gang member, and a vicarious relationship with the heroism of Black Panther Party leaders like Fred Hampton, Rivers would justify his combative Christian campaign to be the "Savior" of "the souls of inner-city kids." Like his friend DiIulio, and unlike Hampton, Rivers considers the main problem of the inner cities to be the black youth living in them and their "urban pathologies." As the antidote to this evil, Rivers would wage Christian warfare on ghettoized black youth, in his Boston base and nationally, youth he identifies as either "menacing" or "antisocial." Rivers offers them salvation or threatens them with condemnation in what has been called "no-nonsense, in-your-face policing." [142] Indeed, Rivers has formed a partnership with "every law enforcement agency in the state," calling for a "full and fair suppression of youth violence." [143] Talking tough, Rivers would sweep the streets clean of kids he deems "thuggamuthas," "young hoodlums" and, in line with the DiIulio "superpredator" theory, "the fourteen-year-old badbutts." He deems this program a "model of youth ministry to at-risk kids." [144]

In his new role as DiIulio's unofficial deputy in the Bush faith-based initiative agenda, Rivers seems freed to pursue his program with a vengeance: "Churches must say clearly to gang-involved youth that we accept zero tolerance on violent crime. That position is non-negotiable." [145] Also nonnegotiable for black youth is what Rivers labeled "a pornographic reduction of male-female relationships, accompanied by the acceptance of hip hop culture." [146] Also nonnegotiable is even the way ghetto kids speak and act, as he tells them, "Take your hat off. . . . [Say] yes, *sir*, we don't speak no Ebonics here." [147]

Under the cloak of Christianity, and clutching the hem of DiIulio, Rivers has been completely embraced by the Right. He has served as a panelist with William J. Bennett at a Manhattan Institute Conference; he has been a select guest at a "faith-based initiative" lunch hosted by President Bush in Austin; and he was one of only fifteen "African American religious leaders" invited to meet with Bush at the White House. [148] Reciprocally, he defiantly champions DiIulio and Bush and repels their black critics with Afro-centric posturing, wedging an inglorious spot for himself in the new Bush World Order. After the meeting with Bush and other black religious "leaders," Rivers issued a joint statement with them, which said, "We are here to declare our uncompromising support for President Bush in this [faith-based initiative] endeavor, and for Professor DiIulio, who has been arguably the most important scholar and policy advocate, black or white, promoting faith-based vision and the institutions that advance secular and civic purposes." [149] In a word, Rivers has become a kind of Bible-toting Colin Powell or militant Clarence Thomas.

Ironically, and given that his church reportedly has no more than thirty members, Rivers lambastes nearly all other black religious leaders and their organizations. He condemns "mainline" black churches as "major crime families," stating that "the way it is now, the black church structure undermines any system of moral or financial accountability. It simply perpetuates a circulation of crooks." On the other hand, while assailing Louis Farrakhan personally, Rivers spoke disparagingly of Islam: "For about 20 years now I have been saying that we in the black church need to take on directly the challenge of Islam . . . to promote the [Christian] faith. . . . To meet the challenge of Islam we need to grow a whole new leadership strata of black Christian intellectuals"—presumably led by himself. [150]

Rivers does not limit his mean-spirited assaults on blacks to black youth or the black church. Indiscriminately damning homosexuality and abortion, Rivers blames the "AIDS crisis" in black America as in Africa—which he has labeled a "sexual holocaust"—on unchecked black heterosexual "promiscuity, infidelity, and rape." Moreover, Rivers claims such supposed irresponsible "behavior" on the part of the African people is "inextricably connected" to the "under-development of Africa." [151]

There is nothing in Rivers's rage about how these terrible conditions came to exist, nothing about the enslavement of blacks, nothing about a century more of Jim Crow, nothing about a struggle to survive the violence of it all, as though the black ghetto, and all that festers in it, were hurled to earth whole from a black hole. Seeing only black "hoodlums" and "thugs" everywhere, whose purported pathologies he would cure with his brimstone, Rivers would be blind and mute to the savagery perpetrated against black children growing up malnourished, without medical care, in dilapidated housing, attending deteriorated schools, living in rat-infested neighborhoods, generation upon generation, trying to grow in abject poverty and wretchedness. Rivers would say nothing about the institutionalized racism and discrimination in employment and other affairs that black children's families face struggling to provide for them, nothing about the police violence perpetrated against their fathers and brothers, nothing about their mothers' low income or—now—no income, nothing about the inundation of their communities with crack cocaine. Similarly Rivers is silent on the impact of the slave trade, colonialism, neocolonialism, and wars waged over oil and diamonds on the people of Africa, whose suffering under AIDS and devastating poverty he would cure with the salt of his self-righteousness.

None of this is the point, however. Rivers's agenda is not really about the "pathologies" of blacks in the United States or on the continent. It is about something else. As Christians, black and white, liberal and Right, battle each other as well as Jews and Muslims and Buddhists for the golden calf of Bush's faith-based billion-dollar budget, Rivers rises above them all, his eyes fixed on the prize. Indeed, he has ruthlessly beat back nearly all his competition, including the Black church, the Muslims, and everybody connected to what he identifies as "the civil rights industry." [152] For Rivers has no real agenda, as he has no real church. Of his close relationship to DiIulio and Bush, he said, It's "a new regime. Some folks have access, other folks do not. That's the way the game goes." [153]

And finally, as Little B began his fourth year of incarceration, and at the very moment he was turning eighteen years old at Alto, the NAACP was giving Bill Clinton an Image Award in Hollywood. [154] Despite the fact that more blacks had come to be imprisoned under Clinton than under Reagan or Bush, despite the ravages of welfare reform, the NAACP gave Bill Clinton an Image Award just as he left office in 2001. Even as Clinton, in an eleventh-hour act of his presidency, pardoned fugitive Marc Rich, the billionaire commodities trader who had sold oil to South Africa during the international trade embargo against its apartheid regime, and commuted the prison sentence of Carlos Vignali, convicted linchpin of a drug ring that transported eight hundred pounds, or 363 kilos, of cocaine from Los Angeles to Minneapolis for sale as crack in the black communities there, the NAACP gave Clinton one of its prestigious Image Awards.[155] In presenting his *special* "President's Award," NAACP president Kweisi Mfume said of Clinton, "He took an unequivocal stand in support of Affirmative Action and strongly condemned the ugly practices of racial profiling and hate crimes."[156]

It was this New Age Racist–era abandonment of principle, this shrugging of shoulders and turning of backs by blacks and former friends, that had set the stage for the unchallenged prosecution of a thirteen-year-old black boy. Newly elected Atlanta prosecutor Paul Howard knew that there would be no liberal protest, no black protest. Nobody—nobody that mattered—was concerned about a Little B anymore. Everybody—everybody that mattered—wanted him to go away, forever. Little B was at once a problem and a solution, expendable and expedient.

This was particularly so in "Black Mecca." Ironically, there were probably more New Age House Negroes concentrated in the political hierarchy of Atlanta than anywhere else in America, where accommodating blacks labored to provide a "crime-free" and "fear-free" place for the big business of white corporations. In addition to Howard and the mayor, Bill Campbell, and police chief Beverly Harvard, public housing director Renee Lewis Glover, Fulton County sheriff Jackie Barrett, and labor secretary Michael Thurmond, the state's former "welfare czar," architect and enforcer of Georgia's merciless welfare reform program, there was the state's attorney general, Thurbert Baker.

As an assemblyman, Baker had not only supported but, as then-governor Zell Miller's administration floor leader, had lobbied other representatives and become chiefly responsible for the success of the "Two Strikes You're Out" crime bill as well as SB 440—the legislation that permitted prosecution of children as adults.[157] Miller rewarded him with appointment as attorney general, filling a vacancy.[158] Later Miller vigorously supported Baker's successful campaign for election to the office with a saturation of television advertisements, wherein Miller reminded his own constituency of how Baker had "led the battle to get two strikes passed" and was now "leading the fight to abolish parole."[159] At the end of each such advertisement, Miller added enthusiastically, in his north

Georgia "good-ol' boy" accent, "One thing I know about Thurbert Baker, as governor, if you give Thurbert Baker a job, he'll git the job done!" [160]

And giving voice to this collection of collaborators was Cynthia Tucker, an editor at the *Atlanta Journal-Constitution*. While Tucker often used considerable editorial space to air what seemed her personal animosities toward the family of Martin Luther King Jr., particularly King's son Dexter, and to attack Coretta Scott King's attempt to retain the copyright of Dr. King's speeches, Tucker more typically railed against blacks in general, thematically condemning blacks wholesale for "fratricidal violence" and "the awful self-abuse of drugs and sexual promiscuity." [161] In one editorial she argued that the "challenges" facing black leaders now were not those of racism but of overcoming blacks' "self-inflicted wounds." That is, Tucker explained with shameful sarcasm, black leaders ought to teach black men "how to be good fathers"; turn blacks from an asserted "cultural ethic that suggests scholarship is 'a white thing' "; reduce the black teen pregnancy rate, which, despite low numbers, Tucker asserted "remain[ed] too high"; and encourage black "investment," attributing black poverty to a "failure to take advantage of the booming stock market." [162] On the other hand, with no history in the Civil Rights movement or related record, Tucker editorialized during the 2000 Martin Luther King celebration that it "would please MLK" to see America so "transformed" that blacks were now national role models for whites, citing Tiger Woods; Oprah, as the "arbiter of reading tastes for millions of white women"; and Condoleezza Rice, who Tucker proudly proclaimed "guide[d] the foreign policy pronouncements . . . of George W. Bush." [163]

In deep sorrow at the end of his long life, W. E. B. Du Bois reflected on what it had all been and meant, this Civil Rights movement of which he had been architect and in which he so long worked as a leader and activist. Sometime before leaving the United States to die in Ghana, Du Bois said, "A class structure began to arise within the Negro group which produced haves and have-nots and tended to encourage more successful Negroes to join the forces of monopoly and exploitation and help victimize their own. . . ." [164]

V
THE REAL CRIME

[13] Trompe L'oeil

Everybody scattered when the deadly shots rang out in front of Henry's market, where, Kenya Woods explained later, she and Darrell had gone to buy a soda. It was that way in the Bluff. The crack-addicted skinny women with fluffy slippers backed into the night. The gold-toothed boys and dealers scampered off. Doors closed. Business shut down, including that in Henry's market, where Myong Suh, the owner, called the police. Zone 1 police came out. Darrell Woods's body was stuffed into a bag. Nobody saw anything. The police went away. The pay telephone on the corner rang. Business resumed. Doors unlatched. People came out, including Valerie Morgan and the other skinny women, including Little B, a boy of the Bluff who had to make money for him and Ta-Ta to eat and get some shoes and stuff.

A shooting death in the Bluff was not newsworthy in the Bluff. In the last month or so, several people had been killed in those blocks around Henry's. A shooting death of a black man in Atlanta was not newsworthy in Atlanta, which maintained one of the highest murder rates in the country. Even when, days later, Maria Elena Fernandez wrote her profile of Kenya Woods as a young widow, accompanied by a color photograph of Kenya and Darrell Woods and their two sons, the only response from official Atlanta was a comment Fernandez extracted from Atlanta police department major Mickey Lloyd. Asked why Woods might have been killed, Lloyd said, "That is one of the big question marks in this one." [1]

Another question seemed to arise in Fernandez's first report of the death of Darrell Woods. It had to do with Kenya Woods's account of the

events that led up to her husband's murder. She and Darrell and the two
children had gone to a Captain D's restaurant for dinner. On the way
home, she had become thirsty and had decided to stop at Henry's to
buy a soda. The question was, why had she passed those dozen or more
places where she might have bought a soda, all those fast-food drive-
through places and gas stations that were between the Captain D's on
Ralph David Abernathy Boulevard where they had bought dinner and
their apartment on Western Avenue above Simpson Road, to go to Henry's? Moreover, it was hard to understand how she had been "attracted
by the lights" of Henry's market from either major street that formed
the southern and northern borders of Griffin Street, Henry's being many
hilly blocks away from both. There was no major street east or west
for blocks that ran parallel to Griffin, along which someone unfamiliar
with the area, as Woods said she was, might have reasonably been driving and been able to notice Henry's, and the few blocks of little Western Avenue, where the Woodses lived, which ran perpendicular to Griffin Street, did not intersect Griffin. It defied logic, then, how Kenya
Woods had accidentally driven her husband and children up to that little
market, which sat on that little corner where all kinds of drugs were so
obviously being bought and sold, to buy a soda.

The other question had to do with what Kenya Woods said she did
after she heard the shots while inside the store. Fernandez reported that
when she heard the shots, Woods did not to take cover, but instead
braved running outside. Moreover, she rushed outside Henry's not to
tend to or to protect her children but "to run after the killer." Later, at
trial, Kenya would add that when she ran outside of Henry's, she first
looked at her husband slumped over in the car and then ran after the
presumed killer. More incredibly, she was only stopped in her pursuit by
an unknown man, who held her back and told her to protect herself. She
turned her attention to her husband, who was either already dead or dying, and finally to her children, huddled in the backseat of her car. Then,
she told Fernandez, "I held him and kept telling him not to go, that I
loved him." [2]

Something was wrong with the landscape Kenya Woods painted. It
was a trompe l'oeil. Beyond her atypical response of going toward
danger, or the bravado of running unarmed after what was believed an

armed killer, or the unnatural inattention to her children, there was the contradiction that would soon be revealed about the matter of Kenya Woods's professed love for Darrell Woods.

Eric Mills, Big E, one of the local drug dealers, was arrested as a suspect in the murder of Darrell Woods. Within hours of his arrest, he told the police, "Little B did it." Jason Morgan, J-Boy, Michael Lewis's half brother, arrested later as a suspected accomplice to the murder, would not refute Mills's assertion.[3] Several thousand dollars in reward money had been offered, most of it put up by Bishop Eddie Long, head of New Birth Missionary Baptist Church. It would be suggested later, at trial, that Darrell Woods had been a member of New Birth.[4] Long's money had inspired area addicts and other desperate inhabitants to claim to have been in the crowd in front of Henry's. Eric Mills was the name, until Mills named Little B.

Little B became an "evil in the city," a biblical referent that reverberated from the pulpit and the press and the mouths of the politicians and echoed through the streets of Atlanta, all along Ralph David Abernathy Boulevard and Sweet Auburn. Yes, it was Little B, the "thug," who was a Martian to Henry Louis Gates, the superpredator invented by John DiIulio and James Q. Wilson, the personification of crime in Atlanta for police chief Beverly Harvard, an embarrassment to Cynthia Tucker Negroes, a blight on the horizon of big business for both Maynard Jackson and Tom Cousins, the hoodlum for whom Rene Lewis Glover's "zero-tolerance" policies had been instituted, the bastard product of a welfare-dependent mother, who could not just say no to crack, and a crack-addicted absent father, the very image of the problem of blacks in America according to the president of the United States, unfit for civilized society as Thomas Jefferson had said in the beginning. Paul Howard seized ambition by the throat, charged the boy as a man, and gave the crowd Barabbas, who was called Big E.

No one seemed to doubt that Michael had killed Woods. The question of motive was filled in by superpredator speculation. Black boys from the Bluff were animals who prowled the streets looking for prey. Howard offered up the theory that Woods became prey because he "disrespected" Little B, the thug, by refusing to turn out his headlights as commanded.[5] Although this theory was never substantiated at trial, and despite the fact that Kenya Woods never said, to the press or in court, that she ever saw the boy or witnessed such an altercation during her trips in and out of Henry's, this became the motive Fernandez set forth in what became her own serialized story about the case. It became *the* "motive." People on the street were now shaking their heads over how that boy Little B had confronted Woods and demanded he turn off his car headlights, and how, when Woods refused, Little B felt he had been disrespected and arbitrarily shot Woods—and, in front of his children, as it came to be chanted.

That the car had only one working headlight might have been relevant, though it was never made public by Fernandez or any other reporter of the case. The pretrial presumption remained, then, that Woods's headlights posed a problem to the drug dealers in the area by subjecting them to being exposed to police.[6]

This theory bordered on the absurd, given first that the Atlanta police department's stated priorities did not include halting the flow and trafficking of drugs in Atlanta, and obviously not in the Bluff.[7] Moreover, everybody in the Bluff and everybody who bought drugs in the Bluff— from the local addicts to the students from the nearby historically black colleges and from Georgia State and Georgia Tech to the white boys sliding through from the rich part of town, Buckhead—understood that. Everybody who sold drugs in the Bluff understood. That certainly included Eric Mills, a fearful figure who controlled a small gang of underlings. In all the years Big E had been selling dope in the Bluff, getting bigger and fatter along the way, he had been arrested and charged with drug dealing—"possession with intent"—only once, and that had been just before Woods was killed there. Mills, with his crew, had sold drugs in the Bluff even through the highly charged weeks of the Olympic Games, the very hub of which was only blocks from the Bluff, and had avoided not only a drug arrest but also a parole violation for his only previous criminal conviction, which was simple possession of drugs.[8] Michael himself had never been arrested for drug dealing, even though he had been out there on those corners for the past two years. Indeed, this relaxed atmosphere was what accounted for the virtual crowd of people, dozens of buyers and users and sellers, about which Kenya Woods would speak over and over, which was standing around or passing through the Bluff at or near the corner of Griffin and Meldrum Streets when Darrell Woods was killed.

In any case, the defective headlight issue would be merely noted at trial by the lead public defender, Gary Guichard, who would fail to inquire about this of the one person alive in the best position to know—the driver of the car, Kenya Woods.[9] Moreover, Guichard would never ask Woods the most obvious question: whether or not she turned off the car headlights, or headlight, when she got out of the car.

Guichard, who dominated the defense, seemed to leave the footwork to his cocounsel, Patrice Fulcher, a recent law school graduate who had never tried a murder case. Fulcher, who seemed to be the only person on the planet who believed Michael was worth something—and, most of all, was innocent—reported that Guichard would not allow her to conduct any of the significant cross-examinations. Indeed, she indicated that Guichard ignored her cross-examination outline for Kenya Woods, wherein, among other things, she proposed asking Woods at the outset about this headlight.[10]

By most accounts—including that of Mills himself—at least one streetlight was lit on that corner that evening. And there were other lights shining on that corner that night, lights in front of the dilapidated apartment building adjacent to Henry's as well as the lights from Henry's itself—lights that Kenya Woods consistently claimed had attracted her to the store.[11] All of this taken together would seem to nullify even the notion that the status of the car's headlights could have been reasonably construed to constitute a motive for murder.

Prosecutor Paul Howard had had to creatively use Michael's record at juvenile court to establish his evil superpredator persona in support of this notion of a motive. Howard, who had been sworn into office only weeks before as the state's first black district attorney, had pledged during his campaign to "prosecute more teens as adults."[12] Now he transformed the deprivation hearings in juvenile court, a dismissed case of simple battery when Michael was ten years old, shoplifting, disorderly conduct, "ungovernability," and "runaway" charges into the history of a street thug. The deprivation hearings were, for course, related to the adjudication of Valerie Morgan, Michael's mother, as unfit, whereby the Department of Family and Children Services (DFACS) came to be his parent, and from which much of the rest arose, particularly the runaway and ungovernable charges. Knowing all of this and making no public statement about it, Howard was complicit in Fernandez's promotion of the false impression that the boy had a history as a "thug." Moreover, the pretrial publicity that painted Michael as a thug because he had been brought before the juvenile court a dozen times was exaggerated by Fernandez's dramatized reports that Michael had been "truant" from school for two years—though he had actually never been charged with truancy. This was the same sleight of hand Howard employed to formally indict the boy as a man for the murder of Darrell Woods.[13]

Adding to this sensationalist image of Michael propagated by the collaboration of Howard and Fernandez was the comparison they drew at every opportunity between this boy and the image of Woods as a hardworking husband and father. Woods exemplified the "good" black, the kind of black then-president Clinton had held up as a solution to "the black problem." Woods was a working black man, married, taking care of his wife, his pregnant wife, and their children.

This, too, was in stark contrast with reality. It was never reported by Fernandez or revealed by Howard and would not be raised at trial by Guichard that Kenya Woods had, more than once, charged Woods with "domestic violence," had called police on him several times over his alleged brutal beatings of her. Moreover, Kenya had tried to leave Woods, most recently in the months before his murder, as documented in the rental applications she had filled out for herself. Finally, Darrell and Kenya Woods had not left their College Park apartment to move to that "bad" neighborhood to save money, as Kenya Woods had claimed and would maintain. Veteran investigator Marvin Dixon had discovered that they had been evicted from two apartments before moving into the Western Avenue place. More significantly, though, before they were evicted from the last place, Kenya had called the police on Darrell for beating her again and, according to the written report Dixon placed in the file, had said, "Get this fucker out of here. . . . I'm leaving him anyway."[14]

In the months between Michael's arrest and his trial, as Fernandez and other reporters published piece after piece condemning him, Dixon was uncovering any number of facts that were revealing another picture as to why Darrell Woods might have been killed and who might have killed him. In addition to the contradictions in Kenya's various statements, in terms of her relationship with Darrell or in terms of how she came to drive to Henry's or why they left their College Park apartment, there was the unused and unexplored statement of the Western Avenue apartment neighbor that Darrell Woods had been beaten up in front of the duplex two days before his murder.[15]

The neighbor could not, or would not, say any more than that about the beating. He speculated, however, that it may have had something to do with the Land Cruiser vehicle that had been parked in the driveway of the Woodses' apartment, behind a chain barrier secured by a lock. It was silver, he recalled, and had a Florida license plate. The same men who beat Darrell, he was sure, later cut the heavy chain and drove the Land Cruiser out of the driveway. Moreover, the owner of the apartment duplex, a black woman who lived outside the area in DeKalb County, told Dixon that she, too, had been curious about that Land Cruiser. And Kenya had acknowledged that there had been such a vehicle parked in front of their apartment, but, she stated, it belonged to her cousin, a student at Emory University, who had left town but who had felt, at the time, that it was safer to leave it there than on the sprawling, elite Emory campus. Guichard did not call for any further investigation into this report.[16]

If Woods had been assaulted days before being murdered, it might have been relevant, at least from the standpoint of the "reasonable doubt" standard for jury deliberations, to pursue who might have done it. Dixon felt many unanswered questions were raised by this purported incident, not the least of which related to the Florida license plate and the fact that the vehicle was parked in an area where drugs were generally sold.[17]

The strong nexus between drug distribution in Miami and Atlanta is well known. Georgia and Florida have a common border, and Miami is unquestionably one of the main ports of entry into the United States of cocaine from Colombia. If at no other point, a few years after Woods was killed, there was a big drug arrest in Atlanta that exposed this criminal connection. U.S. marshals from Miami captured a major Miami cocaine dealer in Atlanta as he was establishing a significant trafficking operation there. The suspect, a young black man named Kenneth "Boobie" Williams, was said to be the head of a drug gang known as the Boobie

Boys, which was under suspicion not only for distribution of as much as $89 million worth of cocaine, "from the Bahamas and Panama" into Florida and Georgia, but also for numerous murders in both Florida and Georgia.[18] Contemporaneous with the Woods murder, however, was another connection. It was known in the street that Big E had a supplier called "Miami Black," who, it was rumored, drove a Land Cruiser.[19]

Several other, similar reports Dixon made were never pursued. There was his interview with a girl who said she had been using one of the pay telephones in front of Henry's when Kenya Woods drove up to the store. She told Dixon, and could have been subpoenaed to tell the jury, that while she was talking on the telephone with her grandmother, she watched Kenya Woods get out of the car. She *saw* that the car had only one functioning headlight. She *never* saw Michael. She *knew* Big E and *saw* him nearby. She went into the store to make a purchase immediately after Kenya Woods did, and watched her buy a can of orange soda. She confirmed that Kenya needed five cents more to pay for the soda and said she had offered Kenya the nickel. She said Kenya had refused her offer.[20]

Dixon was also given information by John Fawcett of the Guardian Chemical Company, a man originally listed as a prosecution witness. Fawcett was to have testified regarding his conversations with the district attorney's lead investigator, John Richey, about a so-called eyewitness named Linda Mitchell or Phyllis McBride, who would testify she did some part-time work for Guardian. Fawcett told Dixon about another witness, however. Fawcett said he knew and had seen the prosecutor's star witness, Eric Mills, sometime during that period. When Fawcett saw Mills, Mills was carrying an "assault rifle."[21] Even though Howard's investigator, Richey, had spoken with Fawcett, Fawcett was never called to testify.

The most startling report Dixon submitted that was never pursued had to do with the last thing the Western Avenue duplex landlady told him. On the night of Darrell Woods's death she had received a call from a woman claiming to be Kenya's best friend. The woman wanted to get the key to the apartment from the landlady because Kenya wanted her to get some things out of it. When the landlady refused to give the friend the key, the woman excitedly explained that Darrell Woods had been killed that very night and that Kenya had asked her to please get some of her things from the apartment. Under the circumstances, the landlady agreed to meet her at the apartment on Western and to open the door for her. While the woman gathered up some things, the landlady told Dixon, she talked to her. Kenya Woods's friend made a remark so shocking that the landlady felt obliged to swear to Dixon she had said it: "I really hope Kenya had nothing to do with Darrell's death."[22]

In any case, none of these connections was ever pursued, or all of these known witness statements remained unexplored, as though it had never occurred to Howard or even Guichard that Darrell Woods might have been killed for something and not for nothing.

Nothing was a superpredator fantasy, an evil boy who killed for sport. Nothing was an evil boy trying either to prove his manhood to others in his "'hood" or to gain entry into a gang operating there. Nothing had no basis in reality. In addition to everything else, there were really no organized street gangs in black Atlanta, despite an attempt made a few years before by a group of pseudo-Crips to establish a presence there.[23] Moreover, as Michael would say of himself time and again, he was not wont to "clique up." Nothing was a hat identified as a black "skull cap" that Michael allegedly wore "all the time," a hat that Howard's team would successfully have deemed as "evidence," which would be, in fact, the *only* piece of "physical evidence" Howard would present against Michael. Nothing was an alternative motive theory that Michael had referred to Kenya Woods as Darrell's "whore," which instead might have instigated the argument the state offered as the motive, an altercation, in any variation, that Kenya Woods herself never said she saw or heard.[24] In other words, the sole basis for this accusation against Michael was Howard's assertion, and the only thing linking Michael to murder was Eric Mills.

In November 1996 Mills had been arrested and charged with two counts of "possession with intent" to sell drugs, a felony. At the time, he was on probation for simple possession of drugs. Among other things, Mills's new drug charge represented a violation of his probation. Conviction of the new charge represented a possible sentence of five to thirty years for *each* count.[25] Given the "two strikes" law in Georgia, however, a probation violation coupled with conviction on the *two* counts of "possession with intent" meant that Mills was facing the possibility of life in prison.[26] Nevertheless, as he would later testify, he was boldly out on the streets of the Bluff in January selling drugs the night Darrell Woods was shot to death.

It is now accepted under the law that prosecutors can bribe witnesses with reduced sentences for their own crimes. This is so even though federal law (18 USC Section 201(c)(2)) makes it an offense to pay a witness to testify and even though the American Bar Association's Model Rules of Professional Conduct make no distinction between defense counsel and prosecutors in the prohibition of paying witnesses to testify.[27] Not surprisingly, when the question was raised in a 1997 federal case as to whether what prosecutors called "plea bargains" amounted to the forbidden "bribery," it was settled in favor of prosecutors. A 1999 ruling by the Tenth Circuit Court of Appeals, on a motion in that case, *United States v. Singleton,* supported the government's argument against a criminal defense attorney that prohibiting "plea bargains" as "bribes" would "make a criminal out of nearly every federal prosecutor."[28] Thus Howard was within the letter of the law when he bargained with Big E. However, nothing in the law supports bargaining for *false* testimony.

With Mills, Howard now had a case that would "make his bones," as they say in the Mafia movies. The arrest was made smoothly, though not necessarily lawfully. Homicide detective Sam Lawter, a former narcotics officer in the area, known in the Bluff as Curly Top, knew where to find him, though Michael did not really live on Holly Street. He lived where he could. Lawter also knew when to find him there, though Lawter would never be asked how he knew. The fact was that J-Boy, too, "stayed" on Holly Street, and sometimes so did Valerie, and sometimes Shalance Battle, mother of J-Boy's children, and most of the time, Larry Gee, known as Hootie—who sold drugs for J-Boy.[29] That day, though, when they came for Michael, he was alone.

When Lawter and his team arrived at the red front door and announced "police," Michael did not try to slip out a window, though he certainly knew how, though he was small enough for such an escape to have been feasible. He did not try to hide inside. He simply opened the door.[30] He was still talking on the telephone with Shalance, with whom he had roamed Cumberland Mall earlier in the day. They put their guns in his face. They seized the handgun that was in plain sight, that was not his, that he had childishly tossed onto a couch out of view from the doorway. They handcuffed him, told him he was under arrest for "murder," and marched him outside. Michael has no recollection of having been given the Miranda warning advising him of his right to counsel and to silence.[31] In any case, as Michael was thirteen years old and had completed only the sixth grade, he could not have reasonably been deemed capable of consciousness of his rights under the law.

Valerie appeared as he was being escorted down the outside stairs. She was dropped off in front from a car that had barely stopped. She insisted she go with her son, though she had long ago lost the legal right to make such a claim about him. Still, they let her ride in the police car with him to the main police headquarters over on Ponce de Leon Boulevard. He was taken to an isolated room, away from his mother, who was not his legal guardian, and questioned, and hounded, and assailed for killing that man—in front of his kids. He looked at them. He had been called names before, all his life, so he watched them, silent, distant, as though he were not himself, waiting, bewildered. Of course he knew that Woods had been killed. Everybody in the Bluff knew. Everybody in the Bluff knew people were killed with terrible frequency in the Bluff. What could he say about it, about this accusation, about Woods, or his kids, or life or death in the Bluff, other than "I didn't kill nobody."[32]

The next day, after he was taken to the juvenile detention facility on Capitol Avenue, they thought to get him a lawyer. The public defender's office was contacted and sent over a Trinidadian. He looked at Michael and the situation and refused to accommodate this afterthought of the police, who had already questioned Michael without counsel. He would review the situation with his superiors, but for now he would not allow the police to use him to cover up their failure to obtain representation for Michael in a timely way. It was too sloppy, he told them, with an accent that Michael remembered.[33]

Georgia's 1994 School Safety and Juvenile Justice Reform Act, commonly referred to as SB (Senate Bill) 440, allowing criminal prosecution of children as young as thirteen years old as adults, was silent on the procedure of arrest.[34] It was clear in assigning jurisdiction in these cases not to the juvenile court but to the superior court, providing discretion only to the district attorney to refuse to prosecute such a case and send it back to the juvenile court. It was clear as to the crimes, the "seven deadly sins," for which a thirteen-year-old boy like Michael could be adjudicated as an adult, which of course included "murder." Yet it gave no direction on the arrest procedure. That is, was Little B a boy or a man at the moment of capture?

Georgia did have guidelines in place, however. The state's Model Law Enforcement Operations Manual clearly outlined "professional standards and requirements for law enforcement operations." Under "Standard Operating Procedures" were guidelines for "processing juvenile offenders." This included kids charged in SB 440 cases. The guidelines established that upon the arrest of a juvenile an arresting officer "shall complete a juvenile complaint form and contact a juvenile intake officer and the district attorney." Moreover, under the section "Questioning the Juvenile Offender," the model procedure is that a "custodial parent, guardian, or attorney should be present." In addition, it states, "Both the parent and child must understand and knowingly waive the juvenile's Miranda Rights . . . regardless of the juvenile's age, the charge, or whether or not he is in custody." [35] In addition to this procedural model for police, the courts have held that the Miranda standard for juveniles is higher than for adults, in that it must be "given without threat or promise of benefit." [36] Each of these principles and rules and recommendations and regulations was violated in Michael's case. Indeed, in the case of this thug, this evil black boy, Lawter and the other Atlanta police who arrested and questioned Michael discarded all concern over adherence to proper procedure, as they trampled all his rights.

As to the presence of his legal guardian during his questioning, the fact was, of course, that the state was his parent, in the form of DFACS—as the Juvenile Court records Howard would brandish documented. Indeed, upon his very arrest, the address of a Fulton County DFACS office was listed as Michael's address on the "Intake Data Sheet," as DFACS was identified there as his "legal custodian." [37] DFACS, however, was never contacted to counsel Michael or act as his parent while he was being questioned by Atlanta police, and soon DFACS itself would obtain a court order to relinquish responsibility for him. He was even isolated from Valerie, for whatever it was worth, and did not have the benefit of legal counsel when they questioned him that first night, counsel the state was obliged to provide given his indigent status, whether he was a child or a man. Even if Michael were considered a child, which he was of course, he was still vested with constitutional protections, independent of a parent or guardian, particularly as to due process under the Fifth Amendment.[38] And there were his rights rising under the United Nations Convention on the Rights of the Child, defined as a person below eighteen years of age, providing for special protection and treatment of children in criminal justice matters.[39]

It would be days before anyone realized that Michael had no legal representation. In the meantime, he simply sat there in a Fulton County juvenile jail cell charged with murder. Not long before his first hearing in the superior court, where he would have to enter a plea, Gary Guichard and Patrice Fulcher, walking the hallways of the county courthouse on other matters, were contacted by cellular telephone to look into the case. As an afterthought to the rushed passage of SB 440, and in the absence of guidelines under the law, Fulton County, like other local jurisdictions, had loosely constructed a system whereby the cases of indigent children charged as adults would be handled by the conflict defender. This was how Michael finally came to have counsel.[40]

A few days later, Guichard and Fulcher accompanied Michael to the superior court hearing, where he pled not guilty to the murder of Woods. Within minutes of entering his plea, as he was now officially stripped of the status of "juvenile," the press gathered there snapped photographs of him, of the face of Little B. The story stayed in the headlines for months, the story and photographs of this evil boy.

Gary Guichard never made any challenge to any of the twelve people who became the jury. He never challenged either of the two alternate jurors. He made no motion to challenge any of them for cause, that mechanism by which a prejudiced prospective juror might be discharged on a showing of bias—a motion which, even had it been objected to by the district attorney and rejected by the court, would have made an important record for Michael's appeal. He did not eliminate any of them via the twelve preemptory challenges the state permits defendants, whereby no cause for dismissal need be shown. Thus, eight of the twelve jurors, and one of the two alternates, who came to judge Michael were admittedly exposed to the mass of pretrial publicity, by which they, each of them, had come to hold preexisting beliefs about the facts of the case.

At the same time, Guichard never objected to any of the first wave of challenges for cause that were made by the state. Those prospective jurors Paul Howard's team eliminated had one thing in common: they had strong feelings about juveniles being tried as adults.[41] On the other hand, *all* of the jurors ultimately seated had no such strong feelings about juveniles being tried as adults.

All of the eight jurors who admitted having heard or read or seen press coverage about either Darrell Woods or Michael revealed that they adhered to the same characterization of the case as was depicted in the media, particularly in the *Atlanta Journal-Constitution* stories. They all had come to court carrying a picture of the case as one in which a bad boy from the street had arbitrarily shot a father in front of his children, on account of which the victim's pregnant wife had lost their baby. This press imagery that had invented and promoted a theory of the case, a motive and facts, was an imagery now embraced by at least eight jurors. It was an imagery the prosecution exploited in the absence of proof. It was an imagery Guichard never overcame, that might have been impossible to overcome given the monumental press exposure by a majority of those who came to sit on the jury.

Joan Breitegam encountered press coverage of the case both at the time of the shooting, back in January, and on the very morning she appeared in court as a prospective juror, driving to court listening to 750 Radio, she said: "They just pretty much every fifteen minutes repeated that the trial was starting today." For Breitegam, the case involved a wife who was "four months pregnant" when her husband was killed, who "lost the baby," and it involved "two other children that watched the murder when it took place." She remembered the name "Little B" as the one "accused of shooting a guy in front of his two children." Guichard asked nothing more. Thus, Breitegam's admission that she had "numerous police friends" went unchallenged as to the testimony of police officers, and she become juror number 1.[42]

Nancy Gaenssley, a "discipline secretary" at a middle school, who would become juror number 6, stating that she did not "recall everything," remembered from the pretrial publicity that "the man's wife had gone into a convenience store to buy something," that "the victim was with his children in the car," that "they were looking for the *defendant*" (emphasis added), and "a few days later he was found." Finally, she remembered hearing that "the victim's headlights were on and that may have had something to do with what happened." When asked what she had heard about Michael, Gaenssley noted, "I didn't remember his real name until, you know, we were in court today, but they just referred to him by his *street* name" (emphasis added). There were no further questions of her.[43]

Juror number 3, Henry Elder, was never questioned in depth as to what he recalled with respect to the press coverage, though he acknowledged reading newspaper accounts of the case and, more significantly, admitted being familiar with the corner of Griffin and Meldrum Streets where Woods was killed. "The main thing" juror number 7, Minnie Martin, remembered from the newspaper stories she read about the case was "that there were children in the car and a wife." She also remembered the name "Little B." Tony Miles, juror number 8, characterized the case from his exposure to all the pretrial publicity as that of "a black guy that was shooting a black guy and that the guy was young, underage." What Judith Lippman, a substitute high school teacher who became juror number 9, concluded about the facts of the case from her reading of newspaper articles at the time, as well as on the day before her appearance in court, was that "the *gentleman*—Mr. Woods was waiting in his car when his wife went into the store to buy something and that he was shot" (emphasis added).[44]

Jeffery Reid, who became not only juror number 11 but also the jury foreman, was a journalist who had worked for CNN at the time of the shooting. Reid stated he knew "a lot about the case." When he heard the first reports over the radio, as he was driving in his car with his little girl, as he recalled it, he was shocked, thinking; "How could—I mean, you know, somebody being shot in front of their kids." When questioned as to his ability to put all the reports out of his mind and "make a decision based on the evidence," he responded, "Well, it's hard to say that you could just totally forget, but you know, I guess so, yes."[45]

The last juror seated, James Jinks, juror number 12, heard "a kid shot a guy because he disrespected him." Jinks, who also admitted being familiar with the corner of Griffin and Meldrum Streets, told the court when asked whether he could be fair, in light of all he had heard,

"Yeah, I could be fair but, in knowing everything that, you know, occurred, I don't know whether—it might be best if someone didn't hear—
that hadn't heard about it at all, because it was just so open." Jinks un-
hesitatingly acknowledged that he had been influenced by the press reports, that he had "emotional feelings for the family and for the kid himself . . . it was bad both ways." When pressed about "the kid," and his
emotional feelings, Jinks acknowledged he was referring to Michael
Lewis and that he had feelings about him because "the coverage went
like the kid was in a street gang and he was kind of pushed into what—
the events that happened, by his peers." He also admitted knowing that
"the kid's" name was Little B.[46]

Finally, there was Donovan Shipp. Though Shipp was not a regular
juror, as he became alternate number 2, his incredible pretrial exposure
to the case, via publicity and other sources, seemed to render him a
prime candidate for dismissal for cause. First, Shipp was involved in a
"prison ministry" at the DeKalb County jail, where, based on the newspaper reports about the case, he and his inmate charges "talked about it
during one of the classes."[47] While this comment went unexplored, as
to what was discussed or concluded in the "class," there were also no
questions posed to Shipp as to the nature of his work in the DeKalb
County jail facility or how he had come to be authorized to minister to
the mostly young and black men housed in that skyscraper complex.
Nothing was asked of him regarding his acknowledged membership in
and ties to Bishop Eddie Long's New Birth Missionary Baptist Church.
This was significant, first because it was Eddie Long who had contracted
with DeKalb County sheriff Sidney Dorsey and DeKalb County district
attorney J. Tom Morgan to operate that prison ministry. This was also
significant because DeKalb County was known for having taken the lead
in the state in SB 440 prosecutions, prosecutions mainly of black boys,
Morgan having stated the reason nearly all the children his office had
prosecuted under SB 440 had been black was because black boys were
the main ones committing crimes.

Shipp went unchallenged, even though he also acknowledged: "If
I'm not mistaken, I think Darrell Woods was a member of New Birth
Missionary Baptist church which I'm a member of."[48] Eddie Long, the
leader of New Birth, not only had "blessed" the new, high-rise jail facility when it opened a few years before, but also was a political ally of Sher-

iff Sidney Dorsey and District Attorney J. Tom Morgan. Moreover, Eddie Long had preached about how Michael represented an "evil in the city." And it was Eddie Long who had put up half of the so-called reward money in the case, money that had driven so many desperate drug addicts out of the bowels of the Bluff to become witnesses for the prosecution.

While four of the twelve jurors and one alternate acknowledged having close friends or relatives in law enforcement and four acknowledged being part of police-community neighborhood watch programs, none was asked what weight he or she might give to police testimony. Two jurors felt that Michael reminded them of someone; one of them, Nancy Gaenssley, the middle-school "discipline secretary," felt that Michael looked like kids with whom she interacted: "Our school is mainly black children, so, you know, you're going to find children who have similar features." Of the jurors who responded positively to whether he or anyone in his family or a close friend had ever been the victim of "juvenile crime," juror number 2 said it was she herself who had been the victim, when a "kid punched [her] in the mouth." [49]

This was the composition of the jury. Before the prosecution opened the trial with its obligatory summary of the asserted facts it would prove to this jury, Judge Cynthia Wright looked out at the jurors and all the attorneys there and said, "Let me thank you all for getting through the voir dire in an efficient fashion." [50] Then, just before delivering the standard and other jury instructions, Wright admonished the jury:

This case, as you well know, has gotten the attention of the media. You've heard us talking about that now for the last three days, and you're going to see persons associated with the media, reporters, cameramen, in the halls and even in the courtroom. The cameras will be in the courtroom.

You're instructed you are to have no conversation with the reporters or the cameramen. If you see any of your fellow jurors disregarding this important rule, please let us know. You're also instructed that you are not to listen, watch, read anything about any coverage regarding this trial. . . . I'm going to ask that you put the press out of your mind. I'm going to ask that you put the cameras out of your mind. I'm going to ask that you put the reporters out of your mind. . . . The cameras will not be focused on you. By Court rule they cannot focus on you, and you are not to focus on the cameras either, please.[51]

Howard had assigned the high-profile case of Little B to Suzanne Ockleberry. Given that the case against Michael rested solely on the testimony of Big E and his accomplices, Howard needed someone like Ockleberry, someone enterprising enough to win despite the character and motivations of Mills and the other so-called eyewitnesses, despite the numerous factual gaps in the case, despite the failure of concrete evidence, despite the procedural violations. Ockleberry would come to relish the press's image of her as a "drama queen" and "the diva of the district attorney's office."[52] She would show herself capable of bulldozing over facts and countenancing the deal made with Mills. As the publicity began to swirl about her, Ockleberry, a black woman who had recently been widowed and, as she publicly characterized it, left alone to raise her two children, claimed that she identified with Kenya Woods's loss, adding her own story to a trial that was looming, as newspaper stories were calling it, as a "made-for-TV" case. The television program *Court TV* had even contacted the court about the trial.[53] It was a case that held the promise of a critical first victory for the new D. A. and a big victory for Ockleberry. Given everything, then, by the time the November 1997 trial date approached, Ockleberry, along with another, less flamboyant black woman assistant district attorney, Phyllis Burgess, had prepared a virtual courtroom assault on Michael.

Ockleberry immediately filed a powerful pretrial motion that the defense be "prohibited" from asking any questions and making any reference at trial to the volatile relationship that had existed between Kenya and Darrell Woods, stating, "It is the State's contention that it is not relevant to any issue in the case." Guichard not only did not object to the motion, he stated, "We would not anticipate going into anything like that unless an issue of impeachment arises."[54] There would be nothing disclosed at trial, then, about the beatings, nothing about trying to leave Woods, no police reports. Guichard simply surrendered this pivotal point.[55] This was a terrible blow to Michael's defense, a blow that was almost singularly fatal.

Ockleberry then moved to restrict the defense from asking any prosecution witness about his or her "prior drug use," that is, prior to the night Woods was killed. Again, Guichard made no objection, stating, "no problem."[56] Nearly every nonofficial prosecution witness Ockleberry would call was involved with drugs as a dealer or a user or an addict and was specifically connected to Big E and his business. To set aside their histories would give credibility to people to whom it was not due and provide some semblance of substance to the case, a case indeed arising from these untrustworthy sources.

On the other hand, the most critical motion that Guichard himself made was easily challenged and dismissed. His last-minute pretrial motion for a change of venue, based on all the pretrial publicity, was simply denied by Cynthia Wright on grounds that it was filed too late.[57] Guichard made no motion regarding Michael's fitness to stand trial, relating to whether he might be suffering from any trauma resulting from having spent his childhood in a crack house or from living on the streets since he was eleven years old, to which DFACS could have attested. The impropriety and unconstitutionality of the arrest procedure were never raised.

Not required to fight other defense motions, Ockleberry's hands were fisted in the pretrial battle over exposing the state's deal with Mills. In July 1997, through his attorney, Mike Moran, Eric Mills, who was still being held in jail in connection with the murder of Woods, pleaded guilty to the drug charges arising from his November 1996 case, originally *two* counts of "possession with the intent to sell." With this plea, Mills had sealed his first deal. That is, what he had pled guilty to was the significantly reduced charge of one count of *simple* possession of cocaine and *one* count of possession with the intent to sell cocaine. By November 1997, more than four months later, as Michael's trial was in its opening stages, Mills had still not been sentenced on this plea. Thus Guichard made a pretrial motion for Ockleberry to reveal to the defense, first, whether or what was the connection between Mills's reduced charge and his testimony against Michael, that is, what had Mills promised to do for that reduced charge. More important, what further benefit had Mills been promised if he performed, as suggested by the suspension of his sentencing? The more profound issue seemed to be, however, why Paul Howard was even willing to bargain with Mills.

The fact was, of course, that without Mills there was no case against Michael. It was Mills, the original suspect in the murder of Woods, who had delivered up Michael's name. It was Mills's statement alone that had made the indictment of Michael possible. There was not one shred of physical evidence against Michael—no fingerprints, bloodstains,

DNA—nothing. There was nothing but Mills, and the corroborating witnesses all of whom were associated with Mills, that connected Michael to the murder. Moreover, victory in this high-profile case was now contingent solely on the testimony of Mills, an admitted drug dealer facing life in prison. Mills had freedom to gain by bargaining with Howard. The question was, then, what was it, in fact, that Howard had to gain by bargaining with a man like Mills for a case that was otherwise groundless.

Sadly, the murder of Woods found significance only because of the arrest of Little B, the sensationalist image of a thirteen-year-old superpredator arbitrarily killing a working black man in front of his children. Without Little B, Woods's murder might have been relegated to the insignificance of the rest of the murders in and around the Bluff, another ghetto shooting, perhaps, probably drug-related. If anyone else, a common drug dealer, had been put on trial for this shooting, the matter would have been obliterated in the "crime blotter" pages of the *Atlanta Journal-Constitution,* if noted at all, and lost in the constantly adjusted homicide statistics of the Atlanta police department. The question lingered: other than offering up a street kid as the killer in this otherwise low-profile murder, what did Mills have to sell that Howard was willing to buy?

In my mind, this raised a number of unanswered questions. If Howard truly believed Michael was guilty, was giving a light sentence to Mills, the original suspect, a bargain that justified the end? Alternatively, was Howard's "proffer" the *sole* basis for Mills's willingness to testify? More darkly, was Howard willing to win this high-profile case by any means, without consideration for the truth of the matter or for justice or for the life of this boy or for the result that Mills would be free to return to the streets with his wares? Even more compelling, was it Mills, the original suspect, the admitted drug dealer who had operated so freely and for so long in the Bluff, who had made an offer to Howard that Howard and the establishment he represented could not refuse?

Without Mills having uttered one sentence of testimony, Howard had already reduced the charges against Mills, a critical reduction from *two* felony counts to *one,* a reduction that made the difference for Mills between the certainty of serving life in prison and the possibility of serving as little as five years in prison. Thus, by the time of the trial, the only unknown issue in this bargain between Howard and Mills was the sentencing of Mills for *one* count of drug dealing.

Time would reveal the deal, which was, in effect, no time for Mills. In the meantime, an attempt was made to uncover the deal in a revelatory pretrial hearing on the matter.

The two white men entered the courtroom of Judge Cynthia Wright together. One was Mike Moran, Mills's attorney in the drug case. The other was veteran assistant district attorney Joe Burford, who had handled the Mills plea bargain in front of Judge Stephanie Manis back in July. Incidentally, it was Burford who had originally been assigned as the prosecutor in Michael's case, but in the eleventh hour Paul Howard had replaced him with Ockleberry. A similar shift had occurred with respect to the judge. While Judge Constance Russell, a black woman, had originally been assigned the case under the superior court's arbitrary administrative rotation system, it had recently been reassigned, without notice or explanation, to Wright.[58] Wright, a plain white woman—the word "average" most described her—who was the former executive counsel to Governor Zell Miller, had little experience with criminal trials.[59] After the men and the court dispensed with preliminary protocol, Guichard presented the issue.[60]

At this point, Counselor, I have made a request to be tendered the document that was under seal, which I understand to be a proffer on behalf of Mr. Mills.

Moran immediately admitted that the district attorney had made a deal with Mills in his drug case that was relevant to Mills's testimony against Michael.

There is a proffered agreement in connection with this case and I— for the record, I do represent Eric Mills and did represent him on the case where sentencing is in abeyance at this point. He has tendered a plea, but he has not actually been sentenced at this point.

. . . It was my position then and it is my position now that [as to] the matters that were contained in the proffered agreement. . . . I did feel that in fairness to my client and for my client's protection I needed to assert attorney-client privilege. . . .

My client's mother conveyed to me that she had been threatened and felt threatened . . . that [her] watchdog . . . had been shot in the head or neck and killed within a week or so of . . . when Mr. Mills tendered his plea.

Even though Mills had, back in January, months before his "plea," made his statement to police that "Little B did it," Moran suggestively connected the alleged shooting of a "watchdog" to Mills's plea bargain in July and somehow, therefore, to the matter before the court, as though Mills were some sort of law-abiding citizen who was under threat not to do the right thing; as though the dog was not known to have protected a known drug house;[61] as though Mills were not a feared, admitted drug dealer sitting in jail on a drug-dealing conviction; as though Mills had not been the original suspect in the murder of Woods; as though it was Mills who needed protection from Michael—all in order to hide the deal. Nevertheless, Moran continued:

. . . [Mills's mother] construed that act as being some sort of signal to her that if Mr. Mills cooperated with the investigation or if he testified, that both she and Mr. Mills would be in jeopardy.

Now, that's a conclusion that she made, but I took that seriously and I conveyed it to Mr. Burford. . . .

My client's mother has since moved from this neighborhood because she takes this act very seriously and . . . is very concerned about the disclosure of any information pretrial. That's the reason that I embodied in this proffered agreement language which essentially prohibited Mr. Burford or the District Attorney's office from disseminating or allowing the proffer to be copied, and that is the reason that I asked the Court to seal the proffered agreement. . . .

. . . My initial preference would be to sit down with all counsel and to outline to them the context and substance of the proffer without turning the proffer over. . . .

I specifically requested at the time that we tendered the plea that the proffered agreement be sealed. . . .

The suspect nature of the "proffer" and legality of sealing it was such that Ockleberry stepped forward to give the court an excuse to keep it sealed.

I think what the Court can do, we've given them Eric Mills's statement, okay. . . . I think that would solve the whole thing, because that's basically all that is. . . . They've got his statement that he made at the time of the arrest. . . .

Guichard responded to the implications of the alleged necessity of keeping the deal a secret.

First of all, Your Honor, I want to say that I respect counsel's desires to address the issue of safety of his client and his client's family. I would like the record to reflect that neither myself nor my co-counsel, nor anyone that I am aware of . . . from my side of the fence had any information as to the plea taking place until quite some time after it.

Then, Guichard, in responding to Moran's rather ridiculous charge about a dog being killed as a warning to Mills, revealed something else. Up until that very moment, only days before trial would begin, Guichard had not advised Michael that Mills had made a deal with the state to testify against him.

I'm not saying that counselor is implicating my client in the shooting of . . . his client's mother's pet, and I just want the record to reflect that the fact of the plea or even the date of the plea was not conveyed by myself or my co-counsel to my client. . . .

Wright interrupted Guichard to refocus the matter to his own motion.

. . . I want to make sure that I'm not losing sight of the request. The whole request was to reveal any deal, right? Mr. Moran is in the courtroom now and I've looked at the agreement and I think the answer from the State was earlier there is no deal.

Now, however, the very definition of the deal, as to what sentence the state intended to give Eric Mills on his reduced drug-dealing plea in exchange for his testimony against Michael, was being lost. Moran seized that.

Your Honor, the only agreement that was had between the State and I was as to the counts to which Mr. Mills would plead and the charges to which he would plead. Mr. Mills had two or three, I believe two. . . . But I believe a plea was tendered to two counts.

As the deal remained sealed, however, Moran took the opportunity to interpret it to Mills's benefit—and the state's benefit.

. . . I've made this emphatically clear to Mr. Mills, the State has not agreed to make any specific recommendation regarding sentence on this case. They [the state] have committed to make the extent of his cooperation and his testimony and the truthfulness, assuming that he is truthful when he testifies, known at the time of his sentencing. . . .

. . . They [the state] have simply reserved the right to make an appropriate recommendation at that time, but . . . there is no number attached to the agreement at this point. . . . It is an open-ended agreement. . . .

Given that, Guichard made a final effort to uncover at least the parameters of the state's sealed deal with Mills.

If Your Honor is not inclined to have the document turned over to defense, then my next best position would be to take counselor up on his offer to sit down with us and outline the details of the contents thereof. . . .

Burford then came forward and, alternatively, revealed the new charges to which Mills had pleaded.

. . . Your Honor, I can tell the Court that there were two cases. . . . Both of those were in front of Judge [Stephanie] Manis. . . .

He [Mills] plead [sic] guilty . . . to possession of four grams [of crack cocaine] and he [pled] guilty to possession with intent . . . of two grams. . . .

Guichard made a final plea to unseal the deal.

Your Honor . . . I think it's appropriate for the record to reflect what Mr. Mills was originally charged with and what was, in fact, [pled] to.

. . . The other thing that I think Your Honor needs to take into consideration is the fact that the sentencing was held in abeyance and let me just remind you that that could constitute a deal whether they want to constitute that as a deal or not.

Judge Cynthia Wright responded by closing off such discussion, forever.

Well, you already know about that now. . . . I think I've heard enough on this. . . . I can understand now why this trial might last two weeks.

The last words belonged to Ockleberry.

I'll shoot myself if it does.

While Cynthia Wright's projection of the trial duration would prove incorrect, for the trial would last only days, the deal with Mills would remain sealed. Mills would be seen on the street only months after Michael's conviction.

After the jury was sworn in, Wright reminded them that the state had the burden to prove its case *beyond a reasonable doubt* and that the defendant did not have the duty to prove his innocence, that they were to deem Michael "innocent until proven guilty." The standard of reasonable doubt was then explained by Wright, though mostly in terms of what it was not.

The State is not required to prove the guilt of the accused beyond all . . . doubt or to a mathematical certainty. A reasonable doubt . . . does not mean a vague or an arbitrary doubt, but is a doubt for which a reason can be given arising from a consideration of the evidence, a lack of evidence, a conflict in the evidence or any combination of these.[62]

Continuing to read monotonously from the standard script, Wright went on to instruct the jury about an issue particularly crucial in this case, judging the credibility of the witnesses.

In passing upon a witness' credibility you may consider all the facts and circumstances of the case, the witness' manner of testifying, the witness' intelligence, the witness' interest or lack of interest in the outcome of the case, the witness' means and opportunity for knowing the facts to which they testify. . . . You may also consider a witness' personal credibility.[63]

Now Phyllis Burgess, Ockleberry's coprosecutor, presented the state's case in an opening statement, in which she was bound by law to lay out the facts alleged and what the state would prove. Incredibly, ironically, particularly in light of the state's own motion to quash all references to the violent relationship between Darrell and Kenya Woods— as well as the state's additional unchallenged motion to disallow all reference to the fact that Kenya's older son was not Darrell's—Burgess began by stating, "This case is about the Woods family."[64] With this, Burgess established the core theme of the state's case, built not on facts or evidence but on imagery, imagery constructed by the press, which imagery at least eight of the twelve jurors had come to the jury box possessing, an imagery founded on lies.

Burgess continued.

This case is about the Woods family, and the Woods family consisted of Darrell Woods. . . . He was a husband and a father. He worked as a . . . machine operator. . . .

He was married to Kenya Woods who . . . at the time her husband was killed . . . was pregnant with their third child. . . . And the evidence will show that on January 21st of this year, that that day started out like most days for the Woods family; that Kenya Woods got her boys up, dressed for school, that Darrell Woods went to work and at the end of the day, like most families, they got back together.

There was no objection by Guichard as to the insertion of the false reference to a "third child" or of the improbability of the younger child having gone to school at the age of two, which, though irrelevant to the facts of the case, was introduced to paint the false picture, as sketched by pretrial publicity, of the good father killed by the bad boy.

Even though Burgess knew, that the Woodses had moved to the Vine City area because they had been evicted, she repeated for the jury the fictional press version of the Woodses' family life, which was also unchallenged.

Kenya had picked the boys up from school, she went and picked her husband Darrell Woods up from work and . . . they decided to stop off at a local fast food restaurant, Captain D's . . . and they drove home to their community. . . . And the evidence will show that the Woods family was not very familiar with this area, that they only lived in this community for about four months. They had moved from a larger more expensive apartment . . . to a smaller inexpensive apartment . . . so they could save money for Mrs. Woods to complete her education. . . . Driving home, they spotted the light of a local neighborhood grocery called Henry's supermarket and they decided to stop to get some soda for dinner.

Finally, Burgess began to set forth what the state claimed it would prove, much of which represented allegations that would never be supported at trial. First, there was her assertion that Michael solicited Woods to buy drugs, which not even the dealers and addicts the state would call as witnesses would contend.

This Defendant walked up to the car where Mr. Woods was sitting and he asked Mr. Woods if he wanted to buy some drugs.

Now came the various claims relating to an invented altercation that would produce the presumed motive for the case. Each of these alleged exchanges would be in conflict with or unsupported by the testimony of the state's own witnesses, even Mills, and would never be attested to by Kenya Woods herself. Indeed, Kenya Woods would never testify to having ever seen Michael, and given the state's argument as now presented by Burgess, it would have been impossible for her not to have seen him.

The Defendant then told Mr. Woods to turn the car lights out. . . .

By this time Kenya Woods had come back out of the store because she needed some change . . . to purchase the soda . . . and when she walked back into the store this Defendant said to Mr. Woods, anymore whores in the car? Mr. Woods said, there ain't no whores in the car.

This Defendant again told Mr. Woods to turn his car lights out. And, members of the jury, you're going to hear that the reason this Defendant wanted the lights out was because in that area there's a lot of drug transactions going on and the lights from the car lit up the area such that if the police were to come by they could see the drug transactions going on.

Burgess then rambled on for some time, presenting alternative versions of an alleged exchange between Woods and Michael, none of which the state would ever substantiate, all of which recalled for the jury the kind of story they had heard all along in the press. She dramatically concluded that Michael "ran up to the passenger door where Mr. Woods was sitting and he stood a few feet away from the door and he raised the rifle, and for no reason whatsoever, he fired two shots into that car." [65]

––––––––––

While Guichard promised the jury in his opening statement to show that the state had accused "the wrong man," he himself indicted Michael at the outset. He put information before the jury—information that would never be introduced as evidence by the state—that Michael had sold drugs on the streets of the Bluff, thus giving credence to one of the state's various claims about the motive. Indeed, Guichard made other irrelevant and otherwise unsupported and detrimental statements about Michael. He told the jury, for example, that Michael did whatever was asked of him by his mother and brother—neither of whom would be called by either the state or the defense to testify—in terms of selling and holding drugs for them or taking responsibility for their crimes. Guichard knew, even at that very moment, however, that he would not and could not present any witness or evidence to support this theory that Michael might be on trial as a "patsy" for some older unnamed person. On the other hand, he knew—but never told the jury—something about Michael's history that might have been more relevant: that Valerie Morgan was a crack addict who had been declared an unfit mother and had lost custody of Michael two years before his arrest, and that the state itself had been his guardian those last two years. There was one more critical and relevant omission from the opening statement about Michael's history. Although Michael himself did not know it then, Eric Mills, the original suspect in the murder of Woods, whom Michael knew well, whom Michael knew had been out on the street dealing drugs where and when Darrell Woods had been killed, had made an undisclosed deal with Paul Howard to act as an eyewitness against Michael in exchange for his own freedom from prosecution.

Instead of using this important opening statement to remind the jury of the state's burden to *prove* the story it had just laid out, instead of pointing out the glaring inconsistencies in the state's opening argument, instead of challenging the state's fabricated theory and motive in the case, instead of letting the jury know there were other suspects and other motives, Guichard offered the jury a theory of the case that seemed to comport with the state's assertion that Michael was a "thug," a theory that effectively implicated Michael in the matter, however vicariously.

. . . The Bluff . . . is an area that is known . . . for violence and drug trafficking. It was into this area and this general environment that Michael Lewis was born and raised. He was . . . exposed to the street life in the area at a very, very early age. He was virtually introduced and fed into this lifestyle by his mother and his brother, his brother whom he looked up to and admired. His mother began what I guess can loosely be referred to as the family business, selling drugs. She passed that business on to Michael's older brother Jason. . . . Michael began to hang out where his mother and his brother hung out, that same obscure dark violent corner in this Northwest Atlanta. He endeavored to be like them. He endeavored to emulate their behavior. . . . He was allowed to hang out with the older crowd, the drug selling crowd, and he became or attempted to become a part of their world. . . . But there was a trade off . . . for them he was a patsy, he was a tool, he was a target, because he was so young. . . . Slowly, steadily, step by step he began to be immersed in that world because he was valuable to them.

When the police were in the neighborhood, when the Red Dogs were around Michael held the drugs. . . . And Michael was rewarded for these activities . . . paid money for taking the blame, as it were. . . . This was his method of survival. . . . Michael grew up virtually unsupervised. . . . In point of fact, Michael is a 13-year-old, now 14-year-old scapegoat. . . .

Dispassionate and quiet, Guichard never urged the jury to look to the state's burden of proof, its lack of physical evidence, for the state would not as it could not present a scintilla of physical evidence connecting Michael to the murder. He never pointed out to the jury at that crucial juncture that there was also nothing that tied the murder weapon to Michael, "found" *after* his arrest at the place where he was arrested, but where numerous people, drug users and dealers, lived. He never showed them how the other piece of "physical evidence" the state would rely on, the black skull cap, represented absolutely nothing at all, as the jury would learn.

The most important issues Guichard failed to raise before the jury had to do with the state's star witness, Eric Mills. The jury had just been instructed to consider, among other things, the personal credibility of a witness and the witness's interest in the outcome of the trial. Guichard could have told the jury, first, about the deal, the state's deal with Mills that was never really revealed, as the law required. He could have reminded the jury that Mills was a known dope dealer, facing life in prison, who was out on that corner of the Bluff where and when Woods was killed. Moreover, Guichard could have forecast for the jury that most of the other so-called eyewitnesses the state would call were drug users or dealers who bought or sold Mills's drugs, some of whom were "high" on Mills's drugs at the very moment Woods was killed. Finally, he could have pointed out to the jury that Mills had been the original suspect in the murder of Woods. He could have alerted the jury to watch Mills, who only after he was arrested as the primary suspect told police Michael Lewis, a boy of the street, was the killer. He could have pointed out to them Mills's clear interest in the trial's outcome, his interest in a conviction of Michael, including exoneration from being himself under indictment for murder and a reduced sentence for dealing drugs, along with whatever else there was in his secret deal with the state.

[14] The Innocence of Little B

So it began. A crowd of strange bedfellows gathered, ready to deliver their thousand cuts, each with his or her own motive, willing to exchange the very life of a boy for their deals with the devil.

Kenya Woods would reveal nothing, of course, of her turbulent relationship with Woods, nothing about his beatings of her. She would never discuss how she felt about all that. It was not required. It had been suppressed. Indeed, not only did she cry as she entered the courtroom to testify, she even cried on the stand recollecting the night her husband was killed.

In her brief appearance, she testified that she drove her children to pick Woods up from work, and then, inexplicably, she said, and for the first and only time, they "went home and talked to the landlord." This was noteworthy because the landlady did not live on Western Avenue. It was even more interesting given that the woman who had said she was Kenya Woods's "best friend" had wondered aloud over and over in her investigative interview why Darrell and Kenya Woods "went back home first!"[1] After that, Woods testified, they "went to get something to eat." From that point, she reiterated the familiar story that she and Darrell and the boys bought dinner at Captain D's seafood restaurant on Ralph David Abernathy Boulevard. Then, she said, they "went to get something to drink." The first store at which she stopped was closed, she said. Then she testified, "We saw another store that's lights were on, so I stopped."[2]

She parked the car in front of Henry's and went inside to get the drink. After "the lady" told her she "needed more change," she stepped out to the car, where Darrell was sitting in the passenger seat. He rolled down the window, she said, and gave her the change. She went back into the store. "I gave the lady the change, she gave me the pop, and I heard some shots." [3]

Soon, though, Kenya Woods broke down in tears, and the jury had to be sent out of the courtroom. She had just testified that when she heard the shots, she looked out the door and "saw someone outside": "I saw somebody running, so I was running and I was saying, Hey, Hey, Hey." [4]

Once Woods regained her composure, she resumed her testimony, or revisited what she had already said. Now she explained that she had moved into the area because the rent was "cheap" and she "could go back to school." Now there was no mention of going home and talking with the landlord. Now, her husband told her, when she asked for the change: "Hurry up, there's way too many people out here and I don't like this area."

Again, however, Kenya Woods said, she went back into the store. Again, she said, "I gave the lady the change and she gave me the soda." Again, at that very moment, she heard shots.

Now, though, she looked outside and saw the window to her car was out, the passenger window. Now, she ran outside to her car. She re-iterated she saw somebody running. "So I was chasing them. I said, Hey, Hey, Hey."

Then Phyllis Burgess asked her,

Do you remember what that person looked like that you saw running?

Kenya Woods responded:

Not really.

She started to run after him but was stopped by someone who held her and told her to "get back, get back." She looked inside the car and then ran back to the store to call for help.

She went back to the car and opened the door. She "looked at the kids to see if they were okay." Then she "stretched [Woods] out." A girl came up, and she asked the girl to help. The girl took the kids into the store. Kenya said she "tried to help [her husband]," but, she said, she could not. "I just kissed him and I told him that I loved him and I held him and I tried to help him." That was her testimony.

Then Phyllis Burgess asked Woods one last question, even though it had already been asked and answered:

Mrs. Woods, the person that you saw running away from the car, can you give any description of that person?

Woods responded:

Yes, Ma'am. He was about my height, which is maybe 5' 2", 5' 3", a little bit chunckier [sic] *than me, and he had on a hooded sweat jacket with some kind of brim to it or something under it.*

Finally, Burgess asked,

Do you recall the color of the brim?

Woods answered:

It was like his face, it was black, black.[5]

It would be a few days later that Guichard would conduct his extraordinarily brief cross-examination of Kenya Woods.[6] The cross-examination did not show any conflict with the direct testimony. Thus, though Guichard never clarified the issue, in the totality of Kenya Woods's testimony, she never identified Michael as the shooter and, indeed, never even saw Michael.

In addition, although Guichard never asked Woods about it, when she testified Darrell told her how nervous he was, she never reported that he mentioned anything to her about turning off the headlights, or headlight. Thus, the absence of such a statement in the record presumes he said nothing about turning out the headlight, and Kenya Woods testified that he did say something. There was also nothing in Kenya Woods's testimony that Darrell said anything about a kid telling him to do anything. She herself said nothing about seeing a kid talking to her husband. She said nothing about seeing a gun in the hands of the person she said she saw running away. Guichard never asked her about any of this, however.

There were other permissible questions that went unasked in the cross-examination of Kenya Woods. Even though Guichard had agreed to forfeit all discussion about Kenya and Darrell's violent history, the caveat that could have opened the door to this line of questioning was for purposes of impeachment of her testimony. Nevertheless, even though Woods testified that she and Darrell had moved from a working-class black enclave of Atlanta to a drug-infested ghetto to save money, Guichard did not impeach that testimony with the eviction papers Marvin Dixon had obtained. Moreover, he asked nothing of her about her recent use of three different Social Security numbers: one for the car, registered to her, and the other two used for the apartments she had tried to rent, alone, sometime after she and Darrell were evicted and before they moved into the Western Avenue place.[7] In other words, Guichard did not seize the moment to question Woods about the nature of her relationship with her husband.

Kenya Woods was not cross-examined regarding the exact route she drove from Captain D's to Henry's, or toward home. Indeed, she testified she could not recall the route, which necessarily would have taken them along any number of major boulevards and avenues where they would have passed all those places where a soda could have been purchased before ending up at a little store buried among the dilapidated residences on a tiny street. This might have led to the question of whether or not she, or Darrell, had ever been to Henry's before that night or knew anybody that might have been at Henry's that night, somebody who might have wanted to hurt Darrell. This question also was never raised.

Moreover, nothing was asked about the Land Cruiser that had been parked in front of their place, or the rumored beating of Darrell two nights before his murder. This might have been investigated in order to ask Kenya Woods about enemies Darrell might have had. One issue Guichard did raise in his cross-examination of Kenya Woods seemed to broach this question, however. He noted that "that day [of the murder] there was damage to the front end and the rear end of the car [she was] driving," to which she agreed. She agreed it had happened "on a prior occasion." [8] Guichard never asked her, however, how or when that damage had occurred or who might have damaged both the front and rear ends of the car. He also never asked her why Darrell was often called Little D.[9]

In addition, Kenya Woods was never asked about the soda she bought, as to what kind it was or what she did with it when she heard the shots outside the store. The storeowner, Mrs. Suh (also known as Canty), would testify that it was a can of soda.[10] The girl on the telephone had told Dixon that it was a can of orange soda. The most important issue about the soda that Guichard never raised, however, surfaced in the testimony of police homicide detective Dale Kelly, the first investigator to arrive at the murder scene. It had to do with Kelly's description for the record of one of the crime scene photographs (State's Exhibit Number 9), which Kelly had directed be taken and which Guichard had seen. Kelly identified the photograph as a view of the inside of the car and continued:

It's the right-hand [passenger] side of the vehicle, the window is busted out of the door, it's standing open, the victim is laying at an awkward angle back towards the driver's seat and in the corner there, facing it, to the left is the drink bottle, it was about a liter bottle of drink the family had stopped to get from the store.[11]

The question was, obviously, how had a liter bottle of soda come to be a part of the crime scene? Was it there before Woods was killed? Even if Mrs. Suh and the girl on the telephone had been mistaken about the can of soda, had Kenya Woods run outside in pursuit of the presumed shooter carrying a liter bottle of soda in her hand? She could not have given it to Darrell before she went back in to the store because, as she testified, "I gave the lady the change and she gave me the soda." The answer would remain unknown.

There was one other issue about the purchase of that soda that was not brought to light. While Kenya Woods claimed that even though she had lived in the area about four months she was unfamiliar with the surrounding area and with Henry's, Henry's was well known in the area. An investigative interview with a next-door neighbor of the Woodses confirmed the store's reputation: "He [the neighbor] stated that no one goes in that store to buy sodas. . . . The only people who hang around that store are people either selling drugs, buying drugs, or drug addicts. He says that as long as he has been living there he has never been in that store and does not plan on it."[12]

Detective Kelly's testimony would reveal one other important fact that went unexplored in the cross-examination of Kenya Woods. The damage to the front end of the car, which Kelly stated was the result of an "accident sometime prior to the incident," had left the car with only one functioning headlight the night Darrell Woods was killed.[13] Neither Kelly nor any one else would address the damage to the rear of the car. And, most significantly, Kenya Woods was never asked whether she, or Darrell, knew Eric Mills.

Similarly, Mills was never asked whether he knew Kenya or Darrell Woods, or had ever seen either of them before, or whether he had any kind of a relationship with either of them.

What was established by Mills's testimony, first, was that he was called Big E on the street and that on the night Woods was killed, and in the place where Woods was killed, he had been out there on the street selling drugs—notably an instance of drug dealing for which he had not been and never would be charged. Mills acknowledged that he had pleaded guilty in July to charges of drug possession and possession with the intent to sell drugs. Incredibly, he denied being a full-time drug dealer, and more incredibly, Ockleberry objected to the "relevancy" of this question and Wright sustained her objection—although no one ever asked Mills how else he made the money by which he lived.[14]

As instructed by Ockleberry, Mills pulled his huge body up from the witness chair, his face flushed, and walked over to Michael and pointed at him as the killer of Woods.[15] That was what he was there to do. While out on the street that night, selling drugs, Big E testified, he saw Michael go to a nearby alley and retrieve a gun, a rifle, and go to the car where Woods was sitting and raise it toward Woods. He had known Little B from the neighborhood all his life. He hollered out, "Don't do that!" Nevertheless, Mills said, Michael shot Woods. He saw him shoot Woods with his own eyes. Then Big E walked away.[16] That was it. That was Mills's brief testimony, testimony that would save him from a lifetime in prison.

Given that the case was built on this testimony, corroborated only by Mills's cronies, and given the absence of physical evidence, Ockleberry also used Mills to spruce up her case with a piece of evidence that was not evidence at all. She asked Mills to describe how the defendant was dressed. "He had on dark clothes," Mills responded. When prompted, Mills remembered a "black skull cap." Ockleberry then produced such a hat from her exhibits and showed it to Mills. Not surprisingly, he identified it as, or as looking like, the hat he claimed to have seen on Michael's head the night Woods was killed.[17] One of Mills's various cronies that came to testify would be the only other witness to mention such a hat.

The other reference to this hat in connection with Michael came through the testimony of Detective Warren Keith Picard, identified as an "undercover" narcotics officer assigned to Atlanta police department Zone 1, which incorporated the Bluff. Picard claimed he had seen Michael numerous times in the area, the last time he recalled, rather exceptionally, being the day after the murder, stating, "He was wearing a black cap, which he always have worn ever since I've known him." [18] And after Picard's appearance, testimony was offered as to how the hat had come into being as an "exhibit." It was "found," Detective Sam Lawter ("Curly Top") testified, on Holly Street, *after* he had arrested Michael. Later that evening he had obtained a search warrant for the apartment there. Lawter said he and his men searched for "weapons, ammunition, clothing that might be evidence," recovering only this one piece of "evidence." He claimed to have "found" the hat on the floor of one of the two bedrooms, which he identified as the defendant's—to no objection, even though numerous people lived and "stayed" there, even though Michael lived nowhere in particular and stayed wherever he could.[19] Indeed, according to the investigation of the case, the night Woods was killed Michael had stayed at the house of a girl named Ebony, as he often did.[20] However, on the basis of Mills's statement alone, and although the hat had no intrinsic merit, as it was not blood-stained or found at the scene or otherwise relevant to the murder of Darrell Woods, Okleberry now requested the court mark the cap Lawter found as "evidence" in this murder case. There was no objection.[21]

While Guichard was more aggressive with Mills than he had been with Kenya Woods, pounding him to "reveal the deal" he had made with the state, in his cross-examination of Mills, Guichard never asked him one question, the one question that ought to have been asked: *Eric Mills, did you kill Darrell Woods?*

Although Mills would surely have denied the accusation, assuming Okleberry would not have leapt from her seat before that to object, to silence him, it was a legitimate question. It was a question the jury needed to consider, given who Mills was, what he did, and his pivotal role in Michael's case, and given that Darrell Woods, like every other murder victim, was surely not killed for nothing but for something.

At the very least Mills might have been asked whether he knew Darrell Woods or had ever sold Woods any drugs. He might have been asked whether he knew Kenya Woods. For, while Mills admitted that he had seen "the female" enter the store, and while he denied ever having seen the car in the area before, he was never asked whether he knew Kenya Woods herself.[22] It was Kenya Woods who drove Darrell Woods along with her children to Henry's that night, who claimed to have stumbled upon Henry's as she claimed to have stumbled upon a "cheaper" place in that area, who never revealed her true relationship with Darrell, which the state itself thought relevant enough to have made a motion to secrete—and not for nothing.

While Mills acknowledged that he knew Valerie Morgan, Michael's mother, he was not asked about his relationship with her.[23] This would have been a logical question, given that Valerie Morgan was a known area crack addict and given the significant though indirect role she was playing in the case. It was Valerie Morgan's alleged statement to the district attorney, a garbled recording of which would never be produced, documented, or otherwise used at trial, that would be used to introduce the murder weapon into the case against Michael.[24] And Morgan herself would never substantiate her statement. Two days *after* Michael's arrest, the rifle identified as the murder weapon was suddenly found in the back of the apartment complex on Holly Street.[25] This weapon successfully wound its way into the case as evidence through the trial testimony of the district attorney's own investigator John Richey, who claimed to have "discovered" the weapon based on a conversation with Morgan. He inferred she had told him where the murder weapon was located after allegedly speaking with her son. Thus, Morgan's alleged unproduced and unrevealed statement was used to legitimize the introduction of the weapon into evidence in the absence of a legitimate search warrant. The point was that Mills was never asked about the extent of his relationship with Valerie Morgan, whether she might have sold drugs for him or held drugs for him, or whether she owed him any money for drugs he had supplied her, or what, under the circumstances, Valerie Morgan might have been willing to do for him, which circumstances included her being, like so many others, terrified of him.

Mills was never asked whether he had sold drugs that day or that night to Bertha Hayes, also a known area drug addict—though of course, based on Ockleberry's pretrial motion, the jury would never be able to know that. Hayes was important as the prosecution witness Lawter would testify had been his main informant, on whose statements alone, he testified, he had obtained the arrest warrant for Michael.[26] Mills was also never asked whether LaTosha Beard, another supporting prosecution witness, sold or bought his drugs, not only because she had been admittedly idling away on that corner that night, "chitchatting" with her aunt, but because LaTosha Beard's aunt had a baby by Mills.[27] He was never asked about that relationship with Beard's aunt, which might have been used later to show that Beard had a compelling interest in providing testimony that would corroborate his version of events that night. He was never asked whether he knew Ikesha Arnold, another local witness, who had been sitting on some steps in front of Henry's with Beard and others that night. Arnold was not only a friend of Beard's, she was the mother of one of the children of J-Boy, Michael's brother, who was also Mills's friend—who would never be called to testify.[28] Mills was never asked whether Linda Mae Mitchell, also known as Phyllis McBride, another supporting character who was a known drug addict, was one of his regular customers or whether he had sold her some drugs that night.

Mills was never asked whether he had ever possessed or used an assault rifle such as the one the man from Guardian Chemical, Fawcett, a prosecution witness never called, had seen him carrying not long before Woods was killed.[29] He was never asked how it was that he operated so freely in and around Henry's market. Mills was never asked whether he knew "Miami Black" or anyone else with a Land Cruiser, or where he bought the drugs he sold. He was never asked about the drugs he sold, whether he sold only cocaine or also crack or heroin or marijuana or Ecstasy, and what were his prices, and how much money he made—even restricting his affairs to the night that Woods was killed—and who were his customers other than the local addicts, and was it not true that most of his customers drove through the Bluff and bought their drugs directly and openly from their cars, day and night, so that the jury might have clearly understood that there were no drug transactions to be hidden on the corner known as New Jack City, understood exactly who this witness was and what his interests were in the outcome of this trial.

Finally, and most significantly, Mills was never asked about his relationship with police detective Sam Lawter, known as Curly Top. While he stated that he did not really know Curly Top, though he referred to Lawter in his testimony in this familiar way, and Lawter would swear he did not know Mills, there was something glaringly inconsistent in their mutual disavowals.[30] It was hard to believe that Lawter, the central police figure in this case, who would testify he had worked in the area a total of thirteen years, five of which as a narcotics officer, and that he was "very familiar" with the corner of Griffin and Meldrum Streets, and who seemingly knew nearly all the other characters who spent their lives there, including Valerie Morgan and Bertha Hayes, would still not know the main drug dealer in the area.[31] Conversely, it was impossible to believe that Mills, who sold drugs every day in the Bluff, in fact, could not know a police officer who had worked in the area, and worked in the narcotics division of the Atlanta police department, for so long. For, despite his claim otherwise, Big E was a notorious drug dealer in the Bluff.

When asked whether he had been present when the police arrived after Woods was killed, Mills testified that he had been—even though he had earlier testified he had walked away. When asked whether he had talked with the police that night, Mills answered no.[32] However, when Guichard later asked Lawter whether Mills was one of the people he spoke with when he arrived at the murder scene, Lawter said yes, adding pointedly, "I found that out later . . . I did not know him at the time."[33] When Mills was asked to whom he gave his statement accusing Michael of the murder, he responded "Homicide"; while Lawter, when asked whether he had taken the statement of Mills, the key prosecution witness, would respond, "A statement was taken. I did not take it."[34] What made their mutual denials of each other even more doubtful had to do with the date both Lawter and Mills testified Mills was arrested as a "party" to the murder of Woods, January 28, 1997, the same date as Michael—though the circumstances of Mills's arrest were never reviewed at trial. The subsequent superior court documents in the disposition of Mills's drug cases would indicate another date of arrest. Judge Stephanie Manis, who had ordered Mills's deal sealed back in July 1997, signed a Final Disposition order for Mills on December 23, 1997—only weeks after Michael's conviction—in which Mills was sentenced under the sealed deal to a total of ten years, though he would be required to serve only three years. He was given "credit for time" served in jail.[35] That credit included the time Mills served in connection with the Woods murder case, which was noted as beginning not on January 28 but on January 22, 1997, the day after Woods was killed, the day the case was reassigned from Detective Dale Kelly to Detective Sam Lawter.

In the end, though, something even worse occurred in the cross-examination of Mills. Guichard, in an excited attempt to force Mills to reveal that he did in fact play a role in the murder of Woods, asked questions that pointed more to Michael than Mills.[36]

The question was did you know anything about it [the shooting of Woods] before it happened, before it was to happen?

No, I did not.

. . . You have testified today that you said Don't do it, Don't do it, directed at my client, right?

Yes.

So . . . You are denying at this time that you encouraged anyone to shoot Darrell Woods?

I didn't encourage nobody to do nothing.

And you are denying right now that you said to anyone Don't let him disrespect you like that?

I didn't tell anyone that.

And you are denying at this time that you said Go over there and handle your business?

Yes, I am. I did not tell him that.

When Mills stepped down, Patrice Fulcher wept, and Marvin Dixon never came back to the courtroom.

Gary Barber, known as Chuckie Boy, admitted he was selling drugs in the Bluff for Big E that night. Indeed, he had been out on that corner "all day," he testified. Like Big E, Chuckie Boy was, at the time of his testimony, in custody on various drug-dealing charges, for which he was facing life in prison. Like Big E, he swore he had made no deal with the state for his testimony, though, also like Big E, he was awaiting sentencing. While he cooperated and testified for the state that he at least saw Michael with a gun, saw him running with a "shotgun," he had to admit he had not actually seen the shooting. Yes, he recognized the hat Phyllis Burgess showed him as the one he saw Michael wearing that night —though he acknowledged to Guichard that a lot of people in that area wore the same kind and color hat—and he agreed with her that he had told Detective Lawter he heard Michael tell someone in the car to turn out the headlights. However, he had been around the corner making a drug sale when he "heard" *three* shots. And while his testimony was predictable, and unsurprisingly he was not asked whether he knew Kenya or Darrell Woods or had ever sold either of them any of Big E's drugs, there was one curious variation in Chuckie Boy's testimony. He swore he and Big E were "on the scene" when Curly Top arrived and that both of them spoke to him that night, the night Woods was killed.[37]

Antonio Johnson, known as Tom-Tom, was selling heroin in the Bluff that night—though this fact would not be revealed through his trial testimony. The jury would learn this indirectly, through the later appearances of Sam Lawter and Detective Brian E. Anderson. Anderson, who claimed affiliation with the DEA (U.S. Drug Enforcement Agency), would testify that an "informant" had told him Tom-Tom had been on the scene when Woods was killed. Anderson would say he knew Antonio Johnson as a result of his investigations into heroin sales and he had located Johnson and taken him to Lawter for questioning.[38] Lawter would testify that he was aware that Johnson had been in the Bluff selling heroin when Woods was killed, and knew, too, at the time he questioned Johnson, that Johnson was facing three pending indictments for heroin sales.[39] Indeed, as a result of this interrogation by Lawter, two days after Michael's arrest, Johnson signed a statement indicting Michael, a statement he vigorously refuted in a heated exchange with Phyllis Burgess at trial.[40]

In the signed statement, Tom-Tom said he had been out on the corner and had seen Michael shoot Woods. In court, he said, "I didn't see it." In his statement to Lawter, Johnson said he saw Kenya Woods drive up to Henry's market. In court, he testified, "The police made me see. . . . They had arrested me. A police officer kept harassing me." When Burgess pressed him to acknowledge his signed statement, Johnson said, "I can't read. I can't read." Moreover, he insisted he had not signed the statement "voluntarily," swearing, in the end, "I didn't see nothing."[41] Later, though, the court would allow Ockleberry to validate Johnson's statement via her examination of Lawter. Lawter's voice would, then, testify for Tom-Tom that he saw Michael Lewis shoot Woods.[42] Johnson himself, though, was never asked whether he sold heroin for Big E.

Like Big E, Chuckie Boy, and Tom-Tom, Larry Gee, known as Hootie, was also facing drug charges, on both possession and sale of cocaine, when he came to court to testify for the state against Michael. Like Tom-Tom, Hootie had been out on the corner known as New Jack City all day, "just hanging out," as he put it. Most of the time, he was with Ikesha Arnold and LaTosha Beard. Like Antonio Johnson, Gee had to be prompted by the state to repeat what he had said in a statement to the district attorney's investigator, Richey, implicating Michael in the murder, much of which he, too, disputed in court. Still, Ockleberry pounded him to admit what was reported in his signed statement, that he saw Michael standing out there talking with two other people around the time Kenya Woods drove up to the store—people he was never asked to name, however. Though he testified that he saw Michael walk across the street, after which he and his friends "walked off," Ockleberry forced him to support his statement in which he said he heard Michael say he was going to "shoot down at that nigger." She reminded him that he had told Richey he saw Michael go to a nearby alley. She insisted he had told Richey he saw Michael come back from the alley, though Gee insisted he never saw that, that he had walked away, that he had gone "behind the Chinese store." Ockleberry became so furious with Gee that she accused him of changing his story after talking with Michael in jail—thus illegally identifying that Michael was in jail, on account of which Guichard moved, unsuccessfully, for a mistrial. Even though Ockleberry finally had Gee declared a hostile witness, and even though he denied ever saying he saw or ever seeing Michael with a rifle, and even though he finally acknowledged he did not see the shooting at all, his overall testimony was corroborative of Mills's and served to implicate Michael. He was on the stand to implicate Michael.

This indicting testimony was not really overcome by Gee's testimony in the cross-examination that he never saw Michael go anywhere near the car. It was not overcome by his confession that he had been using cocaine during that day, and even, as he further admitted, shortly before Woods was killed. It was not even overcome by Gee's acknowledgment that he himself owned a black skull cap exactly like the one found on Holly Street—where he himself lived—that was now evidence, a hat he stated he bought at Henry's, like at least ten other people he knew.[43] This was because the most indicting portions of Gee's signed statement were validated later via the testimony of Richey. As in the case of Lawter as to Tom-Tom's testimony, the court allowed Ockleberry to use Richey to effectively testify for Gee, to affirm statements Gee himself disputed in court, which included Richey quoting Gee as exclaiming to himself his belief that Michael had shot the man in the car.[44] And while Guichard extracted from Hootie the fact that he knew Big E, knew him to be a drug dealer in the area, and the admission that he had been "hanging with" Big E in the Bluff that day, Hootie emphatically denied that Big E was on the scene at the time of the shooting. In that case, Guichard pointed out, Big E was not there to have told Michael "Don't do it." Larry Gee, Hootie, had to agree.[45] It was not enough. Gee had placed Michael on that corner alone at the time Woods was shot.

Although he denied that Big E was his drug supplier, Hootie was never asked what exactly was his relationship with Big E.[46] He was never asked to elaborate on his statement that Big E was not on the scene and how impossible that made it for Big E to be an eyewitness to the murder of Woods, or how, therefore, either he or Big E was lying. Most important, Hootie was never asked about the rifle found by Investigator Richey two days after Michael's arrest on Holly Street. After all, Hootie himself lived on Holly Street. Moreover, he was there when Richey found the rifle, which was the very same day he gave a statement to Richey.[47] Still, Larry Gee, known as Hootie, was never asked whether that rifle belonged to him. And he was never asked whether that rifle belonged to his friend Big E.

———

After the parade of drug dealers came the drug users, though Bertha Hayes would swear she was only "high by drinking" that night.[48] Hayes was, however, a known crack addict. Even though Lawter would assert in his testimony that it was Hayes who had been the chief informant on whose statements he had based his warrant for Michael's arrest, Hayes would never state that she saw Michael shoot Woods.[49] In direct examination by Phyllis Burgess, the following testimony was recorded:

When you talked to Ms. Ockleberry and I about this case, have you been able to remember what you saw that night?

I can't remember everything.

You can't remember everything?

Yes, Ma'am.

Okay. Let me ask you one question, Ms. Hayes. Do you know who shot Mr. Woods, the man who was sitting in that car that night?

Yes, Ma'am.

That's all I have, Your Honor.[50]

Among the issues that arose in Patrice Fulcher's cross-examination of Hayes was the significant discrepancy between the gun she testified was used by the shooter and the murder weapon in evidence. That is, Hayes swore that while standing around getting high she watched the shooting of Woods from nearby and she saw the shooter fire a handgun—as opposed to a rifle. In questioning about this gun, she was resolute that it was a handgun, though she might have been wrong when she told the police it was a .357 magnum pistol: "I don't know what a .357 look like. I know what a .38 look like." The other important point that was revealed in Hayes's testimony was how she described the unnamed murderer of Woods: "I know that he had hit me in the head with a gun, but I don't know if it's the gun that he shot the boy with." [51] What made this significant, though it would never be revealed to the jury, was that in Marvin Dixon's statement about his interview with Bertha Hayes, he had reported, "She did state that she saw what happened that night and that the same person that beat her up was the person who shot Mr. Woods. She said that it was a big guy." [52]

The devastating testimony of Linda Mae Mitchell, also known as Phyllis McBride, was not overcome either by the gross and glaring inconsistencies in her account of the events that night or by the revelation that she was high on drugs. That she was a known crack addict could not be revealed to the jury. Moreover, no one would ask Mitchell-McBride whether she was high at the very moment of her testimony, though some observers thought she was.[53] More important, however, the jury would never learn that Mitchell had frequently used the other name, McBride, that she had stayed from time to time in a nearby county facility for single homeless men and women with chronic mental illness, and that she was delusional, in that she used to tell people in the Bluff that she "saw aliens." [54]

This same Mitchell-McBride was sworn in, nevertheless, to testify as a state's witness, an eyewitness. According to her testimony, while she was standing by a tree in the empty lot on the corner opposite Henry's on the night of the shooting "just talking," as she had been "most of the day," she heard voices coming from across the street. She recognized one of the voices as that of Little B, she testified. Although she was homeless, she said, she usually stayed on the streets of the Bluff, where she had once lived and where she knew everybody, including Michael. She heard Little B ask the man in the car if there were "any more whores

THE INNOCENCE OF LITTLE B 307

in the car," and she heard the man say, "Don't disrespect my wife like that." She heard two other, unidentified voices tell Little B not to let people disrespect him. She knew both Tom-Tom and Big E and saw them standing nearby, talking to each other. She then claimed she saw Michael "come back" to the *driver's* side of the car with a "big gun," and say something about being disrespected and raise the gun. Then, she noticed the children in the back of the car and saw that they were both boys. Finally, she testified, she saw the man looking down as she saw Michael raise the gun and pull the trigger.

The first lie Mitchell-McBride told Patrice Fulcher was that she had never before used the name Phyllis McBride. Then she was exposed to have lied about why she was in the Bluff that night, which was, in fact, as she finally confessed, that she was there waiting for Chuckie Boy who "sold nickels" for Big E. She also admitted that the area she claimed she saw Michael coming from, a set of dumpsters on the side of the store, was, in fact, where she had seen Big E standing with Tom-Tom. Furthermore, Mitchell-McBride was unable to clarify whether Woods was sitting on the passenger or driver's side of the car, though she swore she saw Michael shoot into the driver's side. She was unable to verify when or where she actually saw the children from her alleged vantage point across the street that night, testifying at once that she saw them in the back of the car and out on the street, though she swore she had run off right after the shooting started.[55] Nevertheless, what the state was able to accomplish with Mitchell-McBride was to provide testimony to the jury that recalled and reflected, however fuzzily or fantastically, the imagery of events as painted by the press before the trial.

The incredible thing about Mitchell-McBride's statements about seeing Woods and the children was not only how far the car was from where she said she was standing or that it was nighttime, but that the car's windows were tinted.[56] Moreover, when Woods was shot, those windows were raised. And, the incredible thing about Mitchell-McBride's statements as to what she heard was that while she swore she could hear everything that was said from across the street, she testified that she never heard Big E say, "Don't do that." Nobody asked Mitchell-McBride anything else about Big E, about her relationship with the dealer who supplied the drugs she waited for in the Bluff all day. Nobody ever asked the desperate and homeless Linda Mae Mitchell, or Phyllis

McBride, whether she had received or been promised any of the "reward" money for this testimony.

One of the state's auxiliary witnesses, as it were, was twenty-one-year-old LaTosha Beard. Like other witnesses, she disputed most of the statements Investigator Richey's report attributed to her and argued intensely with Ockleberry over those statements. Also like the others, Beard testified she had been on the scene just "chitchatting" with her aunt and her friend Ikesha Arnold, she said, "sitting up under the store." She saw the car drive up, but insisted that Michael "wasn't even by the car." She insisted, too, that she had only heard the shooting: "I had done walked on the side of the building." While she saw Michael running by the car, he was running with everybody else, "like they was running to duck shots," she stated adamantly, and vehemently rejected Ockleberry's allegation that she had said it was only Michael she had seen running. In the end, though, Ockleberry was able to compel Beard to repeat for the jury that she had told Richey that she had thought to herself: "He shouldn't have shot that man with those kids in the car." In the end, Ockleberry forced Beard to repeat that when she said that, she was referring to "B."

Adding insult to injury was Beard's dramatic self-serving detailed description of how she helped get the children out of the car and took them into the store. While this was not relevant to the question of who killed Woods, it dredged up the kind of emotionalism that would rouse sympathy for the victim's family, obliterating the failure of facts, and produce antipathy for the boy sitting there charged with the murder of their father. Thus, despite her arguments with Ockleberry, Beard showed that she was there as a state's witness to point a finger, however wavering, at Michael.

Beard's powerful testimony as to her subjective surmise that Michael must have killed Woods was never overcome. It lingered even when she emphasized in the cross-examination that she had not seen the shooting; her back was turned and it was too dark, she reiterated. It overshadowed her testimony that she thought she had seen Woods's car out on that corner before that night. It diminished Beard's admission to Fulcher that she had never mentioned seeing Michael at all until Investigator Richey himself pushed her, insisted she tell him she had seen Little B, saying, in his own report, "What was his name, What was his street name, Is his street name Little B?'' And Beard's suggestive testimony that implicated Michael retained its force even when she acknowledged in cross-examination that when she saw Michael running there was nothing in his hand.[57]

What was never revealed about Beard, though, was not merely that she might have had a personal interest in the outcome of the trial given that her aunt, with whom she testified she was "chitchatting" that night, was the mother of a child by Big E. When she was asked about the drug dealing in the area, Beard denied knowledge of such activity, though she admitted that she knew Big E, and she certainly provided corroboration for Big E's story that he was "up the street" when the shooting occurred. Beard was never asked, however, whether she ever sold or held drugs for Big E, which would have raised the question of whether she had other ties to him and other interests to serve in effectively supporting his testimony. Moreover, Beard was never asked whether she had bought or had used or had been high on any of Big E's drugs on the night in question. The most important thing the jury would not know about Beard's interest in the trial outcome, though, was that even as she was testifying about her maternal concern for the children in the car, she was a suspect in the murder of her own baby, who had died from a skull fracture in 1996. This was the same infant who had had to be taken out of a burning house in which Beard had left the child alone. After Michael's conviction, the accusation against her would be dismissed, and her boyfriend would be tried and convicted of her child's murder.[58]

It was eighteen-year-old Ikesha Arnold who brought out the fact that the windows of Kenya Woods's car were tinted. Arnold, a friend of LaTosha Beard, was the mother of a four-month-old baby by Jason Morgan, Michael's half brother—who was, notably, conspicuously absent. The purpose of her appearance, however, was to say that she knew Little B and that she had seen him earlier in the day with a gun. Despite her passionate protestations about even testifying—"*Shit, I don't want to do this!*"—and her arguments with Ockleberry over specifics, Arnold served to provide a piece of damning albeit irrelevant testimony. She was there to put a gun in Michael's hands, and although there was no description of such a gun, she did that.

Although Arnold stated that she was one of the numerous people "all over the area of Griffin Street in front of the store," she really had little to which to attest about the shooting of Darrell Woods. She testified, indeed, that she ran to her house around the corner immediately after Larry Gee warned her and Beard, she said, "someone fixing to shoot." The only other testimony she gave about the events that evening was that she saw the car sitting in front of Henry's, but she added, "I didn't see the Defendant when the car drove up." In fact, Arnold told Ockleberry with great force, "I don't know who killed this man."

That was not the point. Ockleberry focused on her statement to Richey that she had seen Michael earlier in the day in a neighborhood field shooting at birds. Arnold denied that she ever said she saw Michael himself shooting, just saw him standing in the field with other boys, with "Red" and "Black" and "Trigger—none of whom was on trial for this murder—and that they were all shooting at birds. Even when Ockleberry threatened to play a videotape of her statement to Richey to rebut this, Arnold held firm: "No, I didn't tell him he was shooting the gun that day. You can play the tape, I didn't say that." While the videotape player malfunctioned and the tape was never played, it did not matter. In the end, Arnold acquiesced. She testified that she had indeed told Richey she saw Little B put bullets in a gun earlier in the day, standing in a field with other boys, shooting at birds.[59]

While Arnold acknowledged that she knew Big E and had seen him in the area, like Beard she distanced him from the scene, even though Mills necessarily had to be nearby to be the eyewitness he said he was, to have tried to stop the killing, as he said he did, by shouting out, "Don't do that." In any case, Arnold was never asked whether she was on that corner that night holding drugs for Big E or whether she was high on drugs she had bought from Big E. She was never asked about the relationship between her baby's daddy, Jason Morgan, known as J-Boy, and Big E. Indeed, she was never asked about what her role was in the rampant drug operations at the corner of Griffin and Meldrum and what role that might play in her testimony against Michael.

As there was an intriguing connection between all the street corner witnesses and Eric Mills, as drug dealers, addicts, or otherwise, there was something extraordinary about the relationship between the key police figures who emerged in the case and Detective Sam Lawter.

While police officers J. R. Criger and Outhar Keovongkot, who had been in the department's Zone 1 for four and six years respectively, were the first officers on the scene, they were never further involved in the case once it was reassigned to Lawter. Criger and Keovongkot had been on the scene when the ambulance arrived, had checked the victim's pulse, and had secured the area. It was Criger who had transported Kenya Woods and her boys to the police homicide headquarters away from the scene. It was Criger who first interviewed Kenya Woods, notably testifying, "She said she didn't see anything." Moreover, in the entire time they were out on that corner, both officers stated that they were unable to get any responses to questions they posed to the people standing around. Criger stated, "As usual, no one said they had seen anything." Neither reported receiving a call from the pay telephones in front of Henry's. When homicide detective Dale Kelly arrived, not much after Criger and Keovongkot, he took command of the crime scene, directing photographs be taken and making a sketch of the scene. It was he who instructed Officer Criger to transport Kenya Woods and the children. During the hour or so Kelly directed activities at the crime scene, he, too, was unable to get any statement from the numerous people standing around, and he, too, never received a call from the pay telephones in front of Henry's. Kelly was a homicide investigator who had been an Atlanta police officer for eighteen years. This, however, would be the extent of Kelly's involvement in the case.[60]

Lawter arrived about an hour-and-a-half after Criger, Keovongkot, and Kelly, at around 9:00 P.M., he testified. Things changed. Evidently acting in an inferior capacity to Kelly, who worked the same 4:00 P.M. to midnight shift as he, Lawter was told by Kelly to "start interviewing people in the crowd." Evidently, the people still there were more cooperative with Lawter: "There were some people there that I knew. . . . [I] started talking to them." Moreover, within twenty minutes after Lawter's arrival, two hours after the shooting, the pay telephone in front of Henry's rang. Keovongkot answered the telephone and testified that it was for Lawter. Lawter said it was a male voice he did not know but that the man had some information for him. The telephone rang again. Again, it was

for Lawter, and it was the same man, Lawter said. Indeed, Lawter testified, "I received three phone calls that night within a few minutes."
Before he left, he had spoken with several people there. Big E was one
of them, though Lawter testified that he did not know who he was. Of
course, Big E had testified that he had walked away from the scene right
after the shooting.[61]

The next day, January 22, 1997, Detective Kelly was discharged
from the case, and Lawter became the lead detective.[62] A new team of
police now became involved in the case. This included Detective Brian
E. Anderson, whom Lawter said he contacted based on those calls he
had received from the pay telephones in front of Henry's the night before, the night of the murder.[63]

Anderson, a former member of the Red Dog Unit had also been a
Zone 1 uniform policeman for years. However, at the time of the Woods
murder he was on a special assignment with the High Intensity Drug
Trafficking Areas Federal Task Force. Still, Anderson became a part of
Lawter's homicide investigation team. He testified that Lawter contacted him the morning after the killing to have him talk to his area drug
informants to obtain an "identification" for a "suspect" named Little B.
This was a curious comment, given that Anderson later testified that
Lawter involved him in the case because he "knew Little B by sight." It
was stranger still as Detective Warren Keith Picard had just testified that
he, too, had spoken with Lawter the next day and had become involved
in the case because he was the only person who could identify Little B.
"I described the Defendant to him. Nobody knew what he looked like,
so I described him." In any case, in his pursuit of obtaining an identification of Little B, as he put it, Anderson produced Tom-Tom, facing three
federal heroin indictments, who became, of course, a key, albeit reluctant, prosecution witness against Michael. Anderson went on to assist
Lawter in locating Little B, he said, as he became a part of the police
team led by Lawter that went out to arrest Michael, in order, Anderson
said, to identify Michael. And it was Anderson who drove Michael to the
homicide headquarters. It was Anderson who was the only officer who
went with Lawter later that night to search Holly Street, when Lawter
discovered the black skull cap there.[64]

What made Anderson's role perplexing, however, was not simply
that he was not a homicide officer or that he was clearly not the only po-

lice officer who could "identify" Little B. The question was, how had Anderson, who was, as he had rather vaingloriously presented himself, a high-powered special narcotics officer assigned to a federal drug task force and having a background not only with the Atlanta police department's elite Red Dog Unit but also with the DEA, come to be so involved in this murder case? It was true, of course, that he had produced Tom-Tom—whom he and Lawter had together interrogated in a twenty-by-twenty windowless room until Tom-Tom signed the statement indicting Michael.[65] The point was that this was a homicide case, not a narcotics case. On the other hand, of course, there was clearly a drug element embedded in the case somewhere, somewhere in the fact that each of the four so-called eyewitnesses was a drug dealer, each of whom was facing a long prison term at the time of his testimony, and that Chuckie Boy and Tom-Tom and Hootie all had clear ties to Big E, the main witness, the convicted drug dealer with a sealed deal with the state. Perhaps that was what, in the end, made Anderson's role seem curious—his silence about Big E—Big E, who was the very heart of the case against Michael, Big E, who ran drugs openly in the territory of Anderson's task force operations, in those very blocks of the Bluff Anderson was known to have ridden through alone with regularity in his plain clothes and in his unmarked car over the last few years.[66] Of course, nobody ever asked Anderson whether he knew or knew of Big E or what his dealings had been with Big E. He was never asked whether he knew Big E "by sight." He was never asked about Big E at all.

The only other police called to testify had only auxiliary roles in Lawter's investigation. Undercover Detective Warren Keith Picard's connection to the case first seemed to be his claim to be the only person who could identify Little B on sight. His other role was to give weight to the otherwise worthlessness of the black skull cap, which Eric Mills had testified he had seen on Michael's head the night of the murder. Testifying with remarkable recall, and without challenge, Picard stated that he had seen Michael between ten and fifteen times, that each time he had been wearing such a hat, and that the last time he saw Michael, he was wearing the same such hat, which was on Holly Street the day after the murder. Sergeant Genaro Sanchez, commander of the Fugitive Unit, was brought in by Lawter solely to assist in Michael's arrest, which Sanchez testified was indeed the purpose of the Fugitive Unit.[67] In effect, then, while Ockleberry enhanced her case by presenting the jury with the testimonies of a number of policemen, this case was Lawter's case alone.

Interestingly, Lawter had been transferred from the homicide division of the Atlanta police department to the larceny division by the time of trial, for undisclosed reasons. Lawter began his testimony by explaining how he had come to focus his investigation on Little B from the beginning. This was based on the calls he received at the pay telephone in front of Henry's the night of the murder, he said. He stated that the calls were from a "Mr. Douglas," whom he knew, he now testified, but not by that name, and no other name was identified. Furthermore, Lawter testified that it was the mysterious Douglas who gave him a description of Little B, whereupon he contacted narcotics officers, school detectives, and officers in the area, and of course Brian Anderson, to locate the boy. This testimony was quite bizarre. First, Anderson and Picard had each sworn that he was the only one who could identify Michael, and each had testified that Lawter had called him the day after the murder to identify and locate Michael. Moreover, Picard had just testified that he had seen Michael the day after the murder on Holly Street, wearing the infamous hat. Still, Lawter testified, he spent the next several days trying to locate Little B, during which time, he said, he was receiving numerous anonymous calls, all identifying the same suspect, he said, Little B, and telling him about the black skull cap.[68]

It was not until Lawter talked with Bertha Hayes, however, on January 26, 1997, five days after the murder, that he sought an arrest warrant for Little B, which he obtained two days later, on January 28, 1997. Hayes, whom Lawter said he had known for years, told him she was an eyewitness to the murder.[69] Based on Hayes's report, Lawter signed an affidavit at the Atlanta Municipal Court for a warrant to arrest Michael Lewis, aka Little B. Notably, Bertha Hayes, according to her own and Lawter's testimony, could not describe anything about the clothing Michael was wearing when she allegedly saw him. Moreover, the affidavit, naming Hayes as the affiant on whose eyewitness information the warrant request was being made, states that the eyewitness saw the accused shoot Darrell Woods in the head with a *handgun*.[70] Despite these irregularities, Lawter and his men went to Holly Street and arrested Michael for murder.

With all of Lawter's days of investigations, he testified that he never spoke with Kenya Woods. He never took a statement from her. In passing, he noted that she had "made a brief statement," but it was never clarified as to what that statement was or whether it had been transcribed like all the others. He never interviewed her two boys, asserting that he had no experience interviewing children, and never stated he directed anyone with such experience to interview them.[71]

Similarly, Lawter testified that he had never interviewed Eric Mills. Irrespective of the unresolved matter of the conversation he said he had had with Mills the night of the murder, and even considering his testimony that he did not know it was Mills at the time, it was incredible that the lead detective in this murder case had never interviewed the main witness. He did, he stated, have a warrant issued for the arrest of Mills, along with Jason Morgan, as "parties" to the crime. He stated that those warrants were issued on the same date as Michael's, on January 28, 1997—which was in conflict with the arrest date of January 22, 1997, as of which Mills would receive credit for time served under his plea bargain. At any rate, by February, Mills was officially discharged as a suspect in the case, having become the key witness.

This failure to interview Woods or Mills stood in contrast to the extraordinary amount of effort Lawter spent interrogating Antonio Johnson, or Tom-Tom. Of course, it was this interview that provided the state the opportunity to have Lawter testify for Johnson, through the statement he was to have made to Lawter, that he was an eyewitness, even though Johnson himself had vigorously disputed the statement:

Did Antonio Johnson indicate who he saw shoot Mr. Woods?

He said he was there and he saw Michael Lewis shoot Mr. Woods.[72]

Lawter was loosed now to speak for Johnson, and he delivered a monologue of shocking, foul street commentary and a descriptive recounting of the horrible shooting that he attributed to Johnson as quoting Michael in connection with the shooting of Woods.[73]

That Lawter never interviewed Kenya Woods or Eric Mills also stood in stark contrast with the fact that, according to his testimony, he personally interviewed Jason Morgan, who, he said, gave him no information and who was ultimately released from jail on the charge of being a "party to the crime." Lawter also personally interviewed Valerie Morgan, whom he said he knew.[74]

Lawter's testimony revealed that his investigation had been no more than a search for support for the charge of murder against one boy, Little B. He had found that support in the form of testimonials dragged from drug-dealing riffraff and from cronies in the network of the Atlanta Police Department. There was no physical evidence linking Michael to this terrible shooting. There was a gun, found without a search warrant two days after Michael's arrest. There was the hat. That was all. Still, Lawter's investigation was given substance by Ockleberry in closing her long examination of him, wherein she pounded home the theme of her prosecution: guilt by default:

Okay. Now, from January the 21st, that would have been the date you initially got this case and went out to the scene, up until today, have you received any information that is inconsistent with the Defendant being the shooter of Mr. Woods?

Received no information that would be inconsistent with that.

Okay. And that's from all the eyewitness statements, the murder weapon being collected, the shell casing, the cap, all of that, did anything indicate that anybody else was the shooter of Mr. Woods other than the Defendant?

No, Ma'am.[75]

Guichard made an attempt to expose the flimsiness of Lawter's investigation. He had Lawter admit that Tom-Tom had said the gun he saw looked more like an Uzi, grossly different from the original handgun or the rifle identified as the murder weapon. The bigger point, though—Lawter's testimony for Tom-Tom that he had seen Michael shoot into the car—was not addressed. Guichard also brought out that while Lawter had said Little B was the only name he had been given by informants, he had also received and never followed up on reports relating to the names "Little Dairy" and "Red." Of course, neither such person was on trial, and the significance of this was lost in a long debate brought on by Ockleberry's objection.[76]

What Lawter was never required to answer to was the numerous constitutional violations he committed in the arrest and processing of Michael, which would indeed never be brought to light and never addressed. He arrested Michael apparently without giving him the Miranda warning of his right to remain silent and his right to counsel. He never contacted DFACS, even though Lawter knew from the moment of Michael's arrest that DFACS was his legal guardian, as evidenced on the arrest intake sheet. He allowed Valerie Morgan to ride to the police homicide headquarters in the car with him and Michael. He allowed her to remain there, even though she was, and he knew she was, a drug addict who had been adjudicated an unfit mother, because he knew her and testified that he knew her prior to January 1997. He interrogated Michael without counsel. And two days after Michael's arrest, Lawter had Michael sign a form, in connection with an appearance before a Fulton County magistrate, that incorporated the Miranda warning without any identification of the crime, only exacerbating the flagrant violations of Michael's due process.[77]

In my mind it was clear that Lawter had targeted a street kid named Little B. The only cloudy issue was Lawter's motivation.

Unlike Ockleberry, John Richey, senior investigator of the Fulton County district attorney's office, had been involved in the case from the beginning, when assistant district attorney Joe Burford was handling the case, right after Paul Howard took office. Richey had been involved since before Mills made his deal with the state, though interestingly Richey, too, according to his testimony, had been "unable" to interview Mills. It never became clear exactly who handled Mills.

Richey was doing police work, in accordance with some new bureaucratic arrangement between the district attorney's office and the Atlanta police department, Ockleberry established. This explained why, on January 30, 1997, two days after Michael's arrest, it was Richey who went to Holly Street to interview potential witnesses among the people who stayed there. He spoke with Shalance Battle, mother of J-Boy's children, who he concluded was not a witness. He interviewed Larry Gee, or Hootie, in his official car. As a result, and as in the case of Lawter as to Tom-Tom, Richey was now allowed to testify for Gee, over Guichard's objection, to remedy Gee's inconsistent testimony and to punctuate that Gee had told him how, even though he had not seen the shooting, he had thought to himself, "Damn, Little B done shot this man." And this passed for testimony, and it passed for truth.

Richey's main role, however, was to provide testimony in the stead of Valerie Morgan, who even Ockleberry knew would not pass muster on the stand—though what would be attributed to her, however circuitously, might have been overcome by her presence, no matter how wretched. There was only Richey, though, to shape and sanitize the shadow of Valerie Morgan and to validate what nobody else would ever hear her say.

Richey testified that, as she had on the afternoon of Michael's arrest, Valerie Morgan arrived out of nowhere while Richey was questioning Hootie in the car. By then even Richey had to have known she was not Michael's mother in any sense of the word, yet he dubbed her Michael's mother, giving her that value. Only moments after her arrival, he testified further, Michael's mother went inside the apartment on Holly Street. She came back outside and told Richey her son wanted to talk with him. Richey now repeated the conversation he said he had with someone on the telephone there on Holly Street who said he was Little B, who Richey himself "realized," he testified without challenge, was the defendant. Richey said Little B wanted to know, quoting the boy, "If I confess, what would I be facing?" He asked—Richey quoted him again —if he couldn't get "a home arrest or something." Ockleberry under-scored this report with saccharine shock, in a sensationalized sentence: "He asked you could he get house arrest for killing somebody?"

Now Richey drove Valerie Morgan to the jail because, he testified, Michael also told him he would talk with him in person if his mother were there. Ironically, though, Richey would never interview Michael. However, riding in his car with Michael's mother provided him the opportunity to talk with her, he said. He testified that for some reason he asked Valerie Morgan whether she knew where the murder weapon was. Ockleberry now made sure that Richey did not repeat Morgan's al-leged words so as to not violate the hearsay evidence rule. Still, Richey was able to tell the jury that Morgan told him her son had told her where the weapon was. Based on that, Richey continued, he turned his car around and headed back to Holly Street. He and another investigator, who had accompanied him, went right to the murder weapon, found it right there behind the apartment complex on Holly Street, wrapped in blankets. There it was, the murder weapon, presumed to have been sit-ting there that whole week or more since the murder, a long rifle now im-plied to have been carried by a short boy over two miles from the scene of the murder back to a place that was not really his house, a murder weapon that had been sitting there undiscovered even as Michael was arrested, undiscovered during the search by Lawter and Anderson under their search warrant when they found the hat. The murder weapon, sitting there all that time, was now seized by Richey after a conversation with Valerie Morgan that would never be otherwise substantiated, and it was seized without even the necessity of a search warrant and, finally, assigned to Michael.

Building up her theme of guilt by default, then, Ockleberry asked Richey, and seriously, "Based upon the conversation that you had with the Defendant's mother, was there any indication that that weapon belonged to Jason Morgan, Shalance Battle or Valerie Morgan or Larry Gee?" Richey responded, "No, she never gave that indication." Then, and without one scintilla of evidence, with no signed statement or testimony from Morgan herself, and in the absence of Richey's unauthenticated recording of Morgan's alleged statements, Ockleberry brazenly asked Richey, "Based upon what the Defendant's own mother told you, did you have information that anyone else other than the Defendant shot and killed Mr. Woods?" It was only after Richey had predictably responded "No, I didn't" that Guichard objected, which the court sustained, though it seemed lost in the drama.

This theme of guilt by default carried to Richey's report of his interviews the next day with Ikesha Arnold and LaTosha Beard, both of whom, inexplicably, he also met on Holly Street. Once again Ockleberry asked him, "Based upon what Ms. Beard and Ms. Arnold told you, did you have information that anyone other than the Defendant shot and killed Mr. Woods?" Of course Richey responded, "No."

Finally, Ockleberry pressed Richey into service to dispose of other unfinished business, so to speak. Richey was, after all, working for the district attorney. Richey now gave additional testimony for Antonio Johnson, Tom-Tom, augmenting Lawter's testimony for Tom-Tom, based on his own interview conducted November 4, 1997, after the trial had already begun. Richey had Tom-Tom, still facing heroin charges, brought to the district attorney's office for the interview. He told the jury that Tom-Tom had told him he had seen Little B wearing the hat in evidence, something Tom-Tom had not said in direct testimony, and furthermore that Tom-Tom had confessed to him, only days before, that he had in fact seen Little B shoot and kill Woods. Finally, Ockleberry had Richey resound her theme of guilt by default, rhetorically asking him, yet again, "Based upon your investigation, including your conversations with Ikesha, LaTosha, Antonio, Larry Gee, Linda Mae Mitchell, locating the murder weapon in the back yard of where the Defendant lived, talking with the Defendant, including his own mother, did you get any information that anyone other than the Defendant was the shooter of Mr. Woods? . . . Did you get any information that anyone else had a motive to shoot Mr. Woods?" Richey responded, "No, Ma'am, no, Ma'am."

The fact was that the gun Richey and Ockleberry imputed to have belonged to Michael was never identified as belonging to anybody at all. And there were no fingerprints on the gun. Guichard never exposed this in his cross-examination of Richey, never attacked Richey's damaging testimony regarding the gun, never asked him, for example, "Mr. Richey, did you learn anything in all your interviews that said the gun you discovered two days after Michael's arrest in fact belonged to Michael?" More significantly, Richey might have been asked, and never was, if he had investigated whether the gun belonged to Big E.

Guichard never exposed that Richey knew, when he allegedly took a statement from Valerie Morgan, a statement that was now missing, that Morgan was a drug addict, a drug addict who had prostituted herself for drugs, been in and out of jail, and done some time in prison on account of drugs. Moreover, Valerie Morgan was a drug addict who often got her drugs from Big E. Letting stand the imagery of Valerie Morgan as an ordinary mother, however, Guichard gave maternal power to all the devastating testimony Richey attributed to her, how he learned where the gun was after talking with her, how she, as Michael's own mother, had facilitated his alleged telephone conversation with Michael. Guichard never pointed out that, in any case, Valerie Morgan had never been called by the state to testify for herself and that Richey's alleged recording of her reputed statements was, unlike all his other recordings of all the others, inaudible and unidentifiable. Thus the jury was being asked to rely on Richey's testimony, and his testimony alone, as to what Valerie Morgan might have told him and as to what he testified he did based on what she told him. Even assuming that Valerie Morgan had told Richey everything he attested to and suggested, however, Guichard might have pointed out that her statements had to be considered in light of her addictive daily use of drugs and daily state of intoxication, on account of which she had lost legal guardianship of her son, who was sitting there alone facing life in prison.

Guichard also never pointed out how Richey had shown no basis for his testimony that he knew he was talking with Little B over the telephone. He never pointed out the underlying illegality of Richey's alleged conversation with Michael, for had he indeed spoken to Michael by telephone, he had done so even though Michael clearly did not have the benefit of counsel. Indeed, on that very date, January 30, 2001, there was a record that Michael had appeared before a magistrate *without* counsel. Moreover, Guichard might have reminded Richey that even if Valerie Morgan had been Michael's legal guardian, no rights enabled her to speak for or negotiate away Michael's constitutional right to silence.

Guichard never attacked the new and revised statements of Tom-Tom that Richey attributed to his own interview with him only days before, nor did he ask Richey about the outcome of Tom-Tom's heroin cases and whether or not that outcome was related to his testimony on the stand as well as through Lawter and him. He never asked Richey whether he or the district attorney had made a deal with Tom-Tom.

This might have led to questions about Big E. Guichard never asked Richey how it was that he had interviewed every single witness in this case, and even testified for some of them, and had never gotten around to interviewing Big E. He never asked him exactly who it was who had interviewed Big E. And while Richey covered himself with respect to being unable to testify as to the contents of Mills's statement, since he had not taken such a statement, which Guichard was unsuccessful in challenging, Guichard never asked him about the deal with Big E, never asked him to reveal the deal Paul Howard had made with Big E months before, after he, Richey, had been involved in the case for some time.

Guichard's cross-examination of Richey was an anticlimactic series of questions about why Richey had not made sure that the state's witnesses waiting outside the courtroom had not been separated, and another series of questions requiring Richey to confirm simply that he had taken all the destructive statements he had testified he had taken, and another series of questions that pointed out certain factual inconsistencies among the witness statements, inconsistencies that appeared as minutiae in the face of the terrible totality of John Richey's testimony.[78]

Kelly Fite was the firearms expert from the Georgia Bureau of Investigation crime laboratory who testified that the bullets that killed Darrell Woods had come from the weapon Richey found on Holly Street, confirming it as the murder weapon. Guichard had no questions for Fite.

He had nothing to ask Fite about the size of the gun. Fite had testified that the rifle was an "Inland Division of the General Motors .30 carbine . . . World War II vintage . . . manufactured in 1942." [79] The typical Inland .30 carbine, the M1A1, commissioned by the U.S. Army in May of 1942, weighed around 6.2 pounds and was a little over 35 inches, or about 3 feet long. [80] According to Lawter's affidavit for Michael's arrest warrant, Michael was, at the time, thirteen years old and approximately 4'6" to 5' tall. This certainly suggested the gun in evidence was unwieldy for a boy Michael's size. It suggested that a gun this size in the hands of a boy Michael's size could not have been mistaken for a handgun or even an Uzi. These possibilities were never raised with Fite.

Fite might also have been asked to confirm that he had found no fingerprints on the gun. Most important, Fite might have been asked his expert opinion as to the trajectory of bullets fired from the Inland carbine into the car, killing Woods, in relation to the probable height range of the shooter. Moreover, given Fite's testimony that the automatic reloading mechanism on the gun was nonfunctional and that therefore to fire the second bullet the shooter would have had to manually reload it in the gun's chamber by pulling back the operating handle to eject the first cartridge casing, he was never asked about the strength required to pull back that lever. [81] He was never asked about the recoiling characteristics of that gun on firing in terms of the sturdiness of the shooter. All of this might have revealed that the shooter would necessarily have been taller, bigger, and heavier than Little B.

Indeed, Guichard could have learned all of this independently and used it in cross-examining Fite. Marvin Dixon had contacted a county crime scene technician, who had agreed to contract with the Conflict Defender's office to set up the necessary experiments with the rifle and the same or same kind of Mitsubishi Kenya Woods was driving to determine the trajectory of the bullets and to attest to the probable height of the shooter. From his own experience in the field, Dixon felt this test would show the shooter had to have been much taller than Michael.

Guichard rejected this offer on grounds that there was no money in the budget to pay for such an independent expert.[82]

The medical examiner, Dr. Geoffey P. Smith, too, was not required to discuss the trajectory of the bullets that killed Woods, even though he testified that was part of his role in performing the autopsy. Indeed, there were no questions at all of Dr. Smith, even though, for example, while he had agreed with Ockleberry that the shooter was a few feet away from the car when he fired, he stated that he could not establish the range of fire.[83] Smith was never asked, however, about the probable size of the shooter in relation to the estimated range and the trajectory of the fatal bullet. He was never asked about what he found in Woods's stomach, as to whether or not its contents indicated that he had had dinner at Captain D's, as Kenya Woods had testified.

Although Ockleberry attempted to get Smith to state that the bullet that entered the back of Woods's right shoulder blade was the fatal bullet, consistent with the state's theory and Kenya Woods's emotional testimony that Woods had turned protectively toward the boys before he was shot, Smith stated otherwise. He testified that Woods was sitting in the car upright, with the car windows rolled up, when the first and fatal bullet was fired into his right chest. This was significant in its suggestion of the seeming passivity of Woods when he was shot. This passivity seemed inconsistent with a man who had just had an argument with a boy, a man who might have been watchful, therefore, for the boy, who might have watched the boy as he walked away and as he came back seconds later, as the drug dealers and drug addicts had testified, and who, if nothing else, might have been shot ducking down or in fact reaching back toward his kids or putting up his arm or doing something that signaled the instinctive move of a man who saw his killer coming. It seemed implausible, even, that a man would be casually sitting in a car at a crowded drug corner having just had an alleged argument over the dimming of headlights or over disrespect, depending on the report, with a person the drug dealers and drug addicts all alleged went to an alley, or dumpsters, and picked up a handgun, or Uzi or rifle, and dramatically walked back over to the car cursing the man and raising a gun at him, as the position of Woods's dead body attested. It suggested that Darrell Woods had not been murdered by some superpredator street boy with whom he had just had an alleged war of words. It suggested that he had been murdered instead as he sat unsuspecting in the car that night by someone he had no idea might kill him.

In any event, the state rested its case.

———————

Who would believe Michael if he testified was the question Patrice Fulcher anguished over all of the night before the defense would be presented. It was what she cried over, and what she begged Gary Guichard to take into consideration before he did what he had long ago decided, to put Michael on the stand, to have Michael tell that he did not shoot Woods, to tell who he knew had shot Woods, to tell that he had been out on that corner with all the other people, that he had run with everybody else, like everybody else, and had jumped into the car of "Ta-Dow," who remained in hiding, who had eluded even Marvin Dixon.

It was after midnight when she called. We cried together. It was more than a question of believability. It was more than a question of what Ockleberry would do to him, or how comparatively ill equipped Guichard had shown himself to be to defend Michael against what would certainly be Ockleberry's ruthless assault on the boy. It was more than the fact that Guichard had not prepared Michael for such an appearance, as the law required, as common sense required. It was a question of the probable collateral consequences, Michael's own life, his mother's life.

By morning, Fulcher had convinced Guichard it would be devastating to Michael, to his defense, to his very life, to call him to testify. The case was over anyway. Perhaps it had ended when Kenya Woods left the stand with her story unquestioned. More than likely, it had ended once Mills stepped down from the witness stand, after getting up and pointing to Michael as the murderer. Yes, after those two, it was all over but the shouting, as the old people used to say. He was a boy without a boat floundering in a tidal wave of drug dealers with deals, of drug addicts desperately awaiting thirty pieces of silver, of cops who oversaw streets where drugs were dealt wildly, brazenly, all pointing fingers at him, to deflect their own culpability, to themselves stay afloat. Ockleberry had made a case out of no case, had spun something out of nothing. The cumulative weight of this nothing was overwhelming.

The defense Guichard presented was underwhelming. That next morning, he told the court the question of his client's testifying had not been resolved, that normally he would advise a client one way or another, but in the case of this boy, who was, in any case, being tried as a man, he felt he should not offer his advice. He would leave the decision to the boy and, he suggested, with a showing of profound ignorance, that Michael could "talk with some member of his family" about the matter. There was no family, of course. There had been no mother. There had been no father. There had been no brother or sister. There had been no social worker from the government agency that had been his legal guardian. No one had been there for him during the days of trial, from November 7, 1997, through to that final day, November 12, 1997, a total of five days less the intervening weekend. His paternal grandmother, Marian Scott, had come out in the end, and brought with her, for a few hours, her son, who was Michael's father, whom Michael did not recognize at all. Guichard asked the court whether Michael could speak with her, whom he barely knew. Enrobed in some concocted legal justification as a substitute for justice, Judge Cynthia Wright enthusiastically agreed, stating, "I think that's a good idea, and, further, if he does elect to testify, in his grandmother's presence I will also advise him of his rights." [84]

A bit later, the fourteen-year-old stood before the court with his grave decision.

All right, Mr. Lewis. . . . Now I know you've had a chance to talk with your attorney and I know that you have had a chance to talk with one of your family members. And I, for the record, would like to know if you have made a decision yet?

Yes, I have.

Are you going to be electing to testify?

No, Ma'am.

No? . . . Do you understand those rights that I just told you?

Yes, Ma'am.

And do you have any questions?

No, Ma'am.

Do you need any more time to talk with your family members?

No, Ma'am.

. . . All right, then, let's go ahead and get started with the presentation of the defense.[85]

All that was left was the defense presentation of the testimony of Eric Pope, a Fulton County Juvenile Court detention counselor, to which Ockleberry strongly objected. It was Pope who had allowed Michael to make a telephone call on January 30, 1997, to speak with his mother. This was the telephone conversation Richey had referenced in his testimony. Pope testified he was present the entire time Michael was on the telephone. He stated that Michael asked his mother, and Pope stressed this was the exact language, "if he said he did it. . . ." Pope testified the question was never completed, stating that Michael "stopped talking and then he started crying." Under direct questioning by Fulcher, Pope acknowledged emphatically that at no time did Michael ever say to anyone on the telephone that he had killed Woods, and that, indeed, he had maintained his innocence. Ockleberry's cross-examination did nothing to deter Pope or disturb what he had to say. It was, of course, too little, too late.

Finally, Guichard presented a witness to rebut the prosecutor's attempt to construe a connection to Michael and to the murder through the black skull cap's asserted uniqueness. He had an investigator from his office purchase a similar cap and then brought her to court to testify as to how easy it was to find such a hat and therefore how commonplace it was. That was the entire defense.[86]

Given that nothing was done at trial to disturb the pretrial perception of the case, it was for Ockleberry now to simply bring in the guilty verdict. She never worried about her corrupt witnesses, reminding the jury that these were the only kind of witnesses one found in drug-infested communities. She never worried about the glaring inconsistencies in the witness testimonies. She never worried about the facts, or that there were really no facts. She never concerned herself over the fact that her entire case rested on the testimony of a drug dealer with whom a questionable deal had been made.

Indeed, that was the very point she made, and relentlessly, as she launched into her closing argument that would win the first big case for Paul Howard, that would establish her own career, as her unabashed theatricality would overwhelm the night's newscasts.

After setting forth the definitions and the legal nature of the two

criminal charges against Michael, which amounted to the crime of murder, upon which the jury was to deliberate, Ockleberry began by simply
dismissing the fact that there was no evidence—notably not even witness testimony—that connected Michael to the murder weapon:

*Circumstantially, how do you connect it [the gun] up to the Defen-
dant? It was found in his back yard. Circumstantial evidence, no one saw
him with that particular gun. . . . however, you have the direct testimony
of Kelly Fite. . . . Y'all can't disagree he was an expert. . . . He connected
the murder weapon to the crime [sic].*[87]

Now she attacked the idea that her drug-dealing and drug-addicted
witnesses were not credible, urging the jury to look beyond their own
world of law-abiding citizens to appreciate the degenerate types that
haunted the Bluff:

*Linda Mae Mitchell, take her. Very articulate woman to be home-
less. . . .*[88]

Now she forcefully demanded that the jury also ignore the inconsistencies among the testimonies of the state's witnesses. She demanded
that the jury understand they could not discredit witnesses like Mills and
Barber on account of their criminal convictions, even if their testimonies
and convictions and sentences were all interdependent, as they were,
especially if other evidence supported their testimonies, she argued
without foundation:

*Y'all will probably all go back there and say, well, heck, they were all
out there drug dealing, drug selling, drug using, but let me ask you, we
know where this happened at. . . . Who you specs [sic] going to be there?
Drug dealers, drug sellers, drug users.*[89]

Now she returned to emotionalism to cover the barrenness of facts,
invoking the tragic persona of Kenya Woods, who, in fact, had given no
testimony with respect to who had killed Darrell Woods or why he had
been killed, suppressing the fact that Kenya Woods had never testified
that she ever saw Michael:

*And you saw Kenya when she took the stand, Ms. Woods, dis-
traught, hysterical. . . . Just want to get something to drink for dinner. . . .
You go back into the store, you hear shots and you run out and see your
husband slumped over in the car dead, your children balled up in the
back seat of the car. . . . The guilt, if I hadn't stopped for that soda.*[90]

By now, Darrell Woods's family members, including the two boys dressed in their Sunday best, all sitting en masse in the front rows of the prosecutor's side of the courtroom, were openly crying, loudly, in unison. Sitting apart from them, but crying with equal emotion, was Kenya Woods herself. Over an objection by Guichard, but with the complicity of Judge Wright, Ockleberry began whipping them and herself into a frenzy, even invoking testimony that was never made:

She [Kenya Woods] got up on the stand, she couldn't even look at him (indicating [Michael]). That's the person that she believes is responsible for robbing her and her family of their life. . . . I direct your attention over here. Let me show you something, Tracy, Tracy . . . Devon, asleep. Two little kids . . . saw their father being shot, and killed in front of them. They got blood on the shoes. . . . [91]

Ockleberry even trampled over the Constitution itself:

He sat here this whole trial. Have you seen one bit of emotion from him? . . . He has sat there this whole trial and not done a thing, not a tear. . . . This, (indicating [photograph of Darrell Woods]), is what they have to remind them of their father. . . . And he did it. He's never said to you, I didn't do it. . . . [92]

Guichard and Fulcher leapt from their seats, simultaneously shouting, "Objection, Your Honor!" The jury was immediately dismissed, and Guichard called for a mistrial, based on Ockleberry's assault on Michael's Fifth Amendment right to be silent. After putting up a vigorous argument that she had not finished her statement and that she never meant what was so very clear, Ockleberry made a rare concession, convoluted though it was, saying: "I'm sorry, it's my emotion, Your Honor." Guichard made no concession:

I don't think there's any doubt of the meaning of that statement. . . . It doesn't matter to me what she meant. . . . That is clearly, clearly a comment on my client's right to remain silent.

She can't now clean it up and say, oh, I meant this or I didn't mean this. . . . That's clearly and blatantly, Your Honor, a comment of my client's right to remain silent, there's no way around it. . . . There's no way you can cure that, Your Honor, and I'm moving for a mistrial. [93]

Wright sighed. She had not been long in the rough arena of the criminal court, having only recently left the civility of adjudicating civil matters—where she would soon return. Wright seemed tired of this case. She had demonstrated that in every ruling, demonstrated her great desire to end this trial sooner than later—demonstrated that she certainly had no desire to start over. She finally spoke ominously: "I don't know that this warrants a mistrial."

She would take the matter under advisement, in her chambers, and return with a decision, she said. Soon she ruled:

In terms of the motion for a mistrial . . . I believe that there was an objection in the middle of the prosecutor's statement, which she did not complete.

There is case law supporting a grant of a mistrial at this time. There's also case law stating that I don't have to grant a mistrial, but that I can give curative instructions. I'm planning on not granting a mistrial. I am going to give curative instructions.[94]

Her mild admonishments to Ockleberry, before the jury returned, did not seem curative: "I don't want any inflammatory arguments from the State. . . . You either prove your case or you don't prove your case." Guichard's persistence was not curative. "Your Honor, I don't know if I need to make a record. . . ." Wright interrupted him, "I know you object, just say you object, I don't want to hear any more argument on it, please." Guichard made his record: "I do object to the curative instructions, yes, Your Honor." Then, he added, "Please let the record reflect that at the time counsel made her remarks she was in tears and several members of the . . . deceased's family were in tears. . . ."

Wright had the last word, effectively arguing for the state: ". . . The record should reflect that a lot of that argument was going more toward pointing toward the victim's family and not particularly as to . . . the Defendant's right not to testify."[95] Now Wright called back the jury and gave her instruction, which, with no criticism before the jury of the state's flagrant constitutional violations, seemed a bandage and not curative at all, her legalese and her monotone voice, a narcotic:

I am going to instruct you to disregard the last argument made by the State. . . . You need to listen to me, you need to apply the law that I give you. . . . The law in a criminal case is that the Defendant is under no duty to present any evidence whatsoever tending to prove innocence and is not required to take the stand to testify in the case. If the Defendant elects not to testify, no inference hurtful, harmful or adverse should be drawn by the jury, nor should such fact be held against the Defendant in any way.[96]

Ockleberry proceeded, delightedly resuming her performance, stomping her feet, pointing her finger at Michael, prancing about like a holy-roller preacher, dramatically making something of nothing. Dragging an empty wooden chair before the jury, she placed a photograph of Woods in it, telling the jury this was all there was of this good man, this husband and father:

I put this chair here, and it's empty for a reason. This is what is left of Mr. Woods because of the Defendant, okay? I'd ask that you keep that in mind when Mr. Guichard comes to . . . talk to you. . . . [97]

―――――――――

Patrice Fulcher had begged him to allow her to do the closing argument. Despite the stifling of information about Kenya Woods's volatile relationship with Darrell and what it implied, she wanted the jury to consider whether it was reasonable that Kenya Woods had driven her husband and children to Henry's to buy a soda. She wanted the jury to consider that Kenya Woods had lived in the area four months and that it was improbable that she had never seen that corner before and not known that the only business on that corner was drugs. In any case, she wanted the jury to remember that Kenya Woods was the one person closest to the car at all times and that she had never testified to seeing Michael at any point. In addition, Fulcher wanted to show the jury the face of Big E, not Mr. Mills. While they surely knew by now that Big E was a drug dealer, she wanted to emphasize that everybody in the Bluff, as epitomized in the interconnection and testimonies of all the street witnesses, knew and feared Big E. Everybody knew fooling with Big E could get you shot. Owing Big E money could get you killed. Guichard refused.

This conflict in the defense had existed for some time. It had surfaced after Guichard acceded to the state's motion to suppress discussion about the violence in the Woodses' relationship. Fulcher had been furious over Guichard's assent to the state's motion. She had also been furious that her attempts to participate meaningfully in the defense had been thwarted. She had appealed to the head of the Conflict Defender's office, had urged him to see that in her mind the defense was falling apart, that Michael's life was in jeopardy. That effort had been repelled, so Fulcher had sat there frozen as the trial went forward hopelessly.

Now the trial had become a circus, the Woods family sitting before the jury weeping and wailing, Ockleberry inflaming them, Wright silent. Patrice Fulcher still believed something could be salvaged in the closing argument to turn the tide. She had intended to start out by walking over to Ockleberry, standing before her, and applauding her guerrilla theater.

Meekly Guichard approached the jury box. He spoke softly, his voice restrained, his language conservative. After a statement about the seriousness of the case, about the emotional nature of the case, about the "awesome duty" of the jury and how the presumption of innocence was "ingrained in our Constitution," he advised the jury that there was only one issue: "Does the State have the right person." [98]

He started his substantive argument by addressing Ockleberry's charge that the defense had not questioned the gun expert, Kelly Fite. However, he did not debunk Ockleberry's abstruse argument that the reason Fite's testimony had gone unchallenged was because the state had proved that the weapon found in Michael's "back yard" was the murder weapon, and that that somehow proved a connection between Michael and the weapon.

Yes, Counsel is right, we didn't cross-examine Kelly Fite . . . because that's not what we're fighting about. We're not fighting about whether or not that was the weapon that shot Mr. Woods. What we're fighting about is have they proven to you who was holding that weapon when it was fired at Mr. Woods?[99]

Guichard soon turned the jury's attention to Eric Mills.

I argue to you that the central figure in all of this is Eric Mills. Everyone that testified in front of you in some way or another had some connection to Eric Mills. . . . I think it is very important and very crucial that you look at the motivations behind why people came and said to you what they said to you.[100]

Those motivations remained abstract, however, as Guichard went on to argue that the drug-dealer witnesses had been coerced by police to testify, that they had been in police custody even as they testified. That they might have been coerced by the police did not seem to explain why the police might have done so. Guichard might have pointed out, however, that Chuckie Boy, Hootie, and Tom-Tom all had an allegiance to and a fear of Big E, which was perhaps the greater fear. Their testimonies had, more than anything, corroborated the testimony of Big E, the original murder suspect who had become the key witness against Michael, the dope dealer who controlled the blocks they worked, blocks that amounted to the universe of their existence.

At the same time, he might have pointed out the suspect irregularities in the testimonies of Mills and Lawter as to their knowledge of each other. Guichard did show, now, that the deal Mills had with the state was clearly the motivation for his testimony.

Eric Mills pled guilty to two different drug cases on July 31st, 1997. He's awaiting sentencing. . . . Why are they waiting for sentencing? . . . He finally admitted to you that he knew good and well that these prosecutors were going to make some kind of recommendation . . . to the judge that was waiting to sentence him what he did on the witness stand. . . . Sound like motivation to you? Sound like motivation to you. . . . We talked about him making a statement on January 28th . . . that subsequent to him making that statement all of the sudden, all of the sudden the charges against him for party to a crime of murder were dismissed.[101]

Guichard showed, also, that nobody else testified to having heard Mills say, "Don't do it." He pointed out that Mills did not remember the names of any other people in the crowd, any other potential witnesses, until his deal was sealed in July 1997. And while he noted that Mills had originally pointed police to a pistol as the weapon he had seen Michael holding, and that he changed that to a rifle in July when he made his deal, he did not explain why that might have been. He never offered that Mills might have had a reason to direct police to search for a gun that was nothing like the one he knew the murder weapon to be. He never mentioned that Mills, too, frequented the apartment on Holly Street.

Guichard moved on to talk about the variances in the street witness testimonies regarding the type of gun they claimed to have seen: a shotgun, a .357, another pistol, a rifle, no gun. This led to Guichard's other core argument: "The details do matter." He pointed out how the entire case was based on information, from Hayes and presumably Mills, that the murder weapon was a pistol—"a house of cards," as he put it. He showed how not only were there gross differences in the other testimonies regarding the gun but that there were differences in testimony as to what side of the car different witnesses say they saw Woods shot, stating, "Unimportant detail? Significant detail? You decide."[102] On the other hand, he never argued that these inconsistent details might not have been a function of poor memory but a function of lying, of concocting testimony from what these witnesses from the Bluff had heard, or what they had been told by police, or by Mills, in order to get reward money or a better deal on a drug charge or avoid the wrath of Big E. He never argued the possibility, the probability, that these people really saw someone else shoot Darrell Woods and that they really never saw Michael shoot anybody because he did not do it.

He suggested that there were other names among the rumors flying around in this "insulate community," reminding the jury of other police suspects, "Little Dairy" and "Red" and "a black male, teens to early twenties, holding a dirty Harry type gun," suspects floating around as ethereal personages, like the neighborhood rumors he referenced, though none of them was sitting before the jury.

In connection with the rumors and the alleged police pressure on the community, Guichard mounted a compelling argument of how Michael was sitting there as a neighborhood scapegoat:

My client was the youngest person that hung out with that group . . . a very easy person for everybody to blame. . . .

Everybody had a reason to blame somebody. Eric Mills had two pending drug cases. . . . Gary Barber has . . . a pending possession case that he's in custody on. Larry Gee has a sale of drugs case. . . . Antonio Johnson . . . had pending against him at that very moment [of testimony] three heroin indictments.[103]

He never followed through on this argument, however. Given Ockleberry's empty theory that there was no one other than Michael who could have committed the crime, Guichard could have referred back to this theme of guilt by default and shown that these people with motivations, under pressure to give the state somebody, might have indeed come to a collective agreement, for their respective reasons, to give the state the littlest among them.

Guichard did now expose one of the absurdities of trying to connect the murder weapon to Michael on account of its being found on Holly Street, pointing out for the jury that numerous people stayed in *both* apartments there. He argued, too, the ridiculousness of any suggestion that Michael had transported that big gun the two miles or so from the crime scene to Holly Street, of Michael "walking through the streets of Atlanta carrying that gun." [104]

Guichard discussed the black skull cap, jocularly stating, "I swore up and down, I'm not trying this hat on." [105] Arguing not only that the hat was common but that it was not important, he never argued that it was Mills who had connected the hat to the crime. The hat had no blood on it or other independent indicia of involvement in the crime, and it had not been washed or cleaned, which, indeed, Ockleberry would point out later with her characterization of the hat as dirty. Guichard did not point out that there was no proof that this was in fact Michael's hat, as only Anderson and Lawter had "found" the hat in what only Lawter identified as Michael's room.

Finally, Guichard focused on the impossibility of the time of the events described by the various street witnesses:

My client must be some kind of Olympic sprinter . . . going around the corner of Griffin and Meldrum, up Meldrum away from the store, to the left down the alley, apparently allegedly retrieving something, turning around and covering that distance in reverse all in five or six seconds. . . . Kenya Woods testified that she went back into the store . . . and heard shots before she could go back outside. Her testimony very clearly puts that time frame in a very tight area. . . . It's impossible for anyone to have left the scene, got the gun and returned to the scene, just wasn't enough time.[106]

He did not point out, however, that this impossibility of timing included the impossibility that, in the short period of time Kenya Woods testified they were at Henry's before Woods was shot, there had been all the conversation the state's witnesses alleged. Moreover, he did not emphasize that Kenya Woods not only testified that she did not see the shooter, though she ran outside and saw someone running, but, more important, that she never saw Michael talking to her husband, never saw anyone talking to her husband, never was told by her husband anything about a kid disrespecting her or threatening him. All of that could not have been missed by her in that short period of time.

Guichard concluded by finally recapitulating for the jury that Bertha Hayes, on whose statement the warrant for Michael had been issued, never testified that Michael was the shooter, although she swore she knew who had killed Woods, had seen him.

Ockleberry had the final rebuttal by law. She spent the moment echoing her theme of guilt by default:

No one else has been identified as killing Mr. Woods. . . . No one else had the weapon to kill Mr. Woods. . . . He's the only one that had a motive or a reason or a weapon to kill Mr. Woods.[107]

Then Ockleberry made an interesting revelation in referring back to how Kenya Woods came to drive to Henry's, a revelation seemingly inadvertently blurted out on account of last-minute hysteria to bring home a conviction:

This wasn't a rush to judgment. This was a thorough investigation.

Kesha [sic (Kenya Woods)], what did she come up and tell you? She hadn't lived in the area long. . . . She was on her way home after stopping for dinner, and they purchased a soda. She was put up there to tell you that they weren't in that area to buy drugs [emphasis added]. *You saw the soda bottle in the picture.*[108]

Then, more hysterically, she added something that went to the heart of the case, that demonstrated there was no heart in the case:

Don't you think at that point the Defendant had already said something to her, because the testimony is after she came back, his words were There any more whores in the car?

Of course, this was not the testimony of Kenya Woods at all. These were the chimerical words of the press and the prosecutor and drug dealers and drug addicts and cops.

Nevertheless, she pushed ahead. Again, Ockleberry found a way to punctuate for the jury that Michael had refused to testify and had never said he was not guilty—even though that was his very plea.

He had the chance to say I didn't do it. When Richey called him, when he was on the phone with his mother, he could have said I didn't shoot that man, Big E did. . . .[109]

Of course, Richey had not testified that he had called Michael but that Michael was already on the telephone when he spoke with him. Of course, Michael never said Big E killed Darrell Woods.

Ockleberry plowed on. She pointed out how Guichard himself had failed to put Valerie Morgan on the stand to rebut what Richey attributed to her. She argued that while Bertha Hayes had not, indeed, been asked by the prosecutor to name whom she saw shoot Woods, it was unnecessary: "You know who Bertha saw shot . . . Mr. Woods." [110]

Now Ockleberry effectively testified for Michael, herself putting words in his mouth, a collection of street corner quotes she pieced together from the testimonies of Lawter and the drug dealers, using her very blackness to provide ghetto intonations, beginning the end of her final argument by raising the superpredator theory the press had promoted, the image of the superpredator that had been the basis for the law that allowed her to try this boy as a man:

This is the words out of his mouth, excuse me, Fuck, nigger, you must not know where you at. This is New Jack City. Don't you think he said that? He's trying to impress his older friends out there. I ain't going to let nobody disrespect me like that, I got a reputation. . . . [111]

Sanitizing the hat, she exclaimed:

Did they ever ask him to try on that hat to say it was his?[112]

Now she shouted, turning Guichard's own words, taken from his opening statement and cross-examination of Mills, to condemn his client:

Say you get back in the jury room and you believe somebody put him up to do this, you know, that they encouraged him and said Don't take that, Don't let that man disrespect you, say you believe that. That still makes him guilty . . . because nobody pulled that trigger but him.[113]

Pounding home the theme of guilt by default, guilt by failure to testify, trampling the Fifth Amendment, she reminded the jury:

He [Richey] talked to the Defendant's own mother. We said put her on the stand. . . . Again, if I confess. Why didn't you just say I didn't do this, they're trying to pin it on me.[114]

Finally, Ockleberry closed with a dramatic flourish that revealed what the case against Little B was really about, about accommodating a powerful racist political socioeconomic agenda that at once invented and condemned black boys as superpredators. Wildly she snatched the rifle from the evidence table and stomped with it up and down in front of the jury box. She snatched the black skull cap and put it on her head, crouched down with gun in hand, and screamed out that this was how Little B had stolen the life of Darrell Woods. The television news cameras followed her every step.

He spent time talking to you about the fact that, you know, the Defendant's only 13. . . . But there's a couple of things I want to say to that, and that is, when he put this hat on his head like this, okay, and he had this gun in his hand like this, what age did he look? Did it matter? Did it matter? . . .

Because, see, when it comes down to it, your verdict sends a message. You're not only talking to him, you're talking to . . . other 13, 14 and 15 year olds. . . . You're telling them You must take responsibility for your actions. If you find him not guilty, what message do you send to other kids out there that do the same thing. . . . That I can kill someone for no reason and I can go before 12 people who will let me go. . . . Don't worry about his age.[115]

After Wright read all the legal instructions, the jury was discharged at 3:10 P.M. The jury returned with a guilty verdict at 5:05 P.M.

Paul Howard appeared at the courthouse to speak to the cameras when the verdict was issued, in time for the early television newscasts. He would personally appear before the parole board once Michael had spent the mandated minimum fourteen years of his life sentence to make sure he stayed in prison fourteen years more. He would make sure the boy spent the rest of his life in prison. As long as he was in office, he pledged to rid the streets of Atlanta of the Little Bs.

In another week, Michael was formally sentenced to life in prison.

———————

Suzanne Ockleberry would go on to use the Little B case to promote herself and her career, first within the district attorney's office and then outside. Maria Elena Fernandez would use the case to move on to the *Washington Post*. Never trying any major crime cases himself over the next years, losing the famous Ray Lewis Buckhead case, Paul Howard recalled this Little B "victory" to overcome his record, not only to secure a massive budget increase from the legislature but also to win reelection.

Atlanta's first black mayor, Maynard Jackson, speaking for Atlanta's businessmen and their black cohorts, came to be proud: "Paul Howard has brought new life to a district attorney's office that . . . had been stagnant for decades. . . . Howard has shown . . . that he truly cares about justice and victims of crime, and about making this community safer." [116]

———————

Three years later, Ta-Ta and Michael and I were laughing in the visiting room at Lee Arrendale State Prison. Michael was, for a change, housed in the general population, not in the "hole," also called "the block." He was chomping on what I considered unchewable Sugar Babies candies.

"When I was a kid, we used to buy a big Sugar Daddy. I can't even chew the Babies today," I commented.

"Yeah, Miss Brown," Ta-Ta said, snickering, "I understand. That's how my mama lost all her teeth."

"You must not have the same mama I do," Michael said. They doubled over with laugher. "Was it your daddy or mine who knocked out her teeth?" he added through tears of laughter.

"But she did like those Sugar Daddies," Ta-Ta said, doubled over. "She used to get 'em all the time from Henry's."

"Wait a minute. You mean the Suhs actually sold candy and other real stuff there?" I asked. "They really sold sodas? Nobody ever talked about what kind of soda Kenya supposedly bought—if it was a soda she bought."

Ta-Ta brightened, "Just go look at the tape from the video camera."

"There was a security video camera there at that time?"

"Yeah, me and my girlfriends used to check ourselves in the TV at Henry's all the time."

[15] The Appeal

She worked for the telephone company, which was where Judy Skidmore asked me to meet her. The wind was swirling wildly through the corridor of towering office buildings in the developing upscale area called Midtown Atlanta, near downtown, where she was waiting. Her hair and clothes ruffling in the wind, she was still smiling, a short, chocolate-colored black woman alone in front of the big building where she worked. We had never met before.

She had called me several times and left nonspecific messages that did not seem very important. After more than a month, I returned her calls. She wanted to talk with me about the article I had written about Little B, which had become a full-page Sunday feature editorial in the *Atlanta Journal-Constitution.* She wanted to talk to me in person, inexplicably. The summer had passed, and Michael's trial date had been approaching. Perhaps she wanted to help him in some way. As it turned out, the man who had given her my number, Leonard Tate, a local black activist, was not our only mutual contact. A wild woman named Loretto Grier was also someone we both knew.

Loretto—Dr. Grier—a dentist, had been at a small NAACP event I had been asked to attend a month or so before that. It was a community meeting about criminal justice. There, on the stage of the little auditorium at Morehouse College, sitting on the panel gathered to lead the discussion on blacks and the criminal justice system, was Paul Howard. Was this NAACP branch completely mad, I asked aloud, cursing under my breath, walking back out of the auditorium. Loretto was in the hallway, sitting at an information table smothered with leaflets and fliers and petitions. Like everybody in the auditorium, she had heard me. She told me to calm down. Once I explained my rage, she lifted her six-foot frame out of her chair and pulled me back into the auditorium, where we sat together loudly grumbling about Howard, to the embarrassment of most of the sparse audience. Finally, I stood up, and Loretto stood, too, a big and brown and beautiful warrior princess. I shouted out that Howard should not be involved in any matters concerning justice and black people, that he was a duplicitous lackey. Loretto shouted her agreement, challenging any opposing voices. Howard actually responded, "I am not duplicitous."

We left and laughed and became friends. Among the million other things Loretto did was to participate in a black women's group in Macon, where she lived and worked. She asked me to speak there one evening. That was what I was going to do when I picked up Judy Skidmore in front of the big office building. Now, we were going together, going to see Loretto, and on the way we would talk about Little B.

On the drive south to Macon, a straight route of an hour or more on an interstate highway that had apparently smoothed over old dusty roads along a flat and monotonous vista, Judy said very little. She listened to me explain the injustice of the case against Little B. After we arrived at the "Best Chicken" restaurant where I would speak to Loretto's group, Judy simply sat silently with the rest of the women, while the owner served fried chicken to everybody, while I gave my little talk. It was on the way back to Atlanta, as the big trucks with their glaring headlights overwhelmed the two-lane highway, that Judy started to talk.

Softly, carefully, she wondered whether I could write any other articles about similar cases, cases like that of her only child, her son, Kevin. Trucks roared by. She had to repeat the pieces of the story before I heard her. "Oh, Judy, I didn't know."

Kevin had been arrested for armed robbery of a convenience store near where they lived. He had been fifteen years old at the time, which was not so long ago. This was one of the "seven deadly sins" under SB 440, so he had been tried as an adult. Under SB 440, one gun can be attributable to the hands of everybody remotely involved. It had not mattered that the storeowner, the "victim," testified that she had never felt threatened by the boys, or specifically by Kevin. It had not mattered that nobody was hurt at all. It had not mattered that the amount of money involved was only twenty-seven dollars. Once charged with armed robbery, once so convicted, SB 440 required a mandatory minimum sentence of ten years. Her boy was now serving that mandatory sentence in an adult prison.

She wanted somebody to say something about him. She wanted somebody to say that she was a hardworking mother, that she had taught her son all the right things, that he had made a mistake, that he was sorry, that there ought to be other ways to remedy the harm, that this penalty did not fit the crime, that he should not grow up in prison, miss high school and teenage dances and girls and college, that he was a good boy who had done one bad thing, that nobody had been hurt, that ten years was a long, long time.

Judy introduced me to the others, and we formed our small ragtag army of mothers, called Mothers Advocating Juvenile Justice (MAJJ). They were all black mothers with young sons in prison under SB 440 charges. Marva Williams's son Truvoris had a case that paralleled Michael's; his conviction and sentence of life in prison when he was thirteen years old had been overturned, and she was embroiled in the process of preparing for a new trial for him. Billie Ross, who was earning her master's degree, whose husband was a Morehouse College professor, had an only son, Glenwood, who had been sixteen when he was sentenced to the mandatory ten years in prison for a purse snatching that had been deemed an armed robbery, in which the black woman victim could not swear he was the one, though the two nineteen-year-olds in whose car Glenwood had been riding swore, in exchange for light sentences, that he was the only one. Kameelah Shabazz, a customer service manager for an airline, had a son Josh, convicted of a robbery on a MARTA rapid transit train, who had been sentenced to *fifteen* years mandatory time because the white man who had been robbed, who had not even been scratched, told the judge he had felt "terrorized." Valerie Bahar, an apartment complex manager, had a fourteen-year-old son who was facing trial for armed robbery, along with her seventeen-year-old daughter, both of whom would be convicted and sentenced to adult prisons, whose strange and complicated case also did not involve any violence. Soon, Charles Maxwell would join us, the only father among the mothers, a school principal whose son, Chuck, was serving a mandatory sentence of ten years—plus eight years of extended probation—for armed robbery, a case in which, like the rest, nobody was hurt, and there was no gun in evidence. None of these children had ever been arrested previously.

What had happened, what was happening, to the children of MAJJ reflected what was a terrible national trend, we learned. This was not about crime. This was about black children. We pledged to overturn SB 440. We vowed to save our sons and daughters.

"While juvenile crime, including violent crime ha[d] *decreased* in recent years," we learned, "40 states ha[d] changed their laws to allow increased prosecution of juveniles in adult criminal court." This was according to the documentation of the Building Blocks for Youth Initiative, a partnership of organizations that included the Youth Law Center, the American Bar Association Juvenile Justice Center, and the National Council on Crime and Delinquency, supported by, among others, the Annie E. Casey Foundation and the Rockefeller Foundation. Furthermore, the initiative found, "the great weight of these punitive juvenile justice policies [had fallen] disproportionately on minority youth."

Exacerbating the situation, the initiative stated, was the fact that "the evening news [was] regularly filled with stories of young (usually minority) perpetrators, sometimes even referring to these youth as 'superpredators.'" Indeed, the initiative's research, titled "Youth, Race, and Crime in the News," revealed that "the news media unduly connect[ed] youth to crime and violence and that youth of color [were] overrepresented as perpetrators." The research also showed that, ironically, "crime coverage . . . increased while real crime rates ha[d] fallen." This media imagery had contributed significantly to the national support for the racist draconian laws that were hammering away at black kids in the criminal justice system, because "three quarters (76%) of the public say they form their opinions about crime from what they see or read in the news."[1]

In state after state, the rate of incarceration of black children was disproportionally high, MAJJ found. The Justice Policy Institute reported that while minority youth constituted about 53 percent of the youth population of California, for example, 70 percent of juveniles placed in secure corrections were minority kids, mostly black. In Ohio the correlation was 14.3 percent of the state population and 43 percent of the juveniles placed in secure corrections. In Texas black and other children of color made up 50 percent of the state youth population but accounted for 80 percent of juveniles in secure corrections and *100 percent* of juveniles in adult jails. The ratio in Virginia was 27 percent of the population and 57 percent in secure corrections; in New Jersey 29 percent of the population, 85 percent in secure corrections; in Pennsylvania 14.3 percent of the population compared with 87 percent in secure corrections; in Wisconsin 11 percent compared to 75 percent. In the so-called liberal northeast sector of the country there was no difference. In Connecticut, while black and other kids of color represented 15.3 percent of the population, they composed 69 percent of the youth population in secure corrections and *100 percent* in adult jails, and in Massachusetts black and other children of color who were 17.2 percent of the youth population constituted 81 percent of juveniles in adult jails.[2] Overall, in America, black children represented "the largest racial/ethnic proportion of youth held behind locked doors."[3]

This was confirmed by an April 2000 study commissioned by the United States Justice Department and six of the nation's leading foundations. Their comprehensive report documented that there were monumental race disparities in the juvenile justice system and identified this as a national problem, as indicated in the title of the report: "And Justice for Some." The report found that black and Hispanic youth "are more likely than their white counterparts to be arrested, held in jail, sent to court for trial, convicted and given long prisons terms." It also found that black children never sent to juvenile prison before were *six times* more likely than their white counterparts to be sentenced to prison; that among youth charged with violent crimes, black teenagers were *nine times* more likely than white teens to be sentenced to prison; and for drug offenses, black kids were *forty-eight times* more likely to be sentenced to prison than white kids. Furthermore, the long-term custody rate for black children across the nation was *five times* that for white youth, and black children are much more likely than whites to end up in prisons with adult offenders.[4]

According to the Georgia Indigent Defense Council, of the juveniles arrested under SB 440 between 1994 (when the law was passed) and

1998, 80 percent were black children, and 19 percent were white. In both Fulton and DeKalb counties, the arrest rate was 94 percent black. Black youth during the same period represented 33 percent of the youth population in Georgia.[5] This racial trend remained essentially the same through the end of the millennium.[6] The council's report also documented what crimes black youth, mostly boys, were being charged with and convicted of committing. Like most of the sons of MAJJ, 62 percent of the black children convicted under SB 440 were convicted of armed robbery.[7]

The mothers of MAJJ set up our little nonprofit corporation, had a logo designed, focused our agenda on developing our own legislation, toward at least reforming SB 440, and began trying to hold some community meetings among other parents. New mothers joined, but people were mostly afraid. Most afraid were the so-called black leaders, the legislators and churchmen and businessmen and lawyers and other professionals, who in general wanted little to do with a bunch of women and their condemned children.

Though I had no biological child in prison, I had become one of the "mothers" of MAJJ. All of nature's children seem to need or want a mother, and imprinting, even among animals not of the same species, has seemed to accommodate this yearning, especially for swans deemed ugly ducklings. So it was that Michael made me his mother. I had become all he had, so to speak, speaking out for him, trying to get a lawyer for his appeal, sending him money for the prison store, that sort of thing, so he had latched on to me in the first year of his incarceration and had made me Mommie. I had been informed of my new role suddenly, in a letter he had struggled to write me, which, like some of his others, had a funny drawing on it: "How are you doing? Better than ever I hope! I'm maintaining like always. Missing my freedom. So how have things been coming along for you? . . . I'm still working on that rap for you. When you get the rap you are gonna say it's good. . . . Peace out . . . w/b/a/s/a/p [write back as soon as possible] . . . I love you Mother!!!"

Although there were so many glaring issues for Michael's appeal, the most prominent being the prosecutor's blatantly illegal accusation in her closing argument that Michael should have been presumed *guilty* on account of his not having testified, mounting the appeal became extremely complicated. Gary Guichard's boss at the office of the Conflict Defender, Paul Kehir, felt that his office should handle the appeal—unless the issue of "ineffective counsel" was to be raised. It was a moot point.

A private criminal defense attorney would require a lot of money in the absence of the plethora of radical lawyers from another time, the old probono lawyers whose hearts were bigger than their fees. As I began to search out the possibilities, most lawyers I solicited believed that Little B had killed that man in front of his kids and really did not care about representing him.

There was at least one radical lawyer left in Atlanta, I learned, however, and by a stroke of serendipity it turned out that he was my neighbor. Bob Bensing was still a believer, still wore his hair long and disheveled, like his secondhand wardrobe. He was with a group of lawyers called the Southern Center for Human Rights, the focus of whose work was death penalty cases. We met at the newspaper recycling bin in our apartment building, finding mutuality in the bags of newspapers he and his wife, Mary, a physician, had accumulated the way I had. Bob was a part-time Buddhist vegetarian who liked good wine and other things French, and he and Mary and I came to spend any number of evenings drinking lots of French wine, Bob and I lapsing into French conversation from time to time.

Bob could help, I hoped. However, he did not practice criminal law per se; instead, like the rest of the center's lawyers, he worked on big legal issues that affected classes of people. His specialty was prisoners' rights. Bob thought the head of the center, Stephen Bright, might know someone, and Bright, in turn, referred me to Robert McGlasson. McGlasson showed interest, though he was concerned about "attacking" Guichard. In the meantime, Bob put me in contact with Theresa Nelson, head of the Atlanta ACLU, who said they might be interested in supporting Michael's appeal in some way. By the beginning of the new year, 1998, the appeal seemed achievable.

It was Black History Month, and the rain was pouring so, only the echo of Ray Charles singing about it soothed the sound of the relentless beating. It did not seem like a dangerous rain, just relentless, all night and all day. The early February sunset was barely visible, like the sunrise. Though dreary, it was the kind of ordinary moment one remembers forever when somebody suddenly dies. Bob Bensing had been coming back from Valdosta, at the southern tip of Georgia. That very day, he had won his case against the reactionary head of the Department of Corrections, Wayne Garner, an actual monetary victory for the inmates he represented for the violation of their rights, one of whom Bob had been visiting in Valdosta. The car in which he had been riding had hydroplaned, a horrible event captured by a word that sounded like something bird-like and beautiful. Bob had been killed instantly. I wept with Mary for months, as Robert McGlasson sort of went away, like the hope that Bob himself had represented.

Somehow an old friend from my Black Panther Party days, Dennis Riordan, appeared. He was still practicing criminal law in San Francisco, specializing in criminal appeals. Dennis was, in fact, a preeminent lawyer in criminal appellate work. He told me he knew a powerful lawyer in Atlanta, Don Samuel, and not much later he committed himself to overseeing the case, gratis. Samuel was not so enthusiastic. In fact, he made it clear to me that the only reason he would become involved in this case was to work with Dennis, and that he would do what he could for Dennis here in Atlanta, but that was all. For now, he and Dennis needed to see the transcript. It would take one year and numerous motions to the court by Patrice Fulcher, however, to finally get the transcript. By then, even Dennis had moved on to other, bigger cases, and no one else appeared on the horizon.

———

"Lewis, I hope you die in here," a guard told Michael somewhere before the end of his first year at Alto, Lee Arrendale State Prison. I promised him he would not, though there was still no real appeal plan. Michael was not whining about it, though, as he never had and never would, though life at Alto was hard. The warden would actually tell me later that Michael was having a lot of trouble "adjusting." This was a doubly ironic comment given that a few years later this same warden would be dismissed from his position allegedly on account of a criminal accusation of assaulting his wife.[8]

Of the twelve hundred inmates at Alto, thirty-two were under seventeen years old. At fourteen years old, Michael was the youngest when he arrived.[9] Over that first year, he had survived the intimidation tactics of the CERT (Corrections Emergency Response Team) guards in charge of him then, specially trained men in combat boots who sported assault batons on their belts and who escorted him, handcuffed, everywhere. He had suffered what seemed the monthly disciplinary reports, the DRs, that sent him to the hole for indeterminate periods for "insubordination" and "failure to follow" and "verbal threats." And of course Michael had survived and defended himself against attacks from other inmates, all of whom were older than he was.

In addition to everything else, it cost money to survive in prison. Like the others, Michael was actually charged $4.00 for each DR written up against him, which would automatically be deducted from the money in his prison account. Each doctor's visit, which would more than likely be a nurse or medical paraprofessional, cost $5.00. A five-ounce bar of soap cost $.77; a small bottle of hand lotion, $2.05; a large bag of potato chips, $1.19. The greatest expense, however, was a telephone call home, which could only be made collect through the private company Harris TeleCom in conjunction with Sprint and which cost $1.50 for the first minute and nearly $.50 per minute thereafter. Most families bore the hardship of these expensive calls given that they represented the primary communication between themselves and their sons. Without a car, it was virtually impossible to get to the remote corner of the North Georgia mountains where Alto was located to visit their men and boys, and most prisoners' families were poor and did not have cars. Typically, telephone charges amounted to $150 per month, for a few minutes of conversation per day.

As so many black boys growing up in prison had become part of the burgeoning population of young black males in the criminal justice system, the larger black community was suffering in other ways. These boys were doomed to become part of the large number of black males excluded from voting in America on account of prison records, further diluting the power of the black vote. Moreover, the removal of the potential earnings of these boys was further depressing the meager economies of black communities, which would not be recovered upon their release as men whose earnings capacities would be limited by their incarceration history. All of this was acting as an additional disruption to the cohesion of the black family and was leading to the further impoverishment, isolation, and alienation of another generation of black children.

———

> For there began to rise in America in 1876 a new capitalism and a new enslavement of labor.
>
> W. E. B. Du Bois, *Black Reconstruction*[10]

Now, at the end of another century, Michael's incarceration was looming as part of a new scheme of convict labor, free black labor, in America, on which Du Bois had so profoundly reflected a century before. Georgia is one of only three states in America that do not pay inmates at all for their labor.[11]

In South Georgia, in 1999, for example, the private for-profit Environmental Technologies Group made a deal with the Crisp County Solid Waste Management Authority for the free labor of women inmates at the Pulaski County Prison. The women inmates were put to work five days a week, eight hours a day, to sort "recyclables" from garbage trucked into the area from literally dozens of other towns and counties. What made this design more insidious was that Environmental Technologies used this free convict labor to fulfill its own contract with another government agency, the Waste Management Authority. Furthermore, in order to obtain the benefit of this free prison labor, the company laid off fifty minimum-wage workers, among whom were thirty-five women forced off welfare to take the jobs. This deal was concocted in an arrangement made by and among the authority; the company; prison officials; the local state senator, Rooney Bowen; and Georgia's lieutenant governor, Mark Taylor—author of SB 440. Under it, the authority reimburses the prison $122,000 a year in tax dollars for guards to escort the women prisoners to sort through the garbage for Environmental Technologies, which in turn is paid $93,600 in tax dollars to run the $54 million state-owned waste facility. Taylor shrugged off the matter by saying that he had given his approval to the contract because "it was just another constituent request." The head of the authority, Chip Wells, defended the arrangement by stating that this free inmate labor "helps put the facility a little bit closer to being profitable."[12]

This kind of scheme has become so enticing that it has spawned intense lobbying efforts by economically impoverished cities and towns for prison construction—a scheme that necessarily requires more prisoners. In 1999, Nicholls, Georgia, lobbied to have the state build a prison there because, as one city council member put it, "we had to have an industry if we were going to survive . . . [and] a correctional facility would be a nonseasonal, environmentally friendly industry that would provide jobs that we sorely needed." The state gave Nicholls the taxpayer money to build the prison, and Nicholls used the money to contract with and pay private Corrections Corporation of America (CCA) to construct and operate it. This brought Nicholls 215 new jobs and a thousand other benefits, according to the enthusiastic city council. Those benefits have included a new bank building, a Dollar General store, a remodeled "sit-down" restaurant, an expanded convenience store, a new car sales lot, a chicken take-out business, and finally, the prospect of even more employment when the five-hundred-bed expansion is completed.[13]

None of this takes into account the profits made by CCA itself. By 2000, CCA was being paid $33 million a year by the state of Georgia alone to house one thousand prisoners. CCA contracts in Georgia were established earlier by former corrections commissioner Wayne Garner. The only problem the new commissioner, Jim Wetherington, saw with the CCA contracts was that their two existing facilities—though more are being constructed—were not being used to their capacity of fifteen hundred inmates each. On the other hand, another private prison corporation, Cornell Corrections Corporation, had had no problem filling and running its fifteen-hundred-bed private prison in Folkston. This triggered a fear that CCA would fill its empty beds with "dangerous criminals from other parts of the country." Thus the state began exploring using the empty spaces for the "detention" of "illegal immigrants."[14] It is certain, however, that the state will soon resolve this problem, as Georgia ranks third in the nation, behind Louisiana and Texas, in the total incarceration rate of its population—and nearly 70 percent of the state's prisoners are black.[15]

Nationwide, CCA, with facilities in Georgia as well as in Washington State, Ohio, Colorado, Tennessee, and more under contract, has come to virtually monopolize the construction and maintenance of private prisons, paid for and supported by state and local tax dollars. The profitability in this scheme is obvious and has spawned stiff competition for CCA. Among its competitors are not only Cornell Corrections but Wackenhut Corrections Corporation, which dominates the international private prison market. Also competing are CiviGenics, Management and Training Corporation, Correctional Services, the Bobby Ross Group, Marantha Production Company, and others.[16] The profitability in this industry is sweetened by the fact that while these companies are the beneficiaries of millions of dollars from the bottomless well of public tax money, as private corporations they are not subject to public oversight or scrutiny. This unregulated and unchecked operation has created a permissive —and racially charged—atmosphere in private prison facilities, where inmates are and have been vulnerable to cruel and unusual punishments.[17] This was documented in a 1996 videotape made in a Brazoria County, Texas, private prison where guards were filmed "beating, shocking, kicking and setting dogs on prisoners."[18]

Others profiting from this industry are private manufacturers. As the prison population in the United States increased *80 percent* during the 1980s, many manufacturers seized the opportunity to make their products with this controlled cheap labor force.[19] By the 1990s, big U.S. corporations were using inmate labor, including IBM, Motorola, Compaq, Texas Instruments, Honeywell, and Microsoft. Moreover, Nordstrom department stores were retailing jeans and other clothing produced in Oregon prisons for Yoshiba Group, under the marketing slogan "Made on the inside to be worn on the outside."[20] CMT Blues, which is actually located at the maximum security prison Richard J. Donovan State Correctional Facility, not far from San Diego, has inmates make T-shirts under CMT's contracts with Mecca, Seattle Cotton Works, and Lee Jeans, among others.[21] New Hampshire prisons make output chokes for GFS Manufacturing's clients, which include Hewlett-Packard and Siemens. Prisoners in Maryland inspect glass bottles and jars for Revlon and Pierre Cardin. South Carolina prisoners sew graduation caps and gowns for contracts of Jostens for worldwide distribution.[22] Target Stores distribute various prisoner-manufactured items, and prisoners make lingerie for Victoria's Secret.[23] At the Washington State Reformatory, Microjet enjoys a rent-free and benefits-free arrangement, where it employs prisoners to make aircraft components for Boeing.[24] By 2000, more than eighty thousand inmates in thirty-six states were so "employed" by private companies to, as one observer noted, "take advantage of state-supplied facilities and low-wage nonunion workers."[25]

One of the chief lobbyists for using convict labor for private manufacturing is former U.S. attorney general Edwin Meese III, now Ronald Reagan Distinguished Fellow at the Heritage Foundation and chairman of the Enterprise Prison Institute. Meese argues that this scheme is completely justified in that it gives inmates something to do and keeps American businesses from locating outside the country where labor is even cheaper—despite the fact that some inmates must work without compensation.[26]

The high profitability in the burgeoning private prison industry has virtually silenced official criticism, black and white, of the labor exploitation and human rights abuses of people in prison, particularly, it seems, since such exploitation and abuses are suffered by a population of people that is, in the main, poor and black.[27] Indeed, given the profit potential in the use of below-minimum-wage or free prison labor to private enterprise and private prisons, and given that CCA and its competitors are paid by the head, it is in the various profiteers' interests to keep these prisons filled to capacity. The private prison industry is, after all, a "growth industry," in which the only "product" is prisoners. Declining crime rates in the 1990s had portended a problem for CCA and the others, including the various big corporations doing business with them and their Wall Street investment partners, Goldman Sachs and the like. However, under the new mandatory minimum sentences built into the federal "Three Strikes" crime bill and its state progeny, the prison population in America, particularly the black prison population, has increased phenomenally.[28] Indeed, the largest growth in the private prison industry has been in the federal system, which had become, as of 2000, the third biggest prison system in the country.[29]

The number of women in prison *doubled* between 1990 and 1999, a highly disproportionate number of whom were, needless to say, black women.[30] In fact, black women represent the fastest growing group of people being imprisoned in America.[31] Moreover, by the end of the century the arrest rate for juvenile females—mostly black girls—had increased twice as much as that for boys.[32] The increased arrest and incarceration figure among women does not, however, comport with the *decline* in the rate of crimes attributed to women.[33] Similarly, although the juvenile violent crime rate decreased, juvenile criminal arrest rates have steadily increased.[34] Indeed, for each year in the waning of the twentieth century, the FBI's Uniform Crime Report has documented, overall, a consistent dramatic decrease in crime in America.[35]

The greatest contributing factor to the consistent increase in the black prison population rate is victimless nonviolent drug arrests.[36] Black women, for example, who now represent *more than half* of the nation's female prison population, are, in the main, serving sentences for nonviolent drug-related offenses, that is, for illegal drug possession or on account of drug addiction. In New York, for example, 70 percent of all women in prison, the majority of whom are black, are serving time for drug-related offenses. Throughout the nation at the end of the century, black women represented 82 percent of women sentenced for crack cocaine offenses and 50 percent for overall drug offenses. Considering that *two-thirds* of all women in prison have minor children and that over 1 million children have parents in prison in relation to the highly disproportionate number of women in prison who are black, the increased imprisonment of black women, like that of young black men, has had a devastating impact on black families, particularly children.[37]

By the end of the millennium, blacks, about 12 percent of the population, represented 46 percent of all prisoners in the United States of America.[38] The *majority*, 73 percent, had been convicted of *nonviolent* offenses, and blacks imprisoned on drug convictions alone accounted for *38 percent* of the monumental increase in the black prison population. Indeed, nationwide more blacks were sent to state prisons for drug convictions than for convictions for violent crimes.[39] Blacks represented nearly 75 percent of all state prisoners convicted of *simple* drug possession, and the biggest increase in the total American prison population resulted from the convictions of "non-underclass" blacks for drug offenses.[40] All of this represented a 465.5 percent increase in the number of blacks imprisoned for drugs over the last decade of the century, as drug convictions, representing approximately 400,000 people, were chiefly responsible for the steady increase in the total number of people incarcerated in America over the last decade of the last century.[41] These drug convictions were singularly significant to the fact that by 2000, the number of people incarcerated in the nation had risen to over 2 million, giving the United States, representing 5 percent of the world's population, the distinction of incarcerating about *one-quarter* of the world's prisoners and making the country noteworthy as having the highest incarceration rate in the entire world.[42] All of this is very specifically related to crack cocaine.

Even though more whites have been documented to use crack cocaine than blacks, 90 percent of the people *convicted* of federal crack cocaine possession charges are black.[43] In addition, the laws of fourteen states distinguish between the use and possession of crack and powder cocaine. Thus the phenomenal increase in the black prison population on account of crack cocaine charges is a matter of public policy, attributable specifically to the difference in sentencing laws and the application of those laws in relation to powder and crack cocaine, and to blacks and whites: "The result of the combined difference in sentencing laws and racial disparity is that black men and women are serving longer prison sentences than white men and women."[44]

Blacks suffer a high incarceration rate for crack cocaine, on one hand, because, while crack is simply cocaine processed for smoking, and powder and crack produce comparable physical effects, federal law equates five grams of crack with five hundred grams of powder cocaine. That is, possession of five grams of crack is a felony, with an automatic five-year prison term, while possession of five grams of powder cocaine is a misdemeanor, which may carry no jail time at all. On the other hand, the so-called war on drugs has been focused on street-level drug activities, or on the ghetto, where cheap crack became a means to an end, economically and emotionally. For, crack never became a mainstream drug. There are twice as many people using powder cocaine than crack, and many more *millions* of Americans use marijuana. Police across the nation have rounded up black crack addicts, couriers, and small-time dealers—notably in lieu of big-time dealers and importers of large quantities of powder cocaine—as the courts have strictly applied the draconian mandatory crack sentences.[45] Adding to this are the thousands and thousands arrested and convicted under Byzantine "snitch" schemes of criminal prosecutors. New conspiracy amendments to state and federal drug laws, whereby any minor role in a drug transaction can trigger a major indictment, have armed prosecutors with the extraordinary power to convict more and more people without evidence, by making deals for reduced sentences, typically, with big-time drug dealers facing life in prison, to testify against low-level people involved with crack.[46] This overall public policy, set off by sensationalist acts like the 1988 appearance of President George Bush on television announcing the onset of the "war" by holding up what was purportedly a bag of crack, was driven by the efforts of men like John DiIulio and, even more particularly, by right-wing criminologist James Q. Wilson. Wilson recently said, "Putting people in prison has been the single most important thing we've done to reduce crime."[47]

However, even Clinton's drug czar, the four-star general Barry R. McCaffrey, head of the National Drug Control Policy Office, had to acknowledge by the end of the millennium that the country had "a failed social policy [regarding drugs.] . . . We're going to bankrupt ourselves. Because we can't incarcerate our way out of this [drug] problem."[48] But the fact is, that while General McCaffrey referred to the crack invasion of the inner city and the resulting violence as "World War III," he and Clinton—like Bush before him and Bush drug czar William J. Bennett— did nothing in those critical years of the "invasion" to stop the flow of cocaine into the United States. He and Clinton instituted no policy that resulted in the arrest of big-time traffickers and dealers, or bankers and other money launderers, while continuing to send millions and millions of tax dollars to support the dictatorial governments of the primary cocaine-producing countries, Colombia, Peru, and Bolivia.

———

What MAJJ wanted seemed so little, in the end. What we faced, however, was so big. Still, we held a rally in front of the state capitol, calling for the repeal of SB 440. We obtained the support of a few legislators, like Tyrone Brooks, and a few ministers, including the old civil rights warrior Rev. Joseph Lowery. We made up petitions and got signatures of support. We wrote our own legislation. We tried to raise money. We found and communicated with other groups around the country also working for juvenile justice. We visited our children and other children and sent them money and hope. What we wanted was a bit of justice, but it was not coming, even though it was so little.

It began to occur to me that more effort had to be made on behalf of this one child, who was now mine, in a way. In 1999, through another old Black Panther contact, a California lawyer named Dennis Roberts, I found Jim Jenkins. After months of discussions, Jenkins finally agreed to take Michael's case if he had a polygraph test result and $25,000. As far as I was concerned, this meant we were on the road to victory.

The question was, what was the victory. Even if MAJJ could and did really overturn all or part of SB 440, even if—or when—Michael was freed, what did it mean in the face of the monumental problems of which his case was only an indication?

More than a century after the passage of the Thirteenth Amendment, more than 130 years since the legal end of slavery, the black communities of the United States effectively formed a third world enclave of subcitizens within the confines of this richest nation in the world. Indeed, among the richest nations in the world, the United States, as the richest, maintained the highest poverty rate, with blacks at the bottom.[49]

By the end of the century, nearly *one-quarter* of blacks in America were living *below* the poverty threshold.[50] More than half of black children under eighteen years old lived in households headed by single mothers, among whom *more than half* lived in poverty.[51] Black unemployment was more than *twice* that for whites.[52] The income gap between blacks and whites (a 59 percent ratio) remained about the same from the end of the nineteenth century to the end of the twentieth century.[53]

"The sharpest economic gap between blacks and whites in the United States involves wealth," according to the last report of the century by the National Urban League, which reflects "the passing of racial advantage and disadvantage from generation to generation."[54] Besides the individual wealth inferiority of blacks as to whites in terms of income and assets, and its impact on education, inheritance, and self-employment, blacks, either individually or collectively, have little ownership interest in the American economy. At the end of another century, there was no significant black ownership in the American economic complex, *no* black-owned aerospace companies, or airlines, or beverage manufacturers, or electric and gas utility companies, or pharmaceutical companies, or railroads, or telecommunications companies, or motor vehicle manufacturers—even though nearly half the top black-owned businesses in America are auto dealerships. Notwithstanding the sprinkling of blacks in the upper ranks of corporate America, if the revenues of the top black-owned companies were pooled, the collective entity would rank 83rd among the famous *Fortune* 500.[55]

The infant mortality rate of black babies in America has remained more than 50 percent higher than that of white babies.[56] The maternal mortality rate for black mothers is *four* times that of whites.[57] Black women are dying of breast cancer and cervical cancer at *twice* the rate of white women.[58] Black men continue to die of prostate cancer at more than twice the rate of white men.[59] In 2000, 65 percent of children with AIDS were black and 63 percent of women with AIDS were black.[60] And the devastation of crack cocaine remains.

Black children were still cordoned off in America's urban ghettos in the worst public education systems in the country, as the 1954 Supreme Court decision in *Brown v. Board of Education* has died before their very eyes. The result has been a preponderance of black undereducation, the foundation for massive black unemployment and underemployment. At the same time, a whole new generation of black children tries to manage life in a world in which thousands and thousands of their brothers and mothers and fathers are imprisoned.

There has been no twilight of racism falling over America. The dawn of a new age of racism has risen, in which a new forked tongue would lick the country's wounded with new lies, as it would fashion a new language permitting America to comfortably coexist with a continuum of racism and its horrible ramifications. Now stealing the New Age lexicon of self-healing, a gang dominating the social discourse would define the unending oppression of blacks as a matter of "personal responsibility," creating a Wonderland of words wherein a white rabbit deems affirmative action programs as "racist," justifies the end of school desegregation, and places the evil that men do to Little B upon his own head.

The question loomed. What was the appeal that would really free Little B?

When Al Gore tried to be president, like Clinton, he talked about improving "race relations," saying, innocuously, "healing is within our reach."[61]

The new president, George W. Bush, has made his agenda clear. His priorities are "national defense," by which he has promised to increase military spending, reducing the government's commitment to public education with cut-rate vouchers and the like and relegating any commitment to remedy social wrongs to "faith-based initiatives" operated by racists and reactionaries. In other words, only a continuum of oppression awaits Little B and all the millions of children like him.

There lies the proverbial rub. Blacks have hobbled into another century still oppressed, yet still looking to the white man in the White House for help, as though it were from him came strength, as though it were not from him came black oppression. As blacks relied on Lincoln, who tried to colonize and never free black people, blacks have looked to the imaginary benevolence of white men in the White House ever since for deliverance. Blacks have done so even as the presidents and the government and their powerful fellows in society have told us—in their courts, on their streets, in their social practices, under the atrocities of Jim Crow and de facto discrimination; in their violent rejection of the nonviolent efforts of blacks to become as real citizens; in the heartless assaults on and murders of those who tried to lead blacks to freedom, from Nat Turner to Marcus Garvey to Malcolm X to Martin Luther King Jr. to Huey P. Newton; and now in the subtle language of New Age Racism—told blacks that we have served our purpose as slave labor for the development of the American economy and that there is no room for us to exist here anymore. Still blacks would seem to imagine that some great white man in the White House might come someday and do the right thing, be persuaded by moral argument to bring an end to the evil heritage of slavery, right the wrongs of centuries.

If blacks would survive, it seems we must first wake ourselves from this nightmare and come to grips with its reality. If blacks would ever finally march out of the hell of Monticello, where we have lived for seemingly time immemorial, we must look away from the brutal master of this house and become masters to ourselves. We must seize our lives and destinies and collect our due. The goal of *freedom* must return to the top of our agenda, for it is the only business of the slave.

The goal of freedom for all black people, of independence and self-determination, has been reduced over the last decades, however, to anachronism by a growing group of blacks who have found personal comfort in pockets of power or personal power by seizing the tattered reins of black leadership. There has come to be, on one hand, as civil rights leader Whitney Young identified it, "an estrangement of the [black] elite from the [black] masses," even to the degree, as Young argued back in the sixties, of having "stop[ped] regarding themselves as [black]." Indeed, as Young so prophetically stated, "certain middle class [blacks] are now exhibiting an unfortunate tendency to be indifferent if not actually hostile to those black Americans less fortunate and privileged." [62] On the other hand, this "estrangement," as Young warned, has come to permeate the ranks of those defined broadly as black leaders, officials and bureaucrats and endorsed spokespeople, those who in the main possess the privilege of training and time to assume such roles, who establish self-perpetuating goals that do not serve and may be counterproductive to the goal of freedom.

Indeed, the freedom of Little B has come to be written out of the black agenda. The NAACP held a convention in Atlanta in which Colin Powell gave a keynote speech urging blacks to be "worthy of affirmative action" and where a call was made for research into whether the disproportionate ratio of blacks for certain cancer deaths was "genetic." [63] At the same time the Congressional Black Caucus was providing extraordinary support to Bill Clinton, as he was sending millions of blacks to prison and cutting off subsistence support to poor blacks, it included among its legislative priorities getting "more funding for drug prevention" and "increasing access to capital for small businesses." [64] Not long before that, a Million Man March had gone forth with the agenda of "atonement" for black men for their failure as patriarchs, which "God himself [had] imposed" on them, to be "heads of families and heads of communities." [65] Across the nation, local leaders have structured various self-help and rites-of-passage groups to address the purported failures in black boys. And at the beginning of the new millennium black politicos were crying foul and calling for a presidential ballot recount for Al Gore.

So blacks ourselves have come now to bemoan "black-on-black" crime, in total disregard of the activities of the local police or the FBI. We ourselves would rail against black welfare dependence, sanctioning with silence the billion-dollar government subsidization of big corporations. We, too, would lament the "breakup" of the black family as though this were the basis for our oppression, as though it had not come from our oppression, while providing no family for Little B. And while Little B's breast milk was being tainted by cocaine-*contra* deals, some blacks were wondering what was happening to our children.

If Little B would be free, blacks must return to the vision of Booker T. Washington and Marcus Garvey for economic independence, the relentless drive of Du Bois for unconditional freedom and equality, the progressive radicalism of Malcolm X and Huey P. Newton for black liberation. And then there is The Dream.

The history of black struggle suggests the American society may not be capable of accommodating the freedom of black people, that it may be inherently incongruous with the character and structure of America to share its wealth, even with those who represent its very source. For blacks represent a cautionary tale. Over 12 million children in America lived in poverty at the beginning of the new millennium, black children in urban ghettos and Native American children on reservations and Hispanic children in barrios and white children in mountain hollers.

For blacks, a starting point must be reparations for slavery, a just and justified infusion of money to provide food and health care and housing and schools for all the Little Bs. But there is more. There must be more.

In the last days of his life, Martin Luther King Jr., put forth a call to black people—embracing in his great humanity all the other poor people in America—a call for a Poor People's Campaign. It was a call for black people in America to come together and take what was due us as human beings, what had been stolen, a specific call for reparations for slavery, and it was a call for the poor of America, the disfranchised and alienated to join hands in that march, to demand a guaranteed income for all working people, guaranteed health care for all people, and a redistribution of the wealth of this nation—which was, in fact, The Dream.

Speaking, near the end of life, King asked, "Where do we go from here?" and spoke in a voice that resounds as powerfully now as then.

With all the struggle and all the achievements, we must face the fact . . . that the Negro still lives in the basement of the Great Society. He is still at the bottom, despite the few who have penetrated to slightly higher levels. . . . Negroes are still impoverished aliens in an affluent society. . . . For more than half of his American history, he was enslaved. Yet he built the spanning bridges, the grand mansions, the sturdy docks, and stout factories of the South. His unpaid labor made cotton king and established America as a significant nation in international commerce. Even after his release from chattel slavery, the nation grew over him, submerging him. It became the richest, most powerful society in the history of man, but it left the Negro far behind. . . .

Now in order to answer the question, "Where do we go from here?" which is our theme, we must first honestly recognize where we are now. . . . The plantation and the ghetto were created by those who had power . . . both to confine those who had no power and to perpetuate their powerlessness. Now the problem of transforming the ghetto, therefore, is a problem of power. . . .

"Where do we go from here?" . . . We must honestly . . . address . . . the question of restructuring the whole of American society. . . . Now when I say questioning the whole society, it means ultimately coming to see that the problem of racism, the problem of economic exploitation, and the problem of war are all tied together. . . .

And if you will let me be a preacher just a little bit. One day, one night, a juror came to Jesus and he wanted to know what he could do to be saved. . . . Jesus looked at him and said, "Nicodemus, you must be born again. . . ." What I'm saying today is . . . , "America, you must be born again!"[66]

Notes

[1] Black Man-Child

1. Maria Elena Fernandez, "He Never Had a Chance," *Atlanta Journal-Constitution*, January 24, 1997, p. 1.
2. Maria Elena Fernandez, "Teen Suspect a 'Thug,' Police Say," *Atlanta Journal-Constitution*, January 30, 1997, p. 03B.
3. Ibid.
4. Maria Elena Fernandez, "Slaying Suspect's Brother: 'He's Bad,'" *Atlanta Journal-Constitution*, January 31, 1997, p. 01B.
5. Ibid.
6. Maria Elena Fernandez, "Ruined Lives," *Atlanta Journal-Constitution*, February 2, 1997, p. 01A.
7. "Keeping Kids from Killing," *Atlanta Constitution*, January 31, 1997, p. A10.
8. Jeff Dickerson, "Another Black Father Dies," *Atlanta Journal*, February 4, 1997, p. 06A.
9. Dave Kindred, "As Quick as a Heartbeat, Life Is Stolen on Mean Streets," *Atlanta Journal-Constitution*, February 5, 1997, p. 03D.
10. Maria Elena Fernandez, " 'Little B' Faces Judge," *Atlanta Journal-Constitution*, February 6, 1997, p. 1.
11. Gail H. Towns and Maria Elena Fernandez, "Two-Year Truancy Is No Surprise," *Atlanta Journal-Constitution*, February 8, 1997, p. 01E.
12. Fernandez, " 'Little B' Faces Judge."
13. Maria Elena Fernandez and Gail H. Towns, "A Teen's Choice: Accused Killer Wanted Life on the Street," *Atlanta Journal-Constitution*, February 8, 1997, p. E3.
14. Jeff Dickerson, "Pay Now, or Pay Later," *Atlanta Journal-Constitution*, February 11, 1997, p. 08A.
15. Fredrick D. Robinson, "Where's the Outrage?" *Atlanta Journal-Constitution*, February 12, 1997, p. 16A.
16. Maria Elena Fernandez, "Vine City: Repairing Tarnished Reputation," *Atlanta Journal-Constitution*, February 19, 1997, p. 02C.
17. Robinson, "Where's the Outrage?"

[2] The Murder Case

1. Georgia Department of Corrections, "Active Offender Population Statistics by Race," 1996.
2. The Juvenile Advocacy Division of Georgia Indigent Defense Council, "Juveniles Arrested as Adults under SB440: Fiscal year 1998 Final Report," 6; 11.

3. Michael Hinkelman, "Next Fulton DA Should Scrutinize Politicians," *Atlanta Business Chronicle*, November 1, 1996.
4. Maria Elena Fernandez, "Teen Suspect a 'Thug' Police Say," *Atlanta Journal-Constitution*, January 30, 1997, p. 3B.

[3] Evil in the City

1. "Keeping Kids from Killing," *Atlanta Journal-Constitution*, January 31, 1997, p. A10.
2. Pam Belluck, "Chicago Boys, 7 and 8, Charged in the Brutal Killing of a Girl, 11," *New York Times*, August 11, 1998, p. A1.
3. Maureen Downey, "How Should Courts Handle the Unthinkable?" *Atlanta Journal-Constitution*, August 15, 1998, p. A8.
4. Ron Stodghill II, "Justice Minus Joy," *Time*, May 3, 1999, 67.
5. Alex Kotlowitz, "The Unprotected," *New Yorker*, February 8, 1999, 42–53.
6. Stodghill, "Justice Minus Joy."
7. "Children Accused," *Associated Press*, February 10, 1998.
8. "Young Murder Suspect," *Associated Press*, February 11, 1998.
9. Christopher John Farley and James Willwerth, "Dead Teen Walking," *Time*, January 19, 1998.
10. Alymer Ahjohn, NAACP Legal Defense Fund and Education Fund, national headquarters, telephone interview, July 13, 1999; NAACP Legal Defense Fund and Education Fund, *Death Row U.S.A.*, winter 2001.
11. NAACP Legal Defense Fund and Education Fund, "Execution Update," January 30, 1996.
12. Office of Clive Stafford-Smith, Crisis Assistance Center, New Orleans, telephone interview, July 31, 1999.
13. Tracy-Lynn Clough, "States Get Tough on Teens," *Dallas Morning News*, August 31, 1997, p. 1A.
14. Bryan Buchanan, telephone interview, June 1, 1999.
15. Radio Address by the president to the nation, the White House, Office of the Press Secretary, September 10, 1994.
16. Julie Grace, "There Are No Children Here," *Time*, September 12, 1995.
17. *Current Biography* 1961, 273–75.
18. Jay Hughes, "Miss Teen Says Demons Made Him Kill Mother," *Atlanta Journal-Constitution*, June 5, 1998, p. B1.
19. Jay Hughes, "Suspect in Miss. School Deaths Gets Life Term for Killing Mother," *Atlanta Journal-Constitution*, June 6, 1998, p. B1.
20. Rick Bragg, "Forgiveness, After 3 Die in Shootings in Kentucky," *New York Times*, December 3, 1997, National Desk.
21. T. Trent Gegax, Jerry Adler, and Daniel Pedersen, "The Boys behind the Ambush," *Newsweek*, April 6, 1998, 20–26.
22. Scott Johnson, "One Father's Unique Perspective," *Newsweek*, May 3, 1999, 38.
23. Kristen Hays, "Teacher Is Slain; Boy, 14, Charged," *Associated Press*, April 26, 1998.
24. Jeff Barnard, "Bombs Found at Boy's Home; Death Toll Rises," *Associated Press*, May 23, 1998.
25. Froma Harrop, "Strung out in Exurbia," *Atlanta Journal-Constitution*, May 29, 1998.
26. Mark Bixler, "Youth Trial Moving Slower Than Normal," *Atlanta Journal-Constitution*, May 1, 1999.
27. Ron Martin, Cynthia Tucker, and John Walter, "Punishment Too Harsh," *Atlanta Journal-Constitution*, May 13, 1999, p. A18.
28. Dirk Johnson and James Brooke, "Teenagers Didn't Give Off Aura of Murderers," *Atlanta Journal-Constitution*, April 22, 1999, p. 1.
29. Timothy Egan, "The Trouble with Looking For Signs of Trouble," *New York Times*, April 25, 1999, sec. 4, p. 1.

30. Nancy Gibbs, "In Sorrow and Disbelief: Special Report, The Littleton Massacre," *Time*, May 3, 1999, p. 20–36.
31. Craig Schneider, "It Happened Here," *Atlanta Journal-Constitution*, May 21, 1999, p. A1.
32. Leon Stafford, "Shooting Suspect's Hearing Delayed," *Atlanta Journal-Constitution*, July 13, 1999, p. B1.
33. R. Robin McDonald, "Punishing Choices," *Atlanta Journal-Constitution*, August 8, 1999, p. F1.
34. Lori Dorfman, Berkeley Media Studies Group, Public Health Institute, and Vincent Schiraldi, Justice Policy Institute, "Off Balance: Youth, Race, and Crime in the News," April 2001, report of Building Blocks for Youth, quoting from M. H. Barlow, "Race and the Problem of Crime in *Time* and *Newsweek* Cover Stories, 1946–1995," *Social Justice* 25 (1998): 149–82.
35. "America's Assault on Minority Youth," report of Youth Law Center, 1999, quoting from Howard N. Snyder and Melissa Sickmund, "Juvenile Offenders and Victims: A National Report" (Office of Juvenile Justice and Delinquency Prevention, 1995).

[4] Atlanta: Hub of the New South

1. Claud Anderson, *Black Labor, White Wealth* (Duncan & Duncan, 1994), 134, 136.
2. Donald L. Grant, *The Way It Was in the South: The Black Experience in Georgia* (Birch Lane Press, 1993), 33–34.
3. Ibid., 23–24, 35.
4. Darlene R. Roth and Andy Ambrose, Atlanta History Center, *Metropolitan Frontiers* (Longstreet Press, 1996), 33.
5. Grant, *Way It Was*, 126, 154.
6. Ibid., 185.
7. Louis R. Harlan, *Booker T. Washington: The Making of a Black Leader, 1856–1901* (Oxford University Press, 1972), 218.
8. Howard Zinn, *A People's History of the United States* (HarperPerennial, 1995), 202.
9. Bradley R. Rice and Harvey H. Jackson, *Georgia: The Empire State of the South* (Windsor, 1988), 64–66.
10. "Twenty Georgians Who Influenced the Twentieth Century," *Atlanta Journal-Constitution*, October 31, 1999, p. G4.
11. Roth and Ambrose, *Metropolitan Frontiers*, 96.
12. Rice and Jackson, *Georgia*, 93; Doug Cumming, "South's Rise Again Shown After Sixty Years," *Atlanta Journal-Constitution*, June 18, 1998, p. D1.
13. Roth and Ambrose, *Metropolitan Frontiers*, 162; Rice and Jackson, *Georgia*, 98–99.
14. Roth and Ambrose, *Metropolitan Frontiers*, 162–65.
15. Rice and Jackson, *Georgia*, 99.
16. *Metropolitan Frontiers: 1835–2000* (Atlanta History Center, 2000).
17. Roy Barnes, "We Will Not Settle for Second Best," *Atlanta Journal-Constitution*, January 12, 1999, p. C3.
18. Tammy Joyner, "The Two Souths, Economic Success Cut Off from Blighted Rural Pockets," *Atlanta Journal-Constitution*, April 9, 2000, p. P1.
19. Barnes, "We Will Not Settle."
20. U.S. Department of Justice, Federal Bureau of Investigation, *Crime in the United States*, (GPO, 1990); Susan Laccetti, "Violent Crime Up in U.S., Down by 14% in Atlanta: But City's Rate Still Tops the Nation, Report Says," *Atlanta Journal-Constitution*, April 29, 1991, p. A10.
21. Grant, *Way It Was*, 505–7.
22. Bob Holmes, ed., *The Status of Black Atlanta, 1995*, (Southern Center for Studies in Public Policy, Clark Atlanta University), 39.
23. Ibid., 101–2.

24. Roth and Ambrose, *Metropolitan Frontiers,* 209.
25. Holmes, *Black Atlanta,* 107.
26. Ibid., 104; R. Robin McDonald, "Wrong Number; Atlanta Is Not No. 1 in Crime," *Atlanta Journal-Constitution,* May 8, 1996, p. A01.
27. Rice and Jackson, *Georgia,* 116.
28. Lynda Longa and Carrie Teegardin, "Manipulation of Crime Figures Alleged," *Atlanta Journal-Constitution,* May 21, 1998, p. E1.
29. Ron Martz, "Crime Stats: Questions Linger after Atlanta Audit," *Atlanta Journal-Constitution,* January 28, 1999, p. C1.
30. Holmes, *Black Atlanta,* 42, 44.
31. Hollis R. Towns, "Atlanta Housing Authority Seeks End to Federal Audit," *Atlanta Journal-Constitution,* May 3, 1998, p. D7.
32. Larry Conley, "Remaking the Ghetto: Report: Techwood's Legacy Is to Replace 'Hopeless Old Houses,' " *Atlanta Journal-Constitution,* December 17, 1995, p. F2.
33. S. A. Reid, "Options Expanded for AHA Tenants Forced to Relocate," *Atlanta Journal-Constitution,* August 24, 1995, p. D02.
34. Hollis R. Towns, "Housing Chief's Pay $175,000: City Authority's Governing Board Approved Raise in Secret Meeting," *Atlanta Journal-Constitution,* September 25, 1997, p. A01; Hollis R. Towns, "AHA Director: Meeting Not Publicized Right," *Atlanta Journal-Constitution,* October 1, 1997, p. B03; Hollis R. Towns, "Drawing the Line at the Poorest of the Poor: The Doors Are Closing in Neighborhoods of Last Resort: Housing's New Dawn, With Limited Vacancies," *Atlanta Journal-Constitution,* February 15, 1998, p. G08.
35. *Guidelines,* Atlanta Housing Authority Housing Operations Division, Department of Protective Services; Hollis R. Towns, "Makeover for Public Housing," *Atlanta Journal-Constitution,* October 11, 1997, p. C04; Mara Rose Williams, "Federal Grant Pays to Add Phone Lines for Homeless," *Atlanta Journal-Constitution,* December 12, 1994, p. B10; Mark Sherman, "Report: Atlanta Among Cold-Hearted: Advocacy Group Says City Among Toughest That Homeless Face," *Atlanta Journal-Constitution,* December 12, 1996, p. D2; Staff, "Protests Will Not Solve City's Homeless Problem," *Atlanta Journal-Constitution,* December 19, 1996, p. A20.
36. Hollis R. Towns, "Atlanta Housing Programs Win Awards," *Atlanta Journal-Constitution,* June 20, 1998, p. G8.
37. Holmes, *Black Atlanta,* 39; Darryl Fears, "Atlanta Gets $100 Million for Troubled Intown Areas," *Atlanta Journal-Constitution,* December 21, 1994, p. A1.
38. Towns, "Drawing the Line at the Poorest of the Poor."
39. Lucy Soto, "Atlanta Is Riding a Population Rocket," *Atlanta Journal-Constitution,* January 1, 1998, p. A1; Joan Kirchner, "Georgia Tourism Income a Record," *Atlanta Journal-Constitution,* May 10, 1999, p. A1; Michael E. Kanell, "Atlanta Tech: Atlanta Rises to No. 2 on 'Hot Places' List," *Atlanta Journal-Constitution,* May 17, 2000, p. E7.
40. Michael H. Trotter, "America's Public-Housing Capital," *Atlanta Journal-Constitution,* April 20, 1997, p. R03.

[5]   The Bluff

1. Melissa Turner, " 'Defining Moment,' Facility Cements Trend to Create a Destination for Entertainment," *Atlanta Journal-Constitution,* September 12, 1999, p. P15.
2. Sallye Salter, "Developer Tom Cousins: In Prime Position," *Atlanta Journal-Constitution,* July 25, 1999, p. D1; Melissa Turner, "On the Fast Track to Urban Renewal," *Atlanta Journal-Constitution,* June 1, 1998, p. E1.
3. Lerone Bennett Jr., *Before the Mayflower: A History of Black America,* 6th rev. ed. (Penguin Books, 1993), 425, 428.
4. Turner, " 'Defining Moment.' "

5. Carrie Teegardin, "Atlanta's Tarnished Neighborhoods," *Atlanta Journal-Constitution*, March 22, 1998, p. A1.

6. U.S. Department of Housing and Urban Development, Office of Community Planning and Development, *Fulton County, GA, Consolidated Plan for 1995, Executive Summary.*

7. Hollis R. Towns, "Bad Housing Beyond City," *Atlanta Journal-Constitution*, April 29, 1998, p. B1.

8. U.S. Bureau of Economic Analysis, *State Rankings: Personal Income per Capita in Constant (1996) Dollars* (GPO, 1999).

9. Rodger Doyle, "Hard Times in the Delta," *Scientific American*, September 2000.

10. U.S. Bureau of the Census, *Census Bureau Facts for Features* (GPO, 2001).

11. "Race and the Democrats," *International Herald Tribune*, March 18, 1992.

12. U.S. Bureau of the Census, *Crime Rate per 100,000 Population: 1991;* Lyda Longa, "Stadium Safety Survey: Turner Field Area Is Worst," *Atlanta Journal-Constitution*, April 8, 2000, p. E1.

13. Robert D. McFadden, "Enraged Mourners Clash with Police at Slain Man's Funeral," *New York Times*, March 26, 2000, p. 30.

14. Tina Kelley, "Call for Calm after Shooting of Policeman by Colleagues," *New York Times*, January 30, 2000, p. 12.

15. "Los Angeles Board Rules Police Shooting Was Wrong," *New York Times*, February 20, 2000, p. 21.

16. Tammerlin Drummond, "It's Not Just in New Jersey," *Time*, June 14, 1999, 61.

17. United Nations Development Programme, *Human Development Report 1993* (Oxford University Press, 1993).

18. U.S. Bureau of the Census, "Poverty 1999: Table A. People and Families in Poverty by Selected Characteristics: 1998 and 1999"; U.S. Bureau of the Census, *Poverty Thresholds in 1999, by Size of Family and Number of Related Children Under 18 Years.*

19. U.S. Bureau of the Census, *Selected Characteristics of Households, by Total Money Income in 1999;* U.S. Bureau of the Census, *CH-3. Living Arrangements of Black Children under 18 Years Old: 1960 to Present* January 7, 1999; "American Children 2001: Highlights and List of Indicators, Part II: Indicators of Children's Well-Being," Interagency Forum on Child and Family Statistics, 2001.

20. Laurent Belsie, "Job Boom Ripples into Inner-City US," *The Christian Science Monitor*, March 31, 2000; Howard Zinn, *A People's History of the United States: 1492–Present*, revised and updated edition (HarperPerennial, 1995), 569.

21. U.S. Bureau of the Census, *Census Bureau Facts for Features* (GPO, 2001); U.S. Bureau of the Census, *Educational Attainment of Persons 25 Years Old and Over, by Sex, Region, and Race: March 1997,* (GPO, 1998).

22. U.S. Bureau of the Census, "Census Bureau Facts for Features," February 22, 2001.

23. Eddie Salyers, Valerie Strang, "More Than 800,000 U.S. Businesses Owned by African Americans; New York, California, Texas Lead States, Census Bureau Reports," *United Stated Department of Commerce News*, March 22, 2001.

24. Marian F. MacDorman and Jonnae O. Atkinson, Division of Vital Statistics, Centers for Disease Control and Prevention, "Infant Mortality Statistics from the 1997 Period Linked Birth/Infant Death Data Set," July 30, 1999.

25. Hani K. Atrash, Herschel W. Lawson, Tedd V. Ellerbrock, Diane L. Rowley, and Lisa M. Koonin, Centers for Disease Control and Prevention, "Pregnancy-Related Mortality," 2000.

26. Centers for Disease Control and Prevention, Division of HIV/AIDS Prevention, "Commentary," Surveillance Report, vol. 12, no. 2, 2001; Centers for Disease Control and Prevention, "AIDS Cases and Rate in Adult/Adolescent Women, by Race/Ethnicity, reported in 1999, United, States," July 20, 2000.

27. National Cancer Institute, "Breast Cancer: U.S. Mortality Age-Adjusted Rates, Total U.S., 1990–1998," 2001; Centers for Disease Control, "Prostate Cancer (Invasive): In-

cidence and Death Rates, by Race, United States, 1990–1996, Source: National Cancer Institute, SEER Statistics Review, 1973–1996," 2001.

28. The Sentencing Project, "Facts About Prisons and Prisoners—The Growing Corrections System," 2001 Policy Report.

[6] Little B

1. Children's Defense Fund, "Summary: Fair Start," June 28, 2000.
2. Marian Wright Edelman, "The Children's Defense Fund Has Assessed the State of America's Children and Found That America Is Neglecting Its Fifth Child," Children's Defense Fund press release, March 24, 2000.
3. Ibid.
4. Douglas W. Nelson, "Connections Count: An Alternative Framework for Understanding and Strengthening America's Vulnerable Families," in *2000 Kids Count Data Book* (Annie E. Casey Foundation, 2000), 7–8.
5. *Georgia Kids Count Factbook, 1998–99* (Georgians for Children, 1998), 4.
6. Nelson, "Connections Count," 15.
7. Ibid., 8–9, 10.
8. Ibid., 13.
9. Ibid., 16.
10. Edelman, "Fifth Child."
11. Don C. Keenan, "State Foster Care System Crying Out for Attention," *Atlanta Journal-Constitution,* May 29, 1998, p. A19; Christy Oglesby, "Fast-Track Adoptions," *Atlanta Journal-Constitution,* November 5, 1997, local sec., p. 2.
12. Edelman, "Fifth Child."
13. Adam Gershenson, "For Homeless Youths in New York, a Search for Happy Endings," *New York Times,* December 6, 1998, p. 43; Marian Wright Edelman, "The AIDS Crisis in Our Community," *Child Watch,* May 4, 1998.
14. Nat Hentoff, "Integrated Schools: A Dying Dream," *Washington Post,* May 28, 1994, p. A29.
15. Bob Holmes, ed., *The Status of Black Atlanta 1996–97* (Southern Center for Studies in Public Policy, Clark Atlanta University, 1997), 27.
16. Sherrell Evans, "The Ultimate Atlanta School Guide: Parental Involvement, PTA, Funds Big Factors in Effective Schools," *Atlanta Journal-Constitution,* May 23, 1996, p. H12; Children's Defense Fund Fact Sheet, "Key Facts about Education," 2000.
17. Andrew Mollison, "Education: State Schools Cut Math Gap but Racial Divides Are Still Too Great, Test Scores Suggest," *Atlanta Journal-Constitution,* August 3, 2001, p. C4.
18. Ron Martin, John Walter, Cynthia Tucker, Jim Wooten, "Georgia, Read Between the Lines," *Atlanta Journal-Constitution,* March 21, 1999, p. R4.
19. Delbert Ellerton, "Clayton Students Demand Upgrade," *Atlanta Journal-Constitution,* October 20, 1997, p. D4.
20. Sherekaa Osorio, Personal interview, main office, Fulton County Department of Family and Children Services, May 13, 1997.
21. Carmen Ferguson, telephone interview, October 23, 1998.
22. Doris Carnes, telephone interview, November 4, 1998.
23. Carmen Ferguson, letter to Patrice Fulcher, December 16, 1998.
24. Jane O. Hansen, "Did 5-Year-Old Terrell Have to Die?" *Atlanta Journal-Constitution,* October 17, 1999, p. A1.
25. Assistant principal, Bunche Middle School, telephone interview, May 20, 1997.
26. Marcene Thornton, telephone interview, May 20, 1997.
27. Council for School Performance Report, "Atlanta City: Capitol View ES, Elementary School Performance Report (1995–96)," prepared by the Applied Research Center, Georgia State University, January 23, 1997.

28. Council for School Performance Report, "Atlanta City: Bunche MS, Middle School Performance Report (1995–96)," prepared by the Applied Research Center, Georgia State University, January 23, 1997.
29. Office of Reverend W. L. Cottrell, Beulah Baptist Church, telephone interview, June 29, 1999.

[7] Superpredator or Outcast?

1. Kathy Scruggs and S. A. Reid, "Baby Girl Laid to Rest: Family Fends Off Suggestions That Teenage Mother Saw 8-Month-Old Girl Playing with Cockroach Shortly before She Swallowed It and Suffocated." *Atlanta Journal-Constitution*, May 29, 1996, p. C01.
2. Ibid.
3. Ibid.
4. S. A. Reid and Mara Rose Williams, "Child Safety Inspection: Tot's Death Prompts Second Visit to Home, County Health Officials Were Said to Have Seen a Rat and Cockroach," *Atlanta Journal-Constitution*, May 31, 1996, p. C03.
5. Ibid.
6. Mara Rose Williams and S. A. Reid, "Dreams of Faded Glory: Baby's Cockroach Death Puts Focus on Mom, a Great Swimmer Who Lost It All," *Atlanta Journal-Constitution*, June 1, 1996, p. D02.
7. S. A. Reid, "AHA Plans Stepped-Up Inspections, 'Clean Sweeps': New Effort Follows Death of Young Resident Who Choked on a Cockroach," *Atlanta Journal-Constitution*, June 1, 1996, p. D01.
8. S. A. Reid, "Fighting Bugs on Two Fronts, Housing Authority Increasing Inspections, Fumigations" *Atlanta Journal-Constitution*, June 6, 1996.
9. Scruggs and Reid, "Baby Girl Laid to Rest."
10. Jay Croft, "Mom Sues Over Tot Who Choked on Bug," *Atlanta Journal-Constitution*, May 13, 1997, pp. C05, C06.
11. Douglas R. Powell, telephone conversation, Hinton and Powell, Atlanta, June 21, 1997; Civil Case No. E59205; Staff Reports, "Law and Order . . . Atlanta: Death Suit Settled," *Atlanta Journal-Constitution*, July 27, 1997, p. C07.
12. *2000 Kids Count Data Book* (Annie E. Casey Foundation, 2000), 26, 73; *Georgia Kids Count Factbook, 1998–99* (Georgians for Children, 1999), 18.
13. *Changing Concepts of Sudden Infant Death Syndrome: Implications for Infant Sleeping Environment and Sleep Position* (RE9946) (Task Force on Infant Sleep Position and Sudden Infant Death Syndrome, American Academy of Pediatrics, 1998–1999).
14. Ibid., citing Ruth A. Brenner, Bruce G. Simons-Morton, Brinda Bhaskar, Nitin Mehta, Vijaya L. Melnick, Mary Revenis, Heinz W. Berendes, and John D. Clemens, "Prevalence and Predictors of the Prone Sleep Position among Inner-City Infants," *JAMA* 280, no. 4 (July 22/29, 1998): 341–46.
15. Ibid.
16. Georgians for Children epidemiologist, telephone interview, Emory University School of Public Health, May 21, 2001.
17. Renee Lewis Glover, "Perry Homes Hope VI 1996 Application Submitted to the U.S. Department of Housing and Urban Development, Submitted by The Housing Authority of the City of Atlanta, Georgia," September 10, 1996, Exhibit B, Existing Conditions, pp. B-1, B-6, B-7.
18. Rand Wentworth, director, Atlanta Field Office, The Trust for Public Land, interview, 1997.
19. Douglas A. Blackmon, "Atlanta City Council: Large Landfill Will Be Closed by October '93, Neighborhood Cheers," *Atlanta Journal-Constitution*, December 22, 1992, p. C04.
20. Glover, "Perry Homes," p. B-6.

21. Ibid. p. B-7.
22. Ibid., pp. B-3, B-6.
23. Ibid., pp. A-1, B-2.
24. Ibid., p. B-1.
25. Reid, "AHA Plans Stepped-Up Inspections"; Scruggs and Reid, "Baby Girl Laid to Rest."
26. Glover, "Perry Homes," p. G-3.
27. Ibid., p. L-1.
28. Office of the Press Secretary, the White House, "Remarks to the Convocation of the Church of God in Christ in Memphis," November 13, 1993.
29. Lisa Hamm, "Pregnancies among Teens Drop Globally," *Atlanta Journal-Constitution,* February 13, 1997, p. A20; Sey Chassler, "What Teenage Girls Say about Pregnancy," *Atlanta Journal-Constitution, Parade Magazine,* February 2, 1997, p. 4; M. A. J. McKenna, "Pregnancy Rate Drops for Teens," *Atlanta Journal-Constitution,* July 14, 2000, p. E1.
30. Diane Dutson, "Children Having Children Costs Society $29 Bill a Year, Study Says," *Atlanta Journal-Constitution,* June 14, 1996, p. A16.
31. Chassler, "What Teenage Girls Say."
32. G-CAPP Annual Luncheon, February, 1998, Omni Hotel, Atlanta, Georgia.
33. Ibid.; "G-CAPP: Statement of What We Believe," 1998.
34. James Goodman, *Stories of Scottsboro* (Vintage Books, 1995), 15.
35. Ibid., pp. 393–97.
36. David E. Pitt, "More Crimes Tied to Gang in Park Rape," *New York Times,* April 24, 1989, p. B1; "Assault Suspects Don't Seem to Fit Criminal Profile," *Atlanta Journal-Constitution,* April 28, 1989, p. A06.
37. William Raspberry, "America's Black Leadership Must Speak Out on Central Park Attack," *Atlanta Journal-Constitution,* May 2, 1989, p. A09.
38. Jack Warner, "Central Park Story: Stained by Ugly Crime, Stately Green Paradise Hasn't Lost Its Place in New York's Heart," *Atlanta Journal-Constitution,* May 7, 1989, p. A01.
39. Richard Reeves, "Fear and Loathing Rule Streets of Two Scared Cities," *Atlanta Journal-Constitution,* May 8, 1989, p. A11.
40. "Assault Suspects Don't Seem to Fit Criminal Profile," *Atlanta Journal-Constitution,* April 28, 1989, p. A06.
41. "Central Park Safe, N.Y. Police Insist after Near-Fatal Attack," *Atlanta Journal-Constitution,* April 22, 1989, p. A09.
42. "Assault Suspects."
43. "Central Park Rape Was 'Fun,' Teen Coolly Tells Police," *Atlanta Journal-Constitution,* April 23, 1989, p. A07; James C. McKinley Jr., "Official Says Youths Admit Role in Attack," *New York Times,* April 24, 1989, p. B1.
44. "Central Park Rape Was 'Fun'"; "Three Convicted of Raping Central Park Jogger, Teens Cleared of Murder Attempt," *Atlanta Journal-Constitution,* August 19, 1990, p. A1; "Assault Suspects"; Pitt, "More Crimes."
45. "Three Convicted of Raping Central Park Jogger."
46. Ibid.
47. "Assault Suspects."
48. *Betraying the Young: Children in the U.S. Justice System,* Amnesty International, AI Index AMR 51/60/98, November 18, 1998.
49. The Juvenile Advocacy Division of Georgia Indigent Defense Council, *Juveniles Arrested as Adults Under SB440: Fiscal Year 2000 Final Report,* 4, 20.
50. Judith Skidmore, interview, 1998.
51. The *Today* Show, NBC, October 18, 1999.
52. Michael Cromartie, "Kids Who Kill: Conversation with John DiIulio, Ethics and Pub-

lic Policy Center," *Books and Culture: A Christian Review* 3, no. 1 (January/February 1997): 10.

53. John J. DiIulio Jr., "My Black Crime Problem, and Ours," *City Journal* 6, no. 2 (Spring 1996).

54. Richard Zoglin, "Now for the Bad News: A Teenage Time Bomb," *Time*, January 15, 1996.

55. William J. Bennett, John J. DiIulio Jr., John P. Walters, *Body Count, Moral Poverty . . . and How to Win America's War against Crime and Drugs* (Simon & Schuster, 1996).

56. Ibid.

57. Ibid.

58. Ibid.

59. Ibid.

60. Pete Wilson, "Inagural Address," January 2, 1995.

61. House of Representatives, Representative Ron Wyden, "Consequences in Sentencing for Young Offenders Act," *Congressional Record* (January 20, 1995), article 15 of 50, 104th Cong., 1st sess.

62. Naftali Bendavid, "Congress Poised to Mandate That More Youths Be Charged—and Punished—as Adults," *Legal Times* (April 14, 1997): 1.

63. "Super-Predators," *Washington Post*, August 17, 1996, p. A24.

64. Robert Suro, "White House, Hill, GOP Offer Get-Tough Measures on Juvenile Crime," *Washington Post*, May 8, 1997, p. A4.

65. John Leland, "Savior of the Streets," *Newsweek*, June 1, 1998, 20–25.

66. Cromartie, *"Kids Who Kill."*

67. Campaign for Effective Criminal Justice, membership list as of December 6, 1998.

68. Frank Miele, "An Interview with the Author of *The Bell Curve*," *Skeptic* 3, no. 2, 1995, pp. 34–41.

69. Ibid.

70. Richard C. Atkinson, "The 2001 Robert H. Atwell Distinguished Lecture, Delivered at the 83rd Annual Meeting of the American Council on Education," Washington, D.C., February 18, 2001.

71. Miele, "Interview."

72. Stephen Jay Gould, *The Mismeasure of Man*, revised and expanded (W. W. Norton, 1996), 176–88.

73. C. Craig Venter, "The Sequence of the Human Genome," Press Statement, February 12, 2001.

74. Miele, "Interview"; Richard Herrnstein and Charles Murray, *The Bell Curve: Intelligence and Class Structure in American Life* (Free Press, 1994), 338.

75. S. H. Dimwiddie, "Genetics, Antisocial Personality, and Criminal Responsibility," *Bulletin of the American Academy of Psychiatry and the Law* 24, no. 1 (1996): 95–108.

76. Katheryn Russell, *The Color of Crime: Racial Hoaxes, White Fear, Black Protectionism, Police Harassment, and Other Macroaggressions* (New York University Press, 1998), 94.

77. Ibid., 99.

78. *Ethics and Public Policy Center Newsletter*, no. 64 (fall 1998).

79. Russell, *Color of Crime*, 100.

80. Peter R. Breggin and Ginger Ross Breggin, *The War against Children of Color: Psychiatry Target Inner-City Youth* (St. Martin's Press, 1994).

81. *Child and Adolescent Violence Research at the NIMH*, NIH Publication No. 00–4706 (2000).

82. Harriet A. Washington, "Experimenting on Defenseless Children," *Emerge*, October 1998, 28.

83. Philip J. Hilts, "Experiments on Children Are Reviewed," *New York Times*, April 15, 1998.

84. Herrnstein and Murray, *Bell Curve*, 526, as cited in Gould, *Mismeasure of Man*, 377.
85. Russell, *Color of Crime*, xiv.
86. "Teen Suicide: Giving In to the Deadly Impulse," *Atlanta Journal-Constitution*, October 12, 1998, C1, citing National Center for Health Statistics; Rene Sanchez, "Black Teen Suicide Rate Increases Dramatically," *Washington Post*, March 20, 1998, p. A1.
87. President George W. Bush, *A Blueprint for New Beginnings: A Responsible Budget for America's Priorities*, section V.3: "Strengthen and Reform Education," February 28, 2001, pp. 39–44.
88. National Education Association press release, "The President's Budget," March 2, 2001.
89. Bush, *Blueprint*, 39–44, 55–60.
90. Ari Fleischer, White House press briefing, "Faith-Based Programs," January 29, 2001, p. 12.
91. President George W. Bush, Executive Order 13199 of January 29, 2001, "Establishing of White House Office of Faith-Based and Community Initiatives," *Federal Register* 66, no. 21 (January 31, 2001).
92. Ibid.
93. Gould, *Measure of Man*, 19.
94. Miele, "Interview."

[8] Monticello Revisited

1. Barry James, "Paul Touvier, Jailed French War Criminal, Dies at 81," *International Herald Tribune*, July 18, 1996, p. 7; Barry James, "The Final Trial for Vichy?" *International Herald Tribune*, January 6, 1996, p. 2; David Stout, "Paul Touvier, 81, French War Criminal," *New York Times*, July 18, 1996; Greilsamer Laurent, *"L'avocat général a requis la réclusion à vie pour Paul Touvier,"* ["Prosecutor Demands Life in Prison for Paul Touvier"], *Le Monde*, April 20, 1994, p. 13; Greilsamer Laurent, *"Les crimes de Touvier s'inscrivent dans l'histoire de France,"* ["Touvier's Crimes Are Written in the History of France"], *Le Monde*, April 18, 1994, p. 13.
2. Adrienne Koch and William Peden, eds., *The Life and Selected Writings of Thomas Jefferson* (Modern Library, 1993), 243.
3. Ibid., 175.
4. Ibid., 237.
5. Ibid., 238.
6. Ibid.
7. Ibid.
8. Ibid.
9. Ibid., 238–39.
10. Ibid., 239.
11. Ibid.
12. Ibid.
13. Ibid., 239–40.
14. Ibid., 240.
15. Ibid., 241.
16. Ibid., 242.
17. Ibid., 243.
18. Ibid., 243.
19. David Hume, "Of National Characters," 1748, as cited in Emmanuel Chukwudi Eze, ed., *Race and the Enlightenment: A Reader* (Blackwell, 1997), cited in "Opinions on Current Reading," *Journal of Blacks in Higher Education* (summer 1997): 137.
20. Immanuel Kant, "On the Different Races of Man," 1775, as cited in Emmanuel Chukwudi Eze, ed., *Race and the Enlightenment: A Reader* (Blackwell, 1997), cited in

"Opinions on Current Reading," *Journal of Blacks in Higher Education* (summer 1997): 137.

21. Immanuel Kant, "Observations on the Feeling of the Beautiful and Sublime," as cited in Emmanuel Chukwudi Eze, ed., *Race and the Enlightenment: A Reader* (Blackwell, 1997), cited in "Opinions on Current Reading," *Journal of Blacks in Higher Education* (summer 1997): 137.

22. Koch and Peden, *Life and Selected Writings*, 258.

23. Rogers M. Smith, *Civic Ideals: Conflicting Visions of Citizenship in U.S. History* (Yale University Press, 1997), 52.

24. Howard Zinn, *A People's History of the United States: 1492–Present*, revised and updated edition (HarperPerennial, 1995), 35.

25. Ibid.

26. Smith, *Civic Ideals*, 54–55.

27. "Mulberry Row," Monticello Visitors Center, 1999.

28. Barbara Chase-Riboud, *Sally Hemings* (Ballantine Books, 1994), 209, 347; Monticello Visitors Center.

29. Chase-Riboud, *Sally Hemings*, 140.

30. Ibid., 331–37.

31. Smith, *Civic Ideals*, 65.

32. Zinn, *People's History*, 34.

33. Ibid., 35.

34. Smith, *Civic Ideals*, 65.

35. Frederick Douglass, "Narrative of the Life of Frederick Douglass," Chapter 1, as cited in William L. Andrews and Henry Louis Gates Jr., eds., *Slave Narratives*, (Library of America, 2000), 284.

36. Lerone Bennett Jr., *Before the Mayflower: A History of Black America*, 6th ed. (Penguin Books, 1993), 104.

37. Sojourner Truth (Olive Gilbert), *Narrative of Sojourner Truth, a Northern Slave, Emancipated from Bodily Servitude by the State of New York* (Boston, 1850), as cited in William L. Andrews and Henry Louis Gates Jr., eds., *Slave Narratives*, (Library of America, 2000), 576–79.

38. Smith, *Civic Ideals*, 198.

39. Ibid., 199; *Dred Scott v. Sanford*, 19 How. 393 (1857).

40. Smith, *Civic Ideals*, 249.

41. Ibid., 249–50.

42. Zinn, *People's History*, 36.

43. Donald L. Grant, *The Way It Was in the South: The Black Experience in Georgia* (Birch Lane Press, 1993), 87.

44. Smith, *Civic Ideals*, 250; Zinn, *People's History*, 182.

45. C. Peter Ripley, Roy E. Finkenbine, Michael F. Hembree, Donald Yacovone, eds., *Witness to Freedom: African American Voices on Race, Slavery, and Emancipation* (University of North Carolina Press, 1993), 228.

46. Smith, *Civic Ideals*, 261.

47. Zinn, *People's History*, 184.

48. Ibid.

49. Ibid., 187.

50. Zinn, *People's History*, 188.

51. Ibid., 186.

[9]   Post-Emancipation Fight for Freedom

1. Donald L. Grant, *The Way It Was in the South: The Black Experience in Georgia* (Birch Lane Press, 1993), 115.

2. Howard Zinn, *A People's History of the United States: 1492–Present*, revised and updated edition (HarperPerennial, 1995), 215.
3. Ibid., 233.
4. Ibid., 231.
5. Ibid., 213, 230.
6. Lerone Bennett Jr., *Before the Mayflower: A History of Black America*, 6th ed. (Penguin Books, 1993), 87, 233–35, 480.
7. Zinn, *People's History*, 192–93.
8. Bennett, *Before the Mayflower*, 474.
9. Zinn, *People's History*, 193.
10. Ibid.
11. Belinda Hurmence, ed., *Before Freedom: When I Just Can Remember*, (John F. Blair, 1997), 4–5.
12. Bennett, *Before the Mayflower*, 477; Katheryn K. Russell, *The Color of Crime: Racial Hoaxes, White Fear, Black Protectionism, Police Harassment, and Other Macroaggressions* (New York University Press, 1998), 19–20.
13. Russell, *Color of Crime*, 15, 22; Bennett, *Before the Mayflower*, 452.
14. Grant, *Way It Was*, 95–96.
15. Ibid., 96, 97.
16. Bennett, *Before the Mayflower*, 231.
17. Grant, *Way It Was*, 92.
18. Bennett, *Before the Mayflower*, 494–499.
19. Zinn, *People's History*, 271–73.
20. Rogers M. Smith, *Civic Ideals: Conflicting Visions of Citizenship in U.S. History* (Yale University Press, 1997), 348, 357.
21. *Plessy v. Ferguson*, 163 U.S. 537 (1896).
22. Smith, *Civic Ideals*, 378.
23. Bennett, *Before the Mayflower*, 256.
24. Russell, *Color of Crime*, 21.
25. Grant, *Way It Was*, 161.
26. Bennett, *Before the Mayflower*, 502–11.
27. Michel Marriott, "An Image Left Twisting in the Wind," *New York Times*, February 13, 2000, WK 3.
28. Grant, *Way It Was*, 159.
29. Bennett, *Before the Mayflower*, 258.
30. George L. Jackson, *Soledad Brother: The Prison Letters of George Jackson* (Bantam Books, 1970), 127.
31. Kay Mills, *This Little Light of Mine: The Life of Fannie Lou Hamer* (Dutton, 1993), 21.

[10] This Little Light Extinguished

1. Howard Zinn, *A People's History of the United States: 1492–Present*, revised and updated (HarperPerennial, 1995), 566; Public Broadcasting Service (PBS), "The 'Prime-Time' President—the Reagan Presidency: Domestic Affairs," *The American President* (Program 5: "The American Way"), Kunhardt Productions and Thirteen/WNET, New York, April 9, 2000.
2. PBS, " 'Prime-Time' President"; Zinn, *People's History*, 565.
3. Paul Slansky, *The Clothes Have No Emperor: A Chronicle of the American Eighties* (Fireside, 1989), 29.
4. PBS, " 'Prime-Time' President."
5. Slansky, *No Emperor*, 78, 80.
6. Zinn, *People's History*, 565–66, 569; PBS, " 'Prime-Time' President."
7. Zinn, *People's History*, 565, 568; PBS, " 'Prime-Time' President."

8. PBS, "'Prime-Time' President."

9. Zinn, *People's History*, 566–69.

10. Slansky, *No Emperor*, 25–26, 69.

11. Ibid., 44.

12. Martin Luther King Jr., *The Autobiography of Martin Luther King, Jr.*, ed. Clayborne Carson (Warner Books, 1998), 348.

13. Lerone Bennett, *Before the Mayflower: A History of Black America*, 6th ed. (Penguin Books, 1993), 583–84.

14. Clayborne Carson, "Malcolm X: The Deaths of Martin Luther King Jr. and Malcolm X Meant a Missed Chance for a Common Solution," *San Francisco Examiner Magazine*, February 19, 1995, p. 19.

15. Bennett, *Before the Mayflower*, 584–92.

16. Donald L. Grant, *The Way It Was in the South: The Black Experience in Georgia* (Birch Lane Press, 1993), 394.

17. King, *Autobiography*, 343; Bennett, *Before the Mayflower*, 591.

18. Ibid., 595; Zinn, *People's History*, 511.

19. Bennett, *Before the Mayflower*, 597.

20. Ibid., 600.

21. Grant, *Way It Was*, 436.

22. Ibid.

23. Zinn, *People's History*, 553–59.

24. Bennett, *Before the Mayflower*, 611.

25. Gary Webb, "'Crack' Plague's Roots Are in Nicaragua War: Columbia–Bay Area Drug Pipeline Helped Finance CIA-Backed Contras; '80s Effort to Assist Guerrillas Left Legacy of Drugs, Gangs in Black L. A.," *San Jose Mercury News*, August 18, 1996, p. 1A.

26. Ibid.; Gary Webb, "Shadowy Origins of 'Crack' Epidemic: Role of CIA-Linked Agents a Well-Protected Secret Until Now," *San Jose Mercury News*, August 19, 1996, p. 1A.

27. Slansky, *No Emperor*, 126.

28. Ibid.

29. Ibid.

30. Ibid.

31. Aaron Epstein, "Contra Leader Testifies That North Was 'Sort of a Savior' for Rebels," *San Jose Mercury News*, February 24, 1989, p. 2A.

32. "Walsh Accuses Reagan, Meese: Says President Deserved Ouster," *San Jose Mercury News*, August 18, 1994, p. 1A; "Iran-Contra Report Disputed," *San Jose Mercury News*, August 18, 1994, p. 11A.

33. "Money from the Cartel," *International Herald Tribune*, November 28, 1991, p. 4.

34. Bennett, *Before the Mayflower*, 619–25.

35. Zinn, *People's History*, 581.

36. Bennett, *Before the Mayflower*, 627, 629.

37. Ibid., 628, 631, 634.

38. Joseph B. Treaster, "Two Years After Invasion, Panama Drug Trade Flies High," *International Herald Tribune*, August 14, 1981.

39. Michael Isikoff, "Drug Cartel Gave Contras $10 Million, Court Told: Prosecution Witness Startles Noreiga Trial," *Washington Post*, November 26, 1991, p. a1.

40. "Witness Says Bush Did Not Discuss Contras," *Washington Post*, May 4, 1991, p. a15; George Lardner Jr., "Ex-CIA Aide Admits Iran-Contra Role; Fiers Pleads Guilty in Coverup, Says Others in Agency Knew of Funds' Diversion," *Washington Post*, July 19, 1991, p. a1.

41. "Money from the Cartel."

42. Bob Woodward, *The Commanders* (Simon & Schuster, 1991), 376; Susan Okie, "Iraqi Children Face Postwar Disease Threat: Harvard Teams Says 170,000 May Die," *Washington Post*, May 22, 1991, p. a23.

[11] Marching from Monticello

1. CNN Research Library Video, January 17, 1993.
2. Office of the Press Secretary, the White House, Maya Angelou's inaugural poem, January 20, 1993.
3. Lerone Bennett Jr., *Before the Mayflower: A History of Black America*, 6th ed. (Penguin Books, 1993), 441.
4. Otto Johnson, executive ed., *Information Please Almanac*, 49th ed. (Houghton Mifflin, 1996), 643; Bennett, *Before the Mayflower.*
5. Office of the Press Secretary, the White House, "Remarks by the President at Thomas Jefferson Dinner," Benjamin Franklin Room, Department of State, April 11, 1994; Joel Achenbach, "Mr. Jefferson and Namesake: President Clinton Hosts a Belated Salute to His Predecessor," *Washington Post*, April 12, 1994, p. E1.
6. President Bill Clinton, Speech in Little Rock, Arkansas, "All Too Often What Ought to Be Can Never Be for Free," *Atlanta Journal-Constitution*, September 26, 1997, p. A14.
7. Executive Order, Office of the Press Secretary, the White House, "President's Advisory Board on Race," June 13, 1997.
8. Scott Shepard, "Slavery Apology Plan Raises Reparations Issue," *Atlanta Journal-Constitution*, June 17, 1997. "Clinton Decides against Apology for Slavery," *Associated Press*, August 5, 1997.
9. Howard Fineman, "The New Age President," *Newsweek*, January 25, 1993, 22.
10. Office of the Press Secretary, the White House, "Remarks to the Convocation of the Church of God in Christ in Memphis," November 13, 1993.
11. Ibid.
12. Ibid.
13. John W. Wright, general ed., *The Universal Almanac 1997* (Andrews and McMeel, 1996), 215, 216.
14. Howard Zinn, *A People's History of the United States, 1492–Present* (Harper-Perennial, 1995), 632; The Children's Defense Fund, "Key Facts: Children's Health Coverage in 1999," 2000.
15. Joe Klaas, "Three-Strikes Law Is Missing the Mark," Justice Policy Institute (from *Los Angeles Times*), August 25, 1999.
16. Jason Ziedenberg and Vincent Schiraldi, "The Punishing Decade: Prison and Jail Estimates at the Millennium," Justice Policy Institute, 1999; Vincent Schiraldi, "America Imprisons Over a Million Nonviolent Offenders; Nonviolent Prisoners Increasing Faster than Violent Prisoners," press release, Justice Policy Institute, March 25, 1999.
17. Lisa Feldman, Vincent Schiraldi, and Jason Ziedenberg, "Former President Clinton's Prison Legacy Harsher Than Republican Predecessors: More Americans Were Imprisoned Under President Clinton Than Under Any Other U.S. President," Justice Policy Institute Press Release, February 19, 2001.
18. Steven Donziger, "The Prison-Industrial Complex: What's Really Driving the Rush to Lock 'Em Up," *Washington Post*, March 17, 1996, p. C3.
19. Milton S. Eisenhower Foundation Position Paper, "The Immorality of What Doesn't Work," 2000.
20. Thomas W. Lippman, "U.S. Takes New (Old) Path in Narcotics Battle," *Washington Post*, January 12, 1994, p. A01.
21. "Setting Standards," *Washington Post*, April 1, 1994, p. a19.
22. Ibid.; Helen Dewar, "Senate Approves Administration Legislation That Sets Goals for Education," *Washington Post*, February 9, 1994, p. a7.
23. Hugh B. Price, "Education Accountability: First the School Systems—Then the Students," in *The State of Black America 1999*, ed. William Spriggs (National Urban League, 1999), 194.

24. Kenneth J. Cooper, "President Directs Schools to Bar Students with Guns; Law Threatens Elimination of Federal Funds," *Washington Post,* October 23, 1994, p. a8.

25. John F. Harris, "Clinton Calls for College Tax Credit; Proposal Would Allow Refundable Break Worth Up to $1,500," *Washington Post,* June 5, 1996, p. A1.

26. Thomas W. Lippman, Bill Mcallister, "The 1996 Budget: Winners and Losers," *Washington Post,* April 29, 1996, p. A15.

27. Milton S. Eisenhower Foundation and the Corporation for What Works, "The Millennium Breach: Richer, Poorer and Racially Apart," 1998.

28. Office of the Press Secretary, the White House, "State of the Union Address of the President," April 23, 1996.

29. Children's Defense Fund Fact Sheet, "Key Facts About Education," 2000.

30. Milton S. Eisenhower Foundation, "Millennium Breach."

31. "State of the Union Address," April 23, 1996.

32. Donald L. Barlett and James B. Steele, "The Downsizing of the Dream," *Atlanta Journal-Constitution,* September 29, 1996, p. C4.

33. John F. Harris "A Presidential Push for Helping Hands Past, Present: Leaders Open Volunteer Summit," *Washington Post,* April 28, 1997, p. A1.

34. Steven A. Holmes, "Income Disparity between Poorest and Richest Rises," *New York Times,* June 20, 1996, national desk.

35. Carrie Teegardin, "Black Families' Incomes Rising: The Difference between Household Incomes for Black and White Families Is Getting Smaller," *Atlanta Journal-Constitution,* June 11, 1996: A12; William Darity Jr., "History, Discrimination and Racial Inequality," in *The State of Black America 1999,* ed. William Spriggs (National Urban League, 1999), 162.

36. *Current Biography Yearbook* (H. W. Wilson, 1989), 199–203.

37. James Traub, "Newt at Rest: He Doesn't Believe He or His Ideas Were Banished from Washington. Does He Have a Point?" *New York Times Magazine,* October 29, 2000, p. 52.

38. Ibid.

39. Eric Pianin, "Turnabout on Defense Funds: Bipartisan Consensus Supporting Major Buildup," *Washington Post,* May 29, 1999, p. A1.

40. Bob Barr for Congress Brochure, "About Bob Barr," September 15, 2000; Ken Foskett, "The Impeachment Hearings: Barr Brushes Off Charge of Racism, Blasts Clinton: Date With Destiny: Georgia Republican Opens Impeachment Inquiry, Answers Dershowitz Attack," *Atlanta Journal-Constitution,* December 12, 1998, p. A14; Anti-Defamation League Report, "Council of Conservative Citizens, Promoting a Racist Agenda," February 1999.

41. Peter Applebome, "Dueling with the Heirs of Jeff Davis," *New York Times,* December 27, 1998, p. 1WK.

42. Colbert I. King, "Lott's Old Friends," *Washington Post,* December 19, 1998, p. A25; Anti-Defamation League, "Council of Conservative Citizens."

43. Michael Janofsky, "Duke Launches House Quest," *Atlanta Journal-Constitution,* January 3, 1999, p. A4; Anti-Defamation League Report, "David Duke: In His Own Words," May 2000; Jack Anderson, "Skeletons in Duke's Closet Loom Larger," *Washington Post,* September 17, 1990, p. b13.

44. Renae Merle, "Duke, Texas Lawmakers Debate Race, Crime," in *Atlanta Journal-Constitution,* May 3, 1998, p. B1.

45. Special Supplement, "The New South: Politics, Justice, Human Rights," *Atlanta Journal-Constitution,* March 24, 1996, p. 23.

46. Stephen J. Bright, director, Southern Center for Human Rights, "Death in Texas," *Champion* (Journal of the National Association of Criminal Defense Lawyers), July 1999, p. 16; Jason Ziedenberg, Vincent Schiraldi, Justice Policy Institute News Release, "Texas Leads U.S. in Incarceration Growth," October 2000; Special Sup-

plement, "The New South: Politics, Justice, Human Rights," *Atlanta Journal-Constitution*, March 24, 1996, p. 22.

47. Mark Sherman, "Coalition Has Warm Welcome for Bush," *Atlanta Journal-Constitution*, October 2, 1999, p. A3.

48. David Johnston, "Ex-Aide Assails White House Approach on Crime Bill," in *International Herald Tribune*, February 17, 1994.

49. HR3355, A Bill to Amend the Omnibus Crime Control and Safe Streets Act of 1968, known as the Violent Crime Control and Law Enforcement Act of 1994; Lisa Feldman, Vincent Schiraldi, and Jason Ziedenberg, "Too Little, Too Late: President Clinton's Prison Legacy: Executive Summary," *Justice Policy Institute*, February 19, 2001.

50. Bill Rankin, "Federal, State Officials Praise Settlement: After Agreement on Juvenile Justice Reforms, Governor Eases Stance on Civil Rights Attorney," *Atlanta Journal-Constitution*, March 19, 1998, p. C02.

51. Center of Juvenile and Criminal Justice, Justice Policy Institute, "Georgia to Ditch Boot Camp; Commissioner Over Juvenile Offenders Wants to Focus On Training, Education," reprinted from *Atlanta Journal-Constitution*, December 10, 1999.

52. Charles Levendosky, "South Dakota, Other States Brutalize Problem Children," *Casper Star-Tribune*, as reprinted by the Center on Juvenile and Criminal Justice, Justice Policy Institute, Mach 15, 2000.

53. Ibid.

54. Center of Juvenile and Criminal Justice, "Georgia to Ditch Boot Camp."

55. Seth Hettena, "FBI Begins Investigation at Juvenile Detention Camp," *Associated Press*, December 16, 1999; "Criminal Probe Focuses on Boot Camp Guards; Glendening Orders Monitoring of All Juvenile Facilities," *Baltimore Sun*, December 16, 1999, reprinted by the Center on Juvenile and Criminal Justice, Justice Policy Institute.

56. Ruth Marcus, "President 'Determined' to Talk About Crime; Aides Say Clinton, Seeking Defining Themes, May Highlight Issue with Community Visits," *Washington Post*, November 21, 1993, p. a19; Office of the Press Secretary, the White House, "Remarks by the President to Members of the Law Enforcement Community," Ohio Peace Officers Training Academy, February 15, 1994; Center of Juvenile and Criminal Justice, Policy Institute, "Georgia to Ditch Boot Camp."

57. HR3355; Fact Sheet of the Sentencing Project, "Crack Cocaine Sentencing Policy: Unjustified and Unreasonable," 1997.

58. Fact Sheet of the Sentencing Project, "Crack Cocaine."

59. Ibid.

60. Fact Sheet of the Sentencing Project, "Proposed Changes in Crack/Cocaine Sentencing Laws Would Increase Number of Minorities in Prison, Have Little Impact on Drug Abuse," 1997; Bill Moffitt, National Association of Criminal Defense Lawyers, Testimony before the United States Commission on Civil Rights, " 'Three Strikes' Sentencing," July 12, 1996.

61. Marc Mauer, The Sentencing Project Policy Report: "Intended and Unintended Consequences: State Racial Disparities in Imprisonment," 1997.

62. Georgia Department of Corrections Population Statistics, "Active Offender Population Statistics by Race," 2001.

63. HR3355, op.cit.

64. Moffitt, " 'Three Strikes' Sentencing"; The Sentencing Project, "Why '3 Strikes and You're Out' Won't Reduce Crime," 1994.

65. Moffitt, " 'Three Strikes' Sentencing."

66. Greg Krikorian, "Judge Slashes Life Sentence in Pizza Theft Case," *Los Angeles Times*, January 29, 1997, p. A-1.

67. HR3355, Titles XIV and XV; Charles J. Aron and Michele S. C. Hurley, "Juvenile Justice at the Crossroads," *Champion* (Journal of the National Association of Criminal Defense Lawyers), June 1998.

68. Aron and Hurley, "Juvenile Justice."

69. HR3355; Aron and Hurley, "Juvenile Justice."
70. Jenni Gainsborough and Malcolm C. Young, The Sentencing Project Fact Sheet: "Prosecuting Juveniles in Adult Court: An Assessment of Trends and Consequences," 2000.
71. Koch Crime Institute, "Innovative Practices in the Criminal and Juvenile Justice Systems Report: Sentencing—Corrections—Diversion, November 1998"; PBS, *Frontline*, "Juvenile Justice: Child or Adult? A Century-Long View," PBS Online, 2001.
72. Office of the Press Secretary, the White House, "Remarks by the President at the Signing of the Personal Responsibility and Work Opportunity Reconciliation Act," August 22, 1996.
73. Mickey Kaus, "Clinton's Welfare Endgame: Inside the Fight Over Saving the Underclass," *Newsweek*, August 5, 1996, 65.
74. News Services Report, "Welfare Legislation Soon Should Land on Clinton's Desk," *Atlanta Journal-Constitution*, July 25, 1996, A12.
75. Office of the Press Secretary, the White House, "Remarks by the President at the Signing of the Personal Responsibility and Work Opportunity Reconciliation Act," August 22, 1996.
76. Kaus, "Clinton's Welfare Endgame."
77. "Fiscal Facts: An Update on Budget and Policy Issues Affecting Georgia's Children and Families," *Georgians for Children Newsletter* 1, no. 4 (May 1997).
78. Ibid.
79. Laura Meckler, "Power to Punish: Welfare Rules Booting Thousands Out of System," *Atlanta Journal-Constitution*, March 29, 1999, p. A1.
80. Rebecca Carr, "Losing Health Insurance through Medicaid Is Reform's Unintended Consequence; New Report Shows Size of the Crisis," *Atlanta Journal-Constitution*, May 14, 1999, p. B1.
81. Laura Meckler, "Poorest Worse Off, Welfare Study Finds," *Atlanta Journal-Constitution*, August 22, 1999, p. A3.
82. "Gov. Pete Wilson's Inaugural Address," *Congresional Record*, January 18, 1995.
83. Jason DeParle, "What Welfare-to-Work Really Means," *New York Times Magazine*, December 20, 1998, p. 50.
84. DeParle, "Welfare-to-Work"; Annette Fuentes, "Giuliani's Workfare: Slaves of New York," *These Times*, Institute for Public Affairs, December 23, 1996; Rachel L. Swarns, "Giuliani to Place Disabled Mothers in Workfare Jobs," *New York Times*, June 8, 1998.
85. DeParle, "Welfare-to-Work."
86. Adam Cohen, "When Wall Street Runs Welfare," *Time*, March 23, 1998, 64.
87. Ibid.
88. "U.S. Sues to Block Citicorp-Gtech Deal," *New York Times*, July 28, 1998; Jennifer Petersen/All Politics, "Welfare with a Debit Card: States Look to Private Firms to Automate Delivery of Benefits," *CNN* report, August 12, 1998.
89. Cohen, "Wall Street."
90. Donald L. Barlett and James B. Steele, "Corporate Welfare," *Time*, November 16, 1998, cover.
91. Ibid.
92. Richard Joseph, "Summit on Africa Continues What Clinton Began," *Atlanta Journal-Constitution*, May 3, 1998, p. G3.
93. Terence Hunt, "Clinton: U.S. Has Done Wrong by Africa in Past," *Atlanta Journal-Constitution*, March 25, 1998, p. A12.
94. Samar Abulhassan, "Hearing on African Trade Bill Likely to Widen Congressional Rift," *Atlanta Journal-Constitution*, July 19, 1998, p. A8.
95. Christopher Ogden, "Good Will Bill," *Time*, March 30, 1998.
96. Roll Call Report Syndicate, "Votes in Congress," *Washington Post*, May 7, 2000, p. M10.
97. Office of the Press Secretary, the White House, "The Trade and Development Act of

2000: Strengthening Our Economic Partnership with Sub-Saharan Africa and the Caribbean Basin," May 18, 2000.

98. Ogden, "Good Will Bill"; Joseph, "Summit on Africa."
99. Mark Fineman, "The Oil Factor in Somalia; Four American Petroleum Giants Had Agreements with the African Nation Before Its Civil War Began. They Could Reap Big Rewards If Peace Is Restored," *Los Angeles Times*, January 18, 1993, p. A-1.
100. Karl Vick, "Building a Government from Scratch: After Ten Chaotic Years, Somalia Has President," *Washington Post*, November 24, 2000, p. A45.
101. Full text of speech of President William Jefferson Clinton, "All Too Often What Ought to Be Can Never Be for Free," *Atlanta Journal-Constitution*, September 26, 1997, p. A14.
102. Peter Baker, "President Mulls National Apology for Slavery: Proposal Called 'Not a Bad Thing' as Racial Issues Gain Attention," *Washington Post*, June 16, 1997, p. A4.
103. Scott Shepard, "Slavery Apology Plan Raises Reparations Issue," *Atlanta Journal-Constitution*, June 17, 1997, p. A6.
104. Office of the Press Secretary, the White House, "Press Briefing by Presidential Advisory Board on Race," San Diego, California, June 14, 1997.
105. "Clinton Decides against Apology for Slavery," *Associated Press*, August 5, 1997.
106. Terry M. Neal, "In South Carolina, Bush Steps Gingerly around Racial Issues: Texan Tries to Woo Minorities without Offending Conservatives," *Washington Post*, November 11, 1999, p. A14.
107. Sue Anne Pressley, "S. C. Lowers Disputed Flag: Removal Does Not End Debate over Symbol of Confederate Cause," *Washington Post*, July 2, 2000, p. A4.
108. Janet Frankston, "Battlefield Standoff Ends: State to Pay $2.36 Million for Civil War Site," *Atlanta Journal-Constitution*, March 25, 2000, p. F1.
109. John F. Harris and Kevin Merida, "On Affirmative Action, New Perspectives Strain Old Alliances," *Washington Post*, April 15, 1995, p. A01.
110. Ibid.
111. John F. Harris, "Clinton Avows Support for Affirmative Action," *Washington Post*, July 20, 1995, p. A01.
112. William Claiborne, "Affirmative Action Curbed in California," *Washington Post*, June 2, 1995, p. A01; Gary Orfield and John T. Yun, "Resegregation in American Schools," the Civil Rights Project, Harvard University, June 1999.
113. Claiborne, "Affirmative Action."
114. William Booth, "U. of Calif. Ends Racial Preferences," *Washington Post*, July 21, 1995, p. A01.
115. Sue Anne Pressley, "Texas Campus Attracts Fewer Minorities," *Washington Post*, August 28, 1997, p. A01.
116. Bill Ranking and Rebecca McCarthy, "UGA Reviews Racial Policies," *Atlanta Journal-Constitution*, July 13, 1999: A1.
117. Orfield and Yun, "Resegregation."
118. Ibid.
119. Ibid.

[12] The Abandonment

1. David Remnick, "Dr. Wilson's Neighborhood," *The New Yorker*, April 29 and May 6, 1996, 96.
2. Office of the Press Secretary, the White House, "Remarks to the Convocation of the Church of God in Christ in Memphis," November 13, 1993.
3. Remnick, "Dr. Wilson's Neighborhood."
4. Gerald Early, "Williams Julius Wilson: A Leading Scholar of Urban Poverty Has a Prescription for the Ghetto: Jobs," *Mother Jones*, September/October 1996.

5. William Julius Wilson, *When Work Disappears: The World of the New Urban Poor* (Vintage Books, 1997), 75.
6. Ibid.
7. William Julius Wilson, interview, "The Two Nations of Black America," *Frontline*, PBS, 1997.
8. Wilson, *When Work Disappears*, 70–72.
9. Wilson, interview, "Two Nations."
10. Wilson, *When Work Disappears*, 153.
11. Ibid., 210–32.
12. PBS Online Forum, "Dr. William Julius Wilson: *A Look at the Truly Disadvantaged*," November 29, 1996.
13. David Levering Lewis, *W. E. B. Du Bois: Biography of a Race, 1868–1919* (Henry Holt, 1993), 288.
14. Ibid., 9.
15. Henry Louis Gates Jr., interview, "The Two Nations of Black America," *Frontline*, PBS, 1997.
16. Levering Lewis, *Du Bois*, 290.
17. Ibid., 4.
18. Gates, "Two Nations."
19. Ibid.
20. Ibid.
21. Gates, interview, "Two Nations."
22. Jack E. White, "I Have a Scheme: Ward Connerly's Effort to Hijack Dr. King's Legacy Is Full of Black Humor," *Time*, February 3, 1997, 46.
23. John F. Harris, "Clinton Charms Affirmative Action Foes," *Washington Post*, December 20, 1997, p. A01.
24. Peter Baker, "President Mulls National Apology for Slavery: Proposal Called 'Not a Bad Thing' as Racial Issues Gains Attention," *Washington Post*, June 16, 1997, p. A4.
25. Elaine Sciolino, "Woman in the News: Condoleezza Rice," *New York Times*, December 18, 2000.
26. CNN transcript: "Speech by Condoleezza Rice, Gov. George W. Bush's International Affairs Adviser, to the Republican National Convention," August 2, 2000.
27. Ibid.
28. Condoleezza Rice Speech before the Los Angeles World Affairs Council: "American Foreign Policy for the Twenty-first Century," January 15, 1999.
29. Condoleezza Rice, "Promoting the National Interest, in Foreign Affairs, Jan.–Feb. 2000," (excerpt), *New York Times*, December 18, 2000.
30. Ibid.
31. Sciolino, "Condoleezza Rice."
32. Adrian Taylor, "Interview of Prof. Condoleezza Rice, New National Security Adviser of President-elect George W. Bush," TIESWebzine, June 2000.
33. CNN transcript: "Speech by Condoleezza Rice."
34. Dan Balz, "The Republicans Showcase a Rising Star, Foreign Policy Fueled Rice's Party Switch and Her Climb to Prominence," *Washington Post*, August 1, 2000, p. A11.
35. CNN Transcript: "Speech by Condoleezza Rice."
36. Jane Mayer and Jill Abramson, *Strange Justice: The Selling of Clarence Thomas* (Houghton Mifflin, 1994), 13–20, *passim*.
37. Ibid., 50–60.
38. Ibid., 64–76.
39. Ibid. 142–43.
40. Ibid., 20, 44.
41. Dan Balz and Charles Lane, "Divided U.S. Supreme Court Overrules Gore Recount Plea: Decision Appears to Open Path to White House for George W. Bush," *Washing-

ton Post, December 13, 2000, p. A1; Michael A. Fletcher, "Poll: Most Blacks Hold Unfavorable View of Bush," *Washington Post,* December 22, 2000, p. A26.

42. Colin Powell, Chairman, Joint Chiefs of Staff, interview, "The Decision Makers," Frontline, PBS, January 9, 1996.

43. Bob Woodward, *The Commanders* (Simon & Schuster, 1991), 209.

44. Juan Williams, "Race and War in the Persian Gulf . . . Why Are Black Leaders Trying to Divide Blacks from the American Mainstream?" *Washington Post,* January 20, 1991, p. b2.

45. Profile of Colin Powell, "All Politics, 1996," Republican Convention, San Diego, 1996, CNN.

46. Ibid.

47. Ibid.

48. Ibid; Woodward, *Commanders,* 213; Robert Parry and Norman Solomon, "Behind Colin Powell's Legend—Iran-Contra Amnesia," *The Consortium,* 1996; Powell, "Decision Makers."

49. Woodward, *Commanders,* 107.

50. Ibid., 164–91.

51. Parry and Solomon, "Colin Powell's Legend."

52. Woodward, *Commanders,* 226.

53. Haynes Johnson, "Bush's 'Clear Moral Case,'" *Washington Post,* January 25, 1991, p. a2.

54. Tracy Wilkinson, "U.S. Near Accord for Gulf Military Headquarters," *Los Angeles Times,* March 25, 1991, p. A1; Molly Moore, "Volunteers Face Biggest Test: Post–Vietnam War Machine Putting Last Units in Place," *Washington Post,* January 15, 1991, p. a14; Ramsey Clark, "International War Crimes Tribunal: United States War Crimes against Iraq," Commission of Inquiry for the International War Crimes Tribunal, May 9, 1991; Francis Boyle, "U.S. War Crimes During the Gulf War," *New Dawn,* September–October 1992.

55. Clark, "War Crimes Tribunal"; Boyle, "U.S. War Crimes."

56. Woodward, *Commanders,* 376.

57. Michael Parenti, "Ten Years After (Iraq)," *Toward Freedom,* February 2001; Ramsey Clark, "Commission Hears Evidence of US War Crimes," *Green Left Weekly,* May 1991.

58. Clark, "International War Crimes Tribunal: United States War Crimes against Iraq," The Commission of Inquiry for the International War Crimes Tribunal, May 9, 1991, citing Patrick E. Tyler, "Powell Says U.S. Will Stay in Iraq," *New York Times,* March 23, 1991, p. A1.

59. Powell, "Decision Makers."

60. Williams, "Race and War."

61. Laura B. Randolph, "Keeping Promises: Gen. Colin L. Powell Mobilizes a Coalition to Help America's Youth," *Ebony,* July 1999, p. 142.

62. CNN transcript: "Colin Powell Delivers Remarks at the Republican Convention," July 31, 2000.

63. Ibid.

64. Ibid.

65. George E. Curry, "Randall Robinson Disease," *Emerge,* April 1998.

66. Michael Frisby, "Mr. Fix-It: Vernon Jordan Is the Man When Clinton and CEOs Need Help. But Some Ask, What's He Done for Black Folks Lately?" *Emerge,* April 1998, 42.

67. Joel M. Poch, "Workfare—An Analysis of a Doomed Elixir," *New York State Bar Journal,* March/April 1997.

68. U.S. Department of Labor biography: "The Honorable Alexis M. Herman, United States Secretary of Labor"; "Remarks of Secretary of Labor Alexis M. Herman," National Press Club, August 31, 2000.

69. Poch, "Workfare."

70. "States Must Pay Minimum Wage For Workfare, Administration Rules," CNN *All Politics,* May 16, 1997.

71. Press Release, Building Blocks for Youth: "Racial Disparity in Illinois Drug Prosecutions: 99% of Cook County Youth Tried as Adults Are African-American or Latino—Illinois Record Called Worst in Nation," April 2001.

72. "Remarks of Secretary of Labor Alexis M. Herman," National Press Club, August 31, 2000.

73. Courtland Milloy, "The Complexities of Clarence Thomas," *Washington Post,* July 14, 1991, p. d3.

74. Armstrong Williams, "Why I Am a Proud Conservative," *Emerge,* December/January 1998, 84.

75. Courtland Milloy, "Low Standards Let Black Men Fail," *Atlanta Journal-Constitution,* April 21, 1999, p. A11.

76. Leonard Pitts, "Dash of Rhythm Masks the Poison," *Atlanta Journal-Constitution,* November 18, 1999, p. A21.

77. Ernie Suggs, "Noted Author Warns Family to Let MLK Rest," *Atlanta Journal-Constitution,* January 16, 2000, p. G4.

78. Juan Williams, "Race and War in the Persian Gulf . . . Why Are Black Leaders Trying to Divide Blacks from the American Mainstream?" *Washington Post,* January 20, 1991, p. b2.

79. Ellis Cose, "The Good News about Black America," *Newsweek,* June 7, 1999, 29.

80. "More Than 800,000 U.S. Businesses Owned by African Americans; New York, California, Texas Lead States, Census Bureau Reports," 1997, *United States Department of Commerce News,* March 22, 2001.

81. "Net Worth of Nation's Households Unchanged, Census Bureau Reports, 1995," *United States Department of Commerce News,* February 22, 2001.

82. U.S. Bureau of the Census, "Table 13. Earnings of Full Time, Year-Round Workers 15 Years and Over in 1999 by Sex, and Race and Hispanic Origin," March 2000.

83. U.S. Bureau of the Census, "Table 12. Detailed Occupation of the Employed Civilian Population 16 Years and Over by Sex, and Race and Hispanic Origin," March 2000.

84. Cose, "Good News."

85. Shelby Steele, "Engineering Mediocrity," *Weekly Essay* (Hoover Institution), October 30, 2000.

86. Thomas Sowell, "Democrats, Republicans and Blacks," *Creators Syndicate,* September 28, 2000.

87. Interview by Peter Robinson, "Shelby Steele: The Content of His Character," *Hoover Digest Selections,* no. 2, 1996.

88. Barry Kamp, "The Color of Truth," *Vanity Fair,* August 1998, 124.

89. "Samuel L. Jackson Blasts Spike Lee for Criticizing Him for Using the "N-Word" in 'Jackie Brown,' " *Jet,* March 9, 1998.

90. Diane Weathers, "Survival of a Hollywood Marriage: Samuel L. Jackson and LaTanya Richardson, *Essence,* December 1999.

91. "Samuel L. Jackson Blasts Spike Lee for Criticizing Him for Using the "N-Word" in 'Jackie Brown,' " *Jet,* March 9, 1998.

92. Nancy JoSales, "Mix Master," *New York* magazine, May 10, 1999, 22.

93. Ibid.

94. Simon Reynolds, "It Isn't Easy Being a Superman," *New York Times,* October 10, 1999, p. AR29.

95. JoSales, "Mix Master."

96. Ife Oshun, "The Hip-Hop Summit: 'Taking Back Responsibility,' " *About Network, Rap/Hip-Hop,* May 24, 2001.

97. Ife Oshun, "Hip-Hop Summit Resolutions," *About Network, Rap/Hip-Hop,* June 14, 2001.

98. Ife Oshun, "Taking Responsibility: An Interview with Russell Simmons," *About Network, Rap/Hip-Hop,* June 6, 2001.

99. Cheryl Lavin, "It's All Going Oprah's Way," *Chicago Tribune,* December 19, 1985, p. 1.

100. Alex Heard, "Big Phil vs. Grand Ole Oprah," *Washington Post,* February 22, 1987, p. w7.

101. Bill Montgomery, "Williams Arrested in Forsyth County: He Is Charged While Picketing Near Talk Show," *Atlanta Journal-Constitution,* February 9, 1987, p. A01.

102. Sam Heys, "White Bias in America, Part 1: Forsyth County: Past and Present in Forsyth County: It's a Battleground for 'Us' and 'Them,'" *Atlanta Journal Constitution,* February 25, 1987, p. B01.

103. Montgomery, "Williams Arrested"; Monte Plott, "Oprah's 'Live from Forsyth County' Was Stroke of Programming Genius," *Atlanta Journal-Constitution,* February 10, 1987, p. C01.

104. Montgomery, "Williams Arrested."

105. Ibid.

106. Louise Kiernan, "So Much Promise, So Little Gain," *Atlanta Journal-Constitution,* September 24, 1996, p. A8.

107. Tim Wise, "Is Sisterhood Conditional? White Women and the Rollback of Affirmative Action," *NWSA Journal* (Official Journal of the National Women's Studies Association) 10, no. 3 (fall 1998).

108. Liza Mundy, "The Hillary Dilemma: As She Stands by Her Man, the Women's Movement Stands by Hillary Clinton as a Symbol of Women's Right to Choose—a Career, a Home, a Marriage. But What Has She Really Chosen?" *Washington Post,* March 21, 1999, p. W7.

109. "Youth Violence Must Be Curbed, Reno Tells Cities," *Miami Herald,* December 6, 1993, p. 5B.

110. Lynne Duke, "On the Inside Looking Out: EPA Chief Christie Whitman's Agenda: Adjust Self to Changing Environment, and Vice Versa," *Washington Post,* April 23, 2001, p. C1.

111. Ibid; Richard Cohen, "Targets Behind the Wheel," *Washington Post,* March 4, 1999, p. A21.

112. Gail Collins, "The Shadow Story of the Millennium: Women," *New York Times Magazine, Special Issue,* May 16, 1999.

113. Ibid., 126.

114. Emma Edmunds, "There's Something about Mary," *Atlanta,* October 1998, 58.

115. Don O'Briant, "The Door to Tara . . . ," *Atlanta Journal-Constitution,* December 15, 1999, p. D1.

116. Kay Mills, *This Little Light of Mine: The Life of Fannie Lou Hamer* (Dutton, 1993), 273–76.

117. Barbara Ehrenreich, "Silence of the Beltway Feminists," *New York Times,* January 17, 1997.

118. Gloria Steinem, "Feminists and the Clinton Question," *New York Times,* March 22, 1998.

119. Roxanne Roberts, "For Inauguration Celebration, a Group of Diverse Diversions," *Washington Post,* January 13, 1997, p. A1.

120. Judith Shulevitz, "Outside Agitator: Why Was Betty Friedan Ostracized by the Movement She Founded? Two Books Examine Her Life," *New York Times Book Review,* May 19, 1999, p. 18; Ginia Bellafante, "It's All About Me!" *Time,* June 29, 1998, 54.

121. Ehrenreich, "Beltway Feminists."

122. Victgoria Valentine, "Continuing the Legacy," *Emerge,* March 1998, 26.

123. American Civil Liberties Union, "10 Reasons to Oppose '3 Strikes, You're Out,'" 1996.

124. Jacob Weisberg, "Cold War without End," *New York Times Magazine,* November 28, 1999, p. 116.

125. Lance Williams and David Horowitz, "The Unquiet Death of Betty Van Patter," *San*

Francisco Examiner, May 2, 1993, p. D1; David Horowitz, "Elaine Brown: 'A Taste for Violence?'" *San Francisco Examiner,* May 3, 1993, p. B1; David Horowitz, "Black Murder Inc," *Heterodoxy,* March 1993; David Horowitz and Peter Collier, *Smart,* March–April 1990.

126. Office of the Mayor, City of Oakland, "Jerry Brown's Inauguration Speech," January 4, 1999.

127. James Q. Wilson and George L. Kelling, "Broken Windows," *Atlantic Monthly,* March 1982.

128. Office of the Mayor, City of Oakland, "Jerry Brown's Inauguration Speech," January 4, 1999.

129. Phillip Matier and Andrew Ross, "Oakland Rolls Out Welcome Mat for Spurned S. F. Builders," *Oakland Tribune,* June 9, 1999.

130. "Two Brown Appointees Take Seats on Port Panel," *Oakland Tribune,* April 13, 2000.

131. Heather MacDonald, "Jerry Brown's No-Nonsense New Age for Oakland," *City Journal* 9, no. 4 (autumn 1999).

132. Eric Schmitt, "Testing of a President: The Defenders; Citing Unfairness, Black Caucus Stands behind President," *New York Times,* September 13, 1998.

133. Michelle Boorstein, "Impeachment Has Major Implications for Black Americans," *Philadelphia Tribune,* January 22, 1999.

134. Congressional Black Caucus document: "History and Background," 2000.

135. Nancy Benac, Associated Press, "Clinton Thanks Blacks for 'Standing Up' for Him," *CNN ALLPOLITICS,* September 20, 1998; Office of the Press Secretary, the White House, "Remarks by the President to the Congressional Black Caucus, Washington Convention Center, Washington, D.C.," September 19, 1998.

136. Kenneth J. Cooper, "House Republicans Scrambling to Jettison Stereotypes of Party," *Washington Post,* December 11, 1994: a29.

137. Kenneth J. Cooper, "Quick Crime Bill Approval Predicted; Clinton Seeks More GOP Votes," *Washington Post,* August 19, 1994, p. a10; *Jet,* September 19, 1994, p. 16.

138. Michael A. Fletcher, "Black Caucus Urges Probe of CIA-*Contra* Drug Charge; Newspaper Articles Fan Conspiracy Suspicions," *Washington Post,* September 13, 1996, p. A20.

139. Office of the Press Secretary, the White House, "Statement by African-American Religious Leaders," August 16, 1994.

140. Peter Baker, "President Mulls National Apology for Slavery; Proposal Called 'Not a Bad Thing' as Racial Issues Gain Attention," *Washington Post,* June 16, 1997: A4.

141. Katheryn K. Russell, *The Color of Crime: Racial Hoaxes, White Fear, Black Protectionism, Police Harassment, and Other Macroaggressions* (New York University Press, 1998), 187, citing John DiIulio, "My Black Crime Problem, and Ours," *City Journal* 14 (spring 1996).

142. John Leland, "Savior of the Streets," *Newsweek,* June 1, 1998: 20; Editorial, "Rev. Rivers Knows What's Needed Now," *Boston Herald,* June 23, 2000, p. 026.

143. Interview by C. Stephen Evans and Gail Gunst Heffner, "The Word on the Street: Eugene Rivers on Faith-Based Urban Ministry, the Black Church, and the 'Sexual Holocaust' in Africa," *Christianity Today,* May/June 2000; Jose Martinez, "Gangsters Beware: The Rev Is Out to Shut You Down," *Boston Herald,* June 21, 2000, p. 003.

144. Martinez, "Gangsters Beware"; Evans and Heffner interview, "Word on the Street."

145. Remarks by Rev. Eugene Rivers, "'Faith-Based Outreach to Our Capital's Youth,' A Conference Cosponsored by the Manhattan Institute's Jeremiah Project and Empower America," National Press Club, Washington, D.C., July 14, 1999; Martinez, "Gangsters Beware."

146. Evans and Heffner interview, "Word on the Street."

147. Leland, "Savior of the Streets."

148. Rivers, "'Faith-Based' Outreach"; Dana Milbank and Hamil R. Harris, "Bush, Religious Leaders Meet: President-Elect Begins Faith-Based Initiative, Reaches for

Blacks," *Washington Post*, December 21, 2000, p. A6; Mike Allen and Thomas B. Edsall, "Black Religious Leaders Hear Bush's Call: Self-Avowed 'White-Guy Republican' Urges Clerical Push for 'Faith-Based' Program," *Washington Post*, March 20, 2001, p. A6.

149. Allen and Edsall, "Black Religious Leaders."
150. Farah Stockman, "Rivers Walking Turbulent Line," *Boston Globe*, April 4, 2001, p. B1; Leland, "Savior of the Streets"; Kenneth L. Woodward, "The New Holy War," *Newsweek*, June 1, 1998, 26.
151. Leland, "Savior of the Streets"; Evans and Heffner interview, "Word on the Street."
152. Rivers, "Faith-Based Outreach."
153. Dana Milbank, "Bush to Host Black Ministers: Faith-Based Initiatives May Circumvent Civil Rights Leaders," *Washington Post*, December 19, 2000.
154. Greg Braxton, "Clinton a Guest Star at NAACP Awards," *Los Angeles Times*, March 5, 2001, p.
155. Michael Dobbs, "Rich Made His Fortune by Breaking the Rules," *Washington Post*, March 13, 2001, p. A1; "Clinton Pardon of Drug Dealer Comes Under Fire in LA," *Arizona Republic (azcentral.com)*, February 15, 2001.
156. Dave Marks, "NAACP Image Awards Feature Movies, Music, and More," *BlackVoices.com*, March 8, 2001.
157. State of Georgia Office of the Attorney General, biography of Thurbert E. Baker, June 1, 1997.
158. Editorial, "Election Endorsements—Attorney General," *Atlanta Constitution*, October 21, 1998, p. A14.
159. Letter to State Board of Pardons and Paroles, Georgia Department of Law, Office of Thurbert E. Baker, Attorney General, May 6, 1998.
160. Thurbert Baker television campaign advertisement, October 20, 1998.
161. Cynthia Tucker, "Blacks Find Silence Won't Stop Racists," *Atlanta Journal-Constitution*, November 16, 1991, p. A21.
162. Cynthia Tucker, "NAACP: Focusing on the Past Avoids Challenges of the Present," *Atlanta Journal-Constitution*, July 22, 1998, p. A16.
163. Cynthia Tucker, "Black Advances in U.S. Would Please MLK," *Atlanta Journal-Constitution*, January 16, 2000, p. F5.
164. W. E. B. Du Bois, *Socialism & the American Negro* (Folkways Records FH5514), 1972.

[13] Trompe L'oeil

1. Maria Elena Fernandez, " 'He Never Had a Chance,' " *Atlanta Journal-Constitution*, January 24, 1997, p. B1.
2. Transcript of Proceedings before the Honorable Cynthia D. Wright, Judge, Atlanta Judicial Circuit, November 7, 1997, Atlanta, Georgia, volume 4: 689, 693–94; Fernandez, " 'He Never Had a Chance.' "
3. Transcript, November 7, 1997, volume 4: 790; Maria Elena Fernandez, "Slaying Suspect's Brother: 'He's Bad,' " *Atlanta Journal-Constitution*, January 31, 1997, p. 01B; Maria Elena Fernandez, " 'Little B' Faces Judge," *Atlanta Journal-Constitution*, February 6, 1997, p. C1.
4. Michael Weiss and Maria Elena Fernandez, "Youth, 13, Held in Woods Slaying," *Atlanta Journal-Constitution*, January 29, 197, p. C1; Transcript, November 5, 1997, volume 2: 213.
5. Fernandez, " 'Little B' Faces Judge." Transcript, November 7, 1997, volume 4: 673.
6. Transcript, November 7, 1997, volume 4: 673.
7. Atlanta police department bulletin, "Our Mission," May 1, 1995.
8. Transcript, November 7, 1997, volume 4: 775–76.
9. Ibid. 964–66.
10. Patrice Fulcher, interviews, December 2000.

11. Transcript, November 7, 1997, volume 4: 782.
12. Sandra Eckstein, "Campaign '96: Old Hand, New Face Vie for DA: Fulton Contest: The County's Solicitor General Is Running Against a Lawyer Making His First Bid for Public Office," *Atlanta Journal-Constitution,* October 30, 1996, p. C04.
13. Maria Elena Fernandez, "Family Recalls Frugal Life of Slain Victim," January 30, 1997, p. 01B; Maria Elena Fernandez, "Teen Suspect a 'Thug' Police Say," *Atlanta Journal-Constitution,* January 30, 1997, p. 03B; Fernandez, "Slaying Suspect's Brother"; Maria Elena Fernandez, "Ruined Lives," February 2, 1997, p. 01A; Fernandez, " 'Little B' Faces Judge"; Gail H. Towns and Maria Elena Fernandez, "Two-Year Truancy Is No Surprise," *Atlanta Journal-Constitution,* February 8, 1997, p. 01E.
14. Marvin Dixon, interviews, December 26, 2000, and May 7, 2001.
15. Ibid.
16. Ibid.
17. Ibid.
18. Joshua B. Good, "Heat On Alleged Leader of Drug Gang Arrested in DeKalb, Authorities Say," *Atlanta Journal-Constitution,* May 19, 1999, p. B1.
19. Michael Lewis, interviews, 1998–2001.
20. Dixon, interviews.
21. Transcript, November 11, 1997, volume 6: 1147–48; November 10, 1997, volume 5: 877, 881, 897.
22. Ibid.
23. Lewis, interviews.
24. Transcript, November 7, 1997, volume 4: 777–78; November 10, 1997, volume 5: 869–70.
25. Transcript, November 7, 1997, volume 4: 797.
26. Fulcher, interviews.
27. "Snitch: Readings: Paying the Witness," *Frontline,* PBS/WGBH, 1999, citing J. Richard Johnston, "Why Is It OK for the Prosecution, But Not the Defense," *Criminal Justice* (winter 1997): 21–24.
28. "Snitch: The Case That Challenged Lenience Deals," *United States v. Singleton,*" *Frontline,* PBS/WGBH, 1999.
29. Lewis, interviews.
30. Transcript, November 10, 1997, volume 5: 1079; Lewis, interviews.
31. Lewis, interviews.
32. Ibid.
33. Ibid.; Fulcher, interviews.
34. State of Georgia Archive, "Governor Miller's School Safety and Juvenile Justice Reform Act Passes Senate, Goes to House," February 2, 1994, O. C. G.A. § 15–11–28.
35. Georgia Department of Community Affairs, "Model Law Enforcement Operations Manual, Chapter 8: Arrest, Standard Operating Procedure 8–2, Processing of Juvenile Offenders," 1996.
36. Fulcher, interviews.
37. Ibid.
38. *In Re Gault,* 387 U.S. 1 (1967); *Kent v. U.S.,* 383 U.S. 541 (1966).
39. Human Rights Watch, World Report 1999, "Children's Rights, Juvenile Justice."
40. Fulcher, interviews.
41. Transcript, November 5, 1997, volume 2: 169–234.
42. Ibid., 143–46; Transcript, November 6, 1997, volume 3: 385.
43. Transcript, November 5, 1997, volume 2: 154–55.
44. Transcript, November 6, 1997, volume 3: 404–6; November 5, 1997, volume 2: 161–64, 171–74.
45. Transcript, November 6, 1997, volume 3: 546; November 5, 1997, volume 2: 196.
46. Transcript, November 5, 1997, volume 2: 199–201.
47. Ibid., 213.

48. Ibid.
49. Transcript, November 6, 1997, volume 3: 397, 418.
50. Ibid., 648.
51. Transcript, November 7, 1997, volume 4: 656–57.
52. Jay Croft, "To Fulton's DA Diva, All the Courtroom's a Stage," *Atlanta Journal-Constitution,* May 24, 1998, p. F2.
53. Transcript, November 3, 1997, volume 1: 6.
54. Transcript, November 6, 1997, volume 3: 644–45.
55. Fulcher, interviews.
56. Transcript, November 6, 1997, volume 3: 644 45; November 7, 1997, volume 4: 652.
57. Fulcher, interviews, op.cit.
58. Ibid.
59. Jim Wooten, "Forgiveable Loans vs. Jobs," *Atlanta Journal-Constitution,* April 9, 1995, p. D07.
60. Transcript, November 3, 1997, volume 1: 82–95, *passim.*
61. Lewis, interviews.
62. Transcript, November 7, 1997, volume 4: 665.
63. Ibid., 666.
64. Ibid., 671.
65. Ibid., 671–79.

[14] The Innocence of Little B

1. Patrice Fulcher, interviews, December 2000.
2. Transcript, November 7, 1997, volume 4: 688.
3. Ibid., 688–89.
4. Ibid., 689.
5. Ibid., 690–95.
6. Transcript, November 10, 1997, volume 5: 964–65.
7. Marvin Dixon, interviews, December 26, 2000, and May 27, 2001.
8. Transcript, November 10, 1997, volume 5: 966.
9. Maria Elena Hernandez, "The Killing of Darrell Woods: When Dreams Collide," *Atlanta Journal-Constitution,* February 2, 1997, p. B04.
10. Transcript, November 10, 1997, volume 5: 953.
11. Ibid., 998.
12. Dixon, interviews.
13. Transcript, November 10, 1997, volume 5: 1010.
14. Transcript, November 7, 1997, volume 4: 799.
15. Ibid., 792–93.
16. Ibid., 776–86.
17. Ibid., 778–79.
18. Transcript, November 10, 1997, volume 5: 1016.
19. Ibid., 1083–84.
20. Dixon, interviews.
21. Transcript, November 7, 1997, volume 4: 778.
22. Ibid.
23. Transcript, November 7, 1997, volume 4: 800.
24. Transcript, November 3, 1997, volume 1: 61–62.
25. Transcript, November 11, 1997, volume 6: 1162.
26. Transcript, November 10, 1997, volume 5: 1076–77.
27. Transcript, November 7, 1997, volume 4: 738–39; Michael Lewis, interviews, 1998–2001.
28. Transcript, November 7, 1997, volume 4: 698–99, 707.
29. Dixon, interviews.

30. Transcript, November 7, 1997, volume 4: 790; Transcript, November 11, 1997, volume 6: 1126–27.
31. Transcript, November 10, 1997, volume 5: 1058; Transcript, November 11, 1997, volume 6: 1114.
32. Transcript, November 11, 1997, volume 6: 1126–27.
33. Transcript, November 7, 1997, volume 4: 787.
34. Transcript, November 11, 1997, volume 6: 1126.
35. Fulton County Superior Court records, Criminal Action No. Z82809, final disposition.
36. Transcript, op.cit, November 7, 1997, volume 4: 805–6.
37. Ibid., 837–57.
38. Transcript, November 10, 1997, volume 5: 1040–42.
39. Transcript, November 11, 1997, volume 6: 1108.
40. Transcript, November 7, 1997, volume 4: 823.
41. Ibid., 823–35.
42. Transcript, November 11, 1997, volume 6: 1095.
43. Ibid., 1237–38.
44. Ibid., 1150–58.
45. Transcript, November 7, 1997, volume 4: 903–49.
46. Ibid., 946.
47. Transcript, November 11, 1997, volume 6: 1150.
48. Ibid., 1138.
49. Transcript, November 10, 1997, volume 5: 1076–77.
50. Transcript, November 10, 1997, volume 6: 1139–40.
51. Ibid., 1142.
52. Dixon, interviews.
53. Lewis, interviews.
54. Ibid.
55. Transcript, November 10, 1997, volume 5: 864–903.
56. Transcript, November 7, 1997, volume 4: 717.
57. Ibid., 736–72.
58. Dixon, interviews; Lewis, interviews.
59. Transcript, November 7, 1997, volume 4: 697–736.
60. Transcript, November 10, 1997, volume 5: 974–78, 994–1007.
61. Ibid., 986, 1057–63.
62. Transcript, November 11, 1997, volume 6: 1105.
63. Transcript, November 10, 1997, volume 5: 1065.
64. Ibid., 1015, 1032–46, 1083.
65. Ibid., 1051.
66. Lewis, interviews.
67. Transcript, November 10, 1997, volume 5: 1016, 1021.
68. Ibid., 1056–68.
69. Ibid., 1074–77.
70. Affidavit/arrest warrant, Fulton County, Georgia, S. E. Lawter, Complaint #97–021–1958, January 28, 1997.
71. Transcript, November 10, 1997, volume 5: 1069–70.
72. Transcript, November 11, 1997, volume 6: 1095.
73. Ibid., 1096–98.
74. Transcript, November 10, 1997, volume 5: 1079–82; November 11, 1997, volume 6: 1132.
75. Transcript, November 11, 1997, volume 6: 1103–4.
76. Ibid., 1109, 1121–26.
77. Magistrate, Fulton County, "First Appearance," sworn report of Det. S. E. Lawter, January 30, 1997.
78. Transcript, November 11, 1997, volume 6: 1144–98.

79. Ibid., 1223.
80. Riverbank Armory, "United States Army Rifles of the 20th Century," 2001, citing Bruce N. Canfield, "The Army's 'Light Rifle,' " *American Rifleman*, National Rifle Association of America, February 1996.
81. Transcript, November 11, 1997, volume 6: 1228.
82. Lewis, interviews.
83. Transcript, November 11, 1997, volume 6: 1247, 1258.
84. Transcript, November 12, 1997, volume 7: 1266–67.
85. Ibid., 1268–70.
86. Ibid., 1288–89.
87. Ibid., 1305.
88. Ibid., 1306.
89. Ibid., 1308–9.
90. Ibid., 1309.
91. Ibid., 1310.
92. Ibid., 1311.
93. Ibid., 1310–15.
94. Ibid., 1316–17.
95. Ibid., 1317–19.
96. Ibid., 1320.
97. Ibid., 1321.
98. Ibid., 1325.
99. Ibid., 1326.
100. Ibid., 1327.
101. Ibid., 1331.
102. Ibid., 1338–39.
103. Ibid., 1341–2.
104. Ibid.
105. Ibid., 1353.
106. Ibid., 1357.
107. Ibid., 1363–64.
108. Ibid., 1365–66.
109. Ibid., 1371.
110. Ibid., 1373.
111. Ibid., 1375.
112. Ibid., 1378.
113. Ibid.
114. Ibid., 1382.
115. Ibid., 1383–85.
116. Maynard Jackson, "Fulton DA: Doing a Great Job," *Atlanta Journal-Constitution*, May 12, 2000, p. A-18.

[15] The Appeal

1. Lori Dorfman, Berkeley Media Studies Group, and Vincent Schiraldi, Justice Policy Institute, "Off Balance: Youth, Race and Crime in the News," A Report for the Building Blocks for Youth Initiative, April 10, 2001.
2. Mike Males and Dan Mcallair, the Justice Policy Institute, "The Color of Justice: An Analysis of Juvenile Adult Court Transfers in California," 1999; Vincent Schiraldi, director, Justice Policy Institute, "Real Data Necessary to Guide Juvenile Justice," October 20, 1999; Vincent Schiraldi, "The Bias of 'Color Blind' Juvenile Justice," *Los Angeles Times*, June 27, 1999.
3. Eileen Poe-Yamagata and Michael A. Jones, "And Justice for Some," National Council on Crime and Delinquency, April 25, 2000.

4. Ibid.
5. The Juvenile Advocacy Division of Georgia Indigent Defense Council, "Juveniles Arrested as Adults under SB440: Fiscal year 1998 final report," 6, 11.
6. The Juvenile Advocacy Division of Georgia Indigent Defense Council, "Juveniles Arrested as Adults under SB440," March 2001, 5, 10.
7. The Juvenile Advocacy Division of Georgia Indigent Defense Council, "Juveniles Arrested as Adults under SB440: Fiscal year 1998 final report," 7.
8. Interview with director of facilities, Georgia Department of Corrections, 2001.
9. Georgia Department of Corrections, "Active Offender Population Statistics by Age," Arrendale State Prison, 1998.
10. Howard Zinn, *A People's History of the United States, 1492–Present,* revised and updated edition (HarperPerennial, 1995), 205.
11. Facilities Division, Georgia Department of Corrections, 1999 annual report: "Putting Inmates to Work."
12. Rhonda Cook, "Prisoners 'Hired,' So Ex-Welfare Clients Fired. Free Convict Labor Means Trash Sorters Are Recycled Out of a Job," *Atlanta Journal-Constitution,* June 19, 1999, p. A1.
13. Nina Lott, Nicholls city council, "Prison Gives Town New Life," April 24, 1999, p. A14.
14. Ron Martin, Cynthia Tucker, John Walter, "Creating Private Prisons Was Criminally Bad Idea," *Atlanta Constitution,* May 23, 2000, p. A10.
15. David Ho, "U.S. Prison Population Rising," *ABC News.com,* April 20, 2000; Georgia Department of Corrections, "Active Offender Population Statistics by Race," June 2001.
16. Charles W. Thomas, University of Connecticut, "Private Adult Correctional Facility Census, A 'Real-Time' Statistical Profile," December 31, 1999.
17. Angela Y. Davis, "Masked Racism: Reflections on the Prison Industrial Complex," *ColorLines,* fall 1998.
18. Julie Light, "The Prison Industry: Capitalist Punishment," *Corporate Watch,* October 28, 1999.
19. David Leonhardt, "As Prison Labor Grows, So Does the Debate," *New York Times,* March 19, 2000, p.
20. Davis, "Masked Racism." Jennifer Sullivan, "Made on the Inside for Use on the Outside," *Wired News,* December 2, 1997.
21. Light, "Prison Industry."
22. Sullivan, "Made on the Inside."
23. Ibid., Davis, "Masked Racism."
24. Paul Wright, "Profiting from Punishment," *Prison Labor News,* March 1997.
25. Leonhardt, "Prison Labor Grows"; Wright, "Profiting from Punishment."
26. Edwin Meese, "Let Prison Inmates Earn Their Keep," *Wall Street Journal,* May 1, 1996.
27. In 1999, 46 percent of all prisoners in the United States were black. "Facts about Prisons and Prisoners: the Growing Corrections System," The Sentencing Project, 2000.
28. Marc Mauer, the Sentencing Project, policy report; "Intended and Unintended Consequences; State Racial Disparities in Imprisonment," 1997.
29. Deb Vargas, Dan Macallair, Justice Policy Institute Press Release, "JPI Analysis of Bureau of Justice Statistics 'Prisoners 2000' Release," August 9, 2001.
30. Ibid.; Ho, "U.S. Prison Population"; Reginald Stuart, "Behind Bars," *Emerge,* March 1997, 44.
31. Stuart, "Behind Bars"; Davis, "Masked Racism."
32. Juvenile Court Centennial Initiative, Office of Juvenile Justice and Delinquency Prevention, U.S. Department of Justice, "Juvenile Justice System: Girls," February 2000.
33. Ho, "U.S. Prison Population."
34. Shay Bilchik, administrator, 1999 National Report Series, Juvenile Justice Bulletin, U.S. Department of Justice, "Challenging the Myths: Arrest Rate Trends Reflect Changes in Public Attitudes and Law Enforcement Policy," February 2000.

35. Fox Butterfield, "Crime Keeps Dropping Fast, FBI Statistics Show," *Atlanta Journal-Constitution*, May 17, 1999, p. 1.

36. The Sentencing Project, "Facts about Prisons and Prisoners: The Growing Corrections System," 2001 Policy Report; Mauer, "Intended and Unintended Consequences"; Vargas, Macallair, "JPI Analysis"; "Testimony by NACDL [National Association of Criminal Defense Lawyers] member Bill Moffitt before the United States Commission on Civil Rights," July 12, 1996.

37. Stuart, "Behind Bars."

38. The Sentencing Project, "Facts about Prisons and Prisoners: The Growing Corrections System," 2001 Policy Report.

39. Human Rights Watch Report, "United States, Punishment and Prejudice, Racial Disparities in the War on Drugs: Racially Disproportionate Incarceration of Drug Offenders," vol. 12, no. 2(G), May 2000.

40. NADCL Testimony before U.S. Commission on Civil Rights.

41. Mauer, "Intended and Unintended Consequences"; Timothy Egan, "The War on Crack Retreats, Still Taking Prisoners," *New York Times*, February 28, 1999, p. 1.

42. Vargas, Macallair, "JPI Analysis."

43. Egan, "War on Crack"; The Sentencing Project Fact Sheet, "Crack Cocaine Sentencing Policy: Unjustified and Unreasonable," April 1997.

44. The Sentencing Project Fact Sheet, "Crack Cocaine Sentencing Policy: Unjustified and Unreasonable," April 1997.

45. Ibid.; Egan, "War on Crack."

46. Frontline, PBS, "Snitch," written, produced and directed by Ofra Bikel, January 12, 1999.

47. Egan, "War on Crack."

48. Ibid.

49. "2001 Human Development Report," United Nations; U.S. Bureau of the Census, "Poverty: 1999 Highlights," Supplement to the Current Population Survey, March 2000.

50. U.S. Bureau of the Census, "Poverty 1999: Table A. People and Families in Poverty by Selected Characteristics: 1998 and 1999."

51. U.S. Bureau of the Census, "Living Arrangements of Black Children Under 18 Years Old: 1960 to Present," January 7, 1999; "America's Children 2001: Highlights and List of Indicators, Part II: Indicators of Children's Well-Being," Interagency Forum on Child and Family Statistics, 2001.

52. Laurent Belsie, "Job Boom Ripples into Inner-City U.S.," *Christian Science Monitor*, March 31, 2000.

53. William Darity Jr., "History, Discrimination and Racial Inequality," *The State of Black America 1999: The Impact of Color-Consciousness in the United States*, ed. William Spriggs (National Urban League, Image Partners Custom Publishing, 1999), 154.

54. Ibid.

55. Roy S. Johnson, "The New Black Power," *Fortune*, August 4, 1997, 46.

56. Marian F. MacDorman and Jonnae O. Atkinson, Division of Vital Statistics, Centers for Disease Control and Prevention, "Infant Mortality Statistics from the 1997 Period Linked Birth/Infant Death Data Set," July 30, 1999.

57. Hani K. Atrash, Herschel W. Lawson, Tedd V. Ellerbrock, Diane L. Rowley, Lisa M. Koonin, "Pregnancy-Related Mortality," Centers for Disease Control and Prevention, 2000.

58. National Cancer Institute, "Breast Cancer: U.S. Mortality Age-Adjusted Rates, Total U.S., 1990–1998"; "Cervix Cancer: U.S. Mortality Age-Adjusted Rates, Individual States, 1969–1998," 2001.

59. Centers for Disease Control and Prevention, Division of HIV/AIDS Prevention, "Commentary," Surveillance Report, volume 12, number 2, 2001; Centers for Disease Control and Prevention, "AIDS Cases and Rate in Adult/Adolescent Women, by Race/Ethnicity, reported in 1999, United, States," July 20, 2000.

60. Centers for Disease Control and Prevention, Division of HIV/AIDS Prevention, "Commentary," Surveillance Report, volume 12, number 2, 2001; Centers for Disease Control and Prevention, "AIDS Cases and Rate in Adult/Adolescent Women, by Race/Ethnicity, reported in 1999, United, States," July 20, 2000.

61. Scott Shepard, "Racial Healing Would Be a Top Priority, Gore Says," *Atlanta Journal-Constitution*, January 17, 2000, p. A5.

62. Whitney M. Young Jr., "The Role of the Middle-Class Negro," *Ebony*, Special Issue, September 1963, 67.

63. Christy Oglesby and Ernie Suggs, "Powell: Prove Worthy of Affirmative Action," *Atlanta Journal-Constitution*, July 15, 1998, p. A1; Lillian Lee Kim, "Race Gap: Research Sought on Higher Black Cancer Rate," *Atlanta Journal-Constitution*, July 15, 1998, p. B1.

64. Marcus Franklin, "Black Caucus Facing Tougher Fight," *Atlanta Journal-Constitution*, May 21, 1997, p. A10.

65. Minister Louis Farrakhan, "A Call to March," *Emerge*, October 1995.

66. Clayborne Carson and Kris Shepard, eds., *A Call to Conscience: The Landmark Speeches of Dr. Martin Luther King, Jr.* (Warner Books, 2001), 171–99.

Acknowledgments

Only her brother's freedom can be recompense for the commitment to this work provided by Tavia Morgan, who spent so much of her early teen years answering my innumerable questions, guiding me through rough terrain, and keeping me in check with her courage and humanity.

Merci pour tout to Sandy Dijkstra, my agent, who made me believe I could write this book. I am grateful, too, to Helene Atwan, my editor and publisher, who believed in the potential of this book, who bravely agreed to publish it, and who uncompromisingly pushed me to work hard and well to realize it.

My great appreciation goes to Ericka Abram for her significant assistance in the research required, and without compensation and with so much caring. And thanks to Tony Kline and Michael Kennedy for reviewing this material with their brilliant legal eyes.

For my Sisters of Mothers Advocating Juvenile Justice, Judy Skidmore and Marva Williams and Billie Ross and Kameelah Shabazz and Valerie Bahar, and our Brother Charles Maxwell, thank you for sharing your stories, and for caring not only for your sons but all the others, and for working for the freedom of all our children.

Finally, I send out into the universe my undying gratitude to my friend and mentor Calvin Hernton, who did not live to see this publication, though his literary lessons made it possible.